Logos and Eros

Books of Interest from St. Augustine's Press

Logos and Eros

Essays Honoring Stanley Rosen

Edited by Nalin Ranasinghe

ST. AUGUSTINE'S PRESS
South Bend, Indiana
2006

Manufactured in the United States of America.

1 2 3 4 5 6 12 11 10 09 08 07 06

Library of Congress Cataloging in Publication Data

Logos and eros: essays honoring Stanley Rosen/
edited by Nalin Ranasinghe.
p. cm.
ISBN 1-58731-470-3 (hardcover: alk. paper)
1. Philosophy. 2. Plato. 3. Philosophy, Ancient. 4. Philosophy, Modern. 5. Logos (Philosophy) 6. Rosen, Stanley, 1924 –
I. Rosen, Stanley, 1924 – II. Ranasinghe, Nalin, 1960–
BD41.L64 2006
190 – dc22 2006030089

∞ *The paper used in this publication meets the minimum requirements of the American National Standard for Information Sciences – Permanence of Paper for Printed Materials, ANSI Z39.48-1984.*

St. Augustine's Press
www.staugustine.net

Contents

Works on Modern Philosophy

Stanley Rosen as an Educator

Nalin Ranasinghe
Assumption College

> I wished that I could find a true philosopher as my teacher, a man who could raise me above the inadequacy of the age and teach me simplicity in thought and life—to be unmodern in the deepest sense of the word. . . . Modern man is so complex that he is forced to be dishonest whenever he speaks, opines and wishes to act.
>
> —Friedrich Nietzsche, *Untimely Meditations*

I

The inherently difficult task of writing an introduction to a *Festschrift* celebrating the career of one's beloved teacher is further complicated by the fact that—far from being a valetudinarian—Stanley Rosen, despite having already been the author of fifteen books and countless articles, perhaps is now in the most productive decade of his life. Having already published two books, *Metaphysics in Ordinary Language* and *The Illusiveness of the Ordinary,* that are judged to rank among the best philosophical works of the new century, this septuagenarian has just completed a magisterial commentary on Plato's *Republic*. However, we are at a point in this active teacher's career where it is possible to identify and celebrate the grand motifs that he has consistently iterated over his fifty years as a doctor of philosophy.

Even though, as Drew Hyland points out in this volume, his writing style has changed more than once, Rosen has always sought to defend the lifeline between cosmos and logos; he has always insisted that the bond between philosophy and ordinary language is sacred and indissoluble. From this vantage his amazing ability to yoke together and drive the unruly black horse of ordinary language and the ideal steed of metaphysics seems godlike. Accordingly, bearing in mind his teacher's famous assertion that the depth of things resides precisely in their surfaces, it is appropriate that this introduction should begin by describing Stanley Rosen in the place where his unsurpassed mastery of both philosophy and ordinary language are most evident: the classroom.

II

I first took a class with Stanley Rosen almost twenty years ago, at Penn State, in autumn 1985. What transpired in Rosen's seminar that afternoon was something that I have never experienced, either before or since, with any other teacher. My other instructors that semester were Joseph Kockelmans and the late David Lachterman, professors of rare erudition perfectly capable of making difficult texts clear and accessible. However, only Rosen could seamlessly integrate philosophy into ordinary experience while enormously enriching his students' awareness of both. He was an amazing combination of Platonist, stand-up comedian, Dutch uncle and social commentator. Like Socrates, he could bring philosophy down from the heavens and do the most difficult topics justice in the language of the agora—or gridiron. His students saw that Rosen came before them neither to praise ordinary language—at the expense of philosophy, nor to bury it—in abstract jargon. Rosen made me aware of how flat and stale it was to make a living by opposing philosophy to everyday life; Platonism, as he embodied it, was distinguished by a robust sense of reality. A philosopher who cannot use the direct evidence of the everyday exercise of reason to justify the good life is worse than useless; he is dangerous.

This is why Rosen took it upon himself ceaselessly to warn against the nihilistic foundations of what his teacher memorably called "the joyless quest for joy." By thoughtlessly denouncing the so-called elitist experience of excellence, our egalitarian ethos is powerless to defend the very virtues that must sustain a democracy. For one thing, any talk of high and low, noble and base, or good and evil is expressed purely in terms of selfishness, sentimentality, or superstition. Alternately, and even more dangerously, any 'value language' that cannot be quantified is deemed either meaningless or, horror of horrors, judgmental. Consequently we find ourselves 'thrown' in a world in which ordinary speech is hopelessly incompatible with the technical jargon and quantitative measurements that rule and constitute the increasingly artificial and illusory everyday reality we dwell in. Yet Rosen does not zestfully denounce modernity in the stern and pompous tones of Cato the Elder; self-consciously anachronistic speech only serves to widen the gap between eternal verities and present-day exigencies. He is of the view that human beings can only maintain the essential connection between reason and the good by living the good life in the present. Ancient self-knowledge and modern liberality cannot be understood as virtues that mutually exclude each other.

Rosen's metaphysics of the ordinary becomes startling relevant when we realize that the hundreds of billions spent annually on weapons that could blow our planet up many times over are as inconceivable in terms of human experience as the immeasurably tiny particles of matter and energy used by computer technology to hold our world together. Reality today is such that even the President of the United States cannot hope to master all the data at his disposal and gain an accurate worldview without a large number of assistants and deputy assistants, all operating from their own limited and limiting perspectives. Furthermore, by a perverse reversal of Heisenberg's Uncertainty Principle at the macro level, it seems inevitable that the very efforts made to measure and report this chaotic mass of raw matter itself result in distorted pictures of the whole that only further disorient the various entities that constitute it. Consequently, power, no matter how arbitrary or violent, is affirmed for its own sake. Renouncing higher notions of justice and personal integrity, both the technocratic West and the fundamentalist East shamelessly kneel before the altar of necessity. Human society becomes generic and machine-friendly, and the loudly proclaimed advances in human genetics only promise to embody superficially what educational institutions have been doing to the minds of impressionable students for many decades. Under these conditions, when nobility and even uncorrupted speech seem to be all but impossible, a man who can practice ordinary language to remind us of virtue and excellence can only be compared to Teiresias in the underworld "alone retaining his wits while the others flitted around like shadows." Yet such is the dis-ease of this state that even many students fear those rare teachers who can bring them out of Hades.

For fifty years, Stanley Rosen has unceremoniously dragged thousands of students from the ghetto of jargon and compelled them to speak and think in ordinary language. This is why many righteously tolerant academics have been appalled by his use of 'judgmental' language and unprofessional examples to gratuitously indicate the nihilistic foundations of their schizophrenic existence. Now, as then, many highly intelligent students of philosophy prove to be utterly incapable of living their lives in accordance with the principles to which they pay lip service in academese. Nihilism, an unbalanced disposition towards reality, which often results from a death-obsessed 'care' or ego-maniacal authenticity, is preferred over the 'logocentric' procedures of judgment and rank ordering that provide meaning and virtue in a world conspicuously deficient in both qualities. Unfortunately, the question of whether 'being judgmental' is worse than being a hypocrite is one that few care to address in our simultaneously over-tolerant and over-righteous times.

Many students (and professors) still view philosophy as a disease (or a way of being articulately neurotic) at which they just happen to be good. Of course, this sophisticated *diaresis* has no way of distinguishing between Wittgenstein and Woody Allen—and perhaps it shouldn't. In other words, philosophy becomes just a means of paying one's bills; the unquestioned end is normalcy—understood in the most banal and mimetic terms. Any setback will cause philosophers of this variety to not unhappily pursue some other, often more lucrative career path that would better advance either 'family values' or Epicurean lifestyles. Furthermore, following the example of Wittgenstein and the Logical Positivists it has become acceptable, and indeed downright philanthropic, for philosophers to set about the liquidation of philosophy itself—with a view to delivering normal people from its annoying questions and perplexities. Unfortunately, this Socratic 'speed-bump' is the last obstacle to the flattening out of everyday reality and its bifurcation into the extremes of Last Men and Fundamentalists.

By inconsiderately philosophizing in everyday language Rosen makes it far harder for his audience to maintain a 'double-truth' relationship between philosophy and everyday life. He has never treated philosophy as a language game that is played strictly within the pages of scholarly journals and becomes irrelevant or dangerous the moment we re-enter the real world of Xanthippe and Crito. The good must have precedence over being, even in our thoroughly historicized surroundings. Indeed, one could argue that Rosen has always followed Zarathustra's imperative to "be faithful to the earth" and never been seduced by ontic or even ontological exigency. Whilst those least worthy of philosophy only pursue it instrumentally, better but more timorous scholars have sought to make the world safe for philosophy and only succeeded in debasing both philosophy and the world. Vigorously eschewing both of these false oppositions, Rosen believes that true philosophers can and must justify existence through their "robust sense of reality." It follows that 'rank-ordering' is an essential aspect of the distinctive manner in which a philosopher views the world and judges that it is still possible to practice virtue. Even though seeing things as they are certainly is not easy, and the task frequently seems to be as impossible as it was for Socrates or Rousseau to penetrate the encrusted outer shell of Glaucus, Rosen points us towards an abiding structure that, in his own words, "isn't the eternal order but yet is the natural foundation for willing the eternal order to be."[1] It is noteworthy that despite the cryptic language, this formulation is far more positive than its equivalent in the writings of his teacher: eternally recurrent problems that let philosophers stand beyond good and evil to rescue us from the chaotic mire of historicism. By his emphasis on this structure that allows noble deeds and thoughtful words to remain timelessly meaningful, Rosen defends the reality of both ordinary language and human virtue.

Furthermore, despite his passionate interest in moral and political questions, Rosen has consistently been critical of irrationalism and dogmatic skepticism; both poses conveniently conclude that 'everything but judgmental language is permitted' once we are either desperate or 'cool' enough to assume the absurdity of existence or the final inaccessibility of ultimate reality. As a result, the world is delivered up to extremists on both ends of the political spectrum. Contrariwise, Rosen has demonstrated throughout his extraordinarily successful and productive career that ordinary language *is* sufficient to guide human life when it is governed by rational judgment—rather than mindless imitation. Conversely, ideas and facts cannot be separated from each other without consequences even more dangerous than those following the splitting of the atom. Neither does Rosen's model of human existence place man somewhere between an illusory physical world and a wholly transcendent heaven; he prefers to derive the ideas used to measure

1 Stanley Rosen, *Hermeneutics as Politics* (Oxford: Oxford University Press, 1987), 127.

qualitative excellence from human cognitive activity itself—thus deriving depth from surface. In this important regard he once again separates himself from those who pride themselves on their ability to create values *ex-nihilo* by imposing order on the chaotic *hyle* of reality. Rosen's scathing criticisms of historicism and pseudo-aristocratic nihilism are founded in his recognition that it is possible for human beings to take their stand in the real world and resist both fundamentalism and sophistry.

Stanley Rosen, a self-described New Deal Democrat, has remained constant in his political views while instructing three generations of students. Temperamentally unsuited to occupy the Vicarage of Bray, he has never failed to warn against the worst tendencies of the ideology most in vogue among his students—even at the risk of being (wrongly) associated with political views toward which he is least sympathetic. His characteristic defense of prudence in eloquent but seemingly immoderate language has very little resemblance to our contemporary tendency to use insidious methods to promote extremism. Far from being the kind of man who would prescribe Nazism to ward against the corruption of Weimar, his criticisms of nihilism and postmodernism have always been undertaken in the name of moderate enlightenment. It is far nobler to be a Platonist accused of sounding like a Nietzschean than to be a Nietzschean impersonating a Platonist.

Rosen's well-known unwillingness to suffer fools gladly derives precisely from his awareness that many fools are yet capable of excellence; he does not allow a false sense of charity to alienate him (or them) from the experience of quality in the world. His high expectations of others have always been accompanied by genuine authenticity in personal relations with individuals. Having been educated in the company of truly brilliant eccentrics at the University of Chicago in its glory days, and being himself the possessor of an artistic temperament, Rosen has always understood the thin line that separates genius from madness. He has never mistaken an artful plodder with a high I.Q. for a genuine philosopher. In a situation where students typically expect professors either to be their equal or an unapproachable superior, Rosen has refused to play either role in order to gain approval of crowds. Differently put, he has never been known to be afraid of being himself or of speaking his mind. Consequent to this refusal to conform to stereotype, humorless students (and colleagues) at both extremes have decided that he is either unprofessional or an elitist. Their pathetic inability to appreciate Rosen's unsurpassed sense of humor has always served as a kind of *pons asinorum* separating the children who approach him from the goats, sheep, camels and lions making up the intellectual order of rank. By refusing to take himself too seriously, and by never seeking to make disciples, Stanley Rosen always pointed beyond himself. The exaggerations and self-caricatures that made members of the aforementioned menagerie regard him as an egomaniac were in fact the productions of an artist always keenly aware of the enigmatic relationship between image and original. It followed sadly but necessarily that those incapable of understanding this basic Platonic distinction proved that they were unworthy of studying with our greatest living Platonist. Some of the most egregious misinterpretations of Plato have been committed by persons firmly convinced that a philosopher will never write or speak humorously.

III

Of course, any talk concerning Stanley Rosen and the student-teacher relationship is necessarily incomplete without a discussion of his attitude towards his own teacher, Leo Strauss. Since much of Rosen's own work could be regarded as an ongoing response to certain fundamental themes in Strauss's work, and because Rosen himself has had much to say about his former teacher, we could gain valuable insights into the thought of both thinkers by directly addressing this topic. Just as Strauss's amazing success as a teacher is attested to by the large number of disciples garnered by this unprepossessing man, the strange fact that the charismatic and ebullient Stanley Rosen has actively refused to make disciples points to a not unimportant difference in the deepest philosophical beliefs of the these two giants.

Rosen first met Strauss in 1949 shortly after the latter had moved to the University of Chicago, via the latter's stepson, who was an acquaintance of the former. ("You're a poet? My father knows something about poetry. Why don't you go see him.") Rosen at the time regarded himself as a poet. He was also busily engaged in completing the requirements for a Bachelor's degree from Chicago in one year—a feat that was also performed by his distinguished contemporary Seth Benardete. Rosen's hilarious account of his first encounter with Strauss awaits publication, but it suffices to state that on the occasion of their first meeting, after having introduced himself as a poet, Rosen responded to Strauss's inquiry whether he, Rosen, knew what Plato said about poets by saying that he didn't give a damn—because as a poet he knew more about his art than Plato possibly could. This was the unpromising beginning of a very long and animated conversation that ended with an invitation to study with Strauss.

It is highly significant that Rosen was one of a very small number from the Philosophy Department at Chicago to attend Strauss's lectures; Richard Rorty was another. Most of the participants were either from Strauss's own department of political science or the Committee on Social Thought. Among these were intellectual luminaries such as Seth Benardete, Victor Gourevitch, Muhsin Mahdi, and Allan Bloom. In addition, Rosen was the only one of Strauss's students to come to him from poetry. This fact is of course not unrelated to Rosen's interest in language and its often tenuous relationship to everyday reality. By his own account, he was also initially virtually uninterested in politics,[2] an attribute that, needless to say, also separated him from the vast majority of those who attached themselves to

2 See Stanley Rosen, Preface to the Portuguese Translation of *Nihilism*, xxii.

Strauss. Indeed, it has been noted on many occasions that Rosen's interests in metaphysics and epistemology also make him almost unique among Strauss's students. Because of his departmental affiliation, every official course offered by Strauss had to do with political science; however there were several private groups reading philosophical and theological works that he presided over as well.

By his own admission, Rosen attended virtually every meeting of Strauss's seminars over the five years he spent as a graduate student at the University of Chicago. It was soon readily apparent to him that Strauss "transcended the faculty members of the philosophy department in virtually every significant way." Accordingly, after taking his master's degree, Rosen transferred to the Committee on Social Thought where he was able to write a dissertation on Spinoza under the supervision of Leo Strauss. Shortly after completing his degree, marrying, and spending a year in Greece, Rosen secured employment at the Pennsylvania State University and left Chicago. This did not however end his association with Strauss. They corresponded often by letter and in 1958 Strauss visited Rosen and his wife at State College, Pennsylvania. Strauss, who had often defended Rosen against criticisms concerning his student's colorful temperament by giving assurances that he was "getting better", was very pleased at his student's success. He is said to have boasted to colleagues in Chicago that Rosen had "made it" and was now the proud owner of a house and automobile. Rosen continued to visit Strauss on many occasions, the last such visit taking place shortly before the latter's death in 1973. On that occasion, upon hearing that Rosen was preparing a book on Hegel, the ailing teacher pointed him towards what turned out to be a vitally important passage in understanding the full argument of the *Greater Logic*. This incident confirmed Rosen's adamantly held conviction that Strauss's true genius was to be found neither in his pronouncements as a statesman or prophet, nor in his metaphysical or poetic powers, but in his remarkable ability to read a text.

Rosen has stated elsewhere that Strauss rescued him as a teenager from a "transcendentally grounded nihilism." While he came to share a number of his teacher's central views and retained many of them throughout his life, Rosen says he was never at any time a 'Straussian.' Strauss never required him to become one "as a price for the extraordinary benefits he bestowed on his students."[3] Despite fully acknowledging how much he benefited from Strauss's immense learning and "sober madness", Rosen believed that there were certain important differences, largely concerning the issue of esotericism, which caused him to separate himself from the Straussian mainstream. As readers of his writings are well aware, Rosen is in considerable sympathy with the courage and generosity animating the "moderns" in their revolution against tradition and nature. Yet Strauss, who according to Rosen regarded courage as the lowest of virtues,[4] was often critical of what he perceived as Rosen's excessive boldness. It is worth repeating the expression '*epater le*

3 ibid., xxiii.
4 ibid.

bourgeois' (shocking the bourgeoisie) that summed up Strauss's disapproving opinion of his student's more exoteric writing style.[5] We cannot avoid the inference that this criticism had more to do with style than substance.

Even though Rosen's celebrated book *Nihilism* was written to work out the general features of Strauss's analysis of the nihilistic roots of modern philosophy, its "spiritual father", while commending the work highly, also commented that he himself lacked the courage to write such a book.[6] This goes to the heart of the fundamental difference between Strauss, a refugee from Nazi Germany, and Rosen, a native of Cleveland, Ohio. Despite his frequent and stirring invocations of *thumos*, Strauss, the man who rediscovered the long forgotten art of esotericism by reading heretical political theologians, preferred not to express his truest opinions freely on most matters of importance. Some argue that this was due to his fear of corrupting his readers (*epater le bourgeois*). However that may be, it seems not unrelated to their different views on whether it is more desirable and or practical to gain fame or disciples. There are reasons for and against the belief that Strauss, the prudent "ancient", obeyed the Greek warning against seeking fame in one's own lifespan. It is likewise unclear whether Rosen, the courageous and generous "modern", embraced Machiavelli's advice to trust in his own arms—even if the goal was to hold *fortuna* within them.

While Rosen has always defended the phenomenon of esoteric writing, it is his contention that our plight today is such that 'shocking the bourgeoisie' is far less dangerous than allowing them to persist in complacently nihilistic modes and orders already producing a civilizational meltdown. Put bluntly, esoteric writing is useless in a decadent time where success is measured by power rather than wisdom, and even the best students are barely literate, certainly not pious, and often incapable of ever being more than merely good students. Importing esotericism to America is ultimately almost as quixotic as transplanting democracy in Iraq; in both cases one can best deflect the accusation of esoteric knavery by drawing attention to exoteric folly.

IV

An emphasis on rigorous interpretive procedures aiming at the utmost clarity possible, ultimately expressed in ordinary language, rather than reliance upon oracular pronouncements and dogmatic assumptions concerning perfectly constructed texts written by all-knowing Ancients, that could only be decoded by infallible interpreters, starkly distinguishes Rosen's approach from results common to Heideggereans and Straussians. Such procedures only separate

5 ibid.

6 ibid., xxii–xxiii.

student from interpreter while promoting the latter to an intellectual pantheon that confirms his qualitative kinship with the Ancients: "Where I go, you cannot follow." This pious posture also deprives writers from past times of what they would most desire in ours: intelligent readers capable of ascending from the signifier and sign-painter to the signified. The idea that Shakespeare could only have learned about the soul through reading Xenophon by candlelight denies the possibility that an intelligent man may understand a great deal through observing human affairs by daylight.

In other words, while it is quite obvious that many great writers write in such a way that the deeper implications of their works would only be apparent to more astute readers, the view that great works are flawless masterpieces of logographic necessity takes away the only quality that makes interpersonal communication of goodness truth and beauty between very different times and places possible: shared erotic humanity. Consequently, we must deplore the effects of a certain kind of historicism, based upon dark oracles concerning the withdrawal of being or caves below caves, that necessitates revelatory exegesis when unnecessarily befuddled students cry out "Only a god can enlighten us!"

By refusing to resort to obscurantism, and providing constant verbal and non-verbal reminders of his robust humanity, Stanley Rosen has never 'hermenutered' his students and left them incapable of reading for themselves. He recalls Strauss smiling broadly and quoting Nietszche's assertion that the best thing a student can do for his teacher is to kill him. Teacher-student relationships modeled after the doctrine of original sin, which opens up an infinite moral and qualitative abyss between creator and creation, are not appropriate in rational—as opposed to revelatory—contexts. In other words, teachers who produce disciplined disciples often cast a long shadow that makes emulation of the master's virtue by the disciples, or even recognition of it by later generations, all but impossible. Shakespeare put it best in *Julius Caesar*: "The evil that men do lives after them; the good is oft interred with their bones." Accordingly, Rosen's fidelity to Strauss might very well be best assessed by somewhat more esoteric criteria than those used to prove ideological discipleship.

Rosen has stated that Leo Strauss "regarded Heidegger as the enemy of the heritage of Platonism in the late Modern world." Accordingly, he sought to "inoculate his students against Heidegger by training them in the Platonic tradition."[7] It was in the service of this cause that Rosen published two works that took direct aim at Heidegger: *Nihilism* and *A Question of Being*. Yet Rosen's singular experience was that Strauss very rarely mentioned Heidegger by name, even in private conversations and reading groups, and never referred to Heideggerean texts.[8] It was only shortly after leaving Chicago that Rosen became aware of Strauss's

7 ibid., xxiv.
8 ibid.

lecture *An Introduction to Heideggerian Existentialism*—a revised version of which was published in 1989. This document concludes with a description of Heideggerean Being or *Esse* as a synthesis of the Platonic Ideas and the Biblical God. *Esse* is said to be as impersonal as the former and as elusive as the latter.[9] It is curious that Strauss himself, in his famous 1953 lecture *Progress or Return?* claimed that the secret of the vitality of the West depended on the continuance of the unresolved conflict between Reason and Revelation, Jerusalem and Athens.[10] Bearing in mind Heidegger's famous pronouncement in his *Introduction to Metaphysics* (also published in 1953) that the idea of a Christian Philosophy was about as meaningful as a round square,[11] we must entertain seriously Rosen's thought that, despite their respective foci on ontology and politics, the man his teacher called "the only great thinker in our time",[12] exerted a great deal of influence on Leo Strauss.[13] Did Strauss himself have a non-corrupted take on either the round or the square? His recently published early writings point to the heady influence of Freud and Nietzsche; they certainly don't convince us that he was immaculately conceived from the head of Zeus. Does Strauss subscribe to the Nietzschean view that a culture is created *ex nihilo* out of the dialectical interaction between two fictions? Or did he follow Heidegger's example and effectively function as a prophetic interpreter?

Perhaps we could say that Strauss, who claimed to be only a scholar,[14] rejected the poisoned chalice of reason and preferred to find upright shelter in the enduring stormy tension between the impersonal and the elusive. In less poetic words, he preferred political philosophy to metaphysics. Viewed in this light, it is likely that his setting up of the famous quarrel between the ancients and moderns was undertaken with the intention of reconfiguring the debris remaining from Heidegger's *destruktion* of the Western tradition in a way that protected the West from the nihilistic consequences of enlightenment. This solution amounted to forcing both faith and reason to cooperatively assume defensive postures against their common enemy, the juggernaut of technology, instead of exposing each other's deficiencies. Unfortunately, the exigencies of the Cold War forced the

9 Leo Strauss, "An Introduction to Heideggerian Existentialism" in *The Rebirth of Classical Political Rationalism,* ed. Thomas Pangle (Chicago: University of Chicago Press, 1989), 45.

10 Leo Strauss, "Progress or Return?" in *Jewish Philosophy and the Crisis of Modernity,* ed. Kenneth Hart Green (Albany: State University of New York Press, 1997), 116.

11 Martin Heidegger, *Introduction to Metaphysics* (New Haven: Yale University Press, 1958), 7.

12 Strauss, "An Introduction to Heideggeran Existentialism," 29.

13 Stanley Rosen, Preface to Chinese translation of *The Quarrel between Philosophy and Politics,* 1.

14 Strauss, "An Introduction to Heideggerean Existentialism," 29.

West to embrace this very enemy in self-defense. Heidegger warned against this danger, but of course his own doctrines had contributed greatly towards the Western tradition's weakened condition. Rosen himself believes that Strauss was "too pessimistic concerning human creativity, too enamored of nature and so too forgetful of the fact that nature is both good and bad."[15] While we deplore the liberal tendency to celebrate raw potentiality as actuality, this is no reason to embrace the conservative fallacy of justifying, anointing and acclaiming what *is* as what *ought* to be. This is but another form of historicist fatalism. While they might flatter the rich and pander to the powerful, language games of this kind can only breed hubris and stupidity in the real world.

Strauss's preoccupation with such theorists of strife as Thucydides, Hobbes, Machiavelli, and Schmitt as well as his preference for those two noted anti-Socratics Aristophanes and Nietzsche, justify the inference that he esteemed the ancients for their noble pessimism than out of any belief in goodness, truth and beauty. This view is also supported by the fact that his celebrated re-discovery of Platonic political philosophy occurred through the esoteric, atheistic, and decidedly pessimistic medium of Islamic political thought. While Strauss's call for the revival of spiritedness was altogether justified in dark days of the Cold War, Cassandra-like, he drowned out his own warnings that the less immediate but gravest threats were posed by intellectual and religious decadence. In our present hegemonic predicament, the swashbuckling hubris of an Alcibiades is more attractive and consequently a greater danger than the over-prudent timidity of a Nicias. At a time when our foes are unified by their hatred of us, the splendid pseudo virtues of prodigality and optimism are no longer acceptable substitutes for temperance and prudence.

Sadly, despite his prophetic recognition of a looming clash between the Enlightenment and Fundamentalism, the vast majority of Leo Strauss's publications consist of cryptic interpretations of obscure writings; these works have little to say to our unlettered, thoughtless and thoroughly exoteric times. His praise of martial virtue seems redundant besides our sanguine bellicosity, and his guarded revelations of well-concealed wickedness fail to shock our shameless and insatiable appetites. Mindless imitation of imagined hierarchical relationships between infinitely wise oracular teachers, spirited young aristocrats, and invincibly ignorant *hoi polloi* does little good and generates a great deal of mischief in our cynical, superstitious, and materialistic society. Today, the grand alliance promoted by Strauss between Reason and Revelation yields a distressingly large harvest of knowledgeable knaves, lustful libertarians and fanatical fools.

By contrast, subsequent to his bittersweet Socratic recognition that no human being (not even Strauss!) was transcendently wise, Rosen's accounts of the essential connection between reason and the Good provide a richly comprehensive erotic

15 Rosen, Preface to Chinese translation, 2.

Platonism that is agreeable to the generous heart and fevered temperament of modernity. He believes that poetry can mediate successfully between sad reason and crass politics [16] and he has shown that a new robust metaphysic can be derived from the enduring phenomena of ordinary experience. While fully aware that nihilism is a permanent human possibility, Rosen's speech and deeds are animated by his confidence that humans are not inherently incapable of the self-knowledge needed to educate their desires and lead a good life. In one of the most beautiful passages of *Nihilism*, Rosen stirringly reminds us of the contagious example of a virtuous human being:

> The good man . . . is not 'useful for . . .' in the same sense that tools, food, acts even just and beautiful things exhibit utility . . . there is a certain fulfillment, completeness, or perfection which shines forth from such a man, and which we too admire, even perhaps without envy or desire because of its splendor. This is what we mean by 'genuine goodness' or 'purity of character.' The shining of a good man's splendor may illuminate and help us to complete our own lives, whether by virtue of its nobility, or because we are able to see better what to do ourselves when that noble light permeates the otherwise dark contours of our lives.[17]

These winged words best express what Stanley Rosen has meant to many of his students.

16 ibid.

17 Stanley Rosen, *Nihilism* (New Haven: Yale University Press, 1969; South Bend, Ind.: St. Augustine's Press, 2000), 172–173.

Transformations of Enlightenment

Plato, Rosen, and the Postmodern

Alasdair MacIntyre

University of Notre Dame

It is an undeniable truth that Stanley Rosen's philosophical work has not received the attention that it deserves. But the reason why so admirable a set of achievements have not been paid their full due is a good deal more interesting than many such explanations are. In philosophy we generally learn to find our way around by accepting from our elders and teachers some standard account of what the major standpoints are, of how the conversations between them have gone so far, and of what roles it is now acceptable to play, if we are to be recognized as participants in those continuing conversations. And most of us find our place in those conversations by assuming some acceptable role. Not so Stanley Rosen. Rosen has recurrently been the interrupter, the disrupter, the one who insistently points out the inconvenient fact or the disturbing argument, attention to which would make it impossible to continue the conversation along its familiar and established paths, attention to which might even make us fall momentarily into that rare philosophical condition, silence.

Not that silence is characteristic of Rosen himself and happily so. For his chosen part is to put the rest of us to the question, to distract, to disturb. And of course the easiest way to avoid distraction and disturbance is: to ignore its source, to pretend that Rosen is not there. Just this, I believe, is the major explanation for the inadequate recognition of his striking achievements.

There is however another aspect of the resistance to acknowledging Rosen's insights with which I have more sympathy. One of his methods is to take some familiar subject-matter or some well-charted set of disagreements and then to show us by a detailed exegesis of relevant texts conducted with insight and imagination that things are a good deal more complex than we had taken them to be. Yet, if we respond by amending our account to accommodate this complexity, he then often points out some further complexity engendering feature of the argument that we seem to have overlooked, and proceeds in this way until we have just too many issues on our hands all at once. And a refusal to accompany Rosen to this point may arise at least in part from a sense that sometimes some fundamental issue may be in danger of being obscured.

What I am going to suggest is first of all that we are deeply in Rosen's debt for having shown how much more difficult and complex the issues are that divide the defenders of Enlightened modernity from those of its radical critics whose allegiance has been to some position drawn from ancient thought than has sometimes been supposed. Yet I shall also argue that, even when we have given their due to those complexities, fundamental and divisive issues remain. Those issues concern the sense in which and the ways in which nature provides a standard for right action in social and political life.

My account will have five parts. The first will be concerned with the portrait of the Enlightenment's legacy that emerges from Rosen's observations. The second will be about the part that, on Rosen's view, the misunderstanding of Plato has played in the history of Enlightenment and postEnlightenment thought. The third concerns Rosen's own attitudes to the Enlightenment and identifies a central problem for Rosen's position, the problem of how *phronēsis* and law are related. A fourth part addresses that problem. And the final part concerns Rosen's remedy for the excesses of postmodernist thought, the virtue of moderation.

I

Postmodernism is often treated both by its protagonists and by its critics as if it were, almost self-evidently, a revolt against the values of the eighteenth-century Enlightenment. It is to Rosen that we owe the insight that in key part at least postmodernist thought is a sequel to Enlightenment thought, generated from within that thought by the strains and tensions internal to it. Those strains and tensions result from the Enlightened attempt to combine and to implement on the one hand ideals of reason and on the other ideals of freedom and spontaneity.

The ideals of reason prescribe for us a mode of enquiry that enables us to implement and in part to satisfy the human "desire to solve problems and to achieve mastery" (*Hermeneutics as Politics* pp. 150–51). What is to be mastered is nature. But, if human beings are to understand nature and so become masters of nature, "one must reconstitute nature itself" (p. 150) "The nature to be mastered"—and therefore to be reconstituted—"was no longer the Greek *physis*, or the living and even reasonable center of order in man and the world, but a lifeless and so unreasonable extension in the void, moving in accordance with the laws of mechanics but blind to the rational purpose of the human soul. Nature in the sense of matter was thus sundered from soul or mind in God and man" (*The Ancients and the Moderns: Rethinking Modernity*, p. 22). In consequence nature could no longer provide a standard for reason or for virtue. So the prescriptions of Enlightenment become very different from the prescriptions of the great classical thinkers. Nature is now matter to be reconstructed, not a standard for action (on how this contrast is to be interpreted, see Leo Strauss e.g. *Natural Right and History* chapters 4 and 5). But the prescriptions of Enlightenment reason are not restricted to the tasks of understanding and mastery.

The Enlightenment valued both reason and freedom. And one aspect of the "modern celebration of freedom" is that reason is taken to prescribe freedom, a freedom that is the expression of a spontaneity which is, on the Enlightenment view, as fundamental to human nature as reason is. But in fact it is possible to value reason, as the Enlightenment understood it, and to value freedom, as the Enlightenment understood it, only at the cost of generating tension and conflict. And the history of distinctively postEnlightenment thought is the working out of the tensions and conflicts thus generalized, the latest stage of which is postmodernism.

Postmodernism interprets metaphysical reasoning as at once a disguise worn by freedom and an imposition upon, a limitation of freedom. And, since it takes all reasoning to be interpretation, it takes metaphysical reasoning to involve misinterpretation, a misconstrual of reason, a series of philosophical mistakes, the exposure of which is one of the tasks of deconstruction. In so doing the protagonists of postmodernism often see themselves as opposed to the Enlightenment. But, on Rosen's view as I have already indicated, once we have understood the structure of the Enlightenment's thought, we are also able to understand postmodernism as a continuation of that thought, even if, as Rosen puts it, "Postmodernism is the Enlightenment gone mad" (*The Ancients and the Moderns*, p. 20), mad because it presses immoderately towards one-sided conclusions, in which some insights of the Enlightenment are developed in such a way that the Enlightenment's allegiance to truth and reason is abandoned. How then are we to understand the structure of Enlightened thought? Rosen in answering this question has provided us with illuminating analyses of Descartes, Kant, Fichte and Hegel, but it is on Kant that he focuses.

For Kant Ideas and Ideals are products of reason and as such they provide the grounds for our theoretical, practical, and aesthetic judgments (*The Ancients and the Moderns*, p. 48). So the exercise of our freedom is grounded on and constrained by the exercise of reason and understanding. And it may appear therefore—as it does indeed appear to almost all Kantians and Kant scholars—that, on Kant's view, reason has priority over freedom. But this, according to Rosen, is a mistake. "The understanding is in essence the formulation of and obedience to rules. Since there are no rules for the following of rules, or in other words, since reason is the domain of freedom, the understanding must be a 'project' (my [that is, Rosen's] term) of reason. But what grounds or motivates reason?" (*Hermeneutics as Politics*, p. 4). Rosen argues that "on the basis of Kant's texts there is only one answer. Reason is itself constituted, or let us say constitutes itself, in accordance with the will to freedom. The upshot is that freedom both grounds and is grounded by reason" (p. 6). And Rosen goes on to comment that, if "judged by the canons of traditional logic, which Kant accepts, his argument is invalid".

On this conclusion it is worth making two comments. The first is that, if Rosen's interpretation of Kant is correct, what he has shown is not that Kant's argument is invalid, but that it is circular. But I take it that nothing in Rosen's overall argument is affected by this revision. A second comment is that whether Kant's argument is or is not circular does not depend on Kant's acceptance of the canons of traditional or any other logic. And perhaps Rosen did not intend to suggest that it does so depend, but only that Kant's understanding of logic should have enabled him to identify the failure of his argumentative strategy.

Yet well-grounded accusations of circularity, even of vacuous circularity, against Kant would still not be sufficient to make out Rosen's case against Kant. For his claim is not merely that, on Kant's view, freedom both grounds and is grounded on reason, but that in the Kantian scheme freedom is at least at some points—contrary to Kant's own claims—given a priority over reason, that reason has become only what freedom can make of it. And so unsurprisingly it is Fichte who in his revision of Kant "represents the characteristic axiom of the modern approach: freedom is higher than Being" (*The Ancients and the Moderns*, p. 69), although it was Kant who had provided "the classical statement of the theoretical defense of freedom" (p. 70).

So Rosen presents us with a coherent, albeit complex narrative of the development of Enlightenment and postEnlightenment thought. First there is a set of initial seventeenth-century formulations which both introduce a new conception of nature and afford recognition to the desire for freedom with the result that nature can no longer provide a standard for ethics and politics. A second stage is represented by Kant and Fichte, a stage during which the new relationship between reason, nature and freedom is worked out, although not entirely coherently. And a good deal later comes the postmodernist stage in which the rejection of the incoherent theorizing of the earlier stages disguises both for its adherents and its critics the extent to which the original values of the Enlightenment are still being affirmed, albeit without the sobriety of the earlier thinkers.

* * *

The story, as Rosen tells it in detail, is of course even more complex and tortuous than I have suggested and to represent it fairly and fully much more would have to be said, especially about Hegel. But enough has perhaps been said to make it clear why, on Rosen's view, one recurrent attribute of Enlightenment and postEnlightenment thought is a rejection of ontology, a rejection which is understood as a rejection of Platonism. Yet this is an antiPlatonism that depends in key part on misunderstandings of Plato. And, so Rosen argues, this relationship to Plato throws important light on Enlightenment and postEnlightenment claims. Consider from this point of view Kant's Plato, Rosen's Plato, and Derrida's Plato.

Rosen ('Antiplatonism', chapter 3 of *The Ancients and the Moderns*) quotes Kant in the first critique (B596f.) as saying that "What is for us an Ideal, was for Plato an Idea of the divine understanding, an individual object in God's pure intuition, the most complete of each type of possible being and the ultimate ground of all images in appearance. Without our soaring so high, however, we must admit that human reason contains not only Ideas, but also Ideals which indeed do not like the Platonic have creative but rather practical force (as regulative principles)." Kant thus presents us with an account of what divides him from Plato, according to which, while he and Plato agree in according a certain kind of primacy to Ideals and Ideas, Plato takes them to be actual and existent, while he, Kant, restricts their status to that of merely regulative principles for both theory and practice. And many readers have followed Kant in contrasting his thought with Plato's in this way. But Rosen argues that matters are a good deal more complex than Kant or his commentators have allowed. Kant is more ontologically committed than he himself recognized, while Plato is less ontologically committed than either his critics or his defenders have perceived.

Kant, on Rosen's interpretation, leaves open the question as to whether those "heuristic fictions" which are the Ideals are original or images. "If they are genuine originals, then Kant has created the regulative concepts that supply unity and direction to the world of experience . . . If the heuristic fictions are not originals in this sense, then they must be images of the nature of the noumenal world, or more properly, of the teleological nature of the noumenal world as a creation of a divine intelligence or as the Platonic order of eternity. In this case the originals are absent" (*Ancients and the Moderns*, p. 56) and, because they are absent, they are unknowable.

Kant thus, on Rosen's account, still leaves open the possibility that there are indeed ultimate existents, even if we can only be aware of them indirectly through the images that they generate. In so doing however he has moved towards agreement with Plato. For Plato, on Rosen's account, holds that we are aware of the Platonic Ideas, which are pure form, only through recollection and Rosen follows Leibniz in holding that "a recollection of an Idea is already an image and not the Idea itself" (p. 55). Yet of course Kant and Plato thus understood are still in disagreement. For Plato it is crucial that the Ideas are actual and that actuality is more fundamental than possibility, while for Kant possibility is primary, even if it is what is necessarily possible that is fundamental. Rosen comments that, ironically, the quarrel between Plato and Kant could only be resolved by recourse to a quasiKantian argument, one that showed that "the logical condition for the possibility of the world is the primordial and unknowable structure of original and image" (p. 50).

On Rosen's view no sound argument of this kind is however available and it is not just that no sound argument has as yet been advanced. There is here an unresolvable *impasse* in wrestling with which philosophy has made and can make no progress. And the quarrel between the two sides is not so much a quarrel between Kant and Plato, let alone one between the moderns and the ancients, as it is a quarrel internal to Platonism. Plato, that is to say, was not the straightforward expositor of a theory of forms, nor even someone who at one stage of his career had held such a theory, but later criticized and abandoned it. On that interpretation of Plato the dialogue form would be no more than an expository device, one that Plato could easily have dispensed with, whereas on Rosen's view—and on this matter let me endorse Rosen's view—the dialogue form is indispensable, if Plato is to communicate to us what he needs to communicate. What he needs to communicate, according to Rosen, is not at all an ontology, not what postmodernists accusingly speak of as a metaphysics of presence. Why not?

The Plato of the dialogues is to be distinguished from an apologist for an ontology of forms in at least three ways. First, such a defender would be committed to showing that knowledge of forms can be achieved in a way that frees those who achieve it from the limitations and especially the one-sidedness of sense-perception. But the Platonic Socrates, while contrasting the knowledge of forms with the opinions that derive from sense-perception, is unable to characterize that knowledge and its objects without using the language of vision, so that, as Rosen puts it "the famous Socratic distinction between the intelligible (*to noéton*) and the visible (*to horaton*) cannot be sustained. In the first place the intelligible is itself visible to the mind's eye. This is of course a metaphor, but an inescapable metaphor" (*The Ancients and the Moderns*, p. 59). And we may reinforce Rosen's point by noticing that, when the Platonic Socrates contrasts mathematical understanding with knowledge of the forms, one of his two reasons for asserting that mathematical understanding is inferior is that it cannot dispense with diagrams, yet he himself explains what knowledge of the forms is by appeal to a diagram (*Republic VI* 509a–511e) and one that appears to be indispensable.

Secondly, our vision of the Ideas is neither some type of inferential knowledge nor direct, unmediated vision. "It is rather a temporalized image" (*The Ancients and the Moderns*, p. 58). And our images are tied to our particular point of view. "Seeing the Ideas is like stargazing, not astronomy" (*Hermeneutics as Politics*, p. 76). So that the most that we can ever have is "a perspectival and temporally conditioned vision of the eternal" and this "is not a sufficient basis for an ontology" (*The Ancients and the Moderns*, p. 76). "It is not that we do not have glimpses of the eternal, but that the world of movement and change in which we are situated, rules out the possibility of systematic speech about the structure of being" (p. 182). We see with difficulty, although certainly "To see with difficulty is not the same as not to see at all."

Thirdly what we have instead of systematic speech is either poetic and myth-recounting discourse or silence, each of which has a necessary place, for "all discursive analyses are grounded in silent vision" (*Hermeneutics as Politics*, p. 76). And what we can express as the outcome of our discursive analysis must take account of the fact that "there is a disjunction between vision and *logos* or the discursive account of what we see" and that this "disjunction can only be filled by myths" (*The Ancients and the Moderns*, p. 60). So philosophical enquiry can never free itself from myth, can never be a matter wholly of those concepts that are at home in discursive analysis.

The Platonic dialogues then are "a web of speech and silence" and, insofar as they are speech, they are playful speech, "artifactual phantasms of the truth" (*Hermeneutics as Politics*, p. 77). No reader of both Rosen and Plato could fail to remark on the distinction and the originality of Rosen's account. This is not Terence Irwin's analytical Plato nor John Findlay's Neo-Platonic Plato nor Jowett's Victorian Plato. So that we might easily be distracted into asking the not unimportant question: Is Rosen's Plato Plato? Nonetheless I shall treat it as a distraction. For Rosen's Plato provides him with a paradigm of philosophy and, if that particular Plato had never in fact existed, Rosen would have had to invent him.

Philosophy on this view has to steer a course between a dogmatism that ignores the situatedness of all thought and a relativism that obscures the inescapable reference to standards of truth that informs all discourse and every enquiry. It can only steer this course successfully, if those engaged in philosophy recognize the necessary incompleteness of and limit to the findings of discursive analysis. And, if we do recognize this, we will understand that philosophy consists in "the deepening of comprehensive problems that cannot be solved by technical devices of any kind." It is just because there are no such solutions that the issue that, on Rosen's account, divides Kant from Plato cannot be brought to any decisive resolution. Yet that it cannot be brought to such a resolution is itself surely, if Rosen's accounts of Plato and of philosophy are correct, a victory for Plato.

It is my reading of Rosen's reading of the history of philosophy that he takes it to be a series of vindications of this Platonic standpoint in which successive explorations succeed or fail insofar as they avoid or fail to avoid the one-sidedness of both dogmatism and relativism. Yet, although these are very different types of error, their protagonists tend to agree in misinterpreting Plato as an ontologist, the dogmatic party claiming him as an ancestral and prototypical figure, their opponents accepting this characterization, so that they can attack whatever contemporary view they happen to be opposing by attacking Plato. Hence AntiPlatonism is not accidentally a recurrent feature of the history of philosophy, one whose latest representative is Derrida.

Rosen's critique of Derrida's interpretation of Plato makes a number of telling points: that Derrida's canons of interpretation are self-undermining; that Derrida ascribes to Plato a condemnation of writing as such, while Plato in fact only criticizes one kind of writing; and that Derrida fails to construe correctly the relationship between analytic discourse and poetic myth, both in Plato and more generally. This third criticism finds application in part because of a more general failure by Derrida, a failure to recognize that "The perception of forms guides every kind of discourse", so that there is no escape from the kind of standard that Derrida aspires to disown.

Here I interpolate a comment on Derrida that confirms Rosen's diagnosis. Derrida's practice on occasion subverts Derrida's theory. Two kinds of writing in which he engages make this especially evident. First, there are the interviews that he has given and the question and answer sessions in which he has engaged. In these contexts what is revealing is Derrida's remarkable and praiseworthy attempt to make sure that he has grasped the question as the questioner intended it, that he is speaking to the questioner's concerns. In so doing he tacitly acknowledges not only shared standards and a shared goal, but more specifically standards of truth and truthfulness, standards that he finds inescapable in this kind of writing. And this is even more evident in a very different kind of writing, that of his memoirs of and elegies for the recently dead (collected in *The Work of Mourning,* ed. P.-A. Brault and M. Naas, Chicago: University of Chicago Press, 2001). Here it is clear that Derrida is presupposing standards shared not only with the dead, but with those other mourners whom he addresses, standards that once again make it not just intelligible, but inescapable that he and they should grieve for the lost goods of their relationship with those who have died. This is what Derrida himself speaks of as an "ethics beyond ethics" in his farewell to Levinas.

I do not myself think that Derrida is thereby committed to a strictly Platonic account of the standards to which he is conforming. But Rosen is certainly right that there is in Derrida's theoretical works a failure to acknowledge standards that are nonetheless accorded recognition implicitly even in those works and more openly in these other kinds of writing. And this recognition confirms Rosen's view that the attempt to disown such standards is indeed an arbitrary act of will disguised as a hermeneutic insight. Here the two strands in Rosen's thought that I have traced so far come together. For Derrida is the paradigmatic case of the postmodernist thinker whose view of reason disguises both from himself and also from others the extent to which he is an heir of the Enlightenment. And Derrida's AntiPlatonism is a symptom of this condition. But in thus unmasking Derrida Rosen himself speaks both as a friend of Plato and as a friend, albeit a critical friend of the Enlightenment.

II

How then does Rosen stand to the Enlightenment? He agrees with the thinkers of the Enlightenment in their contention that those ancient conceptions of nature that had made it possible to take nature as a standard to which appeal could be made in our moral and political lives have been conclusively discredited by the philosophical and scientific developments of the sixteenth and seventeenth centuries (*The Ancients and the Moderns*, p. 22). And attempts to revive that standard, and with it the classical ideal of the *polis*, by contemporary conservatives would involve absurd consequences: an intolerably strict regulation of public life, an impossible imposition of their standards on the many by the few, indeed "the steady transformation of the city into an armed camp", and beyond that the quelling of any effective type of disagreement. And so the attempt to implement in the modern world what conservatives take to be the paradigm of civic virtue would in fact subvert that paradigm and be self-defeating (*The Ancients and the Moderns*, pp. 9–11).

Rosen thus takes it not only that in the quarrel of the ancients and the moderns we must stand with the moderns, but also that we need to recognize that that quarrel is itself something that takes place only in the modern world and only among moderns. So it is a quarrel in which one version of modernity confronts another, and because Rosen rejects the modernity of conservatism and, like other post Enlightenment thinkers takes it for granted that the ancient standard of nature is no longer available to us, he finds himself committed to rethinking the relationship between nature, freedom and reason in very much the way that Kant did. Indeed, although he does not accept Kant's solutions, he takes Kant's problems with the utmost seriousness. It would perhaps not be going too far to say that Rosen has made Kant's problematic his own, even when he presents Kant too as problematic (see especially 'Transcendental Ambiguity: The Rhetoric of the Enlightenment' ch. 1 of *Hermeneutics as Politics*). Where he takes Kant, and those who have developed certain aspects of Kant's thought one-sidedly, such as Fichte, to be at serious fault is in not having recognized how much they need to learn from Plato. So Rosen's central project is this: to bring Plato's thought to bear on the distinctive issues of modernity, as defined by Kant.

Rosen believes that the successful carrying through of this project has political as well as philosophical implications. For the politics that he fears is not primarily, I think, the politics of conservatism. What then does he fear? Here I need to mention two topics that I have been trying so far studiously to avoid: Leo Strauss and God. Rosen's relationship to Strauss is complex and in much that Rosen writes that relationship cannot be neglected, both on points of detail and on the definition of large issues. Indeed any adequate treatment of Rosen's attitude to the contrasts between ancient thought and Enlightened thought would require an extended comparison with Strauss. But here I remark only that some of Rosen's fears are distinctively Straussian fears, above all the fear of those who, like Alexander Kojève, identify themselves with God. This tendency towards the madness of self-deification belongs to one particular strand of Enlightenment and postEnlightenment thought, that which denies the need to respect limits and glorifies the immoderate. Rosen rejects what he takes to be the irrationality of the immoderate, whether in its conservative or in its postEnlightenment form. So it became essential to Rosen's project to rethink the notions of sobriety and of moderation, so that those virtues may become at home in the modern world, both in our theory and in our practice. The account of the virtue of *sóphrosuné* provided by the Platonic Socrates has to be the starting-point for this investigation, yet in the end it presents us with difficulties. One source of these is the inadequacy of the

Platonic account of self-knowledge. Another concerns the relationship of theory to practice. And both these problems can only be resolved in the course of acquiring an adequate understanding of practical intelligence, of prudence. For to be moderate is to be prudent in one's practice. What then is it to be prudent?

Here we need to remind ourselves once again of Rosen's rejection of what some followers of Strauss have understood as the ancient conception of nature, which was valued by them for providing a standard by which actions could be judged virtuous or vicious, a standard that is external to and independent of the judgments of particular individuals. If therefore Rosen is to provide us—and himself—with an account of reasonable moderation, then he needs to identify a capacity for exercising a type of practical judgment that may be characterized as reason-governed, yet that does not involve appeal to any such external standard. Plato and Aristotle have a name for just such a capacity: it is "*phronēsis*". So the question of what *phronēsis* is and how it functions had to become an item on Rosen's philosophical agenda.

Moreover the ancient conception of nature, on this understanding of it, provided a standard by appeal to which laws could be evaluated. But, if there is no such external standard for legislators, then the questions inescapably arise: How are we to understand the legislator's activity? And what kind of authority do laws possess? Here then was another item for Rosen's agenda. But at once it is evident that the problem of the nature of *phronēsis* and the problem of the nature of the authority of law cannot be investigated in independence of each other. What conclusions one reaches about the one puts constraints upon the conclusions that one can reach about the other. So that the nature and relationship of *phronēsis* and law is a single, if highly complex problem. It is therefore to Rosen's treatment of that problem in his commentary on Plato's *Statesman* that I now turn. But I do so with an eye to yet another problem confronting Rosen.

Rosen, as we have already seen, distinguishes himself from the postmodern heirs of the Enlightenment not only by counterposing his Platonism to their antiPlatonism, but also by his emphasis on the need in an Enlightened person for the virtue of modest sobriety, so that such a one may then become the protagonist of "a modest version of the Enlightenment" (*The Ancients and the Moderns*, p. 21). "The adherence to Enlightenment", he wrote, "must be moderate in various senses of the term, none of them incompatible with courage" and he added "that temperance is the courage of modesty" (p. 20). Rosen therefore owes us a more systematic account of the virtues then he has hitherto provided, an account which will explain the relationship of temperateness, courage, prudence, and respect for law, that is of *phronēsis* and *nomos*. But an obstacle confronts him in giving such an account.

Rosen, like the Eleatic Stranger in the *Statesman*, denies the possibility of governing the life of a city by a standard derived from nature. Rosen, unlike the

Eleatic Stranger, affirms the possibility of combining *sóphrosuné* and *andreia* in a single character. The problem for Rosen is this. If we are to understand how this latter is possible, we shall need an adequate conception of *phronésis*, or so I shall argue. And any adequate conception of *phronésis*, so I shall argue further, requires a rejection of the Eleatic Stranger's account of the relationship of *phronésis* to law. But that rejection requires us also to reject the Eleatic Stranger's assertion that, in Rosen's words, "the city is not in accord with nature . . . in the same sense as it is for Aristotle" (*Plato's Statesman: The Web of Politics* New Haven: Yale University Press, 1995, p. 5). The city, as understood by the Eleatic Stranger, could not be in accord with nature, both because there are "diverse human natures" which are "the raw material out of which the city is constructed," (p. 5), and because there is a "disjunction within nature that they themselves [human beings] exemplify, but which for that reason they can never master" (p. 7). If there are sufficient grounds for agreeing with Aristotle and therefore for disagreeing with Eleatic stranger, as I shall suggest, then Rosen confronts a dilemma. Either he must revise his view that the standard for the life of the city cannot be derived from nature or else he will be unable to provide an adequate account of the virtue of modest sobriety. He will have to abandon one part of his position. What then are the arguments? They begin from the claim that no one can have and exercise the virtues of *sóphrosuné* and *andreia*, unless they have a further virtue, one that enables them to recognize in which situations *sóphrosuné* is called for and in which *andreia.* That virtue is *phronésis.*

The Eleatic Stranger takes *phronésis* to be the virtue of those who have the kind of understanding befitting a king (294a) and contrasts the exercise of phronésis with the rule of law: "Law cannot prescribe with accuracy what is best and just for each member of the community at any one time" (294 a–b), while the *phronétic* human being knows what it is best and just to do here and now. Even the best legislator, so the Eleatic Stranger asserts, has to enact unvarying rules that are able to take account only of some salient features of the situations to which they apply and therefore must fail to make provision for exceptional and varying circumstances.

The relationship between *phronésis* and law, as understood by the Eleatic Stranger, has three important characteristics. First, those who possess perfected *phronésis* have themselves no need of the guidance provided by law. Secondly, conformity to law does not require the exercise of *phronésis* by those who so conform. Acting in accordance with law requires no more than knowledge of what the laws are and motivation to obey them, motivation provided by the penalties attached to disobedience. Thirdly, in a well-ordered city—unlike actual Greek cities—it is recognized that there are two distinct classes of human individual, the few fitted to rule who live by phronésis and the many from whose everyday law-governed lives *phronésis* is absent. On all three counts I shall suggest that the Eleatic Stranger is mistaken.

First, it is of crucial importance that *phronēsis* can only be exercised successfully in determinate social contexts. And, in order for the circumstances in which it is exercised to be adequately determinate, individuals must stand in norm-governed relationships to each other, each individual having relatively firm expectations of others, expectations founded on their knowledge of those requirements that are generally acknowledged in that particular social context. Central to those requirements are the requirements of whatever set of laws have been enacted and continue to be recognized as authoritative. That is to say, it is only in communities that are partially defined by laws that are authoritative for all the citizens that *phronēsis* can be successfully exercised. *Phronēsis* and law are not alternatives, but counterparts.

Secondly, the better the system of laws the more evident will be the need for *phronēsis* not only in acts of legislation and of administration and enforcement by authorized officials, but also by plain persons, by the ordinary citizens. For laws, unlike the commands of tyrannical authority, are upheld by widely shared agreements to respect them, so that a range of civilized interactions and transactions may continue to be possible. And *phronēsis* is needed as a virtue of the everyday life of the ruled just because in any working system of rules, including systems of laws, based on such agreements, there have to be numerous exercises of judgment by plain persons as to whether this or that action is to be accounted a violation of this or that law, or as to how the law is to be interpreted in its application to this or that set of circumstances, or as to the particularities of what is required and what is permitted.

Let me make this point more generally. Philosophers writing about rules and rule-following are sometimes misled by what Wittgenstein called an unbalanced diet of examples. They attend to examples of arithmetical rule-following, performing long division, say, or reciting the prime numbers or the expansion of pi, without recognizing how different most rule-following in everyday practice is. Numerous empirical studies have shown that in many different social contexts there is first of all a gap between rules as explicitly formulated and rules as actually followed and secondly, and even more importantly, that rule-following in complex cooperative activities has to be sustained by frequent acts of creative improvisation. In all such contacts something very close to *phronēsis* is indispensable for rule-following, both an ability to understand what the rules followed really are, since they may be in crucial respects not at all what people say that they are, and an ability to improvise, sometimes in new and unexpected ways. And among the sets of rules for following which these abilities and skills are required are the rules of legal systems. (An example: what is the answer you should give to a police officer in North Carolina, when he tells you that you have been driving at more than ten miles per hour over the speed limit? Bad answers are either "No, I was driving under the speed limit "or" Yes, I was driving eleven miles over the speed limit". One much better answer is: "I am certain that I was driving eight or nine miles over the speed limit", and this whatever the speed at which you were driving. Am I suggesting that it is right to lie? No, I am suggesting that this kind of question and answer is part of an equivocating ritual by means of which some drivers and some police officers sometimes exercise something very like *phronésis* in order to negotiate the statute law of North Carolina.)

What emerges from this is that the relationship of *phronésis* to rule-following and to law-governedness is quite other than the Eleatic Stranger suggests. For the exercise of *phronésis* has to be an aspect of all agency in and through which human goods are achieved and law-governed human community sustained. And in addition the standard by which the laws of particular human societies are to be judged is a standard provided by nature, although not in that sense which both Rosen and the Eleatic Stranger give to 'nature' or to '*physis*'.

To say that nature affords a standard for law or that a city is in accord with nature is to speak of what human beings are by nature, that is, of what their nature as rational animals is. And it is part of our specific nature as rational animals, as both Aristotle and Aquinas tells us, to ask not only what our specific good as human beings is and how it is good and just for us to act here and now in this or that set of particular circumstances, but also what bearing the answer to the former of these questions has on the answer to the latter. In so asking we discover that, each of us needs resources provided by others, each of us needs to deliberate and to enquire in company, so that *phronésis* may inform our actions. But such communal deliberation and enquiry itself requires that certain conditions be satisfied, that each participant in such deliberation and enquiry is able generally to rely on the observance by other participants of certain precepts. For we cannot deliberate together, we cannot learn from each other, unless each of us knows that we all regard ourselves as bound to respect the person and property of others, to speak truthfully, to honor our commitments, to listen carefully and to acknowledge when we are in the wrong. The precepts that thus bind us are the precepts of the natural law, those precepts without which we cannot achieve the good which is ours by in virtue of our nature as rational animals.

So the argument comes full circle. The exercise of *phronésis* requires a recognition of a standard derived from nature and the exercise of the other virtues, including the virtue of modest sobriety, requires the exercise of *phronésis*. It follows that without a standard derived from nature we cannot exercise the virtue of modest sobriety. And hence Rosen confronts a dilemma. But at least in the form in which I have presented it, it will perhaps be less unwelcome than in some other versions. For the appeal to nature as a standard in morals and politics, as I have understood it, does not after all involve any concessions to the kind of postStraussian conservatism that Rosen so rightly condemns. Nor indeed need this appeal be thought of as taking the side of the ancients against the moderns. Rosen has given us excellent reasons for regarding Plato as a contemporary philosopher. I have tried to suggest, although no more than suggest, that Aristotle and Aquinas too are best regarded as contemporaries.

The “Ordinary Experience” of the Platonic Dialogues

Drew A. Hyland

Trinity College

This collection honors “the work” of Stanley Rosen, and the clear assumption of the title, by long tradition, is that the work we address in these essays will be Rosen’s written work. I want to begin, however, by acknowledging first another dimension of Stanley Rosen’s work too often passed over: his outstanding work over the years as the teacher of so many of us. One might easily cite some of the most striking features of Rosen’s teaching: the brilliance of his presentations, his hilarious asides, his sometimes biting irony. But through the brilliance of the teaching, through the hilarity of the asides and the biting irony, Rosen, as some of us like to say, has always been teaching us the simple but profound lesson of how to read: how to read with the most careful attention to detail, how to read with a critical imaginativeness, how to read philosophically. For that, so many of us remain always profoundly grateful.

I might subtitle this paper, with no little irony, “Rosen’s Development,” or even “From the Early to the Middle High Rosen,” since I want to reflect on the relation, on one issue at least, between Stanley Rosen’s early work on Plato, especially the books on the *Symposium, Sophist, and Statesman,* and his later work, with particular attention to his 2002 book, *The Elusiveness of the Ordinary: Studies in the Possibility of Philosophy.* The irony, of course, derives from the fact that Rosen’s own attitude toward the well-known “developmental hypothesis” as an interpretive principle of the Platonic dialogues has not always been, shall we say, gentle. So perhaps a more prudent way to put the point I want to make is to say that an inspection of the connection between the early Plato works and the later work demonstrates that Rosen has learned from himself.

Rosen, as is well-known, was a student of Leo Strauss, although he has surely been a student who has taken Zarathustra’s advice near the end of Part I to heart: “One repays a teacher badly if one always remains nothing but a pupil.” One lesson Rosen did take from Strauss and preserved concerns the crucial importance of the dialogue form itself to any interpretation of Plato’s philosophy. More particularly, Rosen emphasizes again and again in his Plato work the way in which every dialogue, by the way that it locates every philosophic discussion in a specific existential context, in a particular time, a particular place and situation, with interlocutors of varying character, abilities, and limitations, teaches this decisive initial lesson, perhaps the most pervasive lesson in the dialogues, that what may become the extraordinary speech of philosophy always arises, or perhaps always should arise, out of the "ordinary" situations and predicaments of the everyday. Socrates, in a discussion with two generals, leads the conversation into a discussion of the nature of courage. Socrates, in jail and presented with the opportunity to escape, engages his old non-philosophic friend, Crito, in a discussion about the justice of such an escape that concludes that Socrates should stay and die. Socrates, at a party where most of the participants are involved in various erotic and antagonistic relationships, engages in a discussion of Eros. Philosophic speech may, for a variety of reasons and in a variety of situations, *become* abstract, but the lesson of the dialogues is that it never, never *begins* as abstract, or perhaps we should again say, never, never *should* begin as abstract. To put the point another way, philosophic speech, even what may become the most extraordinary philosophic speech (that is, highly technical, complicated, jargon-filled, or abstract speech) always arises out of and is generated by the predicaments of the everyday, of the ordinary, of what comes to be called much later by various philosophers "ordinary language," or "lived experience," or "average everydayness." A second lesson of the dialogues may well be that the more abstract, and so the more distant from ordinary speech, that philosophic speech becomes, the more problematic it becomes as an account of the ordinary experience that was presumably its guiding intention. One thinks here especially of dialogues such as the *Parmenides, Sophist,* or the more abstruse sections of the *Philebus.* The *Sophist* is a particularly poignant example of this problematic. Dramatically, the dialogue is set the day after Socrates has answered the charges against him of impiety and corrupting the youth, the day on which Socrates engages in two dialogues, the *Theaetetus* and *Euthyphro*. As the *Apology* will soon demonstrate, Socrates understands these charges to be based in part upon a confusion of his own philosophic activity with that of sophistry. To say the least, he could use some help, concrete, ordinary language help that he could use in his defense, in distinguishing his philosophic activity from sophistry. Of what help will the highly technical intellectual gymnastics of the various diareses of the sophist by the Eleatic Stranger be in his defense? Indeed, given that one of the "definitions" of what is called the "noble" sophist comes perilously close to Socrates own activity, one could say that the abstract procedure of the Eleatic stranger, far from helping Socrates in his existential predicament, confuses rather than clarifies his problem. The Eleatic Stranger, whatever light he may shed on what much later generations will label problems of "predication" or "participation" or "the logic of negative facts," offers Socrates no help whatsoever in the defense of his life which he now must be preparing.

Rosen is always careful to place his interpretations of Platonic dialogues in their proper existential context and to show how those contexts generate the "philosophical" issues of the dialogue. Indeed, one could say that no one does this better than he does. In his *Symposium* book, his opening discussion of the complex prologue to the dialogue, a discussion that itself covers some thirty-eight pages, thoroughly sets the groundwork for the interpretations of the speeches that follow, interpretations which themselves constantly call attention to the connection between the theoretical positions that are developed and the existential or personal situations of the speakers. In the *Sophist* book, his discussion of the prologue to that dialogue includes a seminal section on the dramatic significance of the dialogue form entitled "Dramatic Phenomenology," a term which Rosen characterizes therein as follows: "Dramatic phenomenology is the artistic reformulation of phenomenological descriptions of speeches and deeds within the context of a unified statement about the good or philosophic life, and hence about the noble as distinct from the base. Such a unified statement is an interpretation of human life." (*Plato's Sophist,* 12–13).

Such a characterization, while it pays due attention to the dramatic portrayal of "human life," brings out implicitly a further complication to Plato's use of the dialogue form of which Rosen is acutely aware. Although the dialogues clearly portray everyday situations and the way in which philosophy might arise out of those everyday situations, they do so in a way that is itself in no way "ordinary." That is, the dialogues themselves are "extraordinary speech" from the beginning. They are extraordinary, first, in the exquisite care with which they are obviously constructed. One can express this provocatively by saying that the dialogues are extraordinary precisely because they are *art*—a term that becomes provocative in part because of the often apparently critical discussions of art that occur within the pages of the dialogues. Ordinary experience is shot through with chance. There is next to nothing left to chance in the Platonic dialogues, certainly including the occasional artistic incursions of what is experienced by the persona within the dialogue as "chance." (If I were a more obedient philosophic grandson of Strauss, I would say "nothing" rather than "next to nothing" is left to chance). So as Rosen often puts it, the dialogues, in the exquisite care with which they are constructed and controlled by their author, are all "fictions," and so are already extraordinary portrayals of ordinary experience. Nevertheless, again, one lesson of these *artificial* constructions, these "dramatic phenomenologies," is to exhibit the way in which philosophy originates in and arises out of the ordinary experience of the everyday.

In his earlier works on Plato, as I have pointed out, Rosen always pays due attention to these dramatic elements, grounding what follows in concrete experience. And yet, I now want to suggest that however detailed his discussion of this background in ordinary experience is, however more detailed it is than almost any of his predecessors, Rosen's discussions of that grounding in ordinary experience remain propaedeutic rather than thematic. By this I mean that in these earlier works Rosen seems comfortable, having pointed out the importance of the everyday situation out of which the philosophic discussion arises, in making the transition to the extraordinary speech of philosophy, and remaining within that realm of extraordinary speech for the balance of his reflection. This is what I mean by saying tfhat the real *theme* of these books remains not the ordinary experience that gives rise to philosophy but the extraordinary speech of philosophy itself. Indeed, often his very way of leading us from the "ordinary" experience of the dialogue to the extraordinary philosophic issues is itself extraordinary. One need only consult as an example the remarkable "Prologue" to the *Sophist* book, with its highly technical and logically sophisticated accounts of the "predicationalist" reading of the dialogue, to see this. In these books, Rosen teaches us perhaps better than anyone before that the dramatic portrayal of the ordinary experience out of which philosophy arises is crucial to understanding the philosophic teaching. Having taught us that lesson, he is content to spend the balance of his books on the most sophisticated, and in that sense extraordinary, analyses of the philosophic issues that *do* arise out of the everyday.

It is this that changes significantly, I now want to suggest, in Rosen's later work, and quite focally in *The Elusiveness of the Ordinary.* This change occurs, I think, in two fundamental ways. First, in the later book Rosen now stays *with* the ordinary at much greater length, makes the issue of the ordinary as the source of philosophy *itself the guiding question.* The transition from the portrayal of ordinary situations to the extraordinary speech of philosophy that he made so easily in the early work now becomes itself the philosophic problematic. And the nature of that transition, Rosen shows at great length, is itself extraordinarily complicated. On the one hand, the extraordinary speech of philosophy does originate in ordinary experience and ordinary language, just as the Platonic dialogues had shown. However, that ordinary situation already contains the seeds of the extra ordinary speech that it generates, indeed demands it. As such, and contrary to the hope of 20th century "ordinary language philosophers," the ordinary language and ordinary experience which generates the extraordinary speech of philosophy cannot itself be the source of the resolution of the problems generated by that extraordinary speech. Rosen formulates this succinctly as follows:

"Very far from being entirely distinct, ordinary language is rather an anticipation of theoretical discourse. . . . For this reason, it is impossible to return to a natural stratum of discursive experience that is theoretically neutral, in the sense that by grasping it accurately, we are able to determine a unique and correct standard for subsequent interpretations of the significance and value of human existence. Precisely if Socrates was right to refer to the human soul as philosophical by its very nature, ordinary or ostensibly pretheoretical speech contains the seeds of philosophical disputation, not the uniformly valid resolution of that dispute. Philosophy originates in, but does not take its final form as, ordinary discourse." (*The Elusiveness of the Ordinary*, 232).

In the chapter from which the preceding quote is taken, entitled "What Do We Talk About?" Rosen is concerned to emphasize the complexity of the situation here, that while ordinary experience and discourse does generate the extraordinary speech of philosophy, the two are neither entirely separate nor can ordinary experience be used as the final arbiter of the extraordinary speech that it generates. "The fundamental premiss of this chapter is extremely simple: everyday experience provides us with the only reliable basis from which to begin our philosophical reflections. But it does so as the source of extraordinary or philosophical speech, not as a distinct and paradigmatic use of language. Our talk about the substances or things that occur within, or constitute, ordinary or everyday experience is therefore philosophical from the outset. Philosophy is accordingly the process of explaining how extraordinary modes of discourse are demanded for an adequate understanding of the ordinary." (233).

I want to emphasize that this focus on the problematic of the relation of ordinary to extraordinary or philosophical discourse is in no sense a "reversal" of his early work—quite to the contrary—but precisely a "development." What had in the early work been identified and acknowledged as an important issue now becomes itself the philosophic problem. The dialogues, in exhibiting again and again how philosophic issues and philosophic speech arise out of ordinary situations and language, do not just teach us an important lesson; they point to an enormous philosophic problem.

Second, however, the grounding of the extraordinary speech of philosophy in ordinary experience and language has implicitly profound implications for the character of the extraordinary speech itself. As my earlier reference to the dramatic problematic of the highly technical diareses of the "sophist" was meant to suggest, the farther that extraordinary philosophical speech gets removed from the ordinary speech that generated it, the more problematic it becomes as an adequate account of that ordinary situation. This is a complicated issue, complicated first by the fact that, as Rosen emphasizes, ordinary discourse *demands* the extraordinary for an adequate account of itself. So philosophic speech can hardly be criticized *per se* for being extraordinary (again a common mistake of later "ordinary language philosophy"). Yet it remains true that the farther it get from ordinary discourse, the more problematic it becomes as an account of the ordinary; in the extreme cases, philosophic speech becomes almost totally detached from ordinary speech, or "merely" abstract.

Rosen, I now want to suggest, seems to have taken this lesson to heart. His early work, as I have already pointed out, moves rather quickly from the ordinary situation and ordinary discourse that he acknowledges to the most extraordinary discourse, extraordinary not least for its complexity and abstractness. This is evident enough in the Plato books, but is nowhere more visible than in his two early but seminal articles on the Ideas, the articles entitled simply "Ideas" and "Wisdom: The End of Philosophy." Those articles are important statements of Rosen's interpretation of the Ideas, what they are about and what they are intended to explain. But they are nothing if not difficult, complex, and extremely abstract.

A few examples should suffice. I risk the injustice of citing these passages out of context because I want to focus not on the position itself or the justification of the position, but the character of the discourse, or the level of abstractness.

Both articles take their beginning from the conflict between what Rosen takes to be a fundamentally Platonic and a fundamentally Hegelian understanding of philosophy—an issue that can only, one might say, be encountered at a high level of abstractness. In the 1962 "Wisdom" article, he opens, interestingly enough, with a theme very similar to the one he addresses in the later *Elusiveness of the Ordinary* book, the relation between everyday experience and philosophy. But it is instructive to see how rapidly he moves to the more complex discourse of philosophy: The article begins, "One of the peculiarities of philosophy is that every attempt to isolate a particular philosophical question, a question about the most familiar aspect of our daily experience, is transformed, the moment we begin to reflect carefully about the meaning of that question, into the universal problem of the nature of philosophy itself. The decision, for example, to concentrate our attention upon the analysis of the 'logic' of ordinary linguistic usage, depends, if it is truly philosophical, upon prior decisions concerning the meanings of 'logic' and 'ordinary,' upon a decision concerning a 'criterion of significance' or the decision process itself: upon the 'meaning of meaning.'" ("Wisdom: the End of Philosophy," [*Review of Metaphysics*, vol. xvi, no.2, December, 1962; page 181]). What is striking about this introduction for our purposes is that the transition from everyday experience to philosophical discourse is literally "momentary." If we leap, again without reference to content or justification, to the conclusion to the article, we see that the level of discursive abstractness, its distance from ordinary discourse, is preserved: "In different terms, philosophy is 'completed' by its own possibility, and this possibility depends upon the actual intelligibility of the Whole. This Whole is in principle the knowable, although we can never really wholly know it. If it were not in principle the knowable, we could know nothing. Or again, whatever we know is made knowable by the intelligibility of what it would be to be wise. The intelligibility of wisdom, or intelligibility as such, is the peace upon which philosophical war depends. And so, no speech is philosophical which denies intelligibility, or the intelligibility of the Whole as the heterogeneously articulated structure in and through which each part is intelligible." ("Wisdom," 211). I cite these passages not in the least to suggest that they are not philosophically intelligible, on the contrary. My point is to observe the very high level of abstractness both of the subject matter and of the discourse itself.

The same is perhaps even more true of Rosen's important early statement of a justification for the notion of Platonic Ideas, the article entitled "Ideas." Note again the already abstract or extraordinary discourse in which the issue is introduced at the beginning of the article: "Is there, or is there not, an eternal, rational structure, order, or ground of the Whole, independent of that complex of subjectivity and change which we may summarize under the name of history? Is the form of Being identical with, or different from, the form of Time? Are there, or are there not, Ideas in the Platonic sense of the term?" ("Ideas," [*Review of Metaphysics,* vol. xvi, no.3, March, 1963;] 407–8). To accomplish his defense, Rosen turns to the paradigm of mathematics, a move which virtually necessitates a high level of abstractness, which I exemplify by one last citation, near where Rosen introduces the mathematical language: "If to be is to be something, each thing is both one and many. Being is somehow a relation of the one and the many, and if we generalize these elements, we may say that the principles of Being are the Monad and the Dyad. But Being (or any particular being), precisely because it is an instance of the Monad and the Dyad, is not only neither the one nor the other, but it is not just the two taken together. We are forced to say that, as the exhibition of the Monad and the Dyad as simultaneously present, each being is some third thing, which I shall call a Triad or Three." (*Ideas*, 410). Again, the point of my citations is to emphasize that however intelligible and even convincing this argument may be to those of us trained in the technical language of philosophy and mathematics, both the content and the language inhabit a discourse very far from the ordinary.

This distance from the ordinary of Rosen's own extraordinary philosophic speech moderates dramatically in *The Elusiveness of the Ordinary*. Fortunately, we can compare it rather directly to the abstract discourse of the two early articles, because in one of the most remarkable sections of the recent book, in a chapter entitled "The Attributes of Ordinary Experience," Rosen develops over the course of ten pages or so an extraordinary introduction to, or almost a transcendental demonstration of, the necessity of something like Platonic "forms." This time, however, it is extraordinary precisely in how closely it stays to ordinary language. It will be impossible to summarize the entire presentation adequately in a short paper, and in any case the journey must be taken it its entirety, but let me cite just a few representative passages in order to make my point about the way in which Rosen's own discourse, while certainly moving into the realm of the extraordinary, nevertheless remains as close as possible to ordinary discourse.

He begins his account as follows: "Unity, regularity, and comprehensiveness are representative examples of the general attributes of ordinary experience. It goes without saying that this road has been frequently traveled before. Indeed, it is my claim that one cannot travel at all except along this very road. The next step in my argument covers more controversial ground, but I believe I can present my argument in relatively straightforward language. The goal is to clarify the characteristics of the intelligibility of the elements of the continuum of experience. As usual, I begin from the commonsense reasoning of everyday life. I contend that this commonsense reasoning is the core of the doctrine of intelligible form introduced by Plato and Aristotle." (*The Elusiveness of the Ordinary*, 274).

We see in this passage both the insistence that his argument will begin from "commonsense reasoning," that its intent is to adequately account *for* that reasoning, and that it can be stated in discourse that is at least close to the ordinary, or as Rosen puts it, "relatively straightforward language."

He accomplishes this by holding closely to the etymological root of *eidos* as "look," and by the stunningly everyday example of the "look" of a cow. "When I ask you, 'What is that?' I am not asking you for the name of a look, because 'that' is not a look; it is a thing, say, a cow, with a look of a certain kind. I do not ask, however, 'what is that look over there?' I ask rather for the name corresponding to the kind of being of which the one to which I am pointing is an instance. The 'look' comes into play only when I ask 'How did you identify that thing as a cow?' How are you able to identify a cow as the kind of thing that we correctly designate by that name? . . . The simplest answer, which not only conforms with but is certified by ordinary language, is 'Because it looks like a cow.' You say that this looks like a cow, not because it is a look but because it *has* a look." (275). Rosen adds a few sentence later, in a wonderful loyalty to ordinary discourse, "We can of course say 'That cow is mooing too loudly' or 'I admire the complexion of that cow' or even 'Hey, you, cow; get out of my way!' But all these statements are intelligible in the last analysis only because we know what it is to be a cow." (275–76).

When he turns next to what is often the extraordinarily complicated and technical problem of how a look (which he soon identifies as "eventually the eidos or Platonic Idea" [279]) is both the same as but different from its instances, he does so in a way that again reminds us of his intent to stay as close as possible to ordinary experience: "I want now to show that it is impossible to identify anything *as* anything unless the look is in one sense separate and in another sense not separate from the instance bearing that look. My demonstration will be based on features of experience that are accessible to every person of normal intelligence." (276–77). His demonstration claims to show, a few pages later, that "So when we say 'there are a multitude of instances of things of that sort,' what we mean to say is that there is a multitude of the same sort of thing, i.e. the concept, or the look, and so eventually the *eidos* or Platonic Idea. And this shows that the look, concept, and so on, is not the same as the instance. In other words, nominalism is unintelligible." (279).

I cite these examples not because I can claim to summarize Rosen's careful argument here, but to bring out how, especially by contrast to the earlier work on the Platonic Ideas, Rosen here stays as close as possible to the discourse of ordinary experience out of which he insists that philosophic discourse arises and for which it intends to account. That too is a lesson Rosen would seem to have learned from the dialogues.

I close, then, with a question or two that, if I am right, is raised by this movement of Rosen's focus, from what I will call his early "leaving behind" of the ordinary experience and discourse out of which philosophy's often extraordinary speech arises, to his later dwelling on and sustaining of the issue of the relation of ordinary to extraordinary discourse itself. Does that shift of focus represent a "development," in the sense either of a change or of something once left behind and now taken up, or even of something once inadequately expressed now given more adequate expression? Or, to cite another possibility, is it rather a certain shift of *rhetoric*, an appeal to a different sort of reader, even as the different dialogues employ very different rhetorics and subject matters to appeal to different readers? That is, have I in this paper cited an instance of "Rosen's development," or an instance of a different rhetoric, a different stroke for different folks? Or, finally, to borrow from Heidegger's favorite metaphor for his own thought, are these different "ways," different "Feldwege" (one thinks here especially of the example of the "cow") on Rosen's philosophical journey?

From Hermeneutics to Common Sense

Stanley Rosen on Precomprehension

Laurent Jaffro

Université Paris 1 Pantheon-Sorbonne

In his most "French" book, Stanley Rosen summed up the history of hermeneutics in this depressing way: The initial object of hermeneutics used to be the word of God. Modernity extended its realm to the word of man. We were then told that God was dead. According to the latest news (in the seventies), man is dead as well. The history of hermeneutics is the story of a double disappearance. Once both objects have vanished, we are left with our own "garrulity".[1] This is why philosophy has been transformed into a theory of textuality or, on the other side, an analysis of language. One might be tempted to conclude that Rosen has nothing more to say on hermeneutics. It is just one of the numerous faces of nihilism. The only way to confront universal chatter is complete silence.

Somehow this was a provocation. Rosen's inquiry into the principles of hermeneutics did not stop at this point. On the contrary, his further works have taken account of the positive aspects of the hermeneutical transformation of philosophy. The rejection of hermeneutics was not his last word; he has since undertaken to examine in a dialectical way the possibility of a philosophical hermeneutics that should escape the risks both of silence and chatter.

I begin with Rosen's main claim that hermeneutics is possible only insofar as it presupposes a common sense or pretheoretical reason. Next I try to scrutinize the nature of this presupposition and I give a glimpse of the difficulties of a philosophical recourse to "common sense". I am aware that Rosen gives preference to other expressions, such as "everyday life" or "ordinary experience". But I stick to "common sense" in this paper because I think that it is an interesting fact that this expression at once has an ancient philosophical pedigree and is commonly used in ordinary language. This puts in a nutshell a central difficulty.

As I have just hinted, Rosen's views on the relation between philosophy and ordinary experience have changed since *Hermeneutics as Politics*—not to mention *Nihilism* (1969), in which he had wondered whether the philosophical recourse to common sense as a criterion was a rejection of philosophy or a

1 "Theory and Interpretation," in *Hermeneutics as Politics (HP)*, Oxford, Oxford UP, 1987, p. 161.

travesty of common sense. In his recent works, Rosen does not renounce the claim that common sense cannot be used as a criterion, but he argues that this point does not entail the refusal of any philosophical recourse to common sense. On the contrary, provided that they do not use it as a criterion, philosophers are correct when they recognize that they necessarily have recourse to common sense as the medium through which they translate, read, and understand each other. Thus in 1996 Rosen presents common sense, not as an accurate and infallible criterion of truth, but as the "ambiguous matrix" of philosophical inquiry.[2] Of course the appeal to the ordinary is not ordinary; but this extraordinary appeal is initiated within the ordinary. To put it another way, in his *Nihilism* Rosen had a point when he noticed that philosophy itself was responsible for promoting the prephilosophical as a standard; but this does not mean that the prephilosophical is merely a reconstruction and that we should put a ban on any recourse to common sense. It is a truism that the prephilosophical, as such, is far from being acquainted with philosophy; but there is no contradiction in its being animated by that which, according to Aristotle, is the beginning of philosophy: wonder. This is concisely formulated in *The Quarrel between Philosophy and Poetry*: "The problem of the relation between philosophy and everyday life is visible within everyday life, even if philosophy's true nature is not".[3]

The method of this philosophy that remains sensitive to the ambiguities of everyday life and is able to discern the potentialities which are concealed in the *doxa*, is called: dialectics. I propose to piece together the dialectical account of hermeneutics, that is, the supreme dialectic which determines the true relations between philosophy and ordinary life in order to assign dialectics to its proper place and function.

From hermeneutics to common sense

In his "Interpretation and the Fusion of Horizons" (1997), Rosen takes the opportunity of a criticism of Gadamer's conception of interpretation to formulate the connection between hermeneutics and common sense. He starts with the two classical conditions of the interpretation of a text. The first condition is that the meaning and value of the text are susceptible of being determined. The second condition is that its meaning and value are not directly accessible, but somehow hidden and doubtful, to the extent that several interpretations are competing.

The first condition does not entail that a text should have one and only one meaning. Of course this meaning can be ambiguous and complex. This simply

2 "Philosophy and Ordinary Experience" (1996), in *Metaphysics in Ordinary Language (MOL)*, New Haven, Yale UP, 1999, p. 230.

3 "Philosophy and Revolution," in *The Quarrel between Philosophy and Poetry*, London, Routledge, 1988, p. 29.

amounts to say that we could not interpret a text if it was impossible to distinguish a right interpretation from a wrong one. The second condition adds that this right interpretation is not obvious, but must be aimed at among a range of several candidates. In short, the classical concept of interpretation supposes that we are able to distinguish a right interpretation from an arbitrary one through the examination of a plurality of probable interpretations.

The essential point is that stating these two conditions of interpretation amounts to founding the possibility of hermeneutics on the ordinary capacities of everyday life. Philosophical hermeneutics is rooted within common sense since the paradigm of the interpretation of a text is our understanding of other people. The two main characteristics of everyday understanding are the risk of misunderstanding and the fact of ambiguity. The risk of misunderstanding corresponds to the first condition; the fact of ambiguity to the second one.[4]

Postmodern hermeneutics considers that there is no risk of misunderstanding because there is nothing to understand. The first condition does not make sense. Nietzschean historicism or perspectivism replaces the ideal of right interpretation with the fact of interpretative affirmation. To interpret is nothing but to create a new meaning or to frame some evaluation. Hermeneutics boils down to "poetry," namely, to the fabrication of meanings of which the hermeneut is the true author. The main effect of this rejection of the first condition is the transformation of reading into writing or the fading of the distinction between reading and writing.[5] Contemporary theories of literature follow Jacques Derrida when they claim that the interpretation of a text consists in writing a new one.[6]

Rosen maintains the conjunction of both conditions in order to preserve the possibility of reading as distinct from writing. If reading merges with writing, how can we say that the reader has to hear and understand anything? The task of the reader, then, would not be to grasp, but to create the "meaning". To put it in other words, the distinction between reading and writing belongs to that kind of fundamental condition which is presupposed by everyday communication.

According to Rosen, what literary theorists call "theory," to describe their own hermeneutical activity, is not *theôria* but *technê*, since it does not consist of the contemplation of transcendent significations, but amounts to the fabrication of new textual objects. Nevertheless Rosen does not advocate here any return to Platonic contemplation against postmodern techniques. He has accepted the importance of hermeneutics and he is aware that we need it to the extent that interpretation cannot be reduced to contemplation. This is why the alternative to postmodern

4 "Interpretation and the Fusion of Horizons," *MOL*, pp. 183–84.

5 In *Hermeneutics as Politics* (*HP*, pp. 143–44) Rosen used to view hermeneutics as a decadent discipline. He has reappropriated the term since then.

6 There is a similar line of argument in Antoine Compagnon's criticism of formalist approaches to literature, in *Le démon de la théorie. Littérature et sens commun*, Paris, Seuil, 1998.

technê is not Platonic *theôria* but Aristotelian *phronêsis*. The ambiguity of the *interpretandum* must be confronted by the "pretheoretical talent of natural reason"[7], that is, the practical judgment which is typical of common sense.

That which is at stake here is the determination of the true relation between "interpretation" and "theory". This is a quite complicated issue since modernity has replaced the ancient vision with a technical construction or creation.[8] The Moderns view theory as a technique or, to use one of Rosen's most favourite expressions, as "poetry". In order to recover the possibility of a true reading, we must renounce the pretension of "theory" and come back to the roots of everyday intercomprehension. We can get out of hermeneutic nihilism only through a revived attention to the ordinary resources of life. The only way to overcome nihilism is, so to speak, from below, that is, from the substructure of everyday life—not from above or through an extra "theory".

Now we can tackle Rosen's criticism of Gadamer, which consists in noticing that he fails to escape hermeneutic nihilism.[9] A central concept in *Wahreit und Methode*, the notion of fusion of horizons (*Horizontverschmelzung*), has the merit of giving a good account of living traditions: we read the past through the present; we apprehend the meaning of an artwork through its successive receptions, not from the original intention of its author. But what is defective in Gadamer's account is the historicist ontology which is associated with his concept of fusion of horizons. This leads him to neglect the reality of the artwork and to hold that it has no value regardless of its interpretations. Gadamer does not pay enough attention to the fact that we are able to compare and grade interpretations of the same work.[10] He regards the various interpretations of an artwork as analogous to the multiple performances of a piece of music; but he fails to account for the fact that they are performances of *the same composition* and that, from this standpoint, some of them may be considered arbitrary.[11] The recourse to the idea of fusion of horizons substitutes the structure of temporality for the presence of the work.[12] Of course the whole process of interpretation is always a succession of receptions, but the question is: receptions *of what*?

The disagreement between Rosen and Gadamer is about the very nature of interpretation. According to Rosen, it does not consist of the *creation* of a new meaning (as hermeneutic nihilism would have it), nor in the *transformation* of meaning, which amounts to the confusion of the objective *interpretandum* with the concerns of the subjective *interpretans* (as it is the case in Gadamer).

7 This was the definition of *phronêsis* in "Theory and Interpretation," *HP*, p. 174.

8 "A Central Ambiguity in Descartes," in *The Ancients and the Moderns. Rethinking Modernity*, New Haven, Yale UP, 1989, p. 22.

9 "Theory and Interpretation," *HP*, pp. 164–65.

10 "Interpretation and the Fusion of Horizons," *MOL*, p. 187.

11 *Ibid.*, p. 195.

12 *Ibid.*, p. 193.

We should be aware that, far from being a creation or a transformation of meaning, interpretation is the art of understanding (as when we meet someone who speaks our language) or of translating (as when we meet some foreigner with whom we manage to communicate).

Rosen and Gadamer agree on the fact that this hermeneutic ability cannot be completely created by the act of interpretation, but is at least partly antecedent to it. A "precomprehension" is supposed as a prerequisite. Gadamer is convinced that in order to account for this precomprehension he can rely on Heidegger's concept of the interpretative structure of the everyday existence of the *Dasein*. He does not notice that the Heideggerian argument remains essentially historicist and sticks to Nietzschean perspectivism.

Against this view, Rosen puts stress on the observation that this precomprehension draws on the resources of that "intercomprehension" which allows us to understand the works from remote epochs.[13] His main claim is that the everyday resources of intercomprehension do not express merely the spirit of this particular age, but what human nature truly is. This is why he explicitly prefers Plato and Aristotle to Gadamer and Heidegger. Let me specify that this preference is not that of the Greeks versus the Moderns. Dialectics is not a frame of mind peculiar to the Athenians, but the philosophical way in which we can be sensitive to the ambiguities of ordinary life, which is political as far as it is a common life. I should add that when Rosen speaks of "Plato *and* Aristotle," this conjunction is a way of hinting at the *disagreemen*t between Plato and Aristotle on the subject of the confrontation of philosophical activity and everyday political life. As he puts it somewhere else, "the entire complex puzzle of the relation between philosophy and ordinary experience is contained within the disagreement between Plato and Aristotle".[14]

Here we have a glimpse of the nature of the presupposition that roots hermeneutics in common sense:

> I hold that we can understand artworks as well as texts of other kinds from epochs other than our own and that we can submit them to new interpretations only because of this antecedent understanding.[15]

The nature of the presupposition

Drawing mainly on "Interpretation and the Fusion of Horizons," I have shown how a critical approach to the concept of hermeneutics sends us back to the question of common sense. Now I examine the way in which hermeneutical philosophy presupposes (or is anticipated by) common sense, focusing on a major essay,

13 *Ibid.*, p. 191.

14 "Philosophy and Ordinary Experience," *MOL*, p. 239.

15 "Interpretation and the Fusion of Horizons," *MOL*, p. 191.

"Philosophy and Ordinary Experience". In this study, Rosen definitely rejects the dilemma which had been formulated in *Nihilism*. Between the extremes of a triumph of common sense over philosophy on the one hand and, on the other hand, of a complete loss of common sense by philosophical madness, a moderate recourse to the ordinary not only is possible, but is required.

A fundamental characteristic of common sense is, first, its heterogeneity.[16] Ordinary life is neither univocal nor homogeneous, but involves a multiplicity of preconceptions on which a technical language can concentrate. Here we find an implicit revival of the Stoic (and Socratic) theme of the confused or at least imperfect anticipation, within ordinary language and everyday usages, of those notions which only an accomplished philosophical education could apply correctly. "We speak ordinarily of the beautiful, the true, the good, the useful, and so on, but also of our desires, hopes and fears, intentions, goals, and the like."[17] It should be noted that Rosen is now more indulgent with moral prolepses (or preconceptions) than he used to be in *Hermeneutics as Politics.*[18] Common sense is heterogeneous insofar as it provides us a diversity of ends and values, without structuring them according to a clear hierarchy, without making sure that they are consistent, without attempting to justify them. This is why common sense appeals to philosophy, but cannot serve as a criterion for it. "Ordinary experience is not a first principle; it is just ourselves."[19] Thus the ordinary should not be identified neither with the "state of nature" nor with the "golden age". As far as it is an anticipation, it cannot exist unalloyed and pure. It is a continuous dimension of our present life. Rosen calls it the "stream of life".[20]

Another characteristic of common sense is its flexibility. Rosen holds that the historical transformations which human nature undergoes do not prove that human nature does not exist, but that it is flexible. Even though the judgments of common sense vary from time to time and from place to place, "what we mean by *common sense* does not change". It would be against common sense to try to define it with mathematical accuracy.[21]

16 Here Rosen draws on Leo Strauss's comments on Socratic dialectics.

17 "Philosophy and Ordinary Experience," *MOL*, p. 223.

18 "Hermeneutics as Politics," *HP*, p. 129: "One could even grant to Strauss that all men prefer virtue to vice, good to evil, justice to injustice, and the noble to the base. This is not philosophically decisive (although it is interesting) until we decide *what* is virtuous, good, just, and noble." See also p. 128: "The clear implication of this passage is that the moral distinctions of everyday life are known to all prior to theoretical reflection, which then raises severe questions with respect to these distinctions. But if these objections are not resolved, then the very hypothesis of a pretheoretical natural standard is not merely questioned but contradicted."

19 "Philosophy and Ordinary Experience," *MOL*, p. 224.

20 *Ibid.*, p. 238.

21 *Ibid.*, p. 224.

These features—heterogeneity and flexibility—signify that the sense of questioning and wonder is interior to ordinary life. Here we meet what I have called the anticipation of philosophy by common sense, which can be described as a relation between life and books: "Life teaches us how to read, or in other words how to decide which books are in accord with our understanding of how to live."[22] The separation between reading and writing entails that the capacities which are required for reading are not identical with writing skills. Moreover, the understanding of a book does not amount merely to the technical mastery of its content, but is necessarily anticipated at the level of everyday precomprehension. The reader is interested in a book from the standpoint of his or her grasp of life, of human nature and of our "common world". Of course books can help us to understand life, but they would be utterly unreadable if life did not involve in itself a precomprehension or anticipation of that which books claim to teach. Without this presupposition of common sense, there can be no moderate and sound hermeneutics. Philosophy cannot break with the common conditions of intercomprehension.[23]

Common sense is the medium through which translations from one idiolect to another are possible. It allows us to compare books, for instance to concern ourselves with the disagreement between philosophers. Without the language of common sense, how could we translate the language of one book into the language of another one?

It is important to note that a certain kind of criticism is associated with the recourse to common sense. If the consequences of a philosophy completely contradict the claims of common sense, we should revise our philosophical views. This criticism is well instanced by Rosen's observation that a theory which would denounce consciousness as a delusion could not be held without that kind of inconsistency which some philosophers call a performative contradiction (this is not Rosen's expression). To put it in a positive way, "the Cartesian appeal to the cogito is thus not a metaphysical argument or first principle but the evocation of ordinary experience."[24] *Hermeneutics as Politics* made use of a similar dialectics to suggest that the surface, unlike the depth, can never be deconstructed.[25]

I think that this argument gives us an important clue to understand the true nature of the "presupposition" or "anticipation" between philosophy and common sense. We recognize here that kind of dialectical argument which Chaïm Perelman used to call a "retorsion" and which is better known as the *ad hominem* argument. This retaliation consists in pointing out an inconsistency between a rule (which the interlocutor holds to be valid) and the circumstances of its utterance.[26] Perelman

22 *Ibid.*, p. 221.

23 *Ibid.*, pp. 225–27.

24 *Ibid.*, p. 225.

25 "Surfaces cannot be deconstructed, since wherever we begin, they are always present as the beginning." "Hermeneutics as Politics," *HP*, p. 88.

26 *L'Empire rhétorique*, Paris, Vrin, 1977, pp. 72–73.

insists on the comical effects of this dialectical argument. The retorsion is well instanced by classical and modern usages: the way in which Aristotle disproves sophistic arguments against the principle of non-contradiction; a well-known point against neo-positivists, namely that, when they claim that *every* meaningful proposition must be either analytical or empirical, it is doubtful whether this particular proposition is meaningful; the Stoic refutation of the Epicurean denial of natural obligations.

The Stoic form of the argument is of great significance, because it makes explicit that moral skepticism rests on the same kind of inconsistency than logical sophistry. Perelman refers to Arrian's *Discourses of Epictetus*, I, 23, 10. In this passage, Epictetus is ironical about the obvious contradiction between Epicurus's advice to the wise—that they should not have children or, if they have children, that they should abandon them—and the counterfactual consequences for Epicurus's own existence if his parents had been Epicurean and followed their son's advice.[27] Perelman might as well have quoted II, 20, 6–11, in which it is observed that Epicurus contradicts himself when he is worried about our being under the illusion that love and care are real things in nature. Whether he likes it or not, Epicurus testifies to the existence of moral norms while he is contesting them.

This particular kind of retaliation is the rhetorical core of common sense. According to Perelman, this argument is not logical, but rhetorical, since the situation to which it applies is not monological, but dialogical. Moreover, it does not directly prove that such and such a principle is true; it just suggests that the interlocutor is wrong when he or she denies it. Irony shows us the way, but does not provide any evidence. If we attach this kind of argument to the philosophical recourse to common sense, then we must consider that common sense is not merely a set of self-evident intuitions, but involves also implicit normative usages. Common sense is demonstrated by what we do and especially by what we do with words.[28]

If we lay stress on the pragmatic—rather than intuitive—dimension of common sense, then it appears that this ordinary knowledge has little in common with Platonic vision. Here dialectical irony leads to a reappraisal of opinion rather than to the contemplation of Ideas. Rosen says that nihilism consists of the transformation of "theory" into "construction". But it remains that the way out of nihilism is not a way back to *theôria*. If my interpretation is correct, we must admit that the fierce criticism which *Hermeneutics as Politics* had addressed to the postmodern destruction of the Platonic sense of "theory" does not lead to a revival of the good old days.

27 *Ibid.*, p. 74.

28 In *The Ancients and the Moderns. Rethinking Modernity* (*op. cit.*, p. 142), it is significant that Rosen "persists in using the term *intuition*" to refer to particular ordinary capacities which he regards as practical dispositions.

Now we may have better grasp of Rosen's statement about the possibility of hermeneutics, which I have already quoted:

> I hold that we can understand artworks as well as texts of other kinds from epochs other than our own and that we can submit them to new interpretations only because of this antecedent understanding.

The retorsion argument calls attention to this inescapable antecedence of (pre)comprehension. The distinction between reading and writing is attested by this kind of retaliation[29]: if I maintain that reading amounts to writing another text, all I can expect from my readers is that they produce new texts; I would have many disciples, but without being read. If the problem of hermeneutics is that of the possibility of reading as "comprehension," distinct from "production," then the way to the solution is shown by the dialectical argument.

In short, what they call the hermeneutical circle (in order to be able to understand, we must be already engaged in a process of understanding) is not a curse, but the ordinary experience of the "retorsion" of common sense. To illustrate this point, Rosen remarks that, unless they contradict themselves, his readers cannot deny the existence of a common, non-technical language, in which we have the ordinary experience of intercomprehension. Other instances of this argument, or at least of the same formal structure, can be found in *The Elusiveness of the Ordinary* (2002):

> Even the nihilist assumes that his or her judgment is rooted in a true perception of human existence. The doctrine would be worthless if it were based upon erroneous reasoning. I do not see how the assertion could be proved, but it is my view that even the philosophical nihilist takes pride in, that is to say, esteems, the capacity to have arrived at the truth, however distressing, and so is not misled by illusion, however gratifying.[30]

> We could not even imagine an alternative, or what Heidegger calls "a different beginning," if there were not some common basis for comparing traditions of for interpreting human existence. This is why it is possible for philosophical hermeneuts to publish thick volumes in which they support the priority of difference for the edification of larger audiences, each member of which has common access to the perspectival nature of human existence.[31]

29 "Philosophy and Ordinary Experience," *MOL*, p. 232.

30 "The Attributes of Ordinary Experience," in *The Elusiveness of the Ordinary (EO)*, New Haven, Yale UP, 2002, pp. 262–63.

31 "Concluding Remarks," *EO*, p. 294.

We recognize here the formal features of the Stoic criticism of Epicureans and Academics[32], of which a modern equivalent is the refutation of Hobbesian "egoism" by eighteenth-century British moralists. As the third Earl of Shaftesbury puts it against the author of *Leviathan*:

> Sir! The philosophy you have condescended to reveal to us is most extraordinary. We are beholden to you for our instruction. But, pray, whence is this zeal in our behalf? What are we to you? Are you our father? [...] It is directly against your interest to undeceive us and let us know that only private interest governs you and that nothing nobler, or of a larger kind, should govern us whom you converse with.[33]

This old argument is employed by twentieth-century "discussion ethics" as well. Jürgen Habermas and Karl Otto Apel point out the performative contradiction in which the skeptic or the "methodological solipsist" is caught when he denies the validity of moral or cognitive norms, which are identical with the norms of every communication. To determine to what extent this argument is correct exceeds the limits of the present paper.

Common sense is not a logical condition of the practical, but rather a dialectical condition of the logical. Here we must turn to *The Ancients and the Moderns*, chapter 7, in which Rosen notices that in Aristotle the defence of the first principle of logic, non contradiction, is not logical but dialectical. Logic excludes formal contradictions, whereas dialectics is a sensitivity to "existential contradictions". These existential inconsistencies are ambiguities in every day life which cannot be formalized. They require from us relevant and appropriate responses, in a word: some finesse.[34]

To this description of the relation between philosophy and common sense, one might object that—like phenomenology—it has been scheduled, but never really fulfilled. One might demand more than a methodology: an effective and direct description of what common sense is.

32 Epictetus's retorsion to Epicurus: "Why do you write so many books, that no one of us may be deceived about the gods and believe that they take care of men; or that no one may suppose the nature of good to be other than pleasure?" *Discourses of Epictetus,* II, 20, 9.

33 Shaftesbury, *Sensus Communis, an Essay on the Freedom of Wit and Humour, in Characteristics of Men, Manners, Opinions, Times* (1711), ed. L. E. Klein, Cambridge, Cambridge UP, 1999, p. 43. See L. Jaffro, *Ethique de la communication et art d'écrire. Shaftesbury et les Lumières anglaises*, Paris, Presses Universitaires de France, 1998, pp. 102–10.

34 "Logic and Dialectic," *The Ancients and the Moderns. Rethinking Modernity, op. cit.*, pp. 118, 142, and especially p. 158: "Dialectics is not a procedure for eliminating inconsistencies and contradictions but rather for making sense out of them."

We should respond, first, that the programmatic and methodological look of this undertaking is the effect of the uneasy and shaky position in which philosophy is with regard to common sense. Philosophy turns its back on common sense, while simultaneously trying to look at it—which is the best way to get a theoretical stiff neck. Indeed philosophy has a therapeutic dimension insofar as it teaches how to endure pains of this sort. Second, this exploration of ordinary experience is not, properly speaking, a description and does not merge into phenomenology. The exact paradigm for this exploration is Socrates's practice of dialectics.

The difficulties of a philosophical recourse to common sense

Stanley Rosen claims that moderate hermeneutics presupposes common sense. I have tried to clarify the nature of this presupposition. The relation between hermeneutics and common sense can be analysed as a "retorsion". The art of retorsion is called "dialectics". This dialectical approach to common sense is neither descriptive nor theoretical, but dialogical and elenchtic. As such, it draws on the capacity of "antecedent" understanding, which is present in opinion, to convert opinion to philosophy.

Then we must face a first difficulty. Dialectics consists in practising retorsion, but not necessarily in knowing that to which the interlocutor is unwillingly testifying. Dialectics points out that I cannot deny some common sense principles without succumbing to some performative contradiction, but does it give me a positive knowledge of these alleged principles? We can employ the *ad hominem* argument—which shows that the interlocutor presupposes what he or she is denying—without having an adequate notion of that which is presupposed. Here is a fine example in Perelman:

> Just as the public, in a provincial theatre, was about to strike up the Marseillaise, a policeman came on the stage to announce that anything which was not on the playbill was forbidden. Someone in the audience interrupted him: 'as for you, are you on the playbill?'[35]

In this example, can we say that the audience has an adequate notion of what "to be on the playbill" means? I doubt it. They have a good notion of what "anything" means insofar as they notice that it should include the policeman, and this is enough for the *ad hominem* argument. But as far as the playbill is concerned, they rely on the policeman's irresponsible declaration and they just return it to him. My point is that philosophers cannot rely on the policeman. They must have an adequate notion of the playbill. To put it in other words, a philosopher can use the retorsion argument to show that skeptics, nihilists, postmodernists, and the

35 *L'Empire rhétorique, op. cit.*, p. 73. My translation.

like, stick unconsciously to that which they are denying; but a philosopher, especially in the Socratic tradition, cannot be happy with this argument unless he or she tries to *know* the reality, principle, norm, and the like, which they deny.

A second difficulty, to put it roughly: is common sense "natural" or is it rather "historical"? Here Rosen discusses the similarities and oppositions between Wittgenstein and Leo Strauss. The "public idiom" is an "historical creature".[36] Wittgenstein opted for the historical and therefore *conventional* character of the ordinary.[37] As for Leo Strauss, in order to escape historicism, he thought it proper to characterise common sense, not as ordinary language, but as *natural* precomprehension. Pretheoretical life is political and is nevertheless natural, because man is a political animal by nature. But we may object to Strauss that the Greek age during which human nature is unveiled, even though it is an exception in comparison with other epochs of which the history is made up, remains historical.[38] Nothing escapes the dominion of historicity, but at the same time we can use the retorsion argument against those who, under the pretext that nothing escapes historicity, claim that everything is relative. Conversely, if we assert that reading presupposes human nature and its natural capacity to understand, we must admit that *any* effective reading has access to this nature. Then we should say, against Strauss, that the Athenian access to this nature is not more authentic than our contemporary access as readers[39]. It is clear that the retorsion argument is useful to draw the attention of the historicist to his or her own contradiction and well suggests that we cannot get rid of nature. Yet the "nature" which the retorsion argument puts forward against the historicist consists of nothing but the practice of dialectics. According to Rosen, there is an "intrinsic connection between ordinary experience and human nature".[40] This nature is not antecedent to the use of language, nor to political life. It is that which is presupposed by every act of understanding, reading, talking. "Nature" is another name for "reason" in the cosmic, non scholastic sense. In this sense, Rosen is not more an Ancient than a Modern.

Another difficulty concerns the relation between philosophy and rhetoric. On the one hand, Rosen claims that the presupposition of common sense is typical of philosophy and that this is one of the major features which differentiate

36 "Philosophy and Ordinary Experience," *MOL*, p. 218.

37 "Wittgenstein excludes the possibility of theorizing on questions of this sort. He begins from the conventional or historical fact of the linguistic community whose members speak in more or less the same way. It is as a member of this community that the philosopher or speech-therapist has access to standard idioms and rules of linguistic use by which to eliminate mistakes arising from misuse of those idioms and rules." "Wittgenstein, Strauss, and the Possibility of Philosophy," *EO*, p. 141.

38 "Philosophy and Ordinary Experience," *MOL*, pp. 220–22.

39 "Concluding Remarks," *EO*, p. 302: "What I mean by ordinary experience is as accessible in late twentieth-century Paris as it was in classical Athens."

40 "Philosophy and Ordinary Experience," *MOL*, p. 231.

philosophy from poetry and rhetoric. On the other hand, I have suggested that we can draw on Perelman's so-called "new" rhetoric to present this presupposition as a retorsion. We must then solve a question of terminology. Rosen constantly underrates rhetoric and often connects it with "poetry"—that is, in his idiolect, technical construction—, while at the same time he relies on a sort of philosophical rhetoric which is essential to his argument. He wants to show that without the presupposition of common sense interpretations are pure creations and, as such, remain inaudible. In my opinion, this argument should not be considered as a depreciation of rhetoric. On the contrary, if we put aside the old caricature of rhetoric as the art of verbal seduction, we should recognize here the deep connection between philosophy and rhetoric: both involve the art of intercomprehension and suppose the precomprehension of the audience. It seems that Rosen admits this rhetorical dimension of philosophy, in a positive sense, when he passes this remark about the risk, for postmodern artworks, of being completely hermetic:

> These works of art are not intelligible, in the first instance not to any external audience, but also not to their creators, since there is no standard by which to distinguish between a true and a false interpretation of one's own creation.[41]

Even though he prefers the idea of dialectics, Rosen searches for a "theoretically correct rhetoric".[42]

To my last point: is common sense a philosophical reconstruction? Twentieth-century philosophies make use of various expressions to characterise it: ordinary experience, ordinary language, everyday life, Lebenswelt, and so on. If we go back to the Ancients and to early modern philosophy, we can put other items on the list: Platonic doxa, Aristotelian endoxa and legomena, Stoic preconceptions, Cartesian bon sens or lumière naturelle, Scottish common sense, Kantian gemeine Verstand, etc.[43] As many expressions as philosophers. It would be against philosophical accuracy to consider that these expressions are synonymous. It is obvious that they are far from being synonymous, particularly if we take into account the gap, to which Rosen draws our attention, between transcendental reconstructions of prephilosophical life and immanentist approaches to the ordinary.[44] Nevertheless, it would

41 *Ibid.*, p. 228.

42 *Ibid.*, p. 233.

43 This list should be completed with William Hamilton's note on the history of common sense. See *The Works of Thomas Reid*, ed. W. Hamilton, II, Note A, Édimbourg, 1863 (6e ed.), pp. 742–803.

44 This point was first tackled in "Hermeneutics as Politics," *HP*, p. 132: "Strauss makes the reasonable claim that unless thinking is regulated by the everyday world of common sense, it soon becomes indistinguishable from the imagination. [...] His opponents make the equally reasonable reply that the everyday world of common sense is *already* a product of theoretical constitution (Husserl) or imaginative

be against common sense to deny that these various expressions have something in common. It might be the case that each philosophy has its own conception of common sense, but, beyond this paradox, it should be common to all philosophies to presuppose such a prephilosophical level. Surely we must admit that every presupposition of the ordinary is accompanied, to a certain extent, by a philosophical reconstruction. But there is a risk here. If the reconstruction outweighs the presupposition, common sense is lost.

In short, philosophy must engage in the hermeneutical turn, but interpretation rests neither on a technical skill nor on a theoretical vision. We must have recourse to philosophy to clarify everyday life; yet philosophy cannot substitute for everyday life, otherwise philosophy would lose the hermeneutical capacity insofar as it is—this is Rosen's main claim—a prephilosophical talent. This point has been concisely formulated in *The Question of Being*:

> Philosophical doctrines are required in order to clarify the obscurities of ordinary life. But no doctrine is worthy holding if it renders everyday life unintelligible or claims that it is an illusion. At the same time, there is no philosophical doctrine or definition of what constitutes everyday life. There will always be disagreement about what needs to be explained and what does not. This is why one must first be wise before one can be a philosopher.[45]

We might consider as well that, if we must *begin* with wisdom, philosophy is far more difficult than we thought at first. For philosophy is an extraordinary enthusiasm; as such it is not easily capable of this ordinary wisdom and is often blind to it. The notions of what is difficult and of what is easy in philosophy do not coincide with the difficult and the easy in ordinary life.

construction (Nietzsche). I would myself observe that common sense, on Strauss's own premise that thought is (divinely) mad, is incompetent to adjudicate a truly 'fearless' (Strauss's term) philosophical thinking."

45 *The Question of Being*, New Haven, Yale UP, 1993, p. 122.

Four Brief Essays for Stanley Rosen

Herbert Mason
Boston University

Discourse

What is the condition of humanity that brings to surface repeatedly the argument of Athens vs. Jerusalem? The Platonic God is not the God of al-Quds, an argument that was absorbed by Jewish, Christian, and Islamic philosophers, and is still with us in the twenty-first century in various forms.

One aspect of the argument, as I understand it, resides in what one calls the self and expresses its opposing sides with what each considers virtues. The argument isn't clear-cut, however, due to two factors, one of which is historical. Greek became assimilated with Jewish thought by many ancient thinkers in centers of learning in Mesopotamia, Syria and Egypt, the process of which was continued successively by Christian and Muslim thinkers. Secondly, philosophical: the virtues overlapped and became, in effect, ratified in the neo-Platonist Christian philosophies. It is an argument that becomes fashionable in symposia and seminars of discourse periodically and ends in this familiar pattern of assimilation. The differentiation can only be made between Plato's and Abraham's notion of God, and between a neo-Hellenistic philosopher's devotion to self-examination and a monotheistic believer's adherence to revelation; between reflection and participation. The question of virtues can be differentiated ultimately only with regard to the self and its full realization through expansion or diminishment.

In the mysticism that steers one through these human conditions there is the reverse of expansion in the face of many temptations. Ultimately, there is a disappearance of self in God's self. God's creativeness, suffering and compassion make this thinkable as a path of life. What turns one from assuming it is unthinkable is the mystery of conversion on which one builds one's life anew without the obsessive qualifications of rational discourse. One doesn't become unreasonable or driven by emotion. One's reason is redirected through recognition of the limits of self, of self's complex tendencies to misunderstand those limits and of self's frequent aversions to simple truth. Compassion to oneself is seeing and acting against the dangerousness of forgotten limits and aversions.

The whole issue for the mystic becomes one's conception of the mastery of self. It is possible as a religious person to examine one's reason critically, thoroughly, decisively, and to become convinced that one is guided in all things by rational self-examination, and yet to live according to an inflation of self in one's daily life. Such is the subtlety of self-deception. Classical mystics, such as the Muslim al-Hallaj and the Christian St. John of the Cross, speak of the emptying of self and the experience of denudation to the point of having and knowing nothing apart from God, yet whom one can't possess and can't know; God who is neither only absent or only present.

The Christian Gospel speaks of the eye of the needle as a parable that mystics might regard as instruction in approaching nothingness rather than merely judging worldliness. The path in question doesn't mean the mystic assumes no responsibility in worldly matters or for the existence of evil in the world, but that one assiduously strives to remove one's attachment especially to the rewards of responsibility as rapidly as one receives them. Spiritually, it is never possible to accept honors for one's actions or thoughts unless one recognizes simply that they are appropriate, not inflationary In terms of the existence of evil, the mystic suffers anguish yet at the same time presumes no ultimate authority based on what he knows. On every level of experience such a one self-abnegates repeatedly as an interior, hidden way of life. One understands something, one doesn't make understanding a substitute for God.

Everything created is perishable. One experiences foretastes of what is imperishable within creation through friendships and love with others one is not entitled to possess. Such is also the teaching of the path of self-diminishment. It is considered mystical only because one can't proceed along its way through unconverted rationality.

Reason is no match for the thoroughly deluded self and becomes quite willing to be a partner in deception, including religious deception based on self-inflation. Yet with a denuded self as partner reason finds value and power in humility. This partnership provides the strength needed for this path.

Argument

To reiterate: one knows of the dissemination of Greek learning (science, mathematics, medicine, the method of logical inquiry of Aristotle's Hermeneutica) in Alexandria, Jundi Shapur, Antioch, Baghdad, Cordoba, via Syriac, Arabic and Latin. Neo-Hellenism provided a diffusion of religious consciousness through historical criticism and philosophical reflection. It was, so to speak, the universalizing of cultic experience, ancient and monotheistic, with some cults resisting its influence and remaining cults, exclusivist, unanalytical, ahistorical; perhaps mystical and, to themselves, faithful to their origins. The civilizing apparatus of neo-Hellenism eluded them and they remained anomalies, quirks on the screen of anthropological analysis. One thinks of the Yazidis of today in northern Iraq or of numerous African, South American and other tribal religions still undocumented by the neo-Hellenistic investigators. They remain very old in appearance and practice and marginalized as witnesses of religious experience. Of course, neo-Hellenism on the other end of the spectrum has made the "universal" religions almost bland, non-experiential, theoretical, academic, even post-philosophical, embarrassed by experience, abstracting of God as Idea, hostile to mysticism, forgetful of origins.

What of the individual religious consciousness, of the personal search for mystical union with God, whether within mainstream religious traditions or without? Has the path, *sui generis*, also eluded neo-Hellenism's reach and cataloguing? Does this ultra-individual, non-tribal *scientia intuitiva* find itself staring across the computerized desert of World Religions at the so-called primitive fidelity, say, of the Yazidi elders, to all appearances Abrahamic, and see itself mirrored, echoed there, like two birds caught and caged far apart yet yearning together to be free? Is salvation to be found in neo-Hellenistic aesthetic collection? Can personal experience any more than tribal ritual be encapsulated in abstract terms? It is a very old question asked early in Alexandria, Jundi Shapur, the Bayt al-hikma of Baghdad, and every department of religious studies in universities since.

Most would argue that such experience, especially mystical experience, must be conceptualized in order, not to be lived by oneself, but to be understood by others curious about religion and searching for Truth. The legend of the cave in Plato moves us still on this issue, pricking our individual consciences. The legend of the cave in the Koran urges us to sleep in God who will awaken us to question one another in good time. Both call for the devoted and the examined life.

To establish a path for oneself one must look critically at one-self and one's human conditions; and for this one must be in part a neo-Hellenist, even as one inclines repeatedly toward mystical union with God. It isn't an either/or situation. One is moving on one's path with a neo-Hellenistic brother at one's side, and he on his path with a brother he considers, with a tinge of skepticism, yet with affection, as a mystic.

Friendship

Friendship is many things and takes many forms, and is fundamentally inscrutable. It is rarely described as a condition essential to one's health, yet it is one of the profoundest antidotes to the sterility of solitude and the psychological disorders that grow therefrom. Its very inscrutability and unpredictability protect it and those who experience it from all forms of obsessive analytical intrusion.

First, friendship can't be prescribed or invented or forced into being. No one knows how or why or when it is conceived, survives birth, grows, and attains longevity. By contrast marriage seems comprehensible and even predictable and arranged customarily as necessary for the continuance of civilization. It is normally required as a means of procreation, nurturing and socializing of the species. Friendship has no such necessary function and may even be considered an impediment to self-advancement in certain hyper-competitive cultures.

In ancient civilizations, if our reading of oral epic literature is correct, friendship is a spontaneous and uncontrived reflection of human aspiration at its highest, noblest level. Greek and Mesopotamian friendship was fundamental to moral and spiritual development: to self-realization and the achievement of wisdom. In Homeric and Gilgameshian worldviews it stood spiritually above marriage and parenthood in the heroic struggle against injustice and the debilitating fatalism of ubiquitous mortality. One was armed best by friendship, not by weapons alone. Friendship vitalized one to accomplish heroic deeds beyond one's individual powers, and its loss, its invariably ironic and tragic loss, due to one's failure to fully grasp its necessity for survival, led to disaster. In both Mediterranean and Mesopotamian literatures the opening of the heart by the loss of a friend to death reveals the only conquest a human being can achieve over mortality: through the sorrow that transforms tragedy into revelatory wisdom.

Is friendship an unforeseen gift, in religious terms a charism received from a transcendent source? The question is important, because the source believed to have produced revelation has also produced the condition of friendship and in the instant of tragedy is blamed for its loss. One asks in quest of understanding has there been a mysterious force guiding and bringing friends together only to separate them? One's trust in human control of life has been transformed, in any case, by loss. Once a friend, one can no longer believe or act as if only enemies exist; yet after loss, enemies abound again. Perhaps if there is a sequel to tragedy found in wisdom, it is the hope that a single friendship can inoculate one against destructive confrontations and fruitless suspicions that lead to spiritual ruin.

Ageing

This is a definite and, to many outsiders looking in with horror at it, a catastrophic condition. There is no way back from it. It happens, unless one is afraid of it to such a degree that one aborts oneself from its experience. Its personal signs are many, both surface and internal, skin and organs, and its social signs are many, both superficial and psychologically devastating. One can no longer do or be seen by others as capable of doing what one used to do. One's being seems to be going through an involuntary and undesired transformation. A force is at work that seems to be coming neither from God nor from others, one that ambushes one wholly by surprise from within. Call it grandly fate or banally time. It has been part of humanity's experience always, and it reminds one of the bond one has across time with ancient humankind, mediaeval humankind, and so forth. It is a unifying revelation; this awesome ambush, that comes with a violence destroying vanities and hopes for further undertakings and involvements, pleasures and diversions, buildings and imaginings. It lays waste and leaves more devastation than the greatest of hurricanes, floods, fires, and wars, and overlooks neither groups nor individuals. Its storm's eye has amazing gifts for both generalization and particularism. No one can escape its watchful focus and its humiliating exposure of everything one presumed oneself to be. It separates one from everything one has achieved, possessed, and extended through others. It has access to everything but thought, and even that can become twisted out of shape through separation from reality caused by age. One turns in age thus to the struggle not merely to preserve thought but to seek its fruition on a further, yet to be experienced level: a level barely imaginable, ironically, but for the gift of age. Yet to reach this level of perception, contemplation and understanding one must transform one's focus of thought to perceive more deeply and more clearly than previously experienced. One must aim literally at the spirit of others and things and oneself, and one must seek knowledge of the source of all, including, and especially, the source of spirit; and one must be prepared, like the most ancient warriors of history and legend, who fought the monsters of forest, sea and selves, to overcome time with the spiritual weaponry of thought, which is, at last, all one really has.

Discourse: For Stanley Rosen

Geoffrey Hill

1

As to whether there persists—enlighten me—
a dialectic: labour into desire.
Forgive my small vocabulary that tries
and abides your patience. What a wonder's
man the philosopher set on his throne.
What a wonder he is, and how
abysmal. I would not have you say
I speak ungratefully; or that there's self
going spare in our unsparing tribute.
Arbeitsknecht by adoption, I never
slam down advice, even to shake the building.
Perhaps (but not likely) I may be still
a whizz at ordinary language and you
mishear things.

2

No, put this way: cancel, expunge, annul,
self-reference. Philosophy keeps up
embarrassment and expense. I'd quit us
of further scars had these now been incurred.
You're magisterial in judgement's gorge
where the rocks are at all angles and the stream
huggers its way through:
let's flip with self-projection's paper boat.
Language not revealing to the elect
only; and wild descenders pierced by good.
So few of us absolved when what we write
sets us to rights on some scam-scale of justice.
You're magisterial in your own conviction.
And a clown with it, and a judge of clowns.

3

Susurrations of winter: voicing stems mistune
a glass harmonica at my good ear.
The alien's close to home, the changeling's not
too much a prodigy or wastrel; lovers
and children not inimical by rote.
Something here even so. Our well dug-in
language pitches us as it finds—
I tell myself
don't wreck a good phrase simply to boost sense—
granted its dark places, the fabled burden;
its loops and extraordinary progressions,
its mere conundrums forms and rites of discourse;
its bleak littoral swept by bursts of sunlight;
its earthen genius auditing the spheres.

From The New Criterion Vol. 21, No. 10, June 2003

The Grammar of the Soul

On Plato's *Euthyphro*

Michael Davis

Sarah Lawrence College

> [O]rder and stability in speech and deed depend on what Socrates calls the Ideas. But speech and deed are not themselves Ideas; they are the functions of the human psyche. The difference between the psyche and the Ideas . . . is sufficient evidence of [the] error in asserting that Plato replaces Being by the eidetic "looks" of what is. This amounts to the assertion that Being in Plato is, or is represented by (the Idea of), the good, in the sense of the goodness or essence of the Ideas. But this is to identify the whole with the domain of the Ideas, or to forget about the psyche (and the receptacle). The goodness of the Ideas rather would seem to be but one manifestation of the good itself; intelligibility does not account for life or intelligence.[1]

I

The *Euthyphro* is the Platonic dialogue about the holy—our relation to the gods. Its setting suggests a certain urgency, for Socrates is about to enter the court where he will hear the charges for which he will later be tried, convicted, and executed. This is the Socrates whom Plato immortalizes in his writings as the paradigmatic philosopher. So, one might say that in the *Euthyphro* the best of men holds a conversation about the highest beings. While this should suffice to indicate the importance of the dialogue, I don't suppose it is perfectly obvious that the way to approach this importance is a discussion of Greek grammar. Nevertheless, this is where I will begin. Forgive me for the grammar lesson you are about to receive.

The English verb has two voices—active and passive. Voice is perhaps the most fundamental feature of the verb since variations in tense, mood, aspect, person, and number must all occur in a voice—"he saw," "we were seen," "she will be seeing," "they may be seen," "to see," " having been seen," etc.[2] Now the

1 Rosen, Stanley, *Nihilism: A Philosophical Essay* (New Haven and London: Yale University Press, 1969; South Bend, Ind.: St. Augustine's Press, 2000), 162.

2 Voice, according to Emile Benveniste [*Problems in General Linguistics* (Coral Gables, Florida: 1971), 146], "denotes a certain attitude of the subject with relation

Indo-European verbal system (we'll pay special attention to Plato's language, Attic Greek, in a moment) has not only active and passive voices; it also has a middle. Active and passive seem simple enough; the one involves actions done, the other actions undergone—"I hit" on the one hand and "I am hit" on the other. But the middle voice is harder; it seems at first to be a sort of fuzzy intermediate, derivative from the other two, that according to one Greek grammar "usually denotes that the subject acts *on himself* or *for himself*."[3] Now, you might be wondering how on earth it would possible for a subject to do anything other than act on or for himself; if so, you understand why the boundaries of the middle voice are notoriously difficult to make out.

It is almost irresistible to think of the middle as a hybrid, a mean between active and passive produced by splitting the difference. This is especially true in Greek where with a few exceptions middle and passive verb-forms are identical, and one can only determine which is meant by the context. A middle, then, would be an active verb in which I am something like the passive object of my own action. In this it is like the reflexive verb in modern European languages which is either translated as passive or as active and taking the reflexive pronoun as an object. *Sich interressieren* means "to be interested" or "to interest oneself." Yet it is of some interest that even here the priority of the passive to the middle is not so clear; *aqui se habla español* is translated "Spanish is spoken here," but a more literal rendering would be "Spanish speaks itself here."[4] In fact, there is every indication that historically in Indo-European languages the original dualism was not active/passive but active/middle. Emile Benveniste describes the dualism this way.

> In the active, the verbs denote a process that is accomplished outside the subject. In the middle . . . the verb indicates a process centering in the subject, the subject being inside the process. . . . Here the subject is the seat of the process. . . ; the subject is the center as well as the agent of the process; he achieves something which is being achieved in him.[5]

One can thus speculate that in Greek some verbs lack a middle-passive form because the action they signal is too other-directed to support one, and some (called deponent verbs) lack an active form because their action is so internalized that it cannot even be contemplated apart from a transformation in the agent. *Aisthanesthai*, "to perceive," is such a verb.

to the process—by which the process receives its fundamental determination." Much of what follows simply summarizes Benveniste's elegant discussion of the middle voice in Indo-European languages.

3 Smyth, Herbert Weir, *Greek Grammar*, 107.

4 I have borrowed this example from an internet posting by Carl W. Conrad, "Observations on Ancient Greek Voice."

5 *Problems in General Linguistics*, 148–49.

Keeping the middle voice in mind, let us turn to Plato's *Euthyphro*. By my quick count, middle-passive verb forms occur 281 times in the 13 pages of the dialogue. Of these, 78 have passive meanings and 203 have middle meanings. This distribution, however, is a little deceiving since 52 of these passive meanings occur in a single argument that extends over only a page and a half (10a–11b)—an argument that itself turns on the distinction between active and passive verbs, and which would therefore be impossible to articulate without an unusual incidence of passive forms. In the eight pages prior to this argument, of the middle-passive forms, 14 are passive and 125 middle; in the four pages after, of 76 middle-passive forms, 12 are passive and 64 middle. Now, verbs are words of action, and, according to Socrates in the *Euthyphro*, "if something comes to be or is affected, not because it is something coming to be does it comes to be, but because it comes to be, it is something coming to be" (10c1–3). Someone is loved (passive) because someone loves (active); accordingly being loved exists because there is loving. Isn't it rather peculiar then, that in a dialogue where Socrates makes such a strong claim about the dependence of passivity on activity in everything that comes to be or is affected—a claim that presumably covers all verbs—there should appear so many verbs that do not fit the paradigm, so that by a proportion of seven to one, verbs with "passive" forms do not have passive meanings? What does it mean that for the purpose of his argument, Socrates ignores the whole range of "activity" described by the middle voice?

This is especially odd given his primary example. Of 52 passives in the argument, 29 involve the verb "to love." The general problem might be stated this way. For both Plato (*Phaedrus* 245c) and Aristotle (*De Anima* III.9) soul is self-moving. When we try to make this intelligible to ourselves, we find ourselves dividing soul into a part that moves, and so is active, and a part that is moved, and so is passive. This of course simply begins a regress, for now we find ourselves asking how the part that moves the other part first moves itself. The middle does not allow itself be deconstructed into active and passive elements. In an attempt to avoid this regress, both Plato and Aristotle turn to love as a way of explaining the self-motion of soul. We are drawn out of ourselves by ourselves.

II

The *Euthyphro* begins with the words "What's new?" or, more literally "What's newer?" Euthyphro is a young man with an eccentric understanding of the divine things and an estimate of his own stature as a religious seer that is so overgenerous as to be comical (for example, he assures Socrates that nothing will come of Meletus's charges against him). Euthyphro is surprised to find Socrates hanging around the Porch of the King, the location for preliminary hearings in judicial cases. He is certain that Socrates must be under indictment, for surely he would not be indicting another. Euthyphro, on the other hand, is not only indicting another; he is indicting his own father, and for murder at that (although the circumstances are arguably unusually extenuating). The dialogue thus begins with a contrast between Euthyphro the zealous agent and Socrates the perennial patient. Indeed, Euthyphro is so paradigmatically the agent, that he makes Zeus's binding of Kronos his model (Oedipus, by the way, also lurks in the wings). Like Zeus (and indeed Kronos as well) Euthyphro assaults his own father. Now, the binding of Kronos (whose name is a pun on *chronos*—time) marks the beginning of the reign of the Olympian gods—gods whose names no longer double as common nouns like *Ouranos* (heaven) and *Gaia* (earth). The Greek gods are peculiar beings; they are at once principles of intelligibility (as Ares is the god of war, his notorious affair with Aphrodite can be understood as an allegory for the complicated relation between love and war—the theme of the *Iliad*), and they are agents in their own right (Ares is a person capable of being attracted to and sleeping with Aphrodite). As principles the gods point to an unchanging eternal order of things. To understand the variety of and relations among them, then, would mean to understand the world. Yet as persons, the gods are agents of the new. While the names of the Olympians no longer point directly to cosmic phenomena, it is probably no accident that the accusative of Zeus's name (*Dia*) might be interpreted as "cause." If the binding of Kronos means the overthrow of time, then Olympian rule stands for what it means to introduce into the world the possibility of causes that are not simply rooted in the past out of which they grow—causes that are not simply effects. These gods, and this is particularly important for the *Euthyphro*, represent what it means that there are souls in the world. Not accidentally, the word *psuchê* soul, does not occur in the *Euthyphro*. In a world without the agency of souls, everything would be rooted so firmly in its past that there would be nothing unpredictable—nothing new—and so Euthyphro's opening question would make no sense. The problem hinted at by the first words of the dialogue, then, is this: How could there be agency in a world so fully intelligible that everything falls into place, has a place, is rooted, and so, in which there is no real change? The gods, at once principles of intelligibility and initiating agents, are the way we human beings formulate this problem to ourselves. And by speaking of gods, without quite realizing it, we have raised for ourselves the problem of soul. The gods are in a way mythic versions of the middle voice of the verb in which the subject "inside the process" "achieves something which is being achieved in him." As we have seen, although the middle is fundamental, it is deceptively easy to construe as deriving from the combination of active and passive.

Euthyphro acts so as to transcend the fact of his having a past; his goal is a sort of parricide, with all the attendant tragic implications. His first impulse is to affirm the purity of his own agency.

> It's laughable, Socrates, that you think it to make any difference whether the one who died is stranger or kin, rather than to be necessary only to watch out for this: whether the killer killed in justice or not. (4b7–9)

And yet he goes on to say that he is charging his father with murder in order to root out the pollution in his household. So Euthyphro attacks the idiosyncrasy of the ancestral for the sake of purifying the ancestral. This seems to be the fundamental character of the experience of the holy—it is an experience of being unclean, of shame, of needing to cleanse oneself. But the principle according to which this cleansing is undertaken is only a purer version of one's idiosyncratic self. Put differently, Euthyphro senses that there is something wrong with an unexamined loyalty to his own—to the particular—simply because it happens to be his own. But his first reaction is to correct the situation on the basis of a piety that consists in a deeper version of an unexamined loyalty to the particular and idiosyncratic. In practice this takes the form of going to the city to adjudicate the conflict. In taking his father to court Euthyphro acts out the actual historical development from the gods of the hearth—ancestor worship—to the gods of the city. When Socrates confronts him with the prospect of losing his case in the city, Euthyphro restates the case in terms of justice—no longer mentioning pollution. But then Socrates calls the gods of the city into question by showing that they too contain within them the tension that is within Euthyphro—i.e. the story of the binding of Kronos by Zeus is precisely a sort of cleansing of the divine by an attack on the divine. Father Zeus replaces father Kronos. Euthyphro's attempt to cast himself as a perfectly responsible agent is thus riven by self-contradiction.

So much for Euthyphro's case; Socrates describes his own case in the following way.

> For he [Meletus], as he says, knows what way the young are corrupted [*diaphtherontai*—this is the first passive verb in the dialogue] and who are those corrupting them. And he runs the risk of being someone wise, and, gazing down at my ignorance, he comes before the city charging me, as though before his mother, for corrupting those of his age. And he alone of the political men appears to me to begin rightly; for it is right first to care for the young, so that they will be the best possible, just as a good farmer is likely first to care for the young plants, and after this also the rest. And so perhaps Meletus is first thoroughly cleansing us who corrupt the buds of the youth, as he says. Next, after this it is clear that having cared for the older ones he will come to be the cause of the most and greatest goods for the city as is likely to happen for one beginning [middle] from such a beginning. (2c3–3a5)

What is so startling about this account is Socrates' presentation of Meletus's understanding of the young in the city as plants to be nurtured or corrupted. [6] Or, put somewhat differently, if the city is our mother, then aren't we perennial children, never passing through adolescence and coming into our own? And if those in the city are so infantilized as to be like plants, altogether affected by conditions that either nurture or corrupt them, how can Socrates, who is after all one of them, be a cause of their corruption or, for that matter, how can Meletus be a cause of their salvation? The first middle-passive verb form with a passive meaning in the dialogue is *diaphtherontai*—Meletus claims to know in what way the young *are corrupted*. But is being corrupted ever simply passive? Shouldn't *diaphtherontai* be a middle so that the young are in part at least responsible for "corrupting themselves?" If we are to judge by Meletus, Socrates is a subject of passionate discussion among young men he has never even met. Great teachers are often like that. Not unlike Aristotle's unmoved mover, they move what is apart from them by example, by way of attraction rather than compulsion, by what they are, not what they do. Being final and not efficient causes they presuppose some principle of motion in the things they move. When you find a movie moving you are only metaphorically grabbed by it. Socrates, an object of intense admiration in Athens, outdoes his ancestor Daedalus—he animates the statues of others.

By modeling himself on Zeus Euthyphro presents himself as pure agent; this is what he thinks his piety consists in. Meletus, on the other hand, attacks Socrates for undermining the passive acquiescence of young and old to the norms of civic life. For Meletus, piety is pure passivity. Strangely, only criminals are agents. Euthyphro is at odds with himself, for he is passive in his emulation of the action of Zeus. Meletus is at odds with himself, for in coming to the rescue of the passivity of civic virtue he is an agent; his piety turns criminal. This tension between agency and passivity sets the stage for the series of arguments about the holy that make up the bulk of the *Euthyphro*.

Socrates playfully sets forth a plan to become Euthyphro's student so that he can arrange a sort of plea bargain. He'll give up Euthyphro to Meletus, the rationale being that Euthyphro, as *his* teacher, must be understood to have corrupted him. Turning Meletus view on himself, Socrates will take refuge in the claim to be a plant. Of course, this begs the question of who corrupted Euthyphro, but Euthyphro doesn't notice, for Socrates has turned his overconfidence against itself. Euthyphro also doesn't notice how absurd the sequence of events in this plea bargain is, for Socrates doesn't claim to have learned anything from Euthyphro prior to being charged, and yet he plans to place the blame on Euthyphro for his own corruption. There can therefore be no causal connection whatsoever between what Socrates is supposed to have done and what Euthyphro

6 According to the Eleatic Stranger, in the age of Kronos human beings were like plants; see *Statesman* 271a ff.

is about to say. What then is the meaning of Socrates' plan? And, since it is clearly ironic and playful anyway, is there a serious meaning behind appealing to the comical, overconfident Euthyphro for help?

Socrates must defend himself against the view of Meletus that time rules everything in the sense that what comes before altogether determines what will follow, the world of Kronos where everything is a plant, a world where the young or new is necessarily simply an outgrowth of the old, and so where it is quite impossible for anything to be new. The rule of time means the rule of necessity. In his defense Socrates will appeal to the man who stands for the reversal of time. Euthyphro/Zeus is a tool for attacking Meletus/Kronos. To the suggestion that he take Socrates' place Euthyphro says

> Yes, *by Zeus* [emphasis mine], Socrates, if he should try to indict me, I would, as I suppose, discover where he is unsound, and our speech in the law court would rather turn out to be about him than about me. (5b8–c3)

That Socrates, who just met Euthyphro, could not possibly have learned from him the vices for which he has been indicted is a joke designed for make us see that something like the suspension or reversal of time is necessary for corruption, for something new, to occur. What Meletus has not considered is how his own ultra orthodox view itself gives birth to an attack on itself. He has not understood how what he charges Socrates with is possible, how it is possible for Euthyphro to turn on his father in the name of the ancestral, how Zeus is possible. Or, more simply, the tradition is much more complex than Meletus realizes.

Socrates' plan is either to learn from Euthyphro what he needs to defend himself or use Euthyphro as an excuse for his own guilt. He begins his course of study with the crucial question.

> Now then, before Zeus [this is the only time Socrates swears by Zeus in the dialogue], tell me what you just now were so strongly claiming to know clearly—what sort of thing you claim the pious to be and the impious, both with respect to murder and with respect everything else? Or is not the holy itself the same in every action, and the unholy in turn the opposite of all the holy, itself like to itself and having some one idea in accordance with all unholiness that is going to be unholy? (5c8–d5)

What follows is generally taken to be the real substance of the dialogue. Socrates elicits from Euthyphro a series of definitions of the holy. None is successful, but at the very least the procedure of asking for the *idea* or *eidos* of something—what it is "itself in itself"—is held to be one of the earliest examples of Plato's legendary "theory of ideas" or "forms." Socrates' insistence on a definition of the holy, as we will see, threatens to subordinate the gods who are active persons to utterly unchanging and passive principles. But we are getting ahead of ourselves.

Euthyphro responds to Socrates' request by saying that the holy is

> just what I am doing now, to go after one doing injustice, whether concerning murders or temple robberies, or to go after one erring with respect to any other such thing, whether it happens to be father, mother, or whoever else, and not to go after him is unholy. (5d8–e2)

Now, Socrates rejects this account on formal grounds, claiming that Euthyphro has only given an example of the holy. Socrates asks for the "*eidos* by which all holy things are holy" (6d10–11), and then the "one *idea*" by which "the unholy things are unholy and the holy things holy" (6d11–e1). This may not seem unfair, but we need to notice that there is surely a definition implied by Euthyphro's example—his extended comparison of his own action to that of Zeus. As Leo Strauss has seen, the implicit definition with which Euthyphro begins is that the holy is imitating the gods—doing what they do.[7] This, the most active of Euthyphro's definitions, shows up only between the lines—indirectly. As it never becomes explicit, it is never refuted. Nevertheless, it affects all subsequent definitions.

When Socrates presses him for a definition in a more acceptable form, Euthyphro replies that the holy is what is loved by the gods, the unholy what is not loved (6e10–7a1). First Socrates changes this to what is god—loved and god-hated (the two formulations are interestingly different); then, he refutes it by showing that by Euthyphro's own account since there are many gods and they are frequently at odds with one another, the same things will be both god-loved and god-hated, and so holy and unholy.[8] To solve the difficulty of diversity among the gods with respect to what they love, Socrates helps Euthyphro reinterpret his first explicit definition. The holy now becomes what all the gods love, and the unholy what all the gods hate (9e1–3). Socrates refutation of this definition is the grammatical argument that we have been haltingly approaching for some time now.

Socrates asks whether the holy is loved by the gods because it is holy or holy because it is loved by the gods. A lot is at stake. If it is loved because it is holy, there is a reason for loving it—a reason which once known would presumably be higher and more lovable than the gods themselves. Our piety might consist in imitating the gods who love the holy, but in loving something higher than themselves they would have ceased to be the gods we hold high. If there are principles of order higher than the gods as persons, the gods are not gods. If, on the other hand, the holy is holy because the gods love it, then the "order" in the world is

7 Strauss, Leo, "On the *Euthyphron*," in *The Rebirth of Classical Political Rationalism* (Chicago and London: 1989), 197–98.

8 In the course of this refutation Socrates introduces a second implicit understanding of the holy—what we dare not deny, in this case that the unjust should be punished (8c–e). This is the first of the definitions that involves fear.

dependent upon their whim. We would have no recourse but to do what the gods say since their power would exceed ours and their reasons for loving what they love would be no more available to us than the new line of argument Socrates announces at 9c–d was available to Euthyphro prior to his having announced it. After all, until Socrates says "this came to mind at the same time you were speaking" (9c1–2); Euthyphro must have thought Socrates was paying attention. It seems that if the gods are altogether active, then we must be altogether passive. And if the gods are passive, then we may be active.

The grammatical argument is rather complicated, but at the risk of oversimplifying this seems to be its gist. Wherever there is an action there is corresponding being acted upon. Socrates gives a series of examples. That there is something carrying is the cause of something's being carried. Leading is the cause of being led. Seeing is the cause of being seen. Similarly loving would be the cause of being loved. Accordingly the cause of something's being loved by the gods is that they love it. But the holy is surely loved by the gods because it is holy and not holy because it is loved. Being loved by the gods is passive in the sense that it does not so much refer to the nature of the thing loved as to the gods' act of loving. By itself it tells us nothing about the holy; accordingly it cannot be right to define the holy as what is loved by the gods. As beautiful as Euthyphro's definition is in its form, it isn't much good to us, for in not telling us why the gods love what they love, it leaves us altogether in the dark about how we should behave.

Now the difficulty with this argument is that, while it makes sense grammatically, finally it doesn't really make sense at all. Socrates' three examples are rather peculiar. He first pairs two participles *pheron* (carrying) and *pheromenon* (being carried). But in the middle *pheromenon* can mean "carrying off for oneself," and *pheron* by itself can mean "fate." At the end of the argument Socrates exhorts Euthyphro to find another definition saying they will not "differ" about the fact that the holy is loved by the gods (11b4). This "differ" is the verb *diapheresthai*, compounded out of the middle-passive form of "to carry." But surely "to differ" is as active as it is passive.

Socrates second example is no more appropriate. *Agomenon*, which here must mean "being led," has meanings as various as "leading for oneself," "taking," and "marrying." And even were this not the case, surely if to be led means to follow, then following is as much an action as leading. One need not be altogether Hegelian to notice that sometimes being followed depends on those who follow. Furthermore the first part of the *Euthyphro* itself provides a striking example of just how active one can be in being led. While Socrates has been following Euthyphro's lead, there is little doubt about who is in control here. And the case is no better with the third example—seeing (*horôn*) and being seen (*horômenon*)—for *horômenon* can mean "to make an appearance,"—to make oneself seen. Furthermore, when Socrates asks Euthyphro at 11a3 "Do you see?" he is asking him if he gets the point. The verb "to see" is active, but in describing what we undergo isn't it in some way passive in its meaning?

The crucial verb, *philein* (to love), is every bit as problematic. Ordinarily in Greek *philein* is non-sexual love; it is used initially of kin and later of friends. The middle-passive participle, *philoumenon*, is nevertheless often used to designate the beloved in a love relation. Is a beloved ever altogether passive; Socrates of all people surely understands flirtation. And what about the active verb? When we fall in love are we doing something or undergoing something, suffering something? Even if the verb means something like "to be a friend of," can one be a friend without at the same time having been befriended? Aristotle, at least, thinks not.[9]

As if the distinction between active and passive were not already sufficiently confused, Socrates deepens the puzzle. Previously we had a "thing leading" and its correlative "thing led"—the active and passive participles of the verb respectively. Now Socrates asks whether something is a "thing led" (passive participle) because "it is led" (finite passive verb) or *vice versa*. In other words, now the participle is being treated as passive, and the activity it is passively undergoing is being treated as active. Put differently, the first stage of Socrates' argument is this: I hit you, therefore you are hit. The second stage is this: You are hit, therefore you are in a state of being hit. In the first stage "You are hit" is taken as passive, in the second stage as active.

This proliferation and relativizing of active and passive modes is brought to a head at 10c in Socrates' general formulation of the point he has been making.

> I wish [middle] to say this: that if something comes to be [*gignetai*] or suffers (is affected) [*paschei*], not because it is something coming to be does it come to be, but it is something coming to be because it comes to be; nor does it suffer because it is something suffering, but because it suffers, it is something suffering.

Once again Socrates makes the active passive distinction in terms of the difference between the finite verb (e.g. "it suffers") and the participle (e.g. "something suffering"). What is so curious about this summation is that in order to express the meaning of the active in general Socrates uses a deponent verb that has an active meaning but only a middle-passive form (*gignesthai*). And in order to express the meaning of the passive in general, Socrates uses a verb with passive meaning but an active form (*paschein*). We are thus led to draw the general conclusion that depending on the situation virtually any verb can be understood to carry active or passive meaning. It all depends the direction from which you see the action. Since the dismantling of Euthyphro's claim that the holy is what is loved by the gods depends on the rigid distinction between active and passive voices, Plato has gone out of his way to call Socrates' refutation into question. Why?

9 See *Nicomachean Ethics* 1155b–56a.

In its subtext Socrates' argument forces us to ask whether all human action is not reaction, and so in some measure passive. This is a way of asking whether all living beings are not necessarily reactive. One cannot kill the father because to attempt to erase your past is to re-affirm its hold on you. There is no such thing, then, as pure will in the world, and *nothing* is simply loved because someone loves it. Action is always reaction *to*. This is the importance of the distinction Socrates makes at 11a7–9.

> And you run the risk, Euthyphro, upon being asked whatever the holy is, not to wish to clarify the being of it for me but to speak of a *pathos*/affect belonging to it.

Socrates seems to say that to define something means not to describe what happens to it but to say what it is in its being or essence—its *ousia*. Euthyphro had tried to say that the holiness of something consisted in its happening to be loved by the gods. Still, couldn't there be something the being or *ousia* of which was to have a certain sort of *pathos*? Isn't this just what we mean by soul, which cannot be anything apart from a power or ability to suffer, or undergo, certain sorts of experiences? Soul is thus inseparable from its affects; its being *is* first to be affected. If we were to understand gods to be perfect souls, they would have to have the perfection of this suffering, undergoing, or being affected. Worshiping them would then amount to worshiping pure receptivity—the fact that there is such a thing in the world as "being affected."

Let's start over. All doing is ultimately something done by a soul, but there is no soul without undergoing or suffering (the *philon*, the loving thing, is the soul, but loving is something that happens to us).[10] All doing is thus first and foremost something undergone, something done to one. Action is necessarily reaction, and so there is nothing new—there are always fathers. Therefore, the question "What's new?" amounts to asking for a doing that is not reactive—an uncaused cause. "What's new?" means "Show me the perfect soul which only acts and does not react." There seem to be three possible responses to this request: 1. There is nothing new; we are only plants or billiard balls, moments in the march of time. 2. There is something new, a soul so active as to be altogether outside of the ordinary temporal order. Or, 3. there is something in between (the first words of the *Euthyphro*, after all, are not "What's new?" but literally "What's newer?"); we undergo and react, but we react unpredictably. The first alternative describes a world in which nothing changes and which would be totally intelligible save for the fact that there is no being in it to whom anything could become intelligible.[11] The second alternative describes a world in which there are beings who affect the

10 At 11b1 Socrates says to Euthyphro, "So if it pleases you [i.e. if it is *philon*/dear to you], don't hide it but once again from the beginning, tell me what is the holy"].

11 See footnote 1 above.

world, but in which, precisely because it possible for the radically new to come to be at any time, there can be no intelligibility. Finally, the third alternative describes our world. We are generated out of a temporal sequence without being swallowed up by that sequence. We are neither willful gods who annihilate time nor plants. We are souls with the power to react. Perhaps one might call it a power of refusal, a "*little* god" within us which does not so much tell us what to do as tell us what not to do.

Euthyphro is frustrated with this refutation, although not altogether sure what exactly has happened to him. In response to Socrates' request that he try again, he replies,

> But, Socrates, I at least do not have a clue how I am to tell you what I have in mind. For whatever we put forward [middle] moves around [middle] and does not want to remain where we place [middle] it. (11b6–8)

To this Socrates replies that what Euthyphro has said are like the statues of his ancestor, Daedalus; so well wrought that they move of their own accord.[12] When Euthyphro accuses him of being the Daedalus, Socrates expresses great surprise. He would like nothing better, he says, than for the argument to stay put, if his cleverness moves them, it is an involuntary wisdom. This interlude is instructive, for it is disagreement about who is the cause of a movement—Socrates or Euthyphro. Euthyphro begins by admitting that he cannot describe what is going on around him—what he has just undergone. For that reason he attributes a will of their own to "our" speeches. Socrates then disavows any responsibility for the movement and claims Euthyphro is its cause. Euthyphro then responds by accusing Socrates; it is as though he says "If you will not admit that they moved themselves and insist on a cause, then *you* are the cause." Socrates does not deny the charge, but says instead that if it is true he must be more uncanny than even Daedalus since he makes the words of others move and he does so without even knowing how he did it. So the alleged cause of the motion of the speeches shifts from the speeches themselves, to Euthyphro, to Socrates, to a hidden part of Socrates of which he himself is altogether unaware. The significance of this movement becomes clear from the way Euthyphro jumps to the conclusion that the speeches have a mind of their own. Animating the speeches is a way to escape blame for the embarrassing situation he finds himself in. While Socrates refuses

12 That Daedalus is the mythic figure at the bottom of this interlude is clearly important. He was a man who fashioned statues of human bodies that they moved themselves. He gives human bodies souls. He is also the man who contrived a way to escape Crete by fashioning wings from wax and feathers; his son Icarus attempted to fly to heaven to be like the gods, and when the sun melted the wax in his wings, he perished. His father, more moderate, took the middle course and made it safely to the Peloponnese.

to let him flee in this way, it is still true that they did not want the speeches to fail, or at least did not know that they wanted them to do so. This suggests that underneath the appearance that these beings are separate from both Socrates and Euthyphro and have a life of their own lurks a part of Socrates and Euthyphro that gives the speeches life without knowing that it does so. It is not the speeches that are uncanny, but the soul in its hidden depths. Euthyphro's animation of the speeches is simply a way of explaining himself to himself by projecting his own hidden power, his soul, onto an external being. In animating their speeches, Euthyphro has revealed how and why we make gods. And by this attempt to make sense of things, he has rendered invisible what is truly at issue here, the soul. Socrates' refusal to follow him in this theogony signals his understanding that the only way to make the soul visible is to work backward from the reified beings to which, out of perplexity about itself, it gives rise.

III

Socrates begins the second half of the dialogue by asking Euthyphro whether all the holy is just, and then whether all the just is holy (11e4–12a2). Euthyphro doesn't understand, and so, after expressing surprise because "indeed younger [newer/*neôteros*] you are than I not less than to the degree you are wiser" (124–25) (Socrates sounds a bit like Yoda here), Socrates introduces two examples of what he means. Just as fear (*deos*) is a class of which awe (*aidôs*) is a subclass and number is a class of which odd is a subclass, so also justice is a class of which the holy is a subclass. There is too much here to treat adequately; it must suffice to say that just as imitation of god was the implicit definition that fueled the first part of the dialogue, fear of god is the implicit definition that fuels the second part. Euthyphro is then led to agree that the holy is that part of the just that has to do with tending the gods (12e). This is refuted because it implies that we make the gods better. In the definition that seeks to correct this one we are demoted from shepherds of the gods to their thralls; piety becomes the art of slavery to the gods (13d) This fails because it presupposes that the gods need us to produce something for them. The next suggestion is that piety involves the knowledge of prayer and sacrifice—notice that the one is passive and the other active (14b). This however degenerates into a business relation between gods and men in which, since they do not need anything, we must perforce cheat them. At the end Euthyphro comes almost full circle and claims once again that the holy is what is loved by the gods (15b).

Euthyphro began the dialogue in such a hyper-active self-intoxicated imitation of Zeus that Socrates openly wondered that he was not afraid lest he be doing something unholy (4e4–8). After the Daedalus interlude the dialogue shifts in a decisive way. Socrates becomes openly active, and the underlying issue becomes the connection between the holy and fear. The shift is not arbitrary.

While the argument of the first part of the dialogue is altogether aporetic, the action of the dialogue consists in placing Euthyphro in a situation where in the face of something he does not understand, his fear leads him to assume the existence of an animate being. He and Socrates together seek a fixed principle of the holy. When they cannot find it, Euthyphro's confidence fades; to protect himself he animates the *logos*. Plato has thereby allowed us to witness the creation of a god—supposedly as an explanation but really out of fear. In the second part of the dialogue we come to see the natural consequences of such animation. First gods are generated as explanatory metaphors—say the cosmos being formed by the coupling of Ouranos and Gaia—and are objects of wonder. We make them gods and not simply principles because as uncaused causes of motion they, there is only one thing comparable in our experience—soul. We thus animate them so that our world will make sense—to gain control over it. But in so doing we must make them far more powerful than the souls of which we have experience. However, in order to be souls, they must share the fundamental feature of all soul—opacity. They thus move from becoming objects of wonder to objects of fear. As Strauss and others suggest, Socrates does indeed intend to move Euthyphro back toward the orthodoxy which he too easily forsook.[13] He will chasten his arrogant soul by making him god-fearing. By the end of the dialogue, Euthyphro, who was about to enter the court to prosecute his father will "go away" (*apienai*—15e). However this is not simply a moral lesson. The movement Euthyphro undergoes points to what one might call a natural history of religion. To understand ourselves we generate gods for their explanatory power as models of perfect agency. But their very perfection as agents threatens to undermine the intelligibility of our world and make it inexplicable. Once this happens we must understand ourselves to be under the control of the same very powerful agents we have generated as tools for our self-understanding. There is no alternative but slavery. Euthyphro's initial claim to be like Zeus leads willy nilly to his becoming a slave to Zeus, a plant. The active voice generates the passive voice as its corollary; the two together obscure the middle voice which is their common origin. Euthyphro is in a way an immature "young" Socrates who easily gives way to Meletus, a decayed "old" Socrates; Euthyphro is Zeus, and Meletus is Kronos. Euthyphro is an active verb and Meletus a passive. Socrates is in the middle voice—at once the only place to be and a very unstable place to be.

Precisely because the Euthyphro is about the soul, it cannot mention the soul. Instead, it presents us with the characteristic motion of soul. It discloses the nature of our souls as simultaneously and necessarily both active and passive, or rather as in the middle and tending to fall apart into active and passive. The dialogue everywhere shows signs of this indeterminate dualism. Definitions, explicit and implicit, of the holy move from imitation of the gods to slave—like

13 Strauss, "On the *Euthyphron*," 204.

obedience, but neither extreme proves stable, for each regenerates its opposite out of itself. The dialogue contains a similar, if less obvious dualism connected to philosophy. On the one hand, this "early dialogue" seems to provide an immature version of the "theory of ideas," according to which philosophy consists in seeking the fixed principles that render the whole intelligible. Yet, the ideas are only half the Platonic formula for philosophy; the other half is a powerful presentation of the person of Socrates as a model for emulation. To be intelligible the whole must contain intelligence; yet if it contains intelligence the whole must be incompletely intelligible. The philosophic counterpart of the question "Why do men worship gods?" is the question "Why do men need living models in order to learn?" Socrates is on trial in Athens because he is followed by the young. Their ardor may have something to do with the theory of ideas, but its more obvious cause is the example Socrates provides of the living soul at work. The young look to Socrates in order to understand themselves. It is the way of the soul to seek itself in what is apart from itself. This is what leads it to resolve itself into active and passive parts, neither of which can really exist by itself only to then attempt to restore its original unity.[14] One might call this the grammar of the soul.

14 The *Euthyphro* therefore means to articulate how the core of Socratic philosophy, the quest for self-knowledge, is at the heart of the human soul, but for that very reason also at the heart of what gives rise to the trial and execution of Socrates. Socrates' indictment by Athens was at the same time a self-indictment.

Platonic Liberalism

Self-Perfection as a Foundation of Political Theory*

Charles L. Griswold Jr

Boston University

> But what is government itself but the greatest of all reflections on human nature? If men were angels, no government would be necessary. If angels were to govern men, neither external nor internal controls on government would be necessary.
>
> James Madison[1]

Introduction

Whitehead famously declared that "the safest general characterization of the European philosophical tradition is that it consists of a series of footnotes to Plato."[2] This statement is true with respect to the history of political philosophy only in the sense that Plato's political theory has continually functioned as a provocation to which almost everyone has felt the need to respond. The footnotes in the history of political philosophy have mostly been negative and critical. The critique of Plato's political philosophy began almost immediately with Aristotle. The third sentence of the **Politics**, in fact, contains an unmistakable, and negative, reference to the equation suggested in Plato's **Statesman** (258e) of statescraft with the art of ruling over slaves, and substantial consideration is given in the **Politics** to attacking various proposals set forth in the **Republic**, **Laws**, and **Statesman**. Luminaries of the liberal Enlightenment, such as Jefferson, Madison, and Adams, were particularly sharp in their criticism of Plato.[3] The most famous

* Published in **Plato and Platonism**, ed. J. M. van Ophuijsen (Washington: Catholic University of America Press, 1999), pp. 102–34, in slightly emended form. French translation too currently in print (see the final footnote).

1 **Federalist** no. 51. **In The Federalist Papers,** with intro. by C. Rossiter (New York: New American Library, 1961), p. 322. (Subsequent references advert to this edition.)

2 Whitehead, **Process and Reality: An Essay in Cosmology**, corrected ed., ed. D. R. Griffin and D. W. Sherburne (New York: Free Press, 1978), p. 39.

3 In his semi-retirement, Thomas Jefferson turned back to the classics, and after rereading Plato's **Rep.** he wrote to John Adams that Plato is "one of the race of

recent scholarly attack is undoubtedly that of Karl Popper, while I. F. Stone's much discussed book presented the attack at a more popular level.[4] For Popper, Plato's views were "totalitarian" and prepared the way for Nazism and Stalinism (certain Nazi theorists did in fact take themselves to be continuing the program of Plato's **Republic**).[5] Even though Popper's interpretation of Plato has been subjected to endless examination and refutation,[6] it remains difficult to free oneself from the long standing judgment that at least in his political philosophy, Plato's views are deeply flawed.

The specific accusations against Plato's political philosophy are fourfold in nature. First, Plato's schemes are accused of being unfair because not committed to a notion of the moral equality of human beings. Plato's theories seem inegalitarian at their core, and the social and political schemes he sets out are hierarchical. Correspondingly, we hear nothing about "natural rights" in Plato.[7] Second, these schemes seem illiberal to the extreme. Especially as presented in

genuine Sophists" whose reputation has survived only because it was incorporated into equally doubtful doctrines of Christian theology. Jefferson adds "It is fortunate for us that Platonic republicanism has not obtained the same favor as Platonic Christianity; or we should now have been all living, men, women, and children, pell mell together, like beasts of the field or forest." Jefferson to Adams, July 5, 1814; in **The Adams-Jefferson Letters**, ed. L. J. Cappon (Chapel Hill: University of North Carolina Press, 1988), p. 433. On Madison, see below.

4 I refer to his **The Trial of Socrates** (Boston: Little, Brown, and Co., 1988). For a critique of Stone's book, see my "Stoning Greek Philosophers: Platonic Political Philosophy and The Trial of Socrates," **Classical Bulletin** 67.1 (1991): 3–15.

5 See Popper's **The Open Society and its Enemies**, 2 vols. (Princeton: Princeton University Press, 1962), vol. I, p. 87 *et passim*. On the appropriation of Plato by Nazi theorists, see R. F. A. Hoernlé's "Would Plato have Approved of the National-Socialist State?" in **Plato, Popper, and Politics**, ed. R. Bambrough (New York: Barnes and Noble, 1967), pp. 32–35.

6 For a sample of the debate, see the essays collected in **Plato, Popper, and Politics**, and those in **Plato: Totalitarian or Democrat?**, ed. T. L. Thorson (Englewood Cliffs, N. J.: Prentice-Hall, 1963); R. Robinson, "Dr. Popper's Defence of Democracy," in **Essays in Greek Philosophy** (Oxford: Clarendon Press, 1969), pp. 74–99. Further discussion may be found in R. B. Levinson's **In Defense of Plato** (Cambridge: Harvard University Press, 1953), and in G. Klosko's **The Development of Plato's Political Theory** (New York: Methuen, Inc., 1986).

7 Averroes, an otherwise sympathetic reader of the **Rep.,** indicated a related disagreement with Plato. Averroes objects to the **Rep.** view that the Greeks are best suited by nature to perfection. See **Averroes on Plato's *Republic*,** trans. R. Lerner (Ithaca: Cornell University Press, 1974), 27.1–14, pp. 13–14. Averroes implicitly indicates that Islamic universalism is at odds with that sort of particularism (46.10–21, p. 46). On the other hand, Averroes appears to accept Platonic communism, among other aspects of the **Rep.** (57.23–58.14, pp. 65–66).

the **Republic**, they seem to leave very little room for political liberties. And this too seems unjust. Third, they are accused of being tied to complex and doubtful metaphysical and psychological doctrines, doctrines that just about nobody wants to defend and which were immediately rejected, in whole or in part, by his best student—Aristotle.

A fourth set of criticisms alleges that Plato's schemes in the **Republic** and **Laws** are simply unworkable or fail to produce the results intended. Aristotle's arguments to the effect that abolishing private property does not remove either strife or the desire for accumulating property fall into this class.[8] In early modernity, Madison takes it as a crucial axiom that "a nation of philosophers is as little to be expected as the philosophical race of kings wished for by Plato."[9] Locke's pragmatic criticisms of a civic religion that is coercively implemented,[10] criticisms echoed over and over again in the liberal Enlightenment by thinkers such as Rousseau, Adam Smith, and Voltaire, are implicitly directed against the kind of scheme for a coercive civic religion set out in great detail in book X of Plato's **Laws**.

To these points about the unworkability of Plato's scheme we may add the objection, articulated by Rawls (among others), that since there exists no popular consensus as to the truth of a single notion of the human good, such a scheme would be politically irrelevant even if its truth could be established philosophically. Large modern commercial republics are characterized by wide, even extreme, disagreement about the human good in the sense Plato's dialogues speak of that good.[11] This characteristic of modern liberal societies is a cause of lament

8 **Pol.** II.1262a37–1264b25. Aristotle also implies at **Pol.** II.1265a10–18 that the scheme of the Laws is fundamentally impossible. With respect to Phaleas' proposal that the possessions of the citizens should be equal, Aristotle notes that "the nature of desire is without limit, and it is with a view to satisfying this that the many live. To rule such persons, then, [requires] not so much leveling property as providing that those who are respectable by nature will be the sort who have no wish to aggrandize themselves . . ." (II.1267b3–7). Here and below I cite from C. Lord's translation (Chicago: University of Chicago Press, 1984).

9 **Federalist** no. 49, p. 315. For a similar point, see D. Hume's "Idea of a perfect Commonwealth," in **Essays Moral, Political, and Literary**, revised edition, ed. E. Miller (Indianapolis: Liberty Press, 1987), p. 514.

10 I refer to the arguments in Locke's **A Letter Concerning Toleration**.

11 See **A Theory of Justice** (Cambridge: Harvard University Press, 1971), pp. 330–31; "Kantian Constructivism in Moral Theory," **Journal of Philosophy** 77 (1980), pp. 518–19; and "Justice as Fairness: Political not Metaphysical," **Philosophy and Public Affairs** 14 (1985), pp. 223, 245. In this and other articles, Rawls took himself to be working from not an *a priori*, permanently true set of political principles, but from "intuitions" and "convictions" implicit in a constitutional democracy ("Justice as Fairness," p. 225). See also the **Theory of Justice**, pp. 243–44: "The principles of justice define an appropriate path between dogmatism and intolerance

for some (such as MacIntyre) and of celebration for others. In either case, Rawls takes it to be a basic fact that must orient any realizable theory of justice. As Rawls put it, a theory of justice must be "political" and based on an overlapping consensus rather than be "metaphysical."[12] Hence "Philosophy as the search for truth about an independent metaphysical and moral order cannot, I believe, provide a workable and shared basis for a political conception of justice in a democratic society."[13]

I think that we can put these various criticisms in focus by noting that they (rightly) take Plato's political philosophy to be a version of what we may call, following Rawls, "perfectionism." Rawls characterizes perfectionism as a form of a teleological theory, namely one in which the realization of human excellence is taken as the good. Utilitarianism is another form of teleological theory, one in which (to put it very roughly) the good is defined as the satisfaction of desires or interests.[14] As Rawls points out, in the various teleological theories, justice—or what Rawls calls "the right"—is taken as that which maximizes the good. Rawls, of course, argued the converse (that the right precedes the good in political theory).[15]

In a preliminary way, let me parse a bit further the notion of "perfectionism." In classical perfectionist theories, such as those of Plato and Aristotle, we are presented with arguments that run something as follows: as political philosophers we are to orient ourselves by a notion of human nature, and in particular by what it would mean to exhibit some relevant aspect of human nature perfectly, or at least as perfectly as is humanly possible. The best human life is exemplified by the person having that trait in the requisite degree. As Aristotle states in the **Politics**: "Concerning the best regime, one who is going to undertake the investigation

on the one side, and a reductionism which regards religion and morality as mere preferences on the other. And since the theory of justice relies upon weak and widely held presumptions, it may win quite general acceptance." The centrality of disagreement to political life is implicit in Madison's seminal discussion of faction in **Federalist** no. 10.

12 Rawls notes in "Justice as Fairness" (p. 245) that "The absence of commitment to these ideals [comprehensive moral ideals such as autonomy and individuality], and indeed to any particular comprehensive ideal, is essential to liberalism as a political doctrine." Should liberalism assume a set of ideals, it becomes "another sectarian doctrine" (p. 246). And "In such a society [a democratic society] a teleological political conception is out of the question: public agreement on the requisite conception of the good cannot be obtained" (p. 249).

13 "Justice as Fairness," p. 230.

14 Rawls, **A Theory of Justice**, pp. 24–25.

15 See for example his "The Priority of Right and Ideas of the Good," **Philosophy and Public Affairs** 17 (1988): 251–76; and his "Justice as Fairness: Political not Metaphysical." Since mine is an essay on Plato and not on Rawls, in citing Rawls here have not taken into account any variations of his ideas offered in his most recent work, **Political Liberalism**.

appropriate to it must necessarily discuss first what the most choiceworthy way of life is" (1323a13–16). Further, the best political polity is that in which this best life is attained as much as possible by all those who are capable of it. Aristotle writes that "a polis is excellent, at any rate, by its citizens' —those sharing in the regime—being excellent; and in our case all the citizens share in the regime" (1332a32–35; cf. **Laws** 707d).[16] Statecraft is the art of bringing about the best life for as many as are capable of it. [17] For perfectionism, political theory is really an extension of ethics. A theory is thus perfectionist in (a) orienting itself by an account of human perfection, and (b) taking the task of statecraft to be that of bringing about human perfection in the polis, either directly or indirectly. A direct perfectionist scheme attempts to bring about excellence in human beings by perfecting human nature, by involving itself intimately in the improvement of the citizenry. An indirect perfectionist scheme attempts to make perfection of human beings possible by supplying the conditions under which individuals can improve themselves.

As noted, perfectionism and utilitarianism share a common teleological orientation, and revolve around what one might loosely sum up under the title of "interests." Both versions of teleological theory insist that various goods are to be judged relative to what they accomplish for human interests.[18] In this sense both are what Joseph Raz calls "humanistic"; they explain and justify the goodness or badness of things relative to their actual or possible contribution to human life and its quality.[19] I interpret Plato's political philosophy as "humanistic" in this broad sense. But perfectionists and utilitarians take "interests" in different ways. First, perfectionist theory views human beings in terms of their potentialities rather than in terms of their *given* interests, wants, or properties. Utilitarians tend to take "interests" as givens rather than as potentialities (though to be sure Mill's deliberations about this point complicate the distinction). Perfectionists orient

16 At **Pol.** VI.1324a23 we read "Now that the best regime must necessarily be that arrangement under which anyone might act in the best manner and live blessedly is evident."

17 Towards the conclusion of the **E. N.** Aristotle tells us that to be a good man is to be properly trained and educated, and that good laws are crucial to that process (1180a14 ff.). The science of legislation has a pedagogical intent and so is oriented by a notion of human flourishing (cf. also **E.N.** 1103b3–25). Cf. **Euthyd**. 292b4–c1: statecraft is aimed to make the citizens happy; and **Laws** 683b.

18 As Mill says in **On Liberty**, "I regard utility as the ultimate appeal on all ethical questions; but it must be utility in the largest sense, grounded on the permanent interests of man as a progressive being." In the C. V. Shields edition (Indianapolis: Bobbs-Merrill, 1976), p. 14. On p. 77 of the same text Mill rhetorically asks: "for what more or better can be said of any condition of human affairs than that it brings human beings themselves nearer to the best thing they can be?"

19 Raz, "Right-Based Moralities," in **Theories of Rights**, ed. J. Waldron (Oxford: Oxford University Press, 1984), p. 183.

themselves not by interests as agents understand them (not by "subjective preferences"), but by interests as agents would understand them had they full self-knowledge.

Secondly, utilitarians and perfectionists are likely to disagree about the nature of the human good. While utilitarians take happiness to be the human good, and evaluate interests relative to that standard, perfectionists take the development of "human nature" to be the good, and see happiness as a consequence of realization of human nature.[20] The import of the perfectionists' commitment to some form of naturalism is perhaps visible in terms of their description of happiness in contrast to the description that utilitarians are likely to give. While the one will talk about virtues understood as excellences of self, the other will talk about pleasure, satisfaction, tranquility.

There exists wide latitude among perfectionists, of course, in the specification of that which constitutes excellence, as well as in the degree of excellence required for a certain level of moral approbation. At the one extreme, Nietzsche posits so high a standard for excellence that only a few can reach it; he tells us that all those who fail to reach it are, in effect, natural slaves.[21] Towards the other end of the spectrum, Aristotle thinks that a basic capacity for deliberative rationality is (putting aside the thorny question of theoretical virtue) the standard for moral excellence and is a capacity whose realization is available to most human beings. Nonetheless, whether in their milder or harsher versions, perfectionist theories tend to be non-egalitarian, for it is felt that human beings do not share equally in the requisite aspect of human nature. That is, stated simply, political liberty and equality seem incompatible with "absolute" standards of excellence. This is a disturbing thought as pressing now as it ever was.

Given what I said earlier, it might seem that any attempt to defend Platonic perfectionism against its critics is wasted time in that it entails a defense of an illiberal, unfair, unworkable, and metaphysically cumbersome political theory. But if the defense is that Plato's political philosophy does not entail these undesirable features, the effort would seem more worthwhile. In the present essay I shall take a few steps up that road, with the aim of showing that, at least according to some dialogues, Plato's political philosophy, while perfectionist, is neither simply illiberal nor inegalitarian. Hence the first part of the title of this paper. I want to suggest that the "Socratic" virtues of toleration and open-minded inquiry can be seen as founded on "Platonic" metaphysics.[22] Interpreters as diverse as

20 See H. Sidgwick's **The Methods of Ethics**, 7th ed., rpt. (Indianapolis: Hackett Publishing Co., 1981), pp. 1–11 (and notes), 114–15.

21 Nietzsche, **Untimely Meditations**, Third Essay ("Schopenhauer as Educator"), section 1, *et passim*. Nietzsche's comments in section 8 about Plato, philosophy, and politics are also germane to my discussion here.

22 I note that by "Socrates" I shall mean, in this essay, the Socrates of the dialogues, not the historical figure.

Popper and Mill have agreed that these virtues are liberal ones, and have thus seen Socrates as a champion of political liberty.[23] Yet our portrait of Socrates comes in good part from Plato, and in Plato's dialogues some of the objectionable propositions mentioned above are put in Socrates' mouth. It seems, furthermore, an extraordinary provocation that the philosopher who wrote so movingly about love, with such sensitivity about our imperfections, and with such praise of the striving for the good, should have thought that a totalitarian, soul crushing political regime did justice to the human condition. These tensions within Plato's dialogues are worth resolving.

The general line of argument here offered is not without precedent.[24] The project of rehabilitating ancient perfectionism along the lines I have indicated has its adherents, as the work of neo-Aristotelians such as Doug Den Uyl, Douglass B. Rasmussen, Fred Miller, Stephen Salkever, Henry Veatch, Bernard Williams, and Martha Nussbaum shows. Their approach comes to something like placing a theory of rights within the frame of what is now called "virtue ethics." Nussbaum has recently argued for what one might call Aristotelian liberalism, thus developing a tradition that includes earlier neo-Aristotelians such as T. H. Green.[25] A return to the ancient vocabulary of "virtue" might be motivated by the perception that

23 Mill, **On Liberty**, p. 30. Popper, **The Open Society**, vol., I, pp. 128–31 *et passim.*

24 I have in mind R. Kraut's work in particular. See his **Socrates and the State** (Princeton: Princeton University Press, 1984), ch. 7. For discussion of Kraut's "liberalized" Plato, see his exchange with C. Orwin in **Platonic Writings, Platonic Readings**, ed. C. Griswold (New York: Routledge, Chapman, and Hall, 1988), pp. 171–82. See also C. D. C. Reeve, **Philosopher-Kings** (Princeton: Princeton University Press, 1988), ch. 4 (esp. pp. 213–34); D. Clay, "Reading the **Republic**," in **Platonic Writings, Platonic Readings**, pp. 19–33. Other efforts along the same general lines may be found in G. M. Mara's "Socrates and Liberal Toleration," **Political Theory** 16 (1988): 468–95; A. de Lattre, "La Liberté Socratique et le Dialogue Platonicien," **Kant Studien** 61 (1970): 467–95; L. G. Versenyi, "Plato and his Liberal Opponents," **Philosophy** 46 (1971): 222–37; S. Salkever, "'Lopp'd and Bound': how Liberal Theory Obscures the Goods of Liberal Practices," in **Liberalism and the Good**, ed. R. B. Douglass, G. M. Mara, and H. S. Richardson (New York: Routledge, Chapman, and Hall, 1990), pp. 167–202; and my "*Politike Episteme* in Plato's **Statesman**," in **Essays in Ancient Greek Philosophy** vol. III, ed. J. Anton and A. Preus (New York: State University of New York Press, 1989), pp. 141–67.

25 See Nussbaum's "Nature, Function, and Capability: Aristotle on Political Distribution," **Oxford Studies in Ancient Philosophy**, suppl. vol. (1988): 145–84. See also her exchange with D. Charles in the same journal, pp. 185–214; and her "Aristotelian Social Democracy," in **Liberalism and the Good**, pp. 203–52. Some of T. H. Green's reflections on the matter may be found in **Lectures on the Principles of Political Obligation** (London: Longmans, Green, and Co., 1895), pp. 47–48 *et passim* (Green refers to Aristotle on p. 47). See also H. Veatch, **Human Rights: Fact or Fancy?** (Baton Rouge: Louisiana State University Press, 1985); B. Williams,

terms such as "moral ought," "moral obligation," "end in itself," and so forth, have lost (as E. Anscombe argued)[26] the original theological context that gave them sense. The question Plato's Socrates insists on is not "what ought I to do?" (this is Kant's question; **CPR** A805=B833) but "what sort of person should I be?" (e.g., **Rep.** 443d–e). The return to classical virtue ethics also seems motivated by the view that pre-Christian ethics offers valuable insights about the centrality of dialogue, knowledge of ignorance, friendship, love, and the virtues, to our thinking about politics and ethics.

The effort to argue for a liberalism on perfectionist principles has found its supporters as well. That effort invariably begins with a critique of Rawls' view to the effect that the right is "prior" to the good and that a theory of justice should be "political" and not "metaphysical."[27] Victor Haksar, for example, argues that perfectionist theory is unavoidable if the liberal intuitions Rawls wants to appeal to are to be defended.[28] Joseph Raz argues for a conception of rights that explicitly bases itself on a conception of human well being. Raz refers to this as the "beneficiary view of rights,"[29] and characterizes his theory as "perfectionist moral pluralism."[30]

Ethics and the Limits of Philosophy (Cambridge: Harvard University Press, 1985); F. Miller, **Nature, Justice, and Rights in Aristotle's Politics** (Oxford: Clarendon Press, 1995); S. Salkever's **Finding the Mean: Theory and Practice in Aristotelian Political Philosophy** (Princeton: Princeton University Press, 1990); and D. Den Uyl and D. Rasmussen's **Liberty and Nature: An Aristotelian Defense of Liberal Order** (La Salle, Ill.: Open Court, 1991).

26 Anscombe, "Modern Moral Philosophy," **Philosophy** 33 (1958): 1–19. The argument is elaborated in A. MacIntyre's writings, most recently **Three Rival Versions of Moral Enquiry** (Notre Dame, Ind.: University of Notre Dame Press, 1990), chs. 7–8.

27 The list of these critics is a long one. M. J. Sandel's **Justice and the Limits of Liberalism** (Cambridge: Harvard University Press, 1982) is no doubt among the most influential discusions. Rawls' claim that he is articulating widespread intuitions of a democratic culture is questioned in W. Galston's "Pluralism and Social Unity," in **Liberal Purposes: Goods, Virtues, and Diversity in the Liberal State** (New York: Cambridge University Press, 1991), pp. 140–62 (especially p. 158).

28 Haksar, **Equality, Liberty, and Perfectionism** (Oxford: Oxford University Press, 1979).

29 Raz, "Right-Based Moralities," p. 183. Raz there remarks that "'X has a right' means that, other things being equal, an aspect of x's well-being (his interest) is a sufficient reason for holding some other person(s) to be under a duty." This view "would fit well with a view which regards the interests of people as the only ultimate value." For fuller discussion, see Raz's **The Morality of Freedom**, III.7. W. A. Galston argues along similar lines in **Justice and the Human Good** (Chicago: University of Chicago Press, 1980).

30 **The Morality of Freedom**, p. 133.

In section I of this paper I shall begin by developing further the definition of perfectionism. I shall then turn briefly to the **Republic**, as that dialogue is clearly problematic for the line of interpretation I am advancing. I shall say just enough to show how I would disarm the objections the **Republic** seems to pose. I will then offer, in part II, a more detailed consideration of the **Statesman** (supported by references to the **Laws**). I shall attempt to show that the **Statesman** not only supports my comments about the **Republic**, but also points us in the direction of a constitutional democracy as the best available *politeia*. In order to move the argument closer to that destination I shall turn, in part III, to the **Phaedrus** (with brief reference to the **Symposium**). Along the way, I shall discuss why, for Plato (in contrast with Epicurus), the pursuit of perfection of self involves concern for political association, and indeed political association of a certain general type. The story line of the paper is that polities compatible with Platonic perfectionism would be considerably more liberal than traditional readings of Plato suggest. Political liberty and equality need not be at odds with with the assertion of the highest standards of human excellence.

The paper is programmatic both in the intentional brevity of the comments on the **Republic** and in leaving for another occasion discussion of connections between Plato's political philosophy and the contemporary debate about liberalism and perfectionism. My argument is compatible with the proposition that there are tendencies in Plato's political philosophy contrary to those I have elicited, and compatible with any of a number of hypotheses to explain any inconsistency of this sort. This observation is especially important with respect to the **Statesman** and the **Laws**; passages in the former about punishing all those who corrupt the youth (299b–c), or in the latter about the Nocturnal Council (909a), will correctly be cited as illiberal to the extreme. I do not overlook or deny the existence of these passages. I am asserting that there are also other passages with contrary implications. To reconcile these various passages, comprehensive interpretations of the dialogues in question would be required. I cannot supply these here, but merely offer, as a sort of promissory note, my belief that these passages can be reconciled, and in a way that is consistent with the thesis advanced in the present paper.

I

Let me begin by distinguishing between two species of perfectionism. I shall call them "communitarian" and "individualist" perfectionism. I take Aristotle to belong to the first species. As already noted, for Aristotle excellence in the city is determined relative to excellence in the soul of the individual. The purpose of the political association is not just to bring out excellence in a few lucky souls, but in all the citizens. Hence the polis exists not for the sake of living, but for the sake of living well, in accordance with excellence. Further, Aristotle argues that excellence in the individual's soul cannot be brought out fully except through rightly structured civic association, and that participation in a rightly ordered polis is not just a means to moral excellence but is partially constitutive of it.[31] Correspondingly, there is room for the notion of the public good in Aristotle's theory.[32] In committing himself to the views that the polis is natural (1253a25), that humans are by nature political animals (1253a2–3), that the polis is a type of association distinct from (among others) the household and family, and that the polis provides a collective good, Aristotle falls into the camp of what I am calling communitarian perfectionists.

I take it that a moral theory is individualistic if it assigns only instrumental value to any collective or public good.[33] Individualistic perfectionism will also hold that the individual's chief ethical end is self-perfection. This is very different from understanding individualism as that doctrine according to which subjective preferences are good reasons for action. Epicurus may be taken as an extreme example of what I am calling individualist perfectionism. Epicurus sees the individual's *autarkeia* not just in self-origination but more importantly in the correctness of beliefs about his or her own ends. For Epicurus, the *summum bonum* is the agent's happiness, understood, roughly, as pleasurable tranquility of mind (*ataraxia*), freedom from pain, and invulnerability to fortune.[34] The emphasis on stability of happiness and imperviousness to luck makes it difficult for

31 The difference between a polis and other sorts of association is not just numerical but qualitative; it has a form of unity particular to its nature and distinct purpose, and Aristotle criticizes Plato at length for failing to appreciate that fact. For Aristotle, Plato insists on the wrong kind of unity in the polis, and fails to see that the hierarchical relationship of master and slave is not of the essence of the polis. These criticisms suggest that Plato does not see the polis as a precondition for the expression of moral excellence. By contrast, the polis is, for Aristotle, a "sort of multitude" consisting of persons of different kind (1261a17–24); and political rule properly speaking is rule of those free by nature and equal, while household management is monarchy (1255b16–20).

32 The public good would be that good (a) which is made available by the polis, (b) the distribution of the whole of which is not subject to the voluntary control of individuals, and (c) which is constitutive of the individual's realization of his or her own excellence and not merely instrumental towards that end. This definition of the public good follows, in rough form, Raz, "Right-Based Moralities," p. 187.

33 In this definition of individualistic moralities I again follow Raz, "Right-Based Moralities," p. 186.

34 See the **Letter to Menoeceus** 128–29, 132–35, in **Epicurus: the Extant Remains**, trans. and ed. C. Bailey (Oxford: Clarendon Press, 1926), pp. 87, 91–93; **Sententiae Vaticanae** LXXVII, p. 117; **Kuriai Doxai** n. XVI, p. 99; and Diogenes' **Lives** X.118, in Bailey p. 165. (Page references to Epicurus' writings refer to the Bailey edition.) This can be interpreted along perfectionist rather than utilitarian lines, for Epicurus seems to see this *summum bonum* as a fulfillment of the way in which our material natures are constituted; and he assigns no place to a principle of the equal value of

Epicurus to explain consistently why even friendship could have an important place in the life of the self-perfected individual.[35] Further, Epicurus understands self-perfection in such a way that all political involvements are judged solely for their instrumental value. Correspondingly, prudence (*phronesis*) functions as the chief virtue for Epicurus; its task is primarily to deliberate about the means best suited to self-interest rightly understood. Justice, Epicurus says, is nothing but a contract; the agent is obligated to be just only insofar as it is in his interest (rightly understood) to be such.[36] What substantive commitments a just contract makes (putting aside the agent's commitment to his own perfection) will depend. For example, an Epicurean might accept slavery as a just institution in some cases, and in other cases not.[37]

In sum, Epicurus' teaching seems at its core apolitical; it leaves no room for anything like the view that the polis is natural (in Aristotle's sense), that human beings are political animals by nature, or that political association is intrinsic to the realization of self.[38]

There is only partial overlap between Plato's and Epicurus' views. On the one hand, the **Phaedrus** shows, as I shall argue, that part of the individual's self-perfection must include care not just for other individuals but for communities. Plato has significantly different notions of "self" and "happiness" than does Epicurus. On the other hand, nowhere is it argued in Plato that the polis is natural (in Aristotle's sense), or that human beings are by nature political animals. Like Epicurus, Plato takes self-perfection to be the overriding *telos* of the human being. It seems that, for Plato, what is due to others is extrapolated from what we owe ourselves once we have rightly understood ourselves (hence the subtitle of

individuals (hence he nowhere points to the happiness of the aggregate of individuals as the *summum bonum*).

35 See **Sent. Vat.** XXIII, p. 109; and for discussion, Mitsis' **Epicurus' Ethical Theory**, ch. 3, especially pp. 117–28.

36 **Kuriai Doxai n.** XXXI, p. 103. See also P. Mitsis' **Epicurus' Ethical Theory** (Ithaca, N.Y.: Cornell University Press, 1988), p. 80.

37 Diogenes Laertius notes that Epicurus owned slaves, and that he both treated them well and manumitted several on his death (Diogenes interprets all this as indicative of the kind of person an Epicurean would want to be). **Lives** X.10 (p. 147), X.21 (p. 155), X.118 (p. 165). In a manner reminiscent of Plato's Socrates, Epicurus does maintain that the pursuit of self-perfection removes motivations at the root of actions commonly labeled unjust. The Epicurean will care little about wealth or power, for example, and so will take no steps to acquiring any.

38 Correspondingly, Epicurus was accused of shirking his civic duty. See Epictetus' **Discourses** III.vii.19–23. On a purely prudential basis it would be possible to spell out a politics most likely to be conducive to the Epicurean's pursuit of self-perfection. For example, in light of Epicurus' emphasis on the role of scientific investigation in clearing the mind of superstition, one would expect that a society that encouraged such investigation would be useful.

the present paper). Where does this way of looking at political theory lead Plato?

Let us turn briefly to the **Republic**. In book II, Socrates is pushed to prove that we are motivated to be just not because justice is instrumentally good, but because it is an intrinsic good. In book IV (433a–b, 443d–e) Plato has Socrates offer what is surely a counter-intuitive definition of justice as the right ordering of the individual's soul, such that the individual minds his own business ("ta eautou prattein"; "doing one's own thing"). Justice is a quality of a perfected soul in that each of its "parts"—the rational, the spirited, and the desiring—does its proper job. The connection between justice as a virtue of self, and justice as conventionally understood (in connection with equality, law, duties towards others, etc.), is the subject of a now well established debate.[39] At least within the **Republic's** "city in speech," however, the argument is that the structure of the polis is isomorphic with that of the soul; justice in the polis is justice of the soul writ large (435a–b; 368c–369a). The political and the psychological are to parallel each other. This "holistic" model to the effect that a political arrangement is good or virtuous insofar as it has the same structure of goodness or virtue that belongs to the soul of an individual leads to illiberal and inegalitarian measures.[40] The idea is that meaningful choice of a way of life cannot be had without an understanding of better and worse ways of life, an understanding reached through philosophical reason. The higher parts of the soul or city should rule over the lower; the lower parts lack the rationality requisite for meaningful self-rule and should therefore be ruled by the higher. Just as knowledge rules in a healthy self, so the philosophers, those persons knowledgeable about the Forms, rightly rule the polis, for the polis' own good.

This scheme runs into difficulties quickly, as many readers have noticed.[41] It leads to the paradoxical result that the majority of the citizens of the just polis are not just. The largest class of citizens seems be that dominated by the "lower" desires; but by definition those individuals are not just, because they lack proper

39 The discussion was inaugurated by David Sachs' "A Fallacy in Plato's **Republic**," rpt. in **Plato II**, ed. G. Vlastos (Notre Dame, Ind.: University of Notre Dame Press, 1978), pp. 35–51. The same volume contains responses by R. Demos.

40 I take the term "holistic" from Nussbaum, "Nature, Function, and Capability," pp. 155–56. As Nussbaum points out, other models also operate in Plato's text.

41 The paradoxes to which the holistic conception leads are examined in B. Williams' "The Analogy of City and Soul in Plato's **Republic**," in **Phronesis**, suppl. vol. 1 (1973): 196–206. In short, Williams points out that the just city must be divided into parts as the soul is, and so that the lowest (and largest) class of the just city is composed of epithymetic people; but these are not just people because they are not ruled by reason. Therefore the just city must have a majority of citizens who are not just. This contradicts the principle (implied in 433–34) that the city is just if and only if its citizens are just.

ordering of the parts of their soul. It is tempting to modify the thrust of the city/soul analogy and say that only the philosopher-rulers in the just city are just. But the just polis seems unjust in its treatment of them by forcing them to rule (a similar problem arises with respect to the guardians, who are forced to do their job whether or not they are happy doing it). In book VII of the **Republic** we are told that, even in the ideal state, philosophers—here taken to be those ultimately perfected human beings—must be "compelled" to rule, and will rule only because it is a necessary thing not a good one (519c, e; 520e). Even in the ideal state, there seems to be great difficulty in harmonizing self-perfection and care by the self-perfected for the polis. Socrates is explicit that such harmony is not to be hoped for in any non-ideal state.[42]

Even if these difficulties were solved, we might want to voice three objections against the **Republic's** scheme. First, Socrates assumes that every person's nature is suited to a particular sort of job (370a, 395a–b). But this is nowhere demonstrated, and much doubt is cast upon it in the **Phaedrus**. Second, he assumes that the rulers of the city can, for a time at least, discern the natures and so the appropriate occupations of individuals (415b). But this would require omniscience on the part of the rulers. Third, it is assumed that philosopher kings could exist. These individuals are not just philosophers in the sense of the term used in the **Phaedrus** and **Symposium** (204a), i.e., of persons who, as *lovers* of wisdom, are lacking the thing they love. The **Republic's** philosophers *are* wise; they have gazed directly upon the Forms. Even if it is just to compel wise philosophers to rule, and even if the just city need not be composed only of just persons, the just city cannot be just unless wise philosophers rule it. But the **Statesman** and **Phaedrus** will show us that there are no philosophers so understood, and this has crucial political consequences.

Further, the preconditions for setting up the **Republic's** third city (which Socrates refers to as"Kallipolis") virtually ensure that it will never come to pass, as is indicated not just by the requirement that the rulers be perfectly wise, but also by the proviso at the end of book VII to the effect that everyone over the age of ten be expelled. At the start of book VIII we learn that this polis-in-speech would not last long anyhow; Socrates throws out an elaborate mathematical joke to "explain" how the polis' inevitable decay comes about (and given that the passage is a joke, the implication is that there is no formula for the right breeding of the guardians and hence no way to sustain the regime past the first generation).

42 E.g., at **Rep.** 497b we hear that "not one city today is in a condition of worthy of the philosophic nature." (Here and below I shall be citing from A. Bloom's translation (New York: Basic Books, 1968). The reasons for which that is true very probably would still hold, in Socrates' view. One reason is stated as a permanent truth: "it's impossible that a multitude be philosophic" (494a; cf. **Stsm.** 292e). This generates the alienation of philosopher from city graphically described at 496b–e. Still, there may be degrees to which *poleis* are unsuitable to the philosophers.

As Diskin Clay has argued, the dialogue is structured in ways that indicate Plato's intention that the closed regime of the middle books of the **Republic** be read as open to question. As he and Charles Kahn have insisted, we ought not in any case to read off Plato's intentions from the utterances of his *dramatis personae* without further ado. The dialogue form entails a lack of transparency with respect to authorial intention. Plato's can have his characters assert all sorts of things without his wishing either to affirm those assertions or to persuade the reader to accept them uncritically.[43] Indeed his use of the dialogue form positively warns the reader against any such uncritical acceptance.

Let us distinguish between two questions. Granted that the Kallipolis is inegalitarian and illiberal: did Plato (a) intend the **Republic** as a blueprint for social action? and (b) does he intend the 'story' (**Rep**. 501e) he tells to be a description of the perfectly just community or, as I will argue is true of the **Statesman** (below), did he intend the reader to see that even a supposedly "ideal" state of affairs suffers from grave defects? For my present purposes, it suffices to focus on the first of these questions. Socrates explicitly gives us the answer at the end of book IX of the **Republic**. He there concedes that the "city in speech" will come to be only by divine chance and adds "but in heaven, perhaps, a paradeigma is laid up for the man who wants to see and found a city within himself on the basis of what he sees" (592b2–3).[44] The city/soul analogy, and the sense in which the city is the soul writ large, must therefore be completely recast. The whole of the **Republic's** effort to define justice seems of value, that is, because of the role of this effort and of the definition in the individual's self-perfection. The emphasis at the end of the **Republic** is on the individual's choice of a way of life; this is a major theme, in fact, of the myth with which the dialogue concludes.

Let me restate the thrust of the preceding paragraph. We learn at the end of book VII (as we shall also learn in the **Statesman** and **Laws**), that the first best regime is unavailable. We have in effect seen the need to reflect on what such a polity would look like; we are provided with opportunities to reflect on how

43 I refer to Clay's "Reading the **Republic.**" Kahn's point is worked out in a number of places, beginning with "Did Plato Write Socratic Dialogues?," **Classical Quarterly** 31(1981): 305–20. For extended discussion of Kahn's interpretive assumptions, see my "Unifying Plato: Charles Kahn on Platonic *Prolepsis*," **Ancient Philosophy** 10 (1990): 243–62. On the general question of the intentions of the **Rep.**, see also D. Hyland, "Plato's Three Waves and the Question of Utopia," **Interpretation** 18 (1990): 91–109. The reading of the **Republic's** Kallipolis as an (almost certainly) unrealizable polis is argued by Clay, Hyland, and also Klosko (**The Development of Plato's Political Theory**, p. 179 and context).

44 This passage echoes a much earlier description in book VI of the philosopher's passion for and absorption in "things that are set in a regular arrangement and are always in the same condition—things that neither do injustice to one another nor suffer it at one another's hands, but remain all in order according to reason—he imitates them and, as much as possible, makes himself like them" (500c2–5).

desirable such a regime would be for us; and thirdly we are led to reflect on the consequences of the fact that we cannot plan on its coming into being. Theory and practice cannot be straightforwardly reconciled, and the 'practical' question about what follows is itself a matter for theoretical speculation. Thus this third reflection is crucial: it leaves us with several pressing questions, such as: what is the *second* best regime? Or in different terms, what is that polity which best "imitates" the ideal? What would it mean to "imitate" an unobtainable ideal? The answer to these questions must take into account a whole range of factors, including facts about human nature and its imperfections, views about how much knowledge is accessible to humans and how we are to "recollect" more of the truth; theories about the different types of regimes and their relationship (perhaps genealogical relationship); arguments about how we might best "pattern" our souls so as to perfect them in the midst of an irremediably imperfect world; and of course, views about what regime here and now best serves the means for the self-perfection Socrates praises at the end of book VII. The political need not and cannot express our personal ideal; what then follows for the politics of self-perfection? What polis does justice to us as erotic and therefore perpetually incomplete beings? Book VIII takes up some of the just mentioned questions, and similar discussions occur in the **Statesman** and **Laws**.

It is within the space of this question about "imitation," opened up by the necessity for deciding what might be the second best, i.e., the best practicable polity, that the case for a relatively "liberal" regime would be made. Plato follows up the the remarkable passage at the end of book VII with a discussion of various regimes, and the analysis of democracy is striking. Democracy is portrayed as degenerate and yet, as Socrates remarks in a frequently ignored passage, it is also a convenient place to look for a polity: "thanks to its license, it contains all species of regimes, and it is probably necessary for the man who wishes to organize a city, as we were just doing, to go to a city under a democracy" (557d). In other words, the sort of philosophical discussion that is the **Republic** can best be undertaken in a democracy. This regime is "sweet" because it is many colored, dispenses a certain equality (558c), and also provides significant political liberty, thereby providing a context for a Socrates. In this *polis* one is not compelled to rule (557e), and this is crucial; in the **Apology** Socrates tells us that he remained alive by staying out of politics (31d). A democracy is permissive enough to allow him both to stay alive and philosophize, at least for a longer time than would other regimes. A democracy allows one to live the life of the private man laudably chosen by Odysseus (620c–d), and by Socrates. Paradoxically, a democracy is in theory to be rejected by philosophy, while in practice it is hospitable even to philosophy's rejection of it in theory. And we live, Socrates told us at the end of books VII and IX, in the realm of practice, not of theory. How the philosopher would rejoin the two is at the heart of the problem of "imitation" here, and I will say more about it in parts II and III below.

If the interpretation I am sketching is accurate, it may seem not merely that the **Republic** is not a blueprint for political action, but that the activities of actually founding a city, of taking part in politics, or of specifying what sort of polity is best in practice, are matters whose value is purely instrumental. We seem returned to book I of the **Republic**, where Socrates asserts that the philosopher would want to hold office only in order to prevent being ruled by a worse person (347c).[45] Taken in isolation, such passages suggest little place in the well ordered philosophical life for care for a *polis*. As in Epicurus, Platonic self-perfection seems to offer us little more than prudence and self-interest rightly understood as a basis for political theory. It seems that while the philosopher may not be compelled to espouse an illiberal and inegalitarian polity such as that of the **Republic**, he or she might do so for prudential reasons.

But that conclusion does not follow, as I shall now try to show with respect to the **Phaedrus.** We shall see that Plato does provide us with an argument showing that love of wisdom does include attachment to others in their collective capacity. But first, let me show how at least parts of the **Statesman** cohere with the interpretation of the **Republic** just sketched.

II

If the comments in the preceding section are well directed, then for Plato political philosophy will orient itself by a distinction between ideal and non-ideal regimes. The "second best" polis theme is explicit in the **Statesman** (below) and **Laws** (712a ff. and context; 807b, 875a–d).[46] It is also to be found in Aristotle's political theory. Plutarch tells us that when Solon was asked if he had left the Athenians the best laws that could be given, he replied "The best they could receive"; and Hesiod's account of the successively degenerating "ages of man" suggest, indirectly, a difference between first best and relatively best conditions. The distinction between ideal and non-ideal regimes, and its political importance, is scarcely unique to Plato. The view that the best *practicable* form of political association will be imperfect or, in a Platonic phrase, be second-best, complicates in interesting ways Platonic perfectionism. It decisively tempers perfectionist social engineering, and turns moderation into a central political virtue.

45 Cf. also **Rep.** 496b–d, where we are told that philosophers despise the business of the city and look beyond it, and that they mind their own business.

46 The distinction between best and inferior regimes is also explicit in Aristotle. But Aristotle does not draw out, in the ways that the Platonic dialogues do, the paradeigmatic status of the "best" regime, the reasons for which that regime is unavailable, and the ways in which the realization that the best is unattainable should condition our reception of non-ideal regimes.

The **Statesman** is part of a trilogy.[47] It is immediately preceded by the **Sophist**, and was to have been followed by the **Philosopher**. At the start of the **Sophist** Socrates turns to the newly arrived Eleatic Stranger (ES) and asks him the question which leads to, and provides the main topics for, the ensuing two dialogues: do people from the ES' region divide the genera "sophist," "statesman," and "philosopher" into three, just as the names indicate? The ES answers affirmatively, and accepts both Socrates' invitation to define each of these types and Socrates' selection of an interlocutor. Having thus given shape to the ensuing conversations, Socrates sits back and listens. A similar scene occurs at the start of the **Statesman**, where Socrates picks a new interlocutor for the ES, a young mathematician named "Young Socrates" (YS).

The **Statesman** attempts to define the genus "statesman" by defining the science he possesses.[48] The ES' rationale is evidently the belief that possession of political science is a sufficient condition for someone's being a statesman (259b). The ES procedes by using the method of diairesis. The first definition of political science is arrived at as a result of a long series of divisions that occupy the first third of the dialogue. Each step of the division is woven together such that the definition of political science is the sum of its genealogical parts. The ES begins by dividing "episteme" (knowledge or science) into "praktike episteme" (as in the art of carpentry) and "gnostike episteme" (as in arithmetic and kindred arts). The ensuing series of divisions yield a startling definition: the statesman is he who possesses the cognitive science of giving his own orders for the nurturing and grazing of the two footed pedestrial hornless non-interbreeding herd of animals (267b–c). In other words, political science is the art of ruling featherless bipeds. This reductive definition omits what is essential about human beings—the soul, the interiority of self, rationality. Young Socrates accepts this definition as satisfactory without qualification.[49]

47 For a much fuller discussion of the **Statesman**, see my "*Politike Episteme* in Plato's **Statesman**," from which these remarks are drawn. A recent study of the **Statesman**, one in substantial harmony with my own interpretation, is S. Rosen's **Plato's Statesman: The Web of Politics** (New Haven, Conn.: Yale University Press, 1995).

48 Since in the **Stsm.** the possessor of statecraft is referred to with masculine pronouns, it seems pointless to do otherwise when commenting on that text.

49 Three brief comments about this initial definition. First, Young Socrates is a mathematician; thus the opening definition of political science as a theoretical branch of *episteme* expresses his own proclivities. Second, the final definition is also Young Socrates'; not only did he assent to each step as well as the conclusion, but the definition expresses his traditionalist notion that the ruler of a *polis* is a "shepherd of the people," to use Homer's characterization of Agamemnon. If the ruler is a shepherd, we are sheep. Third, the definition is tidy in a way that a politically inexperienced mathematician might be expected to appreciate: there is one ruler; the ruled are treated as units to be manipulated as the ruler sees fit; they are inert, things

Many commentators stop here, assuming that YS speaks for Plato. Popper alludes to this opening section of the dialogue when accusing Plato of advocating totalitarianism.[50] This definition is of a piece with the initial definition of the political art (258e) according to which, as the ES says, the art of political rule and the art of ruling over slaves are effectively the same. But in fact Plato has the Eleatic Stranger proceed immediately to reject the definition. In a very Socratic way, the ES has led Young Socrates down the garden path. Young Socrates is thrown into a state of *aporia*. The ES' initial objection is that the definition does not isolate the statesman's art, for "thousands" of other types of people will claim to be "statesmen" in the sense specified so far (267e–268c). That is, the ES focuses on a crucial aspect of political life, namely the existence of widespread and deep disagreement about who should rule, and so about what just rule is. Title to legitimate rule is in doubt, and a successful political arrangement must take into account the liberty of thinking which the phenomenon of disagreement signals. Each person thinks he or she ought to rule. Thus civil strife and dissolution constantly threaten our lives (cf. 273d, 302a, 308a). The **Laws** puts this even more strongly: every person is an enemy of every other person, and each person is also his own enemy (626d; cf. 744d). The problem with the **Statesman's** opening definition of political science, that is, is that it is strangely apolitical. It has little to do with real world politics.

The ES develops his point in a surprising way. He proceeds to recount a long, complicated, and quite bizarre cosmological myth. I think that this myth is the pivot of the dialogue, that on which the competing definitions of statecraft turn. We can read it as a sort of thought experiment whose central point is that the initial definition of the **Statesman** assumes a state of things that does not exist in the sort of world we presently occupy. Among other things, the myth attacks the definition's assumption that an all-knowing shepherd-of-the-people presently exists. We are given to infer that a person who thinks he possesses political science in that sense, who sees himself as different in kind from the ruled, and takes the ruled to be comparable to sheep, is nothing other than a tyrant. Let me fill out this account with a very brief summary of the myth.

The ES says that current stories about a distant golden age are dim recollections of a truth. The cosmos turns in two cycles. The cycle contrary to that in which we now live—let us call it the divine cycle—is governed by the god Kronos. In the divine cycle the god guided and re-energized the cosmos, taking it

to be manipulated, having no potentiality or freedom; the ruler is the measure of the whole.

50 Popper, **The Open Society**, vol. I, pp. 86–87; I refer to section (A) on p. 86 in particular (no doubt Popper there thinks of the **Rep.** too). I note that Aristotle's **Pol.** discussion of Plato's political philosophy is carefully stated; Aristotle repeatedly refers to "Socrates" rather than to "Plato" as the author of the various views he rejects.

and winding it up like a spindle hanging from a thread. Kronos regulated everything along with helper gods, among whom care of the herds of living creatures is divided. Just as now men graze the inferior species, so then the god grazed humans (271e5–7). It was a beautiful era. Everything operated with extreme efficiency and mathematical precision. In those days there was no disagreement or competition among people. Indeed, humans and animals could converse with one another and got along perfectly (272c). There was no private property, no family, no work, no sexuality (people are generated out of the earth), and no war (271e–272a). There was no reason to develop any of the arts, not even the arts of agriculture or of clothes-making; people in those times went about naked and found food without effort. They possessed no sense of shame. I think it safe to infer that there existed no politics in the ordinary sense of the term, and this because there existed no human beings.[51]

This picture of things supplies the background for the **Statesman's** initial definition of statecraft as the rule of the all knowing person over featherless bipeds. The myth suggests that such a scheme would be appropriate to the golden ages and so, first of all, that it is impossible in practice. The first definition holds only for the cosmos' countercycle (274e–275a). As the ES goes on to say, things are radically different in our cycle of the cosmos. At a preordained time, god let go of the tiller of the cosmos. There was a gigantic quake, and a near total destruction of all living things. God retired to his "observation tower" (*periope*; 272e5; a sort of 'ivory tower') along with his helper gods. The cosmos began to unwind, and in the ensuing cycle—our cycle, the human one—the cosmos and all things in it are left to care for themselves. Disagreement, war, competition arise. So do the arts, customs, communities, religion, philosophy, sexuality, and procreation; all are forms of auto-therapy. We live in the best of times and the worst of times. For a while things go well. But unfortunately the universe is ineluctably entropic. It degenerates into chaos, and god once again grabs hold of the tiller and winds up the universe.

The ES pauses to ask YS which cycle is happier. YS is unsure. ES prompts him with this criterion: if the residents of the countercycle (that which Kronos ruled) had philosophy, then they were happier. It seems clear, as I have said, that in the golden age there was no philosophy. The model of statecraft appropriate to the golden age is neither possible nor ultimately desirable, for utopia was not unequivocally good. This is a point that, as I suggested earlier (part I), might be read in the **Republic** as well. It follows that, among other things, our conception of politics must be conditioned by a deep sense of our neediness and a recognition

51 Another strange aspect of life then is as follows: people were born full grown and then became younger. It would thus seem that there was no learning in the countercycle, only forgetting. As the ES says, no one possessed any memory of preceding generations (271e8–272a2); there thus existed no sense of history or continuity with the past, no traditions.

of our fallibility; of the inevitability of self-reliance thanks to god's absence (the art of politics cannot claim divine guidance as the source of its knowledge); by a deep sense of the constant pressure of decay and the tendency to entropy; of the omnipresence of disagreement and of the ever-present danger of war; by the development of *technai* that will save us from the destructive hand of nature; and finally by—to use a Socratic phrase—knowledge of ignorance, by our recognition that no human can or ought to rule as god would. Indeed, the ES defines the tyrant as someone who rules without established law in the belief that he possesses the true political *episteme* (300b10–c4). The tyrant exhibits ignorance of ignorance in the highest degree. That crucial point is a strongly Socratic one. In sum, the **Statesman** points us to a deeply fallibilistic teaching about the human condition and world, and draws the appropriate political consequences.[52]

These consequences include a recognition of the importance of written law. In a now famous discussion, the ES argues that while in a perfect world the ruler could dispense with written law and instead legislate for each and every case, in a world of imperfections and fallible knowledge, written law is best. Since a god cannot rule, it is best for the laws—the result of trial and error, experience, prudence—to rule (294a6–8).[53] The laws ought to rule as justly and impartially as possible, but always with an awareness as to why they, and not a fallible person, rule. With this in mind the ES sets out a hierarchy of imperfect polities relative to the perfect one which they "imitate." The imitative polities may be governed according to law or lawlessly (i.e., without laws, contrary to laws). The question is this: given the cosmological conditions outlined, which polity is the "mean," the timely or appropriate one, for the times?

After a discussion about measure and the rule of law, the ES sets out the types of polities. He remarks that while a monarchy is best *if* it is governed by *good* writings or laws, in a situation tending to lawlessness and intemperance democracy is best, for while it is not capable of the greatest goods, neither is it capable of the worst evils (303a–b). If we order the six regimes he names from best to

52 The ES has told a story that illustrates why the choice of theoretical knowledge as the branch under which to seek political science was a mistake. It abstracted from our fallibility, our limits, from the world's unwinding. Now we infer that statesmanship is a branch of practical science. The ES puts this metaphorically: political science is like the art of weaving woolen cloaks, i.e., the art of uniting the citizens through mores and laws protecting all from hostile nature.

53 As the ES says, "there is no king that comes to be in the cities, as we in point of fact assert, who's of the sort that naturally arises in hives—one who's right from the start exceptional in his body and his soul—they [the citizens] must, it seems, once they've come together, write up writings while they run after the traces of the truest regime" (301d8–e4). I quote here and below from the S. Bernardete translation in **The Being of the Beautiful: Plato's Theaetetus, Sophist, and Statesman** (Chicago: University of Chicago Press, 1984).

worst, we get this sequence: monarchy, aristocracy, democracy according to law, lawless democracy (mob rule), oligarchy, and tyranny. In the light of the cosmological myth, it seems clear that our times make democracy according to law appropriate, for we surely live in a time tending to lawlessness and intemperance. "Precision"—a favorite word in these passages of the **Statesman**—simply does not characterize our lives as political beings or individuals, in sharp contrast to the world governed by Kronos. Further, we are told that the people refer to anyone claiming the title of monarch as "tyrant."[54] Even well intentioned rulers are corruptible by the usual temptations. Plato makes this point explicit in a remarkable passage in the **Laws**, and with a familiar sounding formulation: absolute power corrupts and is not to be entrusted to a mortal, corruptible being (**Laws** 713c, 714a, 691c–d, 875a–d). The point is there made with reference to the same Kronos myth that plays such a large role in the **Statesman**. And as in the **Statesman**, the conclusion is that the laws must rule in such a way as to provide constitutional restraints on absolute power lest the situation devolve into that which plagued Persia (**Laws** 697d–698a). So monarchic rule is not desirable in a non-ideal situation.

The same objection that the ES articulates against the claim by one person to absolute rule would *a fortiori* hold against the claims of a few such persons. And that leaves us with the third best alternative, namely a lawful or constitutional democracy. As ruled by law and structured by institutions that prevent the (corrupting) concentration of power in one or few hands, a polity of this sort would differ fundamentally from the "democracy" criticized in book IX of the **Republic**.

A constitutional democracy might satisfy the demand of each person to rule. A polity of this sort might encourage development of the arts and sciences in that each person is left at liberty to create under competitive conditions. If knowledge is fallible, then the opportunity to improve it must be encouraged (at 299e the ES notes that a system of laws excluding progress in the arts eventually destroys the *polis*). Those arts and sciences are essential for self-preservation in an entropic age. Since civil war is forbidden and all are equal before the rule of written law, politics is to be carried on by persuasion rather than force. That and the diffusion of power that a properly structured democracy ensures should check the lust for power so evident in the political life of an unravelling world. Finally, I note that at 276e the tyrannical art is characterized as "care of those who submit to force," while the political art is characterized as voluntary care of voluntarily participating

54 As the ES says, the people simply "don't trust that anyone would ever prove to be worthy of a ruler of that {kingly} sort, so as to be willing and able as ruler with virtue and science to distribute correctly the just and holy things to all." (301c8–d2). In a comprehensive interpretation of the **Statesman**, I would seek to show that the section on law recapitulates the whole course if the dialogue, and is a highly dialectical section.

citizens. The distinction between political rule and rule over slaves, demanded by Aristotle at the start of the **Politics**, is now granted. In sum, the **Statesman** points us to constitutional democracy composed of free citizens as the "best" regime for the current cycle of the cosmos.[55] This might be interpreted broadly enough to include elements of other polities, as in the **Laws'** mix of democratic, aristocratic, and monarchic models (756e–757a *et passim*).[56] And as the Athenian Stranger stresses in the **Laws**, the lawgiver's aim must be to secure for the *polis* not just internal harmony but freedom and wisdom (701d).[57]

The **Statesman** confirms, I am arguing, my reading of the **Republic.** Yet both dialogues seem to leave us with the impression that the public realm is not a context within which excellence is to be pursued by individuals. The value of the

55 We can connect the ES' account with Socrates' view of things. The ES tells us that it is extremely difficult to separate the true statesman from the "sophists of sophists," the "greatest imitators and greatest enchanters" who falsely claim to be legitimate rulers (291c, 303c). The problem of images and originals is central to our understanding of political life. Now, this is a favorite Socratic theme. And Socrates responds to the problem by cross-examining claimants to wisdom in order to see which of them really possesses wisdom and which only seems to. In the **Apol.**, he recounts that he concluded from his dialogues that no one is perfectly wise; the best one can do is human wisdom or knowledge of ignorance. That sort of self-knowledge entails recognition of one's limitations as human—a pervasive point in the Platonic dialogues. The famous Socratic and Platonic emphasis on dialogue, that is, supports the **Stsm.'s** fallibilistic critique of despotic rule.

56 But how exactly is this polity to be structured? Will it mix in, say, other forms of *poleis*—aristocratic and monarchic elements, as in the **Laws** (756e–757a et passim)? At this point, I think Plato has no a *priori* answer. The answers will be, to borrow a phrase from a founder of American liberalism, "inventions of prudence" (J. Madison, **Federalist** no. 51, p. 322). It will depend on everything from the social and political history of the people in question to the geography of the place. Trial and error will be one of our teachers (300b). This is unsatisfying if one thinks of political philosophy as capable of answering a *priori* detailed questions of constitutional structure or social policy. But one could also argue that a strength of the approach is precisely that it leaves a great deal of room for deliberations about empirical and contingent affairs. The large role that Plato and Aristotle assign "phronesis" in political theory is connected with their conviction that particularities must be given their due in both ethics and political theory.

57 As the **Laws** indicates, Platonic perfectionism would grant significant space to liberty of speech, liberty to trade, to travel, to gather with other citizens, to participate in politics, to the right to own private property. The glaring exception concerns the public expression of atheism, public disagreement with the civic religion, or the creation of private religions. All are strictly forbidden in book X of the **Laws**. I would want to argue that with regard to freedom of religion, Plato either erred, or thought the threat of civil war so great (**Laws** 744d) as to require him to put aside the 'liberal' consequences of his own theories.

polis, once again, seems merely instrumental. To revert to the ES' question as to where happiness is to be found: we seem led to answer that it is to be found in the individual's private life. This is puzzling within the context of a perfectionist theory, as the point seems now to be that there is little perfection to be gotten by means of the state's direct intervention in the lives of individuals. It also seems that individuals have little reason, other than an instrumental one, to care about a *polis*. To see that this is not the end of the story, we need to turn to the **Phaedrus**. If some connection between self-interest and the interest of others can be established at the heart of the non-political, perfecting pursuit of self-knowledge, then we may be able to see in a general way the connection between that pursuit and politics.[58]

III

Close to the start of the **Phaedrus**, Socrates declares that he cares only about self-knowledge.[59] With this striking declaration Socrates presents us in the strongest form with the assertion of the primacy of self-perfection; for that is the goal to which self-knowledge is the means. This emphasis on self-knowledge and self-perfection is, as we know, repeated many times in the Platonic dialogues.[60] In the **Apology**, for example, Socrates characterizes his life as a divinely provoked pursuit of self-knowledge (21a ff.). Yet in the very same dialogue he describes his purpose in a very different way when he portrays himself as dedicated to the

58 Sections of the following discussion of the **Phr**. are adapted, with many changes, from parts {A} and {B} of my "The Politics of Self-knowledge: Liberal Variations on the **Phaedrus**," in the **Understanding the Phaedrus**, ed. by L. Rossetti (Sankt Augustin: Academia Verlag, 1992), pp. 173–90. I am grateful to the press for permission to adapt that article to my present purposes, for a fuller discussion of the **Phr.** and liberalism. The general strategy of turning to the 'discourses on love' for insight into the foundations of Plato's political philosophy has not been followed through, so far as I know, in the detail I have attempted. But moves in that direction are made R. Kraut in "Egoism, Love, and Political Office in Plato," **Philosophical Review** 82 (1973): 330–44 (Kraut refers to the **Symp**.).

59 "I am not yet capable," he says, "in accordance with the Delphic inscription, of 'knowing myself'; it therefore seems absurd to me that while I am still ignorant of this subject I should inquire into things which do not belong to me. So then saying goodbye to these things {the question as to the truth of various myths}, and believing what is commonly thought about them, I inquire—as I said just now—not into these but into myself . . ." (229e5–230a3). Trans. by C. J. Rowe in **Plato: Phaedrus, with translation and commentary** (Warminster: Aris and Phillips, 1986). I shall use this translation throughout.

60 E.g., **Rep.** 578c ("for, you know, the consideration is about the greatest thing, a good life and a bad one"); **Gorg.** 487e11–488a1: the key issue is what quality a person should have and what his pursuits should be.

moral improvement of his fellow citizens, thereby manifesting (so he claims) great civic concern for Athens as well (29d–30b). How do these two sides of Socrates' moral life cohere? If the philosopher cares only about knowing himself, is there any room for his caring for others?[61]

I think we can make some progress here by recalling some of the metaphysical propositions of Socrates' second speech—often referred to as the 'recantation' or 'palinode'—in the **Phaedrus**. In the palinode we learn that Forms are not directly visible to embodied souls; that privilege is reserved to the gods and the disembodied souls that accompany them. For us, Forms are visible only through their images and so through sense perception; we know the Forms only through recollection, through "memory" (*mneme*, 254b5). This theme of recollection (*anamnesis*), which is absent from the **Republic**, accents the partiality and indirectness of our understanding of Forms. The **Phaedrus** insists much more strongly than does the **Republic** that the philosopher cannot escape the cave altogether. In the **Phaedrus**' universe there could be no "philosopher kings" since there could be no "philosophers" in the requisite sense.[62]

The palinode concentrates on Beauty, but also mentions Justice. If Socrates had chosen Justice rather than Beauty as the Form with which to illustrate the workings of eros, how would the account have proceeded? Where would the images of justice present themselves? Presumably they would do so in the words and deeds of other persons individually and collectively considered. Just as the directedness of the soul towards the Forms, and the availability of Forms through images in "this" world, ties the philosopher to a beloved in the case of Beauty, so we can envision that a similar connection would hold in the case of Justice. A philosophical attraction to that Form would tie the philosopher to persons in this world; perfection of self would seem in this event to include attachment to others in their collective capacity—to one or more communities, in effect.[63]

61 I shall refer to the philosopher using the masculine pronoun because Plato does so in the **Phr.**, and to avoid cumbersome switching back and forth. I do not, however, believe that Plato's story here about soul, perfection, and love *has* to be gender specific.

62 The cycle of departure from and return to the cave, narrated so briefly in the **Rep.**, consumes much of the **Phr.**'s palinode. The palinode tells not only about a heavenly scene above the earth, but about the fate of earthbound, fallen souls—a fate that entails forgetfulness of what was seen above, and a struggle to remember. Down here, our intelligence is bound to sense perception, and in different ways. Beauty is the "clearest" of all the Forms, accessible as it is to the sense of sight; Wisdom ("phronesis"), by contrast, is invisible to sight, and very hard to recollect and to love (250d3–e1). The earthly likenesses of Justice and Sophrosyne also lack luster; they are hard to see (250b1–3).

63 Since at 250b *et passim* Socrates indicates that our attraction to Justice is not as passionate as that for Beauty (at least not initially?), I use the word "attraction" rather than "passion" here. That is, the justice which the organization of the laws of a body

The pursuit of Justice cannot be a merely "other worldly" one, particularly if another aspect of the story Socrates tells about lover and beloved holds by analogy with respect to the philosopher and his or her beloved *polis*. An old debate surrounds the issue of whether the lover cares for the beloved for the latter's own sake, or merely as a means to his (the lover's) own perfection. This debate, initiated by an article by Vlastos, lies at the heart of the problem mentioned earlier as to whether or not the *polis* is merely of instrumental value to the philosopher.[64] I wish to propose that the dilemma is a false one. I shall suggest that the relationship between philosopher and polis parallels that between lover and beloved, such that the polis too may be of more than merely instrumental value. While the lover cares about the beloved because he sees in the other an image of both his own perfection and of the Form, he does genuinely care for the beloved's welfare as measured by the latter's potential for perfection (cf. **Rep**. 401d–402d, 518b). The lover does not better himself at the expense of the beloved, but in such a way as to better the beloved as well. The lover does not throw the beloved away at the end of it all; rather, if things go successfully, they become life long friends (256a–b). The beloved's potential is not a mere means to the realization thereof, as though once perfected he is a different self. That potential is itself treated, in the **Phaedrus** and **Symposium**, as a source of wonderment and respect. It is true that a self is held to be worthy of love in virtue of the lovable qualities immanent in it; but I take Plato's point to be that the "separable" nature of these qualities rescues value for soul rather than deprives it of value.[65] A universe in which a self could not be seen as reflecting these eternally perfect and complete qualities would, on this view, leave us with little motivation for valuing a soul deeply.[66] Love and friendship, in turn, are indispensable components of the good life

politic and of the characters of its citizens may exhibit will lack the brilliance present in a particular, potentially philosophical beloved.

64 I refer to G. Vlastos' "The Individual as Object of Love in Plato," reprinted in **Platonic Studies**, 2nd ed. (Princeton: Princeton University Press, 1981), pp. 3–34.

65 Cf. G. Vlastos' "The Theory of Social Justice in the **Polis** in Plato's **Republic**," in **Interpretations of Plato**, ed. H. F. North (Leiden: E. J. Brill, 1977), p. 33. As Vlastos rightly points out there, if Plato were to ask "what is excellence {of soul} for?" we might answer "for humanity." But Plato would want to take the reverse tack, asking "what is humanity for?" and answering with reference to excellence or perfection. And this answer might seem to lead (and does lead in some Platonic dialogues) to a view of justice that is compatible with substantive inequality. But the **Phr.**, as I shall suggest, at least points in another direction. For a very fine response to Vlastos on this point, see A. Kosman's "Platonic Love," in **Phronesis** suppl. vol. II (1976), ed. W. H. Werkmeister, pp. 53–69.

66 My purpose here is neither to defend the just stated point as an exegesis of the **Phr.** nor as a philosophical position in its own right. The former task I undertook in **Self-knowledge in Plato's Phaedrus** (New Haven, Conn.: Yale University Press, 1986), pp. 124–33 (for the debate about the possible "egoism" of this portrayal of love, see

precisely because, rather than in spite of, their being intrinsic to the philosophic activity of *anamnesis*, to being the kind of self that is perfected.

A similar picture may hold with respect to justice. The philosopher will see images of Justice in *poleis*, and therefore take an interest in these *poleis* in the course of trying to understand what justice itself is. A polis that embodies or in its institutions "images" Justice in a high degree would be particularly promising in his eyes. Should he discern in a polis the reflection of the Form Justice, the philosopher would want to bring out a polis' justice in something like the way that the philosophical lover wants to bring out the best in his beloved.[67] As an overflow of his own desire for self-perfection (for justice in his own soul, say), the philosopher will want to perfect his polis. But just as the lover tries to select a beloved whom he divines is of the same type, so the philosopher would grant his attentions to a community in which he or she divined the potential for justice.[68] As the choice of a correct beloved initiates the love affair, and ultimately the friendship, that provides the lover with the context for self-perfection, so a

pp. 128–29). A difficult problem about the relationship between Beauty and Justice lurks here. One might ask, for example, what makes Justice (or an instance thereof) attractive to the philosopher, if not its Beauty, whose motivational property Socrates makes so much of. Perhaps it is the rational order that might partly define what it is to be just that attracts the philosophical soul, an order or symmetry that might qualify as "beautiful." In this event, the correlate to justice in the city would be justice in the soul, that of beauty in the city would be beauty in the soul. Perhaps justice could be seen as exhibiting harmony and unity that are marks of beauty; and this would account for the philosopher's attraction to justice in the city. Beauty would here function almost as the Good does in the **Rep.**

67 For a discussion of the **Rep.** that leads to similar conclusions (though from quite different premises) see. J. Cooper, "The Psychology of Justice in Plato," **American Philosophical Quarterly** 14 (1977), p. 155: ". . . it does not follow that they [philosophers] would always choose to live a contemplative's life . . . . a just person is a devotee of *the* good, not *his own* good; and these are very different things. Knowing the good, what he [the philosopher] wants is to advance the reign of rational order in the world as a whole." A similar point is made with reference to the **Symp.** by R. Demos in "A Fallacy in Plato's **Republic**?", in **Plato II**, p. 55: "To aim at the good is also to aim at the *production* of good things; thus for an individual to aim at justice means that he cares not only for justice in the abstract, but also that justice should be embodied in human beings in general. . . . The health of the soul includes, above all, the fulfillment of its reason: and the concern of reason is that the good soul be exemplified everywhere." See also M. Miller's "Platonic Provocations: Reflections on the Soul and the Good in the **Republic**," in **Platonic Investigations**, ed. D. O'Meara (Washington: Catholic University of American Press, 1985): 163–93. Miller stresses the element of "generosity" on the philosopher's part that results from his vision of the Good.

68 Recall that there are two kinds of "recollection" in the palinode, and that they are connected: e.g., (a) to recognize oneself as a follower of Zeus—i.e., as a

friendship with the right polis may provide the lover with the context for self-perfection as a just human being.[69] And as not just any beloved will help the lover accomplish these ends, so not just any polis will help the philosopher accomplish analogous ends. Perhaps there is a hierarchy of *poleis*—the most potentially just to the most tyrannical and unjust—as there are of soul types (248c2–e3). Indeed, in book IX of the **Republic** Socrates matches up a hierarchy of polities with a hierarchy of soul types.[70] No more than the beloved, then, is a polis a dispensable feature of the philosophers' love of Forms.[71] This I think is the thrust of Socrates' comments about laws and customs in the **Symposium's** ascent passages. There

philosopher—is to see oneself as the type of soul passionate about (b) tracking down or recollecting the Forms present in their images. One cannot apprehend one's own nature directly, without the mediation of the other who serves, in Socrates' word, as a "mirror" (255d6). I am suggesting that, at least in the case of justice, the polis serves as the philosopher's mirror. What dimension of the soul is mirrored and brought to consciousness by the polis? Presumably, the aspect of soul that would be engaged as dialectician and (in a suitably defined sense) pedagogue in the polis (that engagement described in the **Apol**. as being both beneficial to Socrates and to the citizens). Further: in the palinode's account, the beloved is portrayed as confused by the lover, unclear as to what he (the beloved) is loving and as to what he sees reflected in the lover (255d). If the present analogy holds, we would expect the polis to undergo a similar experience when facing the philosopher. The relationship is asymmetrical in each case. Finally: as Socrates shifts between the language of making (252d7, e4) and of discovering (252e1–4) in describing the lover's stance towards the beloved, so too, perhaps, with respect to the philosopher's stance towards the polis: the given polis, as potentially just, is both discovered to be an image of Justice and made into a more perfect image thereof.

69 This is compatible with the **Rep.**'s view that ruling is drudgery (**Rep.** 540a–b); but there are other forms of political activity, such as that described by Socrates in the **Apol.** as an alternative to direct participation in ruling. Aristotle points out that (Plato's) Socrates "praises above all the city's being one, which is held to be, and which he asserts to be, the work of affection," and goes on to allude to the **Symp.** Aristotle rightly points out that the **Rep.**'s scheme dilutes the possibilities for affection by dissolving the family; the implication being that the **Symp.** is inconsistent with the **Rep.** (**Pol**. II.1262b8 ff).

70 I note that at **Phr.** 246e6–247a1 we hear of a multitude of communities in heaven, varying as soul types do.

71 The general point of the preceding paragraphs could be taken much further, of course. For one could argue that (like other Forms) Justice is not an entity that can be defined in and of itself, that in isolation from contexts and examples in which it is (even if imperfectly) instantiated, there is relatively little to *say* about it (except by negation, as at **Symp.** 211d8–e4), however much it may be something one can "see" (**Symp.** 211e1 *et passim*). In the **Phr.** Socrates in fact says nothing about the substantial meaning of any Form, except that vision of it is deeply fulfilling etc. I note in passing that not even the gods care solely about the Forms: they are portrayed, rather,

we are told that the ordering of cities and households with moderation and justice is the most beautiful part of wisdom; a lover of beauty will want to give birth to admirable regimes, and will admire them too as instances of beauty (209a, d, 210c, 211c).

This way of looking at the relationship between self-perfection and community entails giving up the holistic model of the city/soul analogy, according to which a philosophical polis is one ruled by philosophers just as a philosophical soul is one ruled by reason. In light of the **Phaedrus** and **Symposium** we might rather say that while neither a city nor a soul is admirable if ruled by passion, a city is admirable if it enables each of its members to pursue whatever excellence their natures may hold.[72]

The first two speeches of the **Phaedrus**, which portray the beloved as an object to be manipulated, give us an idea as to how persons may be mistreated. Particularly in Lysias' speech, the "other" is reified, reduced to a body, unsouled, having value only in the sexual gratification it can yield. The burden of the palinode, and so of the "ascent" from Lysias' speech, is to show why that conception of the person is inadequate, why it is that someone possessing self-knowledge would not be disposed to demean others in that way. Socrates introduces the notion of "soul" to denote a core function without which we would not be human. He implies that to treat persons as though this were not true of them would be to act ignorantly.[73]

Socrates' palinode takes us some way towards a critique of the reification or objectification of others so prominent in the first speech (that attributed to Lysias) of the dialogue. That speech implies a denial that persons have internality, that they are "subjects of a life" in a way that things and other animals seem not to

as "caring" for the cosmos (246e5–6), contemplating the Forms only intermittently. *Imitatio dei* thus involves more than contemplation.

72 A promising community need not, on this view, be seen as an individual—here the disanalogy between Socrates' account of the love of beauty and my analogous account of the love of justice is important. I note that individuals who are in love with a particular city are not praised by Plato. For they seem to be according the wrong kind of affection to the city, treating it as though it were an individual. Cf. Pericles' funeral speech where we are urged to become the "lovers" of Athens, inspired by the vision of her greatness. Thucydides II.xliii.

73 For some discussion, see **Self-knowledge**, chs. 2–3. In the **Phr.**, souls have a fixed upper limit, at least within cycles of embodiment; a Hera-like soul cannot in principle become a Zeus-like soul. But the lower limit is not fixed in the same way, and souls can act in ways that are, as it were, beneath themselves. They can fail to reach their full potential. They can also come to see, and attempt to realize, their full potential. As self-directing in that sense, persons possess an inner freedom that permits them to become objects of praise and blame, to be held responsible for failing to live up to themselves.

be.[74] By contrast, the whole description, in the palinode, of the experience of falling in love portrays vividly the self as having "inner" experiences, an inwardness articulated here with remarkable subtlety and sensitivity. The "inner/outer" self distinction keeps reappearing in the **Phaedrus** (245e4–6, 275a2–6, 279b9–c1; cf. 235c4–d1), pointing to the presence in each of us of interiority, one might even say individuality or subjectivity, the possibility of a first-person perspective.[75] Plato's version of Kant's imperative will be "hypothetical": treat others with respect (*aidos*) for the selves they truly would be, if you would become a happy, perfected self. This is part of the story as to how Plato will get from "justice" conceived as an excellence of self (i.e., as "virtue") to "justice" conceived of in terms of what is due to others.[76] Conversely, as Socrates says in the **Republic** (443a) as well, the just person lacks the motivations that commonly lead to injustice in the conventional sense—regardless of the presence or absence of incentives conventionally understood. Socrates wants us to see that selfhood should be understood not as "individuality" cut off from others, not as an entity to which other persons are mere means, but as having a kind of being (*ousia*; **Phr.** 245e3) whose good includes the good of others and, indirectly, of suitable communities. A polity that founded itself on a misunderstanding about this nature of the self will not qualify as just; and Socrates would, I think, hold that many conventional regimes fail to pass muster on precisely this ground.[77]

74 I take it to be part of Plato's purpose to show that the speech is internally inconsistent. For the non-lover gives a speech precisely to persuade the beloved, i.e., he assumes the beloved is capable of choice (231d6–7; cf. 233a4–5). In Socrates' first speech we are presented with a demand for definition of terms, a tactic designed in part to make us see that how we value others makes assumptions about what kinds of beings they are, assumptions that if thought through would require that we treat these beings differently.

75 "Individuality" and "subjectivity" are obviously controverted notions, especially in the context of Greek ethics; hence my tentative use of it. I would only note here that they should not be confused with uniqueness.

76 Worked out in the way suggested in the present essay, this way of bridging the gap between justice understood as a quality of self, and conventional justice, leads to rejection of the "holistic" model of justice.

77 The view of soul as self-moved, of learning as recollection, and the critique of motivation that assumes faulty notions of the human good (and so of what it means to be human) at the very least exclude much conventional politics and *poleis* on the grounds of injustice or some other vice. For example, any regime that claims wealth as a title to rule can claim no legitimacy, and Socrates is very harsh on oligarchs and their regime in the **Rep.** VIII. Rule based on brute force is obviously illegitimate as well, for Socrates; it amounts to tyranny in one form another. Any regime that claims virtue is inherited is based for Socrates on a falsehood. And, more subtly, any regime that fails to promote the development of moral excellence rightly understood will be, in various degrees, less than perfect and so less than worthy of approbation. I would

Let me briefly indicate what sort of communities would pass muster. I note, first, that knowledge and self-knowledge are both, for Socrates, types of remembering. Whatever else this may mean, it strongly suggests that the requisite knowledge is to be found "within" and that it has value as appropriated through one's own dialectical or erotic labors. Socrates contrasts to this process knowledge that is poured in from the "outside," as he thinks book-learning to be (275a). The process of Socratic dialectic famously embodies the view that while souls can be helped to learn, they cannot be taught philosophy directly. The application of political compulsion would presumably transform *anamnesis* into rote memorization, perhaps hypocritically performed. The type of perfectionism compatible with Socratic dialectic and *anamnesis* would be indirect, and would recognize the key role of the agent's effort and choice in self-perfection.

Second, recollection is to be undertaken dialectically, for Socrates, and this requires suitable interlocutors.[78] Correspondingly, the question of the polity is not a matter of indifference for the **Phaedrus'** philosopher. The liberties to discuss, to question, to have students of one's choice, to wander outside the city's walls, and to do so in the company of some politically doubtful souls, seem essential.[79]

expect that in criticizing such regimes Socrates would follow his usual practice of searching for internal contradictions, unsupported assertions, and false beliefs. Ultimately he will argue that a person who advocates, say, a tyrannical regime, manifests a tyrannical soul, one which is enslaved to its own fears and desires (**Rep.** 579d–e). This elenchus would narrow considerably the political options Socrates would consider acceptable, and would point, as I have argued, to an important place for political liberties. In the **Phr.**'s account, the tyrant lies at the very bottom of the hierarchy of soul types (248e3) because he is most ignorant of the Forms and is motivated solely by the basest of desires, a motivation that stems from an impoverished conception of his own "self" and, by extension, of what it means to be a "self." He reifies others because he has reified himself. The tyrant is, as it were, Lysias' non-lover armed with ambition and political power.

78 The philosopher must live within the walls of the city and—again, precisely in order to pursue his own perfection—want to live among interlocutors of the requisite soul types (say, types ranging from Phaedrus to Protagoras to Plato).

79 It is significant that at the end of the **Phr.**, a conversation that takes place in the countryside, Plato makes a point of Socrates' and Phaedrus' return to Athens. Plato has them vote for that polis with their feet. Socrates and Phaedrus have wandered out of the embracing walls of the city, but just for this day. At the end of the dialogue, they return to Athens. As the gods return "home" (*oikade*; 247e4) after feasting on the eternal verities, so when finished with their feast of speeches Socrates and Phaedrus return to the home suitable for embodied souls—a polis, indeed a specific polis. That polis is not just a *faute de mieux,* life outside the walls of which would be infinitely preferable. Socrates leaves uncorrected Phaedrus' assertion that he (Socrates) never leaves Athens "at all" (230d2), and provides an interesting explanation: "Forgive me, my good man. You see, I'm a lover of learning, and the country places and the trees

As we have already noted, Socrates points out in the **Republic** (557d) that anyone wishing to set out a regime, as he and his companions have been doing in that very dialogue, would prefer to do so in a democracy.[80]

Finally, while the **Phaedrus** sets out a hierarchy of soul-types on the basis of how much each soul "saw" of the Forms (248d–e), it does not follow that the distribution of liberties among the citizens should be very restricted, such that the best practical polity must be substantively inegalitarian.[81] For accurate institution of the various soul-types as social classes would depend on accurate discernment of the soul-types. And the palinode leaves us—deliberately, in my view—utterly unclear as to how a list of vocations, a list of character types), and various

won't teach me anything, as the people in the city will" (230d3–5). Of course, Socrates *has* been outside the walls—and significantly, for my present purposes, in order to fight on behalf of Athens. And when he and Phaedrus re-enter, they do so armed with a lengthy discussion of rhetoric, a theme to which the polis is relevant.

80 The reason Socrates cites is that a democracy contains many different models of polities. But it does so because, as Socrates says at 557b, it is a city full of freedom and free speech. These goods would also be required to discuss publicly which of the models is best.

81 Presumably those at the top have a better claim to know justice and to be just than those lower down. After the seeker for wisdom and beauty Socrates ranks the law-abiding king, and so on down the latter. This scheme seems to lead directly to a non-egalitarian political polity, for one could argue that those persons who are by nature incapable of recollecting much, and who "forget" even that of which they were capable, thanks to their way of life (248e3–5, 250a3–4), occupy a lower moral rank than the philosophers and ought to be treated accordingly. So the most "philosophical" polity, the one most beautiful in a philosopher's eyes, would seem to be hopelessly far from anything like a regime that recognized basic principles of fairness and equality.

82 At 253b Socrates says that each follower of a given god strives to make his beloved resemble that god. Hera-types look for royal natures, and so forth. One might ask how followers of Ares will "love" their polis, and what Forms (or what understanding of Form(s)) they seek to have reflected in their own soul and their polis. Part of the answer may lie at 252c, where we learn that followers of Ares are possessive to the extreme; if they think their beloved is doing them some injury, they will shed their own and their beloved's blood. Something like this may fit the description of Alcibiades at **Symp.** 213d, and correspondingly the ways in which Alcibiades repaid his "beloved" Athens for perceived injustice towards him (on Alcibiades as a lover of the demos, see **Symp.** 216b). It remains unclear how that sort of account meshes with the "degree of knowledge of the Forms" issue. Things become still murkier if there exists a Form of Injustice (as suggested at **Rep.** 476a), a possibility that risks seriously disrupting the **Phr.**'s account of things. For then the tyrant would be not a person forgetful of Forms who treats the polis as he would treat himself—e.g., as a thing to be reified and manipulated—but a person who remembers a Form (e.g., Injustice) and passionately seeks to have that Form realized. Presumably, that Form exists in the antipode to the hyperuranian place, somewhere "under the earth" (256d6).

quantities of knowledge-of-Forms, are to be coordinated.[82] Indeed, the palinode may be taken to claim that the relative weighing of these factors cannot be rationally understood.[83] Moreover, the palinode also teaches that such weighing is nearly impossible. Given the inherent fallibility of that procedure, the ever present possibility of error on the part of the dialectician, and the limited number of persons one can examine, it seems to follow that any effort to institute an illiberal hierarchy of social classes is deprived of rational justification from the outset.[84]

In sum, the **Phaedrus** suggests that the best practicable polity will be committed to institutions that encourage persuasion rather than coercion, development of self rather than debasement thereof, philosophy and the love of knowledge rather than tyranny and the love of power or wealth, the treatment of others as potentially perfectible in some degree (a degree not inferrable from the person's vocation or social status), and whatever liberties conduce to the above. It will recognize its own limits; in particular, the fallibility of our knowledge, and the necessity that true knowledge be appropriated by the individual. We would thus expect the philosopher to admire a polis whose institutions are shaped by a knowledge of ignorance parallel to his own. For all practical purposes, we may infer, a polis would do better to proceed along egalitarian lines in its organization of political participation (this is of course compatible with a meritocracy in other spheres of social life). The duty to respect liberties could well be expressed in terms of rights (where a right to something is understood as the legitimate claim

83 For substantiation, see **Self-knowledge** pp. 102–03.

84 Whether this interpretation can be reconciled with the **Rep.** is a fascinating question far too complex to broach here. If I am right, the **Phr.** suggests that we abandon the **Rep.** view that the city is good if its parts are related in a way analogous to the way in which the parts of a well-ordered soul are related. Nor, on the present account, does the **Phr.** suggest that the good polis is that all of whose parts are actually (rather than just potentially) good (those would be very few in number). The palinode's teaching is much more fallibilistic than that of the **Rep.**, as already indicated. The **Rep.**'s argument for an inegalitarian regime depends on the premise that moral experts to rule over non-experts; but there are no moral experts in the requisite sense.

85 Even if this answer is accepted, though, it may seem that we have been furnished with no principled way of defining the liberties, or if you like, the rights, of the citizens in Plato's second best polis. Further, these liberties—whatever they may be, exactly—seem placed on a highly insecure basis; and this has been a reason for rejecting perfectionism as a political theory, as noted at the start of the paper. I take it that Plato would want to reply to the second point that the basis is as philosophically firm as it ever gets; no theory is so obviously sound that discussion about its merits ends among philosophers. He might continue to say that political liberties would be as soundly embedded institutionally in a scheme he would devise as in one we might devise. But if one wants something still more specific, something comparable to the American Bill of Rights, one will find Plato of limited help. I expect that he would see precise enumeration of rights as a task for a legislator in a specific situation. I also expect that

to be protected in doing that thing).[85] In a Platonic context, talk about rights would serve as a proxy for the sorts of moral reasons clustered around the notion of self-perfection that I have discussed. When at the end of **Republic** IX Socrates bids us to order our souls by contemplating the "paradigm" of the "city in speech," I think he means us to adopt just this stance towards politics.

IV

Let me close. I distinguished earlier between individualist and communitarian perfectionism. I characterized Epicurus as an extreme representative of the former camp, and Aristotle as a representative of the latter. In which camp is Plato to be put with respect to his political philosophy as represented above? As in the case of the characterization of the lover/beloved relationship, I want to claim that neither alternative alone does justice to Plato's theory. In that friendship for individuals and care for an appropriately defined poleis are intrinsic to a person's development of self—and I have argued that they are such, for Plato—then Plato is in the "communitarian" camp. But in that the qualities by virtue of which we admire persons and polis's are separable—and the Forms are characterized as such in the **Republic** and **Phaedrus**—and insofar as the Forms apprehensible in and of themselves—the great prize Plato promises those who have perfected themselves—then the good is realized in an activity of contemplation of which community is not constitutive. In a perfect world, Platonic perfectionism would be individualist rather than communitarian. In this world, among us, it would be both.[86]

worries (as expressed in the **Phr.**) about the inherent weaknesses of written word might make him reluctant to sanction in any real world situation an enumeration of rights in a constitution. Of course, this is a worry expressed in the American tradition itself. See Madison's comments in the **Federalist** no. 84.

86 I thank Aryeh Kosman, Mitchell Miller, David Roochnik, Amelie Rorty, and David Schmidtz for their very helpful comments on various drafts of this paper. I am also grateful to the Earhart Foundation and the Woodrow Wilson Center for Scholars (Washington, D.C.) for the support of work leading to this paper. Drafts of this paper were delivered at Scripps College (Claremont), Rutgers University, Loyola College (Baltimore), George Mason University, the Graduate Center of the City University of New York, Yale University, the Université de Paris (XII), and the Catholic University of America. I am indebted to audiences at all these institutions for useful discussion and suggestions. Versions of this paper were published as "Le libéralisme platonicien: de la perfection individuelle comme fondement d'une théorie politique," in **Contre Platon: le Platonisme Renversé**, vol. II, ed. M. Dixsaut (Paris: Vrin, 1995), pp. 155–95; and in "Platonic Liberalism: Self-Perfection as a Foundation of Political Theory," in **Plato and Platonism**, ed. J. M. van Ophuijsen (Washington: Catholic University of America Press, 1999), pp. 102–34. The themes addressed here are perennials in the work of Stanley Rosen; may this serve as a contribution to the on-going dialogue with my friend, colleague, and former teacher.

The Nonlover in Aristotle's *Ethics*

Ronna Burger
Tulane University

I. Madness, Sobriety, and the Possibility of Philosophy

> The very possibility of philosophy stands or falls upon the possibility of a philosophical madness that is more sober than sobriety. This is no doubt a deeply problematical formulation. But it is not a puzzle.[1]

Stanley Rosen's essay, "The Nonlover in Plato's *Phaedrus*," helped guide my understanding of the *Phaedrus*, the subject of my first academic project, though I did not understand sufficiently at the time the broad and deep implications of his analysis.[2] The figure of the nonlover, Rosen leads us to see, is not simply Plato's portrait of a seducer; he is the concrete exemplification of how hedonism, utilitarianism, and "technicism" show up in the human soul and stand in the way of philosophy. But the nonlover cannot simply be dismissed: he exhibits, not only why philosophy is impossible without eros, but at the same time, why "the highest erotic function is impossible without the discursive detachment of the nonlover."[3]

Rosen pursued his analysis of the nonlover with a sequel, "Socrates as Concealed Lover," which appears along with the earlier essay in the collection, *The Quarrel Between Philosophy and Poetry*.[4] Together they establish how "the three speeches in the *Phaedrus* constitute an erotic ascent from the nonlover via the concealed lover to the lover in the full or manic sense."[5] The nonlover

1 Stanley Rosen, *The Quarrel Between Philosophy and Poetry: Studies in Ancient Thought*," New York/London: Routledge, Inc., 1988, p. xiii.

2 "The Nonlover in Plato's *Phaedrus*," *Man and World*, Vol. 2, no. 3, 1969, pp. 423–37. In 1981, Rosen wrote a review of six related books on the Platonic dialogues, which included my book, based on my dissertation, on the Phaedrus (*Philosophy and Rhetoric*, Vol. 14, No. 2, Spring 1981, pp. 112–17). His praise and his criticism were both important for me in my work after that starting point.

3 "Socrates as Concealed Lover," *The Quarrel Between Philosophy and Poetry*, p. 97.

4 *The Quarrel between Philosophy and Poetry*, pp. 78–90 and 91–101. Further references to these two essays indicate page numbers in this volume.

5 "Socrates as Concealed Lover," p. 91. The concealed lover contains elements of the nonlover and the lover that allow him, Rosen demonstrates, to mediate between them (p. 95).

represented by the speechwriter Lysias, who is responsible for the initial condemnation of eros, is exposed, in Socrates' revised version of the speech, as a lover in disguise, seeking to win for himself the favors of the beloved. Halfway through his speech Socrates stops, uncovers his head, which he had covered in shame, and prepares to leave, but is held back by his daimonion; afraid, as he claims, of being punished by the god Eros, and ashamed at having presented such a vulgar view of lover and beloved, Socrates sets out to purify himself by offering a "palinode," which will hold up the divine madness of eros as the source of our greatest blessings.

Overshadowed by the grandeur of Socrates' "mythic hymn" in praise of eros, the first two speeches are commonly neglected; Rosen's consideration of those speeches provides a unique way into the most striking problem of the *Phaedrus*. This dialogue, which more explicitly than any other holds up the standard for the written work as a perfectly ordered whole, appears to violate that standard by its own division into two halves: the series of speeches on eros in the first half, culminating in Socrates' praise of divine madness, appears to be only accidentally connected with the sober analysis of rhetoric and dialectics that occupies the second half of the dialogue. The speeches of the nonlover and the concealed lover provide a key to the unity of the dialogue, Rosen argues, precisely insofar as they represent the element of sobriety that must somehow be put together with the seemingly incompatible element of madness if philosophy is to be a real possibility.[6]

Rosen concludes his prefatory remarks to *The Quarrel between Philosophy and Poetry* with a reflection on those seemingly incompatible elements as reflected in the difference between Platonic madness and Aristotelian sobriety. Aristotle's political writings, he acknowledges, might "be commended for insulating politics from philosophical madness," but they could "be criticized for overestimating the power of sobriety and practical intelligence."[7] There is, perhaps, no more striking sign of the apparent split between Platonic madness and Aristotelian sobriety than their treatment of love and friendship: Plato, one might say, merits the title *the* philosopher of eros as much as Aristotle does *the* philosopher of friendship. Not only is eros the central theme of two Platonic dialogues, and present one way or another in almost all the others, but the discussion of friendship in the one short dialogue devoted to that theme is framed and colored

6 "[T]he peak of the dialogue about speech is in fact silence. But the slopes of that peak are discursive, and in two different senses. The way up is not the same as the way down. The way up is the dialectical transformation of base or nonerotic desire into noble or erotic desire, with the concomitant *Aufhebung* of the legitimate element of the nonlover. The way down, after the recollection of the hyper-Uranian beings, is the technical discussion of rhetoric and dialectic." ("Socrates as Concealed Lover," p. 99).

7 *The Quarrel Between Philosophy and Poetry, Preface,* p. xii.

by the issue of the lover's relation to his favorite.[8] Aristotle, as is well known, devotes the longest segment of his inquiry into human happiness to the theme of friendship, with eros mentioned only in scattered remarks, mostly derogatory.

One hears, in those remarks, the echo of the nonlover of the *Phaedrus*, above all in the insistence the incompatibility of passionate love and friendship. Aristotle, it is true, does not put those remarks into a speech delivered by a fictional character; but he gives us reasons to question whether, or to what extent, he is endorsing the nonlover's understanding of eros as he represents it. That understanding is not, in any case, not Aristotle's last word. There is, I want to propose, a development in the sequence of seemingly casual remarks about eros,[9] and the pattern is furnished by the *Phaedrus*: the condemnation of eros in favor of the sobriety of perfect friendship turns out to be only the first stage of the discussion; a "palinode" that leads us to rethink the account of friendship brings in its wake a transformation of eros, which leads finally to recognition of the erotic moment that belongs essentially to philosophic friendship. Perhaps, this conclusion suggests, Platonic madness and Aristotelian sobriety are not quite so starkly contrasted as the surface of their works make it seem.

II. Eros and *Philia* in the *Nicomachean Ethics*

1. Perfect Friendship and the Disappointments of Eros

No one, Aristotle announces in opening the discussion of friendship, would choose to have all the other good things in life but without friends (8.1.1156a5–6). No comparable claim is made about anything else in the *Ethics*. But the general agreement about the desirability of friendship does not settle, or even address, the disputed issue of what it is. At the core of the dispute is the question whether friendship is primarily a relationship between likes or unlikes (1155a33–b2). The attraction of likes or unlikes, while spoken of in the language of human experience, lends itself readily by metaphor to serve as a cosmological principle.[10] Making a

8 The discussion about friendship that Socrates conducts with the two young friends, Lysis and Menexenus, is preceded by his opening conversation with a young man in love with Lysis, whom Socrates advises on how to speak to his favorite so as not to approach him like a hunter who makes his quarry harder to catch (Lysis 203a–206d). The discussion of friendship ends with the proposal that "one's own" is alike the object of eros, philia, and desire (221e).

9 References to eros or related terms appear in 8.1 (1155b3–4), 8.3 (1156b2–3), 8.4 (1157a6–13), 8.6 (1158a11–12), 8.8 (1159b15–17), 9.1 (1164a3–8), 9.5 (1167a4–6), 9.10 (1171a11–12), and 9.12 (1171b29–31), with a very different treatment up to 9.1 from that which appears in 9.5 and later.

10 As Euripides no less than Heraclitus and Empedocles testify (1155b2–8). Cf. *Lysis* 214a–b and 215e, where the notion of *philia* as a relationship between likes or opposites belongs to a cosmological account.

Socratic turn, Aristotle dismisses such speculations about the whole of nature and sets out to analyze friendship as a strictly human phenomenon: the inquiry is to focus on the questions whether there is more than one form of friendship and whether all people can be friends or only the good.

The two questions prove to be integrally connected: a division of kinds (*eide*) allows friendship to be construed so broadly as to encompass relationships between individuals who are not good, however paradigmatic friendship between the good may be. The classification of friendship into kinds requires an articulation of principles, which Aristotle finds in the motives of our attraction to others: however messy a mixture all our actual relationships may be, the difference between liking someone because we find him good, or pleasant, or useful yields a tripartite division of pure types of friendship (8.2.1155b17–20). This expansion of *philia* is in part guided by ordinary language: we call people "friends" who like each other for all these reasons (8.4.1157a26–30). But beyond ordinary language, the analysis captures some kind of generosity of nature: we are allowed, or compelled, by our political nature, even if we are not simply good, to participate, however defectively, in this most necessary and desirable experience.[11]

Distinguishing the motives of our attraction to others establishes a division of kinds without yet determining what friendship as such is. Aristotle finds the key to that question in the common opinion that an inanimate object cannot be a friend. We do not wish for such an object to be in good condition, unless it is with our own interest in mind; but *they say*—Aristotle does not confirm the claim—that one should wish the good of a friend for his own sake (8.2.1155b31–32). Good will, however, is not enough; it must be reciprocated if it is to count as friendship, and even that is not sufficient, unless both persons are aware of each other's regard. Something inanimate cannot, of course, return our affection or have any awareness of it to begin with. The *philo-sophos*, however drawn he is to becoming wise, cannot be in the precise sense a *friend* of wisdom. Strictly speaking, he is a "lover of wisdom," in whom *sophia* arouses eros, while remaining indifferent to it.[12]

Friendship, then, is a relationship of two individuals bound by a reciprocal, mutually acknowledged affection and genuine goodwill for each other. This is a comprehensive conception that is supposed to encompass three species: we can wish the good for a friend, Aristotle tries to argue, "on account of" any one of the

11 The internal structure ascribed to friendship, which incorporates a set of eide that fall short of the "perfect" or "complete" form (*teleia philia*), prepares for the treatment of happiness at the end of the Ethics, which includes a "secondary" form of *eudaimonia* that falls short of the "perfect" standard (*teleia eudaimonia*) (10.7.1177b23–25, 10.8.1178a9–10).

12 In the *Lysis*, Socrates questions the necessity of reciprocity if it precludes the possibility, not only of "friends of horses" (*philippoi*), or quails or dogs, but also "friends of wine" or gymnastics or wisdom (*philosophoi*) (212d–e).

qualities-goodness, pleasantness, or usefulness-that has attracted us to him (8.2.1156a4–5). In doing so, however, we are wishing the good for our friend "with regard to" one of those qualities (8.3.1156a10). But liking someone for the utility or pleasure he supplies to us, and wishing him well with regard to that pleasure or utility, is not really liking him and wishing him well for himself. A friendship motivated by pleasure or utility seems incapable, in that case, of living up to what friendship aims to be, as expressed in its supposedly comprehensive definition. Such a relationship is bound to be precarious: an association motivated by usefulness dissolves as soon as one party ceases to provide the benefit the other seeks from him, while one motivated by pleasure is as unstable as the taste that initiated it. This is especially clear, Aristotle suggests, in the volatile relationships of the young, who look to friendship for pleasure. It is in this context that the erotic relationship first appears: as an association guided by feeling and motivated by pleasure, it is especially appropriate to the young, who end their attachments as quickly and passionately as they fall into them, often changing in the course of the day (8.3.1156b2–4).

Friendship has the promise of enduring over time only when one feels affection for the person himself and wishes him well for his own sake.[13] This is the core of *philia* as the comprehensive conception expresses it; but it looks as if it could be fulfilled only by the highest kind-the friendship of the good, who are alike in virtue (8.3.1156b7–14). Who are "the good" and what is the virtue they possess alike? The *Ethics* has rarely referred to "the good" simply, and they are not identified now as the decent or the serious, the prudent or the wise; the virtue they have in common remains unnamed. The friendship of the good seems to be an abstraction, which we fill in, for the most part, by recognizing, from the more concrete account of the inferior forms of friendship, what it is not. Especially problematic is the question of what need two individuals would have for one another, each of whom is supposed to be good in himself and, in all essential respects, like the other. Whatever makes them want to be together as friends, it is certainly not any awareness of defectiveness or longing: they are not driven to try to complete themselves by union with each other, as if they were two halves of one whole.

The affection such friends feel is based, presumably, on nothing but their mutual recognition of the goodness in each other. Their relationship is distinguished from the inferior forms of *philia* because their aim is not to get pleasure or profit from each other; yet their association is in fact both beneficial and pleasant, not just in their own eyes, as all friendships are, but simply so (8.3.1156b13–18). The friendship of the good is a standard, therefore, not just as the highest type, but as comprehensive: it is *teleia philia* (1156b7–8), and the

13 Of course, even character, Aristotle eventually admits, can change in ways that make the preservation of a friendship impossible (9.3.1165b14–35).

ambiguity of this characterization-complete friendship or the most perfect friendship-is essential to its status.[14] It is *philia* in the primary sense (8.4.1157a31), not just because it is best, but because it encompasses all the grounds for friendship. And it is only to the extent that they resemble this primary form that relationships aimed at pleasure or utility count as forms of *philia* at all.

While both inferior species can be identified as friendship by analogy to the primary form, relationships motivated by pleasure, Aristotle stresses, bear a much closer resemblance. This is evident from the typical relationships of youth in contrast with those of old age. Older people, who are likely to seek profit in friendship, may genuinely wish each other well, but they don't necessarily take pleasure in each other's company and therefore do not want to spend their time together. Young people, on the contrary, being drawn to friendship by pleasure, are eager to "live together" (*suzen*); but it is living together that makes the potential of friendship an actuality. Pleasure, then, is the instrument through which nature drives us toward the actualization of friendship (8.5.1157a6–8, 16–18). Friendships based on pleasure are closer to the primary form for another reason: such relationships are more likely to obtain between individuals who are alike, whereas relationships based on utility are almost by definition between unlike individuals, insofar as each seeks in the other what he lacks and needs. With each partner engaged in calculating the profit to be gained from their association, the very claim to be friends seems to invite deception, or self-deception, about the grounds for their association. Friendships based on utility, consequently, provide the most fertile ground for complaints and recriminations.[15]

Aristotle calls upon *eros* as the paradigm of a relationship motivated by unlike and potentially conflicting aims (8.4.1157a6–16).[16] The association of lover and beloved thus stands in the sharpest contrast to the perfect friendship of the good, with two like partners each directed toward the other in the same way. But even a friendship based on pleasure or utility could display some strength and stability, Aristotle allows, as long as each partner received the same or similar benefit from the other; at least this would be the case, he adds, when it is pleasure from the same source that the two friends offer each other, as in a friendship between two witty people. In an erotic relationship, by contrast, the lover's

14 This ambiguity first appeared in the characterization of happiness as "*teleios*" (1.7.1097a28–b1), then as a characterization of the *teleia* virtue in accordance with which some activity of soul constitutes the human good (1098a16–18). Cf. the ambiguity of *teleios* in the "dictionary" of *Metaphysics* Δ (1021b31–1022a1).

15 An examination of these complaints and recriminations is undertaken in chapter 13 of Book VIII (see especially 1162b5–6).

16 As an attraction of opposites, the erotic relationship presented here is the human equivalent to the cosmological principle expressed in the verses Aristotle originally cited from Euripides: "Earth longs for rain" when dried up, and "Awesome heaven filled with rain longs to fall to earth" (8.1.1155b3–4).

pleasure comes from gazing at the beloved, but the beloved's from receiving the attentions of the lover, and when the bloom fades, the former lover no longer finds pleasure in the sight of the individual who was once his favorite, and he, as a consequence, no longer receives the lover's attentions.[17] It is possible, Aristotle grants, that in some cases the two remain friends, if they have come in the course of time to appreciate each other's character; but friendship in that case is a replacement for, and not an integral feature of the erotic relationship. Aristotle speaks here in the language of Lysias' non-lover, who tries to seduce a beautiful boy by persuading him of how much more advantageous and enduring a relationship he offers, with each partner looking to his self-interest, than any association with the lover, who is by his own admission out of control.[18] As the concealed lover in Socrates' revision argues, the lover is not only harmful in every way to his favorite, but also most unpleasant, and the only way he induces his favorite to endure him is by the promise of future benefits; but he is bound to forget those promises once his passion ceases, and mind and moderation take over from eros and madness.[19]

This depiction of the erotic relationship continues with its last appearance in Book VIII (8.8.1159b16-19). The essential nature of friendship, as proverbial wisdom has it, is "equality and similarity" (*philotes* is *isotes* and *homiotes*); but this is most perfectly instantiated by those who are alike in virtue, whereas relationships based on utility are likely to hold between opposites, since each turns to the other seeking something he lacks. One might "drag" into this class, Aristotle remarks, the relationship between lover and beloved, or between a beautiful and an ugly person. Lovers, consequently, appear ridiculous when they demand to be loved: if they were worthy of it, that would make sense, but what if there is nothing lovable about them? If *eros* is subject to the requirement of justice, it must be on the distributive principle, and the lover can only expect to be loved to the degree of his worth. This is, once again, the argument of the nonlover, who tries to dissuade the beloved from feeling obligated to requite the lover's feelings just because the lover happens for the moment to have those feelings. If the beloved were to look to his self-interest, he would realize that he should grant his

17 The relationship is even more unstable, Aristotle observes, when lover and beloved exchange pleasure for gain; but such a relationship as later described (9.1.1164a3–11) looks indistinguishable from the exchange of pleasures just depicted.

18 See *Phaedrus* 231a–b. According to the nonlover, he can devote himself to the interests of the beloved in a way the lover never could, precisely because, as Rosen puts it, he "acts from freedom rather than necessity, in a sober and businesslike manner, which does not interfere with an efficient and technically accurate calculation of profits and losses" ("The Nonlover in Plato's *Phaedrus*," p. 87).

19 See *Phaedrus* 240e–241b. Cf. Rosen's account of how "the concealed lover 'rationalizes' the prudential calculation of the nonlover by explicit emphasis upon the subordination of desire to knowledge" ("Socrates as Concealed Lover," p. 99).

favors, not to those who beg for them, but to those who are able and willing to repay him; and the non-lover, who has never neglected his own advantage and has no regrets, should be in just such a position.[20]

Eros seen through the eyes of the nonlover makes one more appearance in the *Ethics*, in the first chapter of Book IX (1164a2–12). At this point-in the midst of an extended examination of the complaints and conflicts that plague relationships of diverse sorts—friendship as "equality and similarity" looks like a distant ideal; the real question now is whether friendship can be achieved at all between unequal partners. That seems to depend on the possibility of applying the principle of distributive justice, in an assignment of rewards proportionate to deserts: for such a friendship to be established and maintained, the inferior party must bestow fondness relative to the worth of his superior. If affection could be measured and controlled in this way, the association that results would be some kind of imitation of the relationship between two individuals who are simply equals, which is supposed to characterize friendship at its best. Aristotle calls upon the erotic relationship, once again, to illustrate the problem. In economic associations, money provides a common measure that makes exchange possible, but lover and beloved have nothing analogous: each is trying to enter into an exchange that will serve his individual interests without any common measure to render their offers commensurate.[21] The lover complains that his love is not requited—however unlovable he may be—and the beloved that the lover fulfills none of his promises. The one is seeking pleasure, the other utility, and neither loves the other person in himself. The erotic relationship thus exhibits the defectiveness of the two inferior forms of friendship together, and it looks, thus far, as if there is no higher standard in the case of *eros* equivalent to the perfect friendship of the good. A transformation in this understanding of eros, equivalent to Socrates' palinode, proves to require, as its necessary condition, that *philia* too undergo a reinterpretation.

20 See *Phaedrus* 233d–234a. The whole argument, Rosen proposes, is a legitimate criticism of the general teaching of the *Symposium*, which identifies the erotic man as the most needy: to gratify the most needy, the nonlover argues, is to gratify the worst rather than the best. The nonlover's exoteric teaching—"one should gratify those on whose pensions (*ousia*) one can rely"—contains an esoteric teaching—"one should gratify those who already possess the good or ousia in the ontological sense (233e–234c). In sum: the baseness of Lysias' speech contains a serious teaching, or rather two serious teachings, in however ironical a form. As always in Plato, the low prefigures the high . . ." ("The Nonlover in Plato's *Phaedrus*," p. 90).

21 "There is to be an exchange of goods," Rosen explains, "or a wholesale rather than a retail business contract" ("The Nonlover in Plato's *Phaedrus*," p. 87). Intimacy with the non-lover, Socrates warns at the end of his second speech, is mixed with "mortal and thrifty economizing," which begets a lack of freedom in the soul (*Phaedrus* 256e).

2. The Friend as an Other Self

Just when the discussion of friendship seems to be completed—having descended from the perfect friendship of the good to an analysis of the various conflicts and disappointments that come with our attachments to others—it starts all over again in the fourth chapter of Book IX, with the idea of the friend as an "other self." This new beginning marks a decisive moment, not just in the analysis of friendship, but in the understanding of the human being that underlies the argument of the *Ethics* as a whole. The aim at the outset of the inquiry was to discover happiness or the good for a human being; but the *human* good was first identified, "in outline," as an "activity of the *soul* in accordance with complete or perfect virtue" (1098a16–18), and human virtue, in turn, was declared to be that of the *soul*, not of the human being as a whole. We do not realize how much has been taken for granted until the designation of the friend as an other self in Book IX leads, for the first time, beyond the abstraction of the soul to the notion of the human being as a self. That it has taken so long to arrive at this subject comes as a surprise. Even more surprising is the claim about how it is to be understood: the self, we are now told, is, or is most of all, mind.[22] This might be appropriate for the contemplative self that appears in the tenth book: it is far from obvious how it fits the self that emerges in and through the relation to the friend.

The self comes to light through a reconsideration of the whole preceding discussion of friendship: all the features thought to characterize the harmonious relation between two friends are now found to belong, in their primary form, to the inner state of the decent person (9.4.1166a3–29). Such an individual desires the same things with his whole soul (1166a13–15);[23] he wishes the good things for himself, because he does so for the sake of the intellectual part (*to dianoetikos*), which seems to be just what each individual is; he wants his life to be preserved, but most of all the life of the thinking part (*to nooun*), which is what each individual is, or is most of all. Only such an individual, precisely because he alone can be said to have, or to be, a self, can be related toward a friend as he is toward himself, for the friend is an other self (*allos autos*, 9.4.1166a3–34). Friendship with another is the extension of an inner harmony, which has been traced in turn to the identification of self as mind, or mind most of all.

22 See especially 9.4.1166a15–27; cf. 9.8.1168b34–1169a4.

23 Now that its place has been taken over by mind, "*psyche*" appears only in this statement about the decent person and once again to describe the base person whose soul is in a state of faction (1166b20). "*Psyche*" will appear again in Book IX only in the proverbial formula "one soul" (9.8.1168b7) and in the description of the blameworthy lover of self who indulges the irrational part of his soul (1168b20). It occurred just once in Book VIII, in an aside comparing the relation of master to slave with that of body to soul (8.11.1161a35). "*Psyche*" has, in fact, more or less disappeared from the *Ethics* after Book VI and it will be conspicuously absent from the description of the contemplative life in Book X.

The base person, in contrast, is one whose soul is filled with faction (1167b7–20): always desiring one thing and wanting another, he cannot share in his own joys and pains. Such a person cannot be said to have, or to be, a self at all. This characterization entails a radical alteration of the premise at work throughout the whole preceding investigation. Until this point, the akratic person, who knows the right end but lacks the self-restraint to carry it out, has been distinguished from the base or vicious one. The base or vicious individual was supposed to be someone whose recognition of the right end is so destroyed that his bad desires are in harmony with wrong judgment; but such an individual is, apparently, no longer a real possibility. Everyone, it is now presupposed, has some inkling of the good; the base person is someone who fails to desire with his whole soul the good he perceives, and the consequence is the internal dissension that makes friendship with another difficult or impossible.

The self, in its relation to the friend as an other self, is invoked one last time, as the discussion of friendship draws to a close with the question whether friends are required for happiness. The issue seems to be settled almost immediately with a simple observation: no one would choose to have all the other goods if he had to enjoy them alone, since the human being is by nature political and meant to live together with others (1169b17–22). Yet what our political nature means is perhaps not so obvious, since Aristotle apparently finds it necessary to offer a series of arguments to demonstrate why we need friends for happiness. In doing so, he introduces a new understanding of *eudaimonia*, which requires, we discover at this late point, a kind of self-consciousness about one's life that was never acknowledged before.

There is, we are now told, a particular pleasure, essential for happiness, that comes with our awareness of ourselves acting. The pleasure has, in fact, a double source, in contemplating actions that are decent and also one's own; but since we are more able to contemplate others than ourselves, the good person needs serious friends, in whose actions he can somehow see his own (1169b31–1170a4). Aristotle offers what he calls a "more natural" variant on this argument (1170a13–b19): it addresses the question of the need for friends on the most primary level, which concerns what it is to be alive. For all animals, being alive is being aware; for non-human animals that means perceiving, for humans it means perceiving and thinking. Perceiving or thinking brings with it an awareness of doing so; that means we are aware of our own being, and that is pleasant. But if the perception of one's own being is desirable, and the friend is an other self (*heteros autos*), the perception of his being is as desirable, or nearly so.[24]

24 What we might have expected from this argument is the conclusion that one needs self-awareness for happiness but can only acquire it through the awareness of one's friend. Instead, the argument seems to assume a primary awareness of oneself that can be extended to awareness of the friend. The perception of one's friend's life and its goodness enriches what must already be perceived as a desirable life of one's own;

Therefore, the argument concludes, one should "perceive together" (*sunaisthanesthai*) with one's friend one's own being and that of one's friend. But this comes about, as one last remark clarifies, through living together; and while living together for cattle would mean feeding together, for human beings it means sharing speeches and thoughts.

The opening argument located a pleasure in our awareness of the decency of our own actions, which is made more available through contemplation of the actions of one's friend; this "more natural" argument indicates how the friend can be, not just the object of my apprehension, but recognized as another subject, undergoing the same experience of awareness I have of myself. In the contemplation of action, the friend could be nothing more than a mirror for the self; only in speaking together is it possible to discover the differences that individuate us.[25] Sharing speeches and thoughts is motivated by and in turn produces an awareness of one's partial perspective or incompleteness: it introduces into friendship the possibility of some kind of longing, which the friendship of the good seemed to preclude. The emergence of the dialogic self, for this reason, provides the condition for the appearance of a new understanding of eros in relation to which the *Ethics*' account of friendship will be completed.

3. Eros Transformed

Eros, once it is no longer defined by contrast with the friendship of the good, ceases to be construed as a relationship between unlike partners with conflicting ends; in fact, the beloved as an active subject drops out and the only feature that remains from the original portrait is the emphasis on vision. The context in which this new understanding first appears is an analysis of goodwill (*eunoia*, 9.5). Goodwill, though it is necessary for friendship, is not sufficient; we can feel goodwill even toward a stranger. It seems to be the starting point, but only the starting point, of friendship, in the same way, Aristotle proposes, as the pleasure of sight is the *arche* of loving: no one loves without first being pleased by the looks (*idea*), but one may enjoy the form (*eidos*) without necessarily loving. Only when one longs for what is absent and desires its presence can one be said to love (1167a5–8). From its starting point in the lover's gazing at the beloved, *eros* necessarily turns into longing; it is essentially an experience of distance, absence, and incompleteness. Friendship, in contrast, as it develops out of good will into being together, is an experience of union, presence, and fulfillment.

and friendship is necessary to the extent that a life without that enriched perception would be missing something desirable. As Aquinas puts it, the deficiency that would result if the happy person did not have this awareness of a friend's life is contrary to the notion of happiness that calls for sufficiency (Commentary on the Ethics 1912, translated by C.I. Litzinger, Dumb Ox Books, Notre Dame, Ind., 1993, p. 578).

This contrast between eros and friendship appears one last time when the "natural argument" for the necessity of friends is resumed and completed in the final chapter of Book IX:

> As seeing is most choiceworthy for lovers, and they choose this sense over the rest, as that in accordance with which *eros* is and comes to be, isn't it thusly, for friends, living together that is most choiceworthy? For friendship is *koinonia*. And as one stands in relation to himself, thus he is toward his friend; but just as the perception about himself, that he is, is choiceworthy, so it is in regard to his friend; but the *energeia* of this comes to be in living together, so this is reasonably what friends seek most of all. (1171b29–1172a1)

Seeing and "being together with" are two elements joined in the Platonic conception of eros, however paradoxically.[26] Aristotle has split them, and assigned one to eros, the other to *philia*: what sight is for lovers, living together (*suzen*) is for friends. Sight, in fact, which was originally only the starting point of *eros*, now seems to be its very being as well. The vision that is so desirable to lovers is not, then, only an initial experience that arouses longing, but the very object of that longing. It is not the contingent absence of a particular individual that evokes such desire, nor his presence that would fulfill it: the beloved, on whom the lover fixes his gaze, must point beyond himself to something else that is at a distance and necessarily remains so. The lover takes pleasure, Aristotle observed, in the sight of the looks and form of his beloved-the *idea* and the *eidos* (9.5.1167a5–6): eros, Aristotle suggests through his language, elevates the vision of the loved one into the sought-for object of *theoria*.[27]

The lover, who is defined by his longing for the vision of what is absent, cannot be completed by union with the beloved; friends, on the other hand, are defined by their living together in "communion" (*koinonia*). The discussion of friendship concludes with a description of the forms that living together might take: some friends drink together, some play dice together, others practice gymnastics together and hunt together (*sugkunegousin*) or philosophize together (*sumphilosophousin*) (9.12.1172a1–6). Aristotle completes his account of

25 The friend was originally designated an *allos autos* (9.4.1166a32), suggesting the replication of myself in an other; as a partner in dialogue he becomes *heteros* autos, forming a pair with me precisely because of the difference that makes him genuinely other.

26 See, for example, *Symposium* 211d–e. Cf. Seth Benardete, "Socrates and Plato: The Dialectics of Eros," Carl Friedrich von Siemens Stiftung, 2000, p. 19.

27 It is the lover's sight of the godlike face of his beloved or "some idea of the body," according to Socrates' account, which inspires his recollection of beauty itself, as he once glimpsed it on his flight to the "hyperuranian beings" (Phaedrus 251a). Aristotle speaks of the sight of the idea and eidos; what is strikingly absent is the beautiful, as that which provokes erotic madness.

friendship with an allusion to Socratic philosophy, whose definitive mark, one might say, is the enigmatic connection between the hunting of the beings and the hunting of beautiful youths.[28]

Hunting begins with the recognition of what one lacks and the desire to attain it, even while recognizing its propensity to escape from one's grasp. The longing for what is absent was supposed to differentiate *eros* from *philia*; it seems to have become in the end the basis for a certain kind of *philia*, between those who "philosophize together." That friendship can only be understood in light of its incorporation into itself of *eros*—not, apparently, the *eros* of each for the other, as lover and beloved, but the eros they have in common that motivates their desire to live together. This is, admittedly, not exactly a praise of the divine madness of eros. But Aristotle's argument has traversed a great distance since the nonlover's condemnation of eros. In every other form of friendship, the fulfillment of being together stands at odds with the longing of *eros*; in the friendship of those who philosophize together, *philia* and *eros* are conjoined, and necessarily so. Philosophic friends live together by sharing speeches and thoughts, which seems to be at once the realization of the political nature and the rational nature of the human being. All other activities friends engage in, which only accidentally require sharing speeches and thoughts, now look like various ways of aspiring to the standard of *sumphilosophein*.[29] Through its incorporation of eros, the friendship of those who philosophize together alone fulfills what *philia* aims to be.

28 See, for example, *Lysis* 206a and 218c, *Laches* 194b, *Protagoras* 309a, *Republic* 432b, *Symposium* 203d–204b, *Sophist* 222d–e.

29 Aristotle's apparently casual set of examples of how friends might spend their time with each other included drinking together, playing dice together, and practicing gymnastics together. All these activities seem to serve, at various moments in the Platonic dialogues, as an image for philosophy (cf. for instance, the first two books of Plato's *Laws, Republic* 487b, 503b–504a.).

Democracy in Motion

Some Reflections on Herodotean Politics

Clifford Orwin

University of Toronto

Reputations with posterity are notoriously difficult to foresee. Still, I feel confident in predicting that Stanley Rosen's will not rest on his early essay on Herodotus. He has simply written too much of value since, about too many other great thinkers who, moreover, loom larger than Herodotus for people of today and (ultimately) for Professor Rosen himself.

This being said, Professor Rosen resembles the elephant of the fable of the blind men. Your experience of him depends on the side on which you approach him. While I too have learned from his work on the likes of Plato, Montesquieu, Hegel, Nietzsche, Heidegger, and Wittgenstein, I don't regard myself as competent to pronounce on it. I may be able to say something useful about Herodotus, however. So I thought that I could make no more sensible contribution to honoring Professor Rosen than by taking up that old but remarkably youthful essay of his.[1]

Once having done so, however, I found myself in the grips of an optical illusion. For my whole adult life I've looked up to Professor Rosen as older than myself by an academic generation, an outstanding contemporary not of mine but of my teachers. Yet in turning to his essay on Herodotus, I behold a Rosen nearly a generation younger than I find myself now. The grizzled veteran eyes the brash upstart. Warily, at first, but with increasing respect.

While Professor Rosen's essay on Herodotus expresses his understanding of the work as a whole, he limits his systematic exposition to its first three books. In what follows, I will build on his contribution as I pursue one of his leads into a later book. Guided by Professor Rosen's reflections, we will review the celebrated debate of the regimes (3.80–87). We will then turn to Book Five, territory untraversed by Professor Rosen, to compare the most famous analyses of democracy uttered by Herodotus in his own name with those of his Persian debaters.

1 "Herodotus reconsidered," *Giornale di Metafisica* 18 (1963): 194–218. Reprinted (minus most of its footnotes) in Herodotus, *The Histories*, Norton Critical Edition, ed. Walter Blanco and Jennifer Tolbert Roberts (New York: W.W. Norton and Company, 1992), 332–56. As the first version is widely unobtainable, I will confine my in-text references to the second.

I

Predictably, Rosen's claim in expounding Herodotus is that the latter was more than just an historian; i.e., more than the "scientific" historians of ca. 1960 mistook him for being. Today the literature on Herodotus is strewn with the preoccupations of postmodernism, but in 1963 a more positivistic view of history still prevailed. That Rosen published his study in the *Giornale di Metafisica* itself expressed the vast distance between his Herodotus and that of the latter's professional custodians, as did his decision to begin the study with a theoretical discussion. Having raised with the assistance of Thucydides the question of how "history . . . differ[ed] from, and [was] related to, *philosophy.*" (emphasis in the original, 334), Rosen asserts that "this problem takes its decisive form in the work of Herodotus." The extraordinarily rich paragraphs that follow, which compare Herodotus with Thucydides and each of them with both Homer and Plato, conclude with a magisterial pronouncement.

setdown

> For Homer and Herodotus, there is something in the nature of things which forbids the public transcendence of the ancestral. At this point the public and private teaching correspond. . . . The absence, or allusive presence, of philosophy on the surface of Herodotus' writings is thus a prelude to Thucydides' silence about philosophy. The inquiries of Herodotus and Thucydides are a preparation for modern "history" insofar as both men are antagonists to philosophy in the Socratic sense. . . . Both are related to Heracleitus, and consequently to each other, in the following way. Herodotus' teaching is in essence the teaching of Homer, and Homer, as Socrates points out, makes all things subservient to motion. One could not say the same about Thucydides, but his main theme is also *kinesis*. . . . With the massive exception of Parmenides, the pre-Socratics . . . like the thinkers of modernity, are obsessed with *kinesis,* and *kinesis* is the father of history. (337–38)

End setdown

"*Kinesis* is the father of history." Herodotus has his own way of putting this.

setdown

> I will go forward in my account, covering alike the small and great cities of mankind. For of those that were great in earlier times most have now become small, and those that were great in my time were small in the time before. Since, then, I know that man's good fortune never abides in the same place, I will make mention of both alike. (1.5)[2]

2 Except where otherwise noted, translations of Herodotus are those of David Grene (Chicago: University of Chicago Press, 1987).

End setdown

> Thus much of cities; what, however, of regimes? In the very first pages of his work, Herodotus speaks of human beings both Hellenic and barbarian (whose great deeds he seeks to rescue from the abyss of becoming and therefore forgetfulness) (1.1). The distinction among regimes is not as significant for his work as that between Hellenes and barbarians. The very existence of non-monarchic regimes is peculiar to the Hellenes. Among the Hellenes, however, despite their common ways in most other respects, differences of regime are crucial. The co-operation of Athens and Sparta to preserve the freedom of Hellas in the face of the Persian threat presupposes their common Hellenism. Yet it also discloses strengths unique to the regime of each city that complement those of the other. It is only from this interplay between their sameness and their differences that the salvation of Hellas arises.

Sparta's mixed regime was of course peculiar to her. By contrast, several cities known to Herodotus were democracies at least some point in their respective histories. Athens was unique among them, however, in realizing the potential of democracy. While he cites her at 5.78 as demonstrating the excellence of *isagoria* ("an equal say for all"), no other "isagoric" city appears to have equaled her in the respect there indicated.

Be this as it may, both Sparta and Athens have known great changes not only of magnitude but of regime, and Herodotus presents the former as having depended on the latter. Sparta became solid and therefore powerful only through the reforms of Lykourgos (1.65; cf. Thucydides 1.18); Athens dynamic and therefore powerful only through those of Solon and Kleisthenes (5.78). While Herodotus may not go so far as to say with Aristotle that a city that changes its regime becomes thereby in the crucial respect a different city (*Politics* 1276ab), he does stress that the Sparta and Athens of "after" the transition to their current regimes were unrecognizable as those of "before." Both, having been "small," have become "great" thanks to these regimes.

II

As it is primarily through war that cities wax and wane, so it is in war that the effects of the different regimes are starkest. It is therefore on their suitability for war that the cases for the different regimes must rest, if not wholly then at least substantially. This already emerges from the "debate of the regimes" at 3.80–82. This discussion among Persian grandees over which regime it would be best to establish in Persia is the oldest such dispute in Hellenic and so in world literature.[3] It is also justly one of the most celebrated episodes in Herodotus.

3 1 Samuel 8 doesn't qualify because no alternative to kingship is considered; but consider Josephus, *Antiquities of the Jews* 6.35–44 [and cf. 4.223–24], for a

When the confusion had settled, five days later, the conspirators against the Magians held a debate about the entire condition of affairs. Here speeches were made that some of the Hellenes refuse to credit, but the speeches *were* made for all that.

Herodotus does not here elaborate this remark. As later emerges, however, if Hellenes will find these speeches incredible it is because as Hellenes they ascribe to barbarians an unquestioning acceptance of despotism (6.43).

In fact, however, as Rosen shows, and as others have since elaborated, the debate is thoroughly embedded in its "Persian" narrative context. As the conspirators against the Magi have consulted together at every earlier stage of their endeavor, so would we expect them to do so now. There is rough parity among them, the Persian nobility being one whose members are deemed equal ("peers," *homoioi).* There is presently no king to overawe them, nor can a new one emerge except by their doing. For with the overthrow of the false Smerdis, Persia finds itself not only without a king but even without a monarchic regime. While the Hellenes of Herodotus' day might reasonably take Persian despotism for granted, the supposed date of this debate is a century earlier. The Persian polity was still quite young at that time (only fifty years from its origin), and had known only three kings, of whom the second and third had been mad and a usurper, respectively. Only the founder, the great Cyrus, had so acted as to enhance the prestige of monarchy, and after just one generation of unworthy successors, his line was now completely extinct.[4] As for the plausibility of Persian grandees entertaining such typically Hellenic notions as democracy and oligarchy, remember that of all peoples the Persians are the most ready to adopt foreign practices (1.135).

Not only is it plausible that the Persians would conduct this debate under the circumstances in which they do, but it's questionable whether any other people would have done so. Certainly Herodotus' Hellenes evince no comparable open-mindedness on the question of the best regime. In the debate, after all, both democracy and oligarchy, regimes never practiced among the Persians, get their day in court, and monarchy must vie with them on equal terms. Among the Hellenes, by contrast, for whom oligarchy or democracy is the rule, the case for monarchy is never heard.[5] It is not to the Hellenes, then, that Herodotus' reader

reworking of the passage in Samuel that supplies this defect on the basis of the intervening Hellenic discussions of which this in Herodotus was the first. (The *Antiquities* dates from ca. 95 C.E.)

4 We hear at 3.88 of a daughter of Cyrus' murdered son the true Smerdis, but there is evidently no royal succession through the female line.

5 The only systematic exploration of the theme of rule by one is the great speech of Sokles the Corinthian (5.90). As a discussion of the advisability of instituting a monarchy, the conference of the Lakedaimonians and their allies at which Sokles speaks parallels the debate of the grandees. The issue, however, is not whether any

must look to find a reasoned debate in which democracy is called upon to vie on even terms with its rivals. Hellenic hatred of despotism serves not to encourage free debate but to suppress it.[6]

So it is that only among these Persian grandees do we find the conditions necessary for democracy to receive a fair hearing—no less and no more. Only here, with all regime options fleetingly open, does each contender make itself heard in the absence of an already established order which *ipso facto* would have served to suppress debate.

The previous councils of the conspirators have disclosed striking differences among them. That Otanes should now advocate democracy and Dareios monarchy or despotism seems fully in character for both. Otanes had been the first to confirm beyond all doubt that the ruling Smerdis was an impostor, and had accordingly been the one to initiate the conspiracy against him (3.68–70). At no point, however, does he display the ambition to become the ruler himself. He is indignant at the notion that he, a Persian noble, should be ruled by a Median Magus, but he never evinces an inclination to take his place. The subject of his speech, appropriately, is the evil of being ruled, and his suggestion, that one can avoid being ruled by abolishing monarchy.

At the same time the onward rush of the events of the conspiracy has disclosed Otanes as lacking in decisiveness (3.71–78). Though Dareios was the last of the seven grandees to enlist in the conspiracy, he was the only one after Otanes himself to do so entirely at his own initiative. Dareios, moreover, enters on this bold course without even the certainty that the ruler is a usurper that Otanes had gone to such risk to achieve. In every crisis that has arisen thus far, Dareios has succeeded in wresting the ascendancy from Otanes—a fact that augurs poorly for the latter's prospects in the current debate.

of the cities present should acquiesce in monarchy in its own case, but whether they should assist Sparta in reimposing tyranny on fledgling democratic Athens. There is no disagreement among the speakers in this debate on the badness of tyranny for the city subjected to it; it is precisely because tyranny will cripple Athens that the Spartan king Kleomenes wishes to inflict it on her. Hippias, the once and (so he hopes) future tyrant whom Kleomenes is bent on restoring, responds to Sokles' fierce attack on tyranny by threatening the assembled cities with the specter of a powerful Athens. He implicitly accepts Sokles' claim that tyranny sucks the life out of a city. While (or because) tyranny knows no limits—Periandros went so far as to violate the corpse of his wife and then, to appease her angry spirit, shamed all the women of Corinth—the city subject to it is easily limited. The cities assembled at Kleomenes' behest thus share a common interest in avoiding tyranny and in imposing one on Athens. In the end, however, the enormity of the evil to be inflicted on Athens deters them.

6 In fact Sokles' animus toward the rule of one drives him to abstract even from the distinction between democracy and oligarchy, the better to unite the partisans of both in unwavering hostility toward tyranny.

Otanes' brief against monarchy is powerful. He begins by appealing to his fellow conspirators' experience of the *hybris* of both the madly murderous Kambyses (3.16–38) and the usurping Smerdis (3.61–79) His subsequent argument anticipates that for which we celebrate Lord Acton: he insists that absolute power corrupts absolutely even the very best of men. In vain do you assert that as the best man you are worthy of monarchy; even if your claim to be the best is valid, your claim to rule is not, for the virtue on the basis of which you lodge it will not survive your accession to the throne. Tacitus' famous epigram on the Emperor Servius Galba ("Greater than a subject he seemed, while he remained a subject, and all would have acclaimed him worthy of rule, had he never ruled")[7]—is true of every pretender to kingly virtue. There is therefore no plausible argument for the rule of the one best.

The specific case against monarchy runs as follows. The advantages of the king breed insolence or outrage (*hybris*), and envy is inbred in (or natural to, *emphyetai*) all. So monarchy fosters the former without (as one might have supposed) appeasing the latter. In elucidating the psychology of this, Otanes openly calls the monarch a tyrant. Possessing all good things, he ought to be free of envy (*aphthonos*). In fact, however, he begrudges the lives of the best or most virtuous of his subjects but not those of the evildoers, and so himself is best (*aristos*) at entertaining slanders. This is the distinctive "virtue" of a monarch: that he is receptive to slander of the virtuous. Monarchy is the enemy of human excellence: under it the best men fare the worst. (We might compare the jealousy of the gods according to Solon or Amasis with the jealousy of the monarch according to Otanes.) Is Otanes suggesting that precisely because the monarch is the man who has everything in terms of material goods, he envies all the more fiercely whatever of others he cannot possess, namely their virtues?

Besides which of all men the monarch is the most discordant, dissonant, or out of tune (*anarmostotaton*; the term is a musical one). Does Otanes mean by this self-contradictory? Measured praise is too little for the monarch; unstinting praise, too much. He resents the former, suspects the latter, so it is impossible to honor him without incurring his wrath. But the greatest (i.e., worst) things to be said of him are that he overturns ancestral customs, raping women and executing men without a trial. So monarchy, even where ostensibly guided by law (as it is among the Persians) is inherently lawless. Just as the distinction between the best man and others proves irrelevant to the case for monarchy, so does that between kingship and tyranny, between legitimate rule and usurpation. All kings flout the law; all are tyrants.

The worst evils arising under monarchy thus emerge as not incidental but endemic to it. They proceed from the unworthiness of human nature as such to bear monarchic power.

7 Histories, 1.49.

The question is whether Otanes' praise of democracy is as conclusive as his condemnation of monarchy. "But when the multitude rules it has first of all the fairest name of all (or finest or noblest or most honorable: *kalliston*), equality before the law (*isonomia*). . . ." So the first argument in favor of the rule of the multitude is from its name, and is therefore a merely nominal argument. While the regime that Otanes praises sounds very much like demokratia, that isn't the name under which he chooses to praise it. If *isonomia* is the finest name, then *demokratia* must not be. But why not? Is it that while implies the rule of the people, one distinct class in the city, over the other citizens (who thereby become subjects rather than citizens), *isonomia* obscures this problem? The equality of each before the laws implies that no citizen is subject to any other, all being subject to the laws, and Otanes can think of nothing finer than the abolition of this subjection.

Otanes' second reason in favor of *isonomia* is "that it does none of the things the monarch does." The superiority of *isonomia* no longer figures as merely nominal, but it does emerge as wholly negative: it is the best regime just insofar as monarchy is the worst one. What distinguishes *isonomia* is the absence of the concentration of power definitive of monarchy. *Isonomia* features election by lot, rotation in office, the accountability of officeholders, and an assembly in which all deliberate about what is common. The officeholders do not rule, they merely execute; only the community as a whole enjoys the final say about what concerns it as a whole.

There is something somehow "modern" or "liberal" in the negativity of Otanes' approach. Politics emerges from his speech as a matter not of aspiring to the heights but of avoiding the depths. Monarchy is the worst alternative because it inevitably fosters oppression; best will be the regime that reliably minimizes it. That regime is *isonomia,* conceived as the regime that is not a regime, in which all rule and therefore none do, because no one is ruled by anyone else. Now this is precisely the goal of the modern political project at least until the Nietzschean reaction against it: most visible, doubtless, in Marx, but fully present already in Hobbes.[8] Perhaps the modern thinker whom Otanes most anticipates is Montesquieu, who shares the negative political orientation of Hobbes but for whom the *summum malum* from which to take our political bearing is not the state of nature but despotism, that scourge of actual societies.

Democracy as Otanes has sketched it is not a regime in motion. He presents it as stable internally, and as at rest externally. In both respects he presents his preferred regime as static rather than dynamic, and in both respects the subsequent speakers will set out to refute him.

8 See Harvey C. Mansfield, Jr, "Hobbes and the science of indirect government," *American Political Science Review* (1970) and my "On the sovereign authorization [in Hobbes];" *Political Theory* 3.1 (1975).

The problem that Otanes has set out to resolve is that of domestic oppression; this explains why relations with other societies receive no mention in his speech. Yet has he solved even this first problem? He sketches what we would call the "rule of law;" it is before the law that all are equal. But this abstracts from the question of the origin of the law.[9] Evidently Otanes would place this origin in *to plethos,* "the multitude," which figures both at the beginning of his account of *isonomia* and again near the end. "The ruling multitude, on the other hand, is called by the fairest of names." "So let us put an end to monarchy and exalt the multitude, for all things are in the majority."

Yet this last statement discloses the ambiguity of the term *plethos.* By it Otanes acknowledges that under *isonomia* the final authority in the city is *to pollon,* not the *plethos* as such but only the greater part of it. The *plethos* so understood is merely the majority, which as such contains not all but only some things, and quite possibly not the best ones.

As the rule of the minority by the majority, of one part of the city by another, is not Otanes' *isonomia* as liable to abuse as any other kind of rule? And if so, does not the question of the character of the ruling part necessarily take center stage, for all of Otanes' efforts to avoid it? If it was on the character of the monarch—which is to say ultimately on the highly fallible nature of human beings as such—that the case against monarchy rested, must not the *plethos* be made to answer for its own character? It is just this weakness on which the following speaker, Megabyzos, will seize.

Megabyzos is the most obscure of the three speakers on this occasion. He plays no other role in the work, either before or after, except as one of the seven conspirators. We learn no more of him than that he was co-opted into the conspiracy by Gobryas, who seems the noblest of the conspirators—I conclude this on the basis alike of his speech at 3.73 and his action at 3.78–and that he himself fathered the noblest Persian of all, Zopyros (3.150–60). On the basis of this little that we do learn about him it ought not surprise us that he champions aristocracy in this debate.

Megabyzos' rhetorical strategy is to endorse Otanes' sweeping condemnation of monarchy while claiming that it applies *a fortiori* to the rule or power *(kratos)* of the *plethos.* Nothing is less intelligent than the crowd (*homilos)* which just a sentence later becomes the "unbridled plebs" *(demos akolastos).* The truth of the

9 While the universal kingship of *nomos* or convention (3.38) points to the primacy of claims of knowledge of the divine (Rosen, 339–40), political *nomoi* among the Hellenes were not generally held to be descended from the divine. (Here the laws of Crete and Sparta were the notable exceptions.) Nor, evidently, among the Persians, or else the current debate would not be possible for them. The authority of the ancestral, which is that of the divine, has fallen into suspension: while Dareios will appeal to it at the culmination of his defense of monarchy, still not it but the will of the conspirators reigns authoritative for the decision at hand.

rule of the whole is indeed the rule of a part. Megabyzos unmasks isonomy as a euphemism for democracy.

While Megabyzos does offer an affirmative case for aristocracy, we will follow Rosen in stressing the extent to which his speech conforms to the pattern set by Otanes: the few best are qualified to rule for the inverse of the reason that the unbridled plebs is not. At the core of Megabyzos' speech lies his concern with mind *(nous)* (Rosen, 348–49).

> Nothing is more witless or insolent than a useless throng; for men to flee the insolence of the tyrant only to fall upon that of the unrestrained people is nowise to be borne. When the tyrant acts, he does so knowingly, but the mob acts in ignorance. For how could it understand when it was neither taught, nor can it see for itself, the noble and fitting, but dashes upon the [public] business like a torrential river.[10]

The *demos* is motion, and therefore *hybris* incarnate; lacking as it does the principle of mind, so it does all moderation. This fine paragraph of Megabyzos evokes a matching one from Rosen.

> The intensity of Megabyzos' concern for intelligence is matched by the degree of violent stupidity which he attributes to the mob. Here again we have the repudiation of motion: the rabble is the political equivalent of the chaotic beginnings, the flowing river of Homer, Hesiod, and Heracleitus. (349)

Democracy brings descent into chaos; reversion to what to a modern reader will recall Hobbes's state of nature. Democracy can be said to triumph only in a negative sense: as power unguided by intelligence, it is a formidable foe to itself only. "Let those who mean evil (*kakon . . . nooei)* to the Persians be subject to the *demos*." Just as the English *mean* is cognate with *mind,* so Megabyzos employs an idiom for intention that is cognate with *nous.* Let not the Persians but those minded on evil toward them fall under the sway of the people and so into mindlessness. As a rushing torrent of popular passion, democracy does not sound peace-loving, but a city subject to it would be hampered not helped in its capacity to wage war. Megabyzos advances the argument beyond where Otanes had left it by introducing the issue of foreign policy. Democracy looks worst where the stakes are highest, for there so too would be the penalties for mindlessness. Megabyzos' aristocrats, conversely, would be as pre-eminent in mind as the people is lacking in it; resplendent in domestic matters for their justice, they would save the city in foreign ones through their superior prudence.

To Magabyzos' critique of democracy Dareios adds one of his own. If his speech were to follow the pattern established by Otanes and refined by Megabyzos, it would discredit oligarchy by tarring it with the same brush as

10 The final two sentences of this translation are Rosen's (348–49).

monarchy and democracy. It would go on to introduce a fourth and previously unmentioned regime as preferable. Dareios does begin as expected by indicating that he will quarrel with Megabyzos' account of oligarchy. (This he has already begun to do simply by following Herodotus himself in characterizing Megabyzos as a spokesman for oligarchy, thus implying that aristocracy served him a euphemism for a reality much less prepossessing.) But Dareios cannot stick with the pattern of Otanes' and Megabyzos' speeches, for he has no fourth regime up his sleeve to promote. Rather he wishes to return to the regime that both of the previous speakers had agreed in blackening. His challenge is to defend the only regimes of which so far only ill has been spoken.

How is Dareios to respond to Otanes' powerful indictment of monarchy, in which Megabyzos has fully concurred? His ingenious solution is to argue that if we take each of the three regimes at its best, monarchy will prove to far outstrip the others. He thus seems to defer to his colleagues' praise of their respective choices; he need only show that monarchy at its best trumps both oligarchy and democracy at theirs. So stated this strategy might remind us of Aristotle's account in the *Politics*, according to which of the three "correct" regimes—i.e., of the rule of one, few, and many at their finest—the rule of the one most virtuous, monarchy in the true sense, comes to sight as the best of all.[11] Is this what Dareios means? Not exactly.

Dareios begins with a brief but fervent praise of monarchy, on the premise that the king is the best of men, combining wisdom with decisiveness. This is indeed to take monarchy at its best, as Dareios implies no concession that things might be otherwise with monarchy or that it might be prone to abuse or decline. He effectively ignores Otanes' claim that the greater decisiveness and expedition of the monarch compound the evils of monarchy.

What then of Dareios' claim to take not just monarchy but democracy and oligarchy at their best? Here "taking each regime at its best" assumes quite a different meaning. However promisingly each may begin, it contains within itself the seeds of its ineluctable decline, a decline from which there is no escape except by means of monarchy. Oligarchs, however "aristocratic;" i.e., however avid to display their virtue on behalf of the common interest, will for this very reason fall to quarreling. "Each wishing to be chief of all and for his judgment to prevail," bitter enmity will result. The desire of the oligarch to serve the public is inseparable from his ambition to be first in serving the public; each ambitious oligarch naturally tends toward monarchy. From this arises violent strife among them, and the eventual emergence of one of them as monarch in fact. "And in this manner monarchy is shown to be best," i.e., better than oligarchy, the instability of which is such that its inevitable outcome is monarchy.

11 Such at least is Aristotle's initial, schematic statement (*Politics* 1279ab). His elaboration of it, which consumes the rest of Book 3, is complex and highly ambivalent.

But what of democracy? As Rosen was the first to discern, Dareios expresses a certain inclination in favor if not of democracy, then at least of the people as a class in contradistinction to the intriguing few (cf. Machiavelli, *Prince,* Chapter Nine). He presents the people as sinned against, not sinning: the problem with democracy is that designs contrary to the good of the people are always arising, doubtless from those ambitious few who would form the regime were it an oligarchy and who therefore conspire on behalf of oligarchy. In response a champion of the people arises, perhaps not the most sincere of ones. Having repulsed the subversive designs of the "evil-minded," he goes on to subvert the regime himself, in the direction not of oligarchy but of kingship. This account is well grounded in the Hellenic experience of tyrants like Peisistratos who began as defenders of the people against the old landed families. Dareios somehow casts himself in this role of a king who will rule primarily at the expense of those who most vigorously contend for rule, the few, while maintaining the support of the people (Rosen 349–50).

Monarchy is best, then, in relation to both oligarchy and democracy, because even at their best their defects are such as to plunge the city into strife from which only monarchy can save it. "Aristocracy "is not Megabyzos' regime of mind because aristocrats will never be of the same mind, or if they are, it will only be in the sense that each will be of a mind to rule. Regimes of the few no less than those of the many are given to random and destructive motion.

But what clinches Dareios' case against both democracy and oligarchy is his appeal to the example of Cyrus the Great, the great benefactor of the Persians to whom they owe their freedom as a people. The cornerstone of Dareios' position is a consideration absent from Otanes' speech and merely implicit in that of Megabyzos when he wishes democracy on Persia's enemies. It is the primacy of foreign policy over domestic and therefore of the demands of war over those of peace. However alluring the notion of a city free of the exactions of a ruler, the first concern of any people must be freedom from domination by other peoples. Flux among factions at home will only subvert the Persians' ability to maintain themselves in the flux that pervades the world outside.

III

What, however, is Herodotus' own view of these matters? In particular, what is his verdict on democracy? Does he accept Otanes' case in its favor, or does he incline toward the critiques of Megabyzos and Dareios? Or his is own position somewhere in between, or even somewhere else entirely?

Neither the space remaining to me nor the state of my understanding will permit me to address this question fully. I do propose to make a beginning, however, and to do so in the most obvious way. We will examine the two most famous remarks on the *grandeur et misère* of popular government that Herodotus offers in his own name. As we might expect, these recall aspects of the earlier schematic debate. They also advance the perspective on democracy as the politics of motion ascribed to Megabyzos by Professor Rosen.

We will begin then with Book Five, Chapter 78, Herodotus' famous praise of *isagoria.*

Now the Athenians increased [in power]. This makes it clear that not in one respect only but in every way for all to have an equal say is a serious business, seeing that while they were under tyrants the Athenians were no better in war than any of their neighbors, yet once free of the tyrants they were first by a wide margin. This makes it clear that while they were held down they willing played the coward, since they were working for a master, but once liberated each one strived eagerly on his own behalf.

This passage features yet another term for popular government, and the one Herodotus takes up when he himself wishes to extol it. So again we will refrain from calling the object of his praise democracy, because we must assume that this distinction of terms is significant. *Demokratia* proclaims that the *demos* collectively rules, that *kratos* or power rests with it (so Megabyzos at 3.81). *Isagoria,* equality of speech, calls attention to a different feature of popular rule: that each citizen enjoys an equal say in public matters. It captures the significance of the transition to popular rule not from the perspective of the demos as a whole but from that of each of the citizens.

Earlier we had occasion to comment on the "modernity" or "liberalism" of Otanes' praise of democracy. By that we meant its negative orientation: Otanes anticipates modernity by casting politics as a matter not of aspiring to a lofty good but of avoiding a paramount evil. Herodotus' own presentation is different. Rather than restate the case for popular rule offered by Otanes, he offers an implicit retort to the *critique* of that case presented by Megabyzos. His brief for the ascendancy of the people is not primarily a negative one. While Otanes argues for democracy by stressing the evils of rule by one, Herodotus underlines the benefits of participation by all. Each, in working for the city, is working for himself, not for any other; and each, in working for himself, is working for the city.

From this it will appear that Herodotus' view of citizenship and of the classical city as its locus is far removed from those of Rousseau and his mentor Montesquieu. His presentation foreshadows not the Rousseauian argument for citizenship as the transformation of nature but the early liberal one in favor of the emancipation of nature, which is to say of the individual. For Herodotus as for Locke and Adam Smith, he will contribute most willingly to the common benefit who least understands himself to be sacrificing for it. The common is most common when experienced as most private, for then each devotes himself wholeheartedly to an end which both is and is not identical with that of his comrades.

For this reason Herodotus understands the private as necessarily prior to the emergence of the common in the political sense of that term. It is because the

Hellenes, unlike certain of the more primitive peoples in the work, display a highly developed sense of the private, that the Athenians, underachievers under the tyrants, become such whirlwinds when granted *isagoria.* As *isagoria* emerges only by contrast with tyranny, so the common itself emerges only by contrast with the private. But in both cases the contrast is an imperfect one, for the common is at the same time a certain development *within* the private. Under the tyrants, politics was a zero-sum game; what was good for the tyrant and his clique was bad for everyone else, but under *isagoria* what is good for each is good for all. If, as Herodotus here claims, *isagoria* is a serious or zealous matter *(chrema spoudaion)*, that is because only it unleashes the *spoude*, the seriousness or zeal, of each of the city's citizens. "Once freed each *was eager* (*proethymeeto*) to undertake deeds on his own behalf." Without denying that the sequel will reveal some problems to be ironed out—it's not as if Herodotus presents Athens as superior in all respects to Sparta—the initial indication is that this emancipation which is at the same time the politicization of the individual's ambition on his own behalf is a highly positive development.

Still, while this aspect of Herodotus' teaching parallels in some respects the project of early modernity, we must note a crucial distinction. Not for him or his Athenians the devolution of human strife from the political plane to the economic or "social" one. The accomplishments of the new Athens unfolded on the field of battle rather than in any peaceful pursuit. They increased their own city at the direct expense of others. Freed of tyranny, they took to acting like so many tyrants. That for which the Athenians were eager (*proethymeeto,* a term cognate with *thymos)*, was victory over other cities; that was the good of which each conceived himself now to enjoy an equal share by virtue of his equal say. Viewed in contrast with the rough *spoude* of the Athenians, liberal acquisitiveness seems a designer passion, carefully crafted to split the difference between *thymos* and *eros*—while "pacifying" both by promoting only "peaceful" competition.

Herodotus delivers his positive judgment of the new dispensation after showing us just one example of Athenian democracy in warlike practice (5.77). An astonishing example it is, however, as the very first action of the unencumbered Athenians to win two major battles in a single day against the Boiotians and Chalkidians. This is the deed that strikes such fear into the Spartans that they mount their abortive attempt to replace *isagoria* with the Peisistratids (5.90).

Someone else whose eye is on Athens is Aristagoras of Miletus. Aristagoras is determined for crooked reasons of his own to organize a revolt of the Hellenic cities of Asia Minor from the Persian King. Rebuffed in his requests for assistance by the Spartan king Kleomenes (5.49–51), Aristagoras turns next to Athens as the second most powerful Hellenic city (5.97). (This confirms how quickly Athens has risen in the world under the aegis of democracy.)

Aristagoras' plan for a revolt is a bad one. He easily enlists the Athenians in it. "It seems," notes Herodotus drily, "that it is easier to fool many men than one;

Kleomenes the Spartan was only one, but Aristagoras could not fool him, though he managed to do so to 30,000 Athenians" (5.97)

So we must balance Herodotus's recent high praise of the Athenians with his deftly ingenuous comment here. Of course it was not for their wisdom that he had lauded them earlier, but for their energy, which, as we saw, was essentially their feistiness. It's just that feistiness that is on display here. The fact is that even prior the appearance of Aristagoras on their doorstep, the Athenians have "resolved to be openly at enmity with the Persians," who, following in the footsteps of the Spartans, have arrogantly demanded of them that they take back the exiled tyrant Hippias (5.96). So what we see now is that same spiritedness which the Athenians had previously displayed against their Hellenic neighbors, newly focused on a still more formidable enemy. It is not Aristagoras who deceives the Athenians so much as their own anger at the Persians; he is merely the right machinator in the right place at the right time.

Still, this episode raises many questions about democracy. Is the people as feckless as it is energetic? Herodotus, who so recently seemed not only to endorse Otanes' praise of democracy but to strengthen it by stressing the potency of the people in foreign affairs, now echoes Megabyzus, whose rejoinder to Otanes offered the most hostile critique of democracy to be found in the work. In particular his likening of the people in its mindlessness to a raging torrent resonates in the present case: one feature of such a torrent is that it is subject to diversion. The very vigor of democracy now appears its Achilles' heel: we can expect its worst wounds to be self-inflicted. While Otanes had presented a vision of democracy in which leadership nowhere figured, we can now see that Megabyzus was right in pointing to leadership as the crucial problem. While Otanes had implicitly rejected strong leadership as tending toward the oppression of the people, Megabyzus deplores its absence from democracy. Obviously Herodotus here endorses that view: led by its anger, the people is only too susceptible to being led by its nose.

Which is to say that Herodotus' point of view, the great strength of democracy—its success at mobilizing the previously private passions of the citizens on behalf of the public—is at the same time its potentially fatal flaw. Two incidents, one from before and one from after the democratic transformation at Athens, demonstrate both the power and the ambiguity of the politicization of the private.

On an unspecified earlier occasion, the Athenians had sent an expedition against their longtime foes the Aeginetans from which only one man returned to tell the tale. The women of the city, however, were not having any of his tale. Swarming him in the midst of the public assembly, each in turn, asking what had become of her husband, stabbed him with the iron pin of the brooch that fastened her garments. And so he died. The male citizens, finding this violent outburst even more upsetting than the disaster itself, passed a law forbidding their women from wearing costumes fastened by brooches.

The corresponding incident from the democratic epoch of Athens is as follows. Late in the Persian Wars, after the Persian defeats at Artemision and Salamis and the King's flight back to Persia, his viceroy Mardonios attempts to detach the Athenians from the Hellenic confederacy. At this stage the Athenians have abandoned their city a second time (having regained it once but finding themselves unable to hold it for want of support from the other Hellenes), so the entire city is camping out wretchedly at Salamis. Mardonios, seeing that even at this late hour Hellas would be his for the taking if only Athens would step out of his way, makes her an offer too good to refuse. The Athenian Lykidas moves before his fellow members of the council that this proposal be put before the people. But when the latter hear of his motion, they surround him and stone him on the spot (9.5). " [And] when the Athenian women heard what was happening, one woman summoned another and took her along, and they went at their own prompting to [his] house, where they stoned to death his wife and children." Obviously the Athenian women have adjusted to the loss of their brooch-pins.

In predemocratic Athens, even the most extreme behavior of the city's women is normal in a certain sense. The widows remain domestic beings, each responding to the general calamity as one to herself only. The intensity of their private grief bursts all public bounds.

In the affair of Lykidas, on the other hand, the rage of the women, in emulation of that of their husbands, erupts on behalf of the public. They are more terrible than Madame Defarge, for no memory of private injustice suffered extenuates their vengefulness. It is entirely civic or disinterested. If they remain somehow feminine it is in their vigilant attention to the private sphere: their men would not have thought to stone Lykidas' widows and children. This is to say, however, that the men would have respected the boundary between public and private, while the women quite obliterate it. There could be no more extreme instance of the democratic politicization of the private. Yet the obduracy of the Athenian people, in tandem with the prudence of Themistokles, made the largest contribution of any city to the salvation of Hellas (7.139).[12]

So Herodotus' praise of *isagoria* at 5.78 proves to refute Megabyzos' critique of *demokratia* only imperfectly. To be sure Megabyzos was wrong in thinking that the torrent of popular energy was destructive only and that therefore its emancipation should be wished only on one's enemy. (In fact democratic Athens proves Persia's most formidable enemy.) Yet as the episode of Aristagoras suggests, and the stonings of Lykidas and his family confirm, the surge of popular passion tends naturally to overflow its banks. Otanes' presentation of *isonomia* had been entirely too bloodless; if the people's proneness to folly had escaped him, so too had its uncouth vitality and stubbornness. Having eulogized the rule of the

12 To be sure the obduracy of the people depended on that of their gods (cf. especially 8.51–53, 8.65, 8.77, 8.143 [but cf. 8.144], 9.7, 9.42–43, 9.65, 9.100–101, 9.116–20)

plethos as free of the vices of the rule of one, he had nothing further to say. His grasp of democracy was only a negative one. Megabyzos, on the other hand, had recognized the lack of leadership as democracy's greatest problem. The emancipation of nature is at the same time the greatest power and the verge of chaos: it threatens "the political equivalent of the chaotic beginnings."

Without passing beyond Book Three, Rosen in his essay has "tried to show how Herodotus' conservative formulation of political freedom is linked to his acceptance of the pre-Socratic (or pre-Parmenidean) teaching about nature or the origins."

> Man is free just because of his independence from the gods, because of the chaotic origins. This motion is man's nature as well, it leads to the political expansion and rise of civilization which culminates in the Persian war. (351)

> Ultimately, it is impossible to restrain the force of motion; as Yeats put it, "things fall apart, the center cannot hold." But Herodotus will do his best to hold things together. (352)

We might say then of democracy that it is the regime in which the truth about man and the world comes closest to being apparent. As the most dynamic it is in a sense the most natural regime. Yet it is also the most liable to self-destruction. Not only Herodotus but the democratic statesman who takes his bearings from him "will do his best to hold things together." When Rosen speaks of "Herodotus' conservative formulation of political freedom" he means to imply the political necessity of veiling the truth of the natural primacy of motion, which is identical with that of man's independence from the gods. If Rosen's Herodotus is intransigently political, it is because he is (unlike the Herodotus of the scholars) intransigently philosophical. Philosophy is higher than politics but depends on politics: "true freedom depends upon the theoretically lower but practically indispensable public freedom." Piety must inform and limit the public conception of freedom, yet precisely in so doing it obstructs the way to freedom in the true or private sense.

If Professor Rosen is right about this, then nothing could be truer or further from the truth than the old perception of Herodotus as credulous in matters of piety. In fact we will find him as skeptical of piety as he is solicitous of it. But precisely in having followed Professor Rosen in identifying piety as Herodotus' pivotal theme, I have disqualified it as a topic for an occasional essay, however celebratory that occasion. Therefore my piece will end here. May it have served to remind the reader of that early study of Herodotus on which Professor Rosen's reputation won't rest.

Aristotle's Commonsensical Cosmology

David Roochnik

Boston University

Aristotle's cosmology is, on the one hand, dead as a doornail. After all, among his other claims are these: the heavenly bodies go around the earth on a fixed circular path; they are ontologically superior to, more "honorable" and "divine" than bodies found on earth; they are weightless and eternal. We know these statements to be false, even laughably so. The sun, not the earth, is the center of our solar system, the planets do not move in circular orbits, matter is homogeneous, and stars have both weight and a history. Given these facts, what can Aristotle's cosmology possibly teach us today? Can it ever be anything more than an antiquarian's relic?

The task of this essay is both to examine and defend the philosophical value of the arguments Aristotle makes on behalf of his cosmology in *De Caelo* I.1–3. As such, it is a test, or perhaps a limit, or a worst case scenario for the study of his thought in general. While a contemporary "virtue ethicist" will, for example, readily grant the significance and value of the *Nicomachean Ethics*, an analogous claim made for his cosmology seems impossible. Unlike ethics, western science seems to have progressed so far that it has left Aristotle deeply buried in the dust. This paper will suggest otherwise.[1]

The strength of Aristotle's cosmological argumentation lies in its reliance on ordinary experience and commonsense, concepts explored in depth in Stanley Rosen's *The Elusiveness of the Ordinary*.[2] Simply put, *De Caelo* begins with the phenomena of ordinary experience, and then by means of the syllogism, which itself emanates from ordinary experience, projects these phenomena onto the heavens. The result is thus a commonsensical cosmology, an articulated world in which human beings find themselves essentially at home. Citing the four features of ordinary experience Rosen identifies, one could say that the Aristotelian "heavens" exhibit "the inner connection between truth and goodness, the exemplification of a unified process, regularity, and comprehensiveness" (259) that we are familiar with here on earth.

1 A early inspiration for this paper comes from Paul Feyerabend's essay, "In Defence of Aristotle" in *Progress and Rationality in Science*, G. Radnitsky and G. Andersson (eds); Boston: Reidel, 1978, pp. 144–80.

2 All quotations from Stanley Rosen, *The Elusiveness of the Ordinary* (New Haven: Yale, 2002) will be indicated simply by a page number in parenthesis.

The following sketches the arguments in *De Caelo* I.1–3 that conclude with the statements that the heavenly bodies move in circular orbits and are ontologically superior to those found below the moon. The first three premises contain basic elements of his physics.

1. There are three, and only three, magnitudes or dimensions: Lines are those magnitudes divisible in one way (*eph' hen*: 268a7) or direction; surfaces, in two ways; and bodies, in three. Body is therefore the complete (*teleion*: 268a22) magnitude.[3] As we will discuss below, this coupling of the "three" and the notion of completeness, or wholeness, is crucial to the entire argument.

2. Some bodies are natural, some not. Natural bodies have the principle of motion in themselves, and move "according to place" (*kinêsis kata topon*: 268b17), i.e., achieve locomotion. There are two general forms of simple locomotion because there are only two simple magnitudes, namely straight and circular lines. Because motion proceeding on straight lines has two directions, up or away from the center (*apo tou mesou*) and down or towards the center (*epi to meson*), there are three forms of simple motion. Thus, just as "body was completed (*apetelesthê*) by the number three, so now is its motion" (268b25).

3. There are four simple bodies: fire, earth, water and air. There are also complex bodies compounded of these. Each of the simple bodies has a natural form of locomotion, which is also simple. Fire and air move upwards in straight lines, while earth and water move downwards in straight lines. Because there are three forms of locomotion, there must be "a simple body naturally so constituted as to move in a circle in virtue of its own nature" (269a7).

These dense passages are difficult to unpack. They rely on Aristotle's definition of a natural being as one with the principle of motion and rest within itself (see *Physics* II.x), his doctrine of the four elements, i.e., his proto-chemistry, and his notion of a natural place and a corresponding natural motion. Implicit as well is the location of the earth at the "center" of the world. For the moment, however unlikely these assertions may seem, let them stand as is. They will be discussed near the end of this essay. What is most relevant now is the way Aristotle argues. In that regard, let us move forward.

4. The simple body that moves in a circle must be composed of a fifth element unlike the four sublunary ones, all of which naturally move in straight lines.

3 All citations from *De Caelo* come from the Loeb Edition, translated by W.K.C. Guthrie (Cambridge, 1986). As is always the case with Loeb citations, line numbers are not entirely precise.

5. Circular motion is "primary" because the circle, unlike any other figure composed of straight lines, is complete (*teleion*: 269a20). An infinite line cannot be complete for the obvious reason that it has no end (*telos*), and a finite line segment can always be extended (269a23). Because "a motion which is prior to another is the motion of a body prior in nature," heavenly bodies are "more divine than and prior to" (269a32) sublunar ones.

6. Aristotle sums up: "Thus the reasoning (*sullogizomenos*) from all our premises goes to make us believe (*pisteuseien*) that there is some other body separate from those around us here, and of a higher (*timiôteran*) nature in proportion as it is removed from the sublunary world (269b15)."

What is striking about these arguments is, as Aristotle himself indicates in 6., how "syllogistic" or "logical" they are. By assuming that there are three kinds of simple locomotion (up, down, around) and that the four sublunary elements all move in straight lines, a "slot" is open and must be filled: something must move in a circle, and by this reasoning only the heavenly bodies are available to perform such a task.

In order to attribute the qualities of weightlessness and eternity to these bodies, Aristotle argues as follows:

7. The heavy is "that whose nature it is to move towards the center, the light that whose nature it is to move away from the center" (269b25). Because all simple bodies have only one natural motion, the heavenly bodies moving in a circular orbit have no weight.

8. The opposite of up is down, and of down up. But the circle has no opposite. Because "everything that is generated comes into being out of an opposite" and "opposites have opposite motions" (270a15), the heavenly bodies moving in circular orbits are neither generated nor perish. "It looks then as if nature correctly exempted from the class of opposites that which was to be ungenerated and indestrucible" (270a20).

To appreciate the nature of Aristotle's argumentation, it is useful first to consider some objections to it. Recall, for example, Francis Bacon's classic complaint in the *New Organon* I.13: "the syllogism is...no match for the subtlety of nature. It commands assent therefore to the proposition, but does not take hold of the thing." For Bacon, syllogistical science fails to apprehend the truth about nature because it is essentially anthropomorphic. It projects human understanding onto a field in which it does not belong. More specifically, "the human undestanding is of its own nature prone to suppose the existence of more order and regularity in the world than it finds." Bacon's example of this tendency to error is Aristotelian: "Hence the fiction that all celestial bodies move in perfect circles" (I.45).[4]

On the one hand, Bacon is quite right in his diagnosis: Aristotle's cosmological arguments are syllogistic. Because there are three forms of simple motion, something must move in a circle and logic, not ruthlessly empirical observation, dictates that this cannot be composed of a sublunary element. Such argument does indeed "suppose" a strong sense of "order and regularity." Because wholeness is triadic, and because the "cosmos" is just that, namely an ordered whole, there must be three dimensions and three forms of simple motion. The heavenly bodies move in a circular orbit because the argument dictates that something must.

Bacon is also right to characterize this sort of reasoning as anthropomorphic. It projects a human conception of order onto the heavens. As we shall see, rather than being its weakness, this is precisely the argument's strength.

Aristotle's cosmology discloses celestial phenomena as they show themselves in ordinary experience. It explains the shape of the human, naked-eye, earth-bound, and commonsensical encounter with the world around and the sky above. To elaborate, let us return to the first claim made above, namely that there are only three dimensions, and that threeness and completeness form a conceptual pair. Aristotle defends this, the crucial premise of the entire argument, with the following:

(1) "There is no magnitude not included in these [the three dimensions]; for three are all (*to ta tria panta einai*) and 'in three ways' (*to tris*) is the same as 'in all ways' (*pantêi*). For just as the Pythagoreans say, the all and all things has been determined (*hôristai*) by the number three. For end (*teleutê*), middle (*meson*) and beginning (*archê*) hold the number of the all, and their number is three. Hence it is that we have taken this number from nature, as it were one of her laws (268a9–13)."

The entire argument rests on the proposition that "three are all." This in turn depends on Aristotle's conception of the "all" or the "whole."[5] A whole is a unity of parts, a structure constituted by a beginning, a middle and an end. Aristotle neither explains what he means here nor defends his claim. He must, then, take it as a given. But of what sort? I suggest it is a given of our ordinary experience

4 I do not suggest that Aristotle alone devised the notion of circular orbits. The Babylonians probably conceived of the great circle or belt of the zodiac with its twelve constellations. Anaximenes had a notion of the rotating sphere. Eudoxus conceived of the sun, moon, and five planets occupying a set of ideal concentric spheres uniformly rotating the earth.

5 In this context the two words can be treated as synonyms, although Aristotle differentiates them in *Metaphysics* V.xxvi. Clearly his definition of the "whole" in that context applies to the pan as discussed in De Caelo.

which, just as Rosen has it, requires unity or wholeness. To elaborate and explain, we must look elsewhere in Aristotle's writings.

Consider, for example, how Aristotle initially defines tragedy in the *Poetics*: it is an "imitation of an action (*praxeôs*) that is serious, complete (*teleias*) and of a certain magnitude . . ." (1449b25). Later he reformulates: "tragedy is an imitation of an action that is complete and whole (*holês*: 1450b25)," and he defines a whole in the same terms he uses in *De Caelo*: "that which has a beginning, middle and an end" (1450b27).[6]

A good tragedy must have a unified plot (*muthos*) structure. Plot, "the arrangement (*sunthesin*) of the incidents" (1450a5), is also described as an "imitation of the action" (1450a4), and so it becomes the central element, or as Aristotle calls it, the "soul" (1450a37), of tragedy as such. Without a unified narrative or plot, a drama is no more than a string of episodes. It is not only a bad piece of work, but also a lifeless one.

A good tragedy requires narrative unity because it is an imitation of a *praxis*. Like many of Aristotle's critical terms, this one is equivocal. In the broadest sense, it can refer to any kind of "doing" whatsoever. It names, for example, the activities of animals (*Historia Animalium* 487a10). In the narrowest sense, such as is found in *Nicomachean Ethics,* III.1 (the discussion of the voluntary and involuntary), it refers only to those specific actions human beings perform. There is, in addition, an in-between sense, namely as a human life conceived neither as an isolated action, nor as a sequence of merely biological activities, but as the consistent and characteristic pattern of activity a human being engages in over a long period of time. This is the sense Aristotle has in mind when he says in the *Politics* (1325a32) that "happiness is a *praxis*." Happiness does not occur in an isolated or single moment. It is the work of a life-time. This sense of *praxis* comes close to what Aristotle calls *energeia* in his definition of happiness in the *Ethics* as "*energeia* in conformity with virtue" (1098b31).[7]

A tragedy imitates a *praxis* (or a portion of *praxis*) in this last sense. It must have a unified plot structure because *praxis* conceived as a human life is a unified whole. In a chronological sense, a life has a beginning, a middle and an end. We begin in childhood, we mature, and at the end of our lives we decline. In order for our lives to have any sort of practical unity and meaning, there must be a coherent structuring of these parts. Human life, in other words, must have a narrative structure. We must be able to tell our "stories." When it comes to an excellent human being, such a story would have three main chapters: a childhood spent in the successful absorption of a set of good habits inculcated by an attentive community; a middle age spent flourishing, i.e., doing everything well that an

6 Translations from the *Poetics* are my own. The Greek text is S. Butcher, *Aristotle's Theory of Poetry and Fine Art* (NY: Dover, 1951).

7 Translations from the *Nicomachean Ethics* are my own. The Greek text is I. Bywater, *Aristotelis "Ethica Nicomachea"* (Oxford: Clarendon Press, 1962).

excellent human being can and therefore should do; and an old age facing decline and its inevitable suffering as well can possibly be expected.

As Rosen puts it, "the stories that we tell about ourselves are made possible by certain pervasive traits of ordinary experience" (259). Primary among these traits are "unity and regularity" (266). For human life to have "meaning and value" (267) it must be a unity of parts; it must be a whole. Consequently it must have, broadly speaking, a beginning, middle and end.

To return to *De Caelo*: Aristotle begins with the phenomenon of wholeness as threeness. He then projects this phenomenon onto the cosmos as such. Although it is not chronological, the world has a story: it makes sense. The various elements fit in their proper place. Again, Rosen is helpful in articulating this Aristotelian, this anthropomorphic, move.

> The unity and regularity of praxis, the domain of intellectual activity through speeches and deeds, is itself dependent upon the unity and regularity of existence, to which we sometimes refer...as the order of nature (266).

Consider a second example. In the *Nicomachean Ethics* Aristotle defines moral virtue as "a stable disposition involving choice and consisting in the mean relative to us" (1106b36). (The word *meson* (1106b7) can also be translated, as it is in *De Caelo*, as "center.") The mean is in-between excess and deficiency. So, for instance, courage is the mean in-between fearing too much (cowardice) and not fearing enough (recklessness). Like its narrative counterpart, the moral life is structured triadically. The moral life can be lived well because moral questions can be answered well. An excellent human being has good judgment and so when facing a moral question-e.g., should I give money to the beggar?-can attain the right answer. Because a right answer is possible, two wrong answers are also possible. One can give too much or too little to the beggar.

Aristotle no more defends (in a logical sense) the notion of the moral mean in the *Ethics* than he does the statement "three is all" in *De Caelo.* He takes it as a given. This is because he has such a strong sense of the intelligibility and the meaningfulness, which in turn require the wholeness, of the moral life. To explain, consider his argument on behalf of the "highest good" in *Ethics* I.2:

> If then among our actions there is some end which we wish for because of itself, and because of which we wish for everything else, and if we do not choose everything because of something else-since if we did it would go on indefinitely, and as a result desire would be empty and vain-clearly this would be the highest good (1094a18-22).

This argument is an enthymeme. Its suppressed premise—suppressed because Aristotle takes it as evident—is that desire is not empty or vain, that life has meaning. Therefore, the sequence of ends or goods—A is for the sake of B, which is for the sake of C, and so on—cannot be infinite. It must stop, and so can in principle be completed.

Aristotle allows this supposition because he takes it to be phenomenologically evident. Human beings consistently appear to act as if their decisions matter and their desires are neither futile nor pointless. If the sequence of ends or goods were infinite, then no good or end, and hence no desire, would matter more than any other After all, compared to (divided by) infinity any finite good is equivalent to nothing. In short, human life, as it is actually experienced, appears to have meaning.

(To be specific: the English "meaning" has two basic senses. The first is the semantic, as in "the word 'table' means 'a flat top placed on legs.'" And there is the purposive: "I meant to turn the lights off." Both senses are operative in the phrase "life has meaning:" it is both purposive and its purposive structure can be explained or articulated.)

Because life is experienced as meaningful, good judgment on moral matters is possible. Therefore, Aristotle implicitly argues, a mean in-between excess and deficiency is the basis or the target of such good judgment. The moral life is intelligible: it is presented in ordinary experience as a triadic whole.

Rosen again captures these features of ordinary life. "At all levels of conscious activity, we prefer correctness or truth to incorrectness or falsehood. . . . Human activity is intrinsically a process of 'trying to get it right'" (262). From these commonsensical observations, Rosen infers, "The goodness of reason is directly visible at the level of ordinary experience" (260).

These remarks are thoroughly Aristotelian in spirit. When it comes to practical decisions, "trying to get it right" implies hitting the "center" or the "mean:" not too much, not too little.

A third way in which triadic wholeness is given to us by the phenomena is more directly related to *De Caelo*, namely the human experience of place (*topos*) and the directionality attendant upon it. Because we occupy, and are aware of occupying, a place in the world, and because we can move from place to place, we experience ourselves as located in a center that is flanked. We experience place directionally. Above us is up; below us is down. To one side of us is left, to the other is right.

These directions, which are meaningless or arbitrary in a modern physics of infinite space, are constitutive of Aristotle's cosmos. As mentioned above, there are two forms of simple locomotion corresponding to two simple lines: the straight and the circle. Air and fire naturally move up, "away from the center." Earth and water move down, "towards the center." The moon is above us, the earth below our feet. (Furthermore, the universe revolves from right to left, from east to west: see II.11.)

The kind of reasoning exemplified above (and the examples could be multiplied)[8] provides a Baconian critic with a ready target, one almost too easy to hit. Aristotle attributes what seem to be merely anthropomorphic and arbitrary characterizations of directionality—to the left *of me*, right *of me*, above and below *me*—to the cosmos itself. On the one hand, such criticism is again quite right. On the other, if Aristotle's cosmology can be defended as anything other than an interesting relic, it would have to be along just these phenomenological lines. The cosmos, as we experience it from earth, does have a center. The earth is the center, not of an infinite universe, but of our lives. The sun rises in the east and moves across the sky, setting in the west. The stars are above us because in order to see them we must tilt our head backwards, and look up and away from our own bodies on earth. They must be made of "different stuff." After all, unlike anything else on earth, they do not move in straight (or compounded) lines, and they do not fall down. Fire does naturally move upwards. After all, in lighting a cigarette we position the match under it.

To return to *De Caelo*: Aristotle's argument on behalf of triadicity continues with the following:

(2) Natural language supports the contention that "three is all," for of two things we say "both" not "all." This latter term we employ only when at least three are in question. In speaking thus, we are accepting "nature herself for our guide" (268a11–20).

Aristotle summons a feature of natural language, more prominent in Greek than English (because of the former's use of the dual), to solidify his cosmological argument. Of two objects, we typically say "both" rather than "all." If I ask you, "which of your eyes hurt?" you might answer "both do." You would not say "all do." If I ask you, "which of your fingers hurt?" you might well say "all do." From this observation of ordinary language, Aristotle concludes that threeness is constitutive of "allness" or "wholeness." Again, this is because an all or whole is a unity of parts, and this requires a beginning, middle and end. These terms need not be interpreted chronologicaly or linearly. The key is that there must be some "middle," some connection between the other two. As Rosen puts it, "unity is in fact a unity of differences" (271). In order for a pair to become an all there must be more than just the two items: there must be a principle, a means of uniting them in their difference. There must be a third.

In a different vein, but also relying on the epistemic value of ordinary language, Aristotle says this:

8 Human temporality of course provides another example. Time is experienced triadically, with a present–a center, where we are now–flanked by the past and future.

> It seems too that the name of this first body has been passed down to the present time by the ancients, who thought of it in the way as we do, for we cannot help believing that the same beliefs (*doxas*) recur to men not once nor twice but over and over again...Thus they, believing that the primary body was something different from earth and fire and air and water, gave the name *aither* to the uppermost region, choosing its title from the fact that it 'runs always' (*aei thein*) (270b15–25).

Of course, the Baconian critic would find it a horrible mistake to project features of Greek or English onto the "screen" of non-human nature. This, however, is a central principle of Aristotelian "phenomenology." The phenomena for Aristotle, as several commentators have argued, are drenched in language.[9] How something appears is not only closely related to what "we" say about it, but also suggestive of the nature of reality itself. The fact that "we" do not call a pair an "all" has epistemic force. Indeed, this use of the "we" is common in Aristotle. "We," for example, speak of four causes; this is evidence that by nature there are four causes. (See *Physics* 195a4.) "We" have ten basic modes of predication. There really are ten categories. (See *Categories* 1b25.)

(3) Aristotle cites religious phenomena on behalf of his cosmological claim: "[We] make use of [the three] even for the worship of the gods" (268a15).

Even if this is a reference to the Greek practice of taking oaths to the heroes, gods and to Zeus, its significance goes further. As Aristotle will later assert, "all men have a conception of the gods, and all assign the highest place to the divine" (270b5). Because gods are above there must be a mediation between heaven and earth. In other words, there must be a beginning, middle and end. Whether this takes the form of animal-human-divine, or mortal-*daimon*-immortal (see *Symposium* 202d), or father-son-holy spirit, religious thinking proceeds triadically.

Speaking specifically about this tendency, but in a way that summarizes much of what has been discussed so far, Aristotle says this:

> From what has been said it is apparent (*phaneron*) why, if someone trusts our hypotheses (*ei tis tois hupokeimenois pisteuei*) the primary body of all is eternal, suffers neither growth nor diminution, but is ageless unalterable and impassive. It seems that the argument (*logos*) gives witness (*marturein*) to the phenomena (*ta phainomena*) and the phenomena give witness to the argument. All men have a conception of gods, and all assign the highest place to the divine (270b5).

9 Consider G.E.L. Owen, "Tithenai ta Phainomena," and W. Wieland, "Aristotle's Physics and the Problem of Inquiry into Principles," both in *Articles on Aristotle, Vol. I*, ed. J. Barnes (1975: Duckworth), pp. 113–40.

The *logos* gives witness to the phenomena, and *vice versa*. Both the phenomena and the phenomenology can be trusted to inform us of the way things are.

The phrase "saving the phenomena"–*sôzein ta phainomena, salvare phenomena*–has long been associated with the history of astronomy and its goal of empirical and predictive adequacy. The phrase is inspired (although not used) by Aristotle. But as is apparent from the discussion above, his conception of the phenomena goes far beyond observations of planetary motion. As we have just seen, it includes ordinary language, religion, the naked-eye, earth-bound, finite human experience of space and time. Such is the commonsensical cosmology. Stars are above us and are made of special stuff, water always flows downwards, and the earth is the center of existence...our existence. The world makes sense because wholeness, structured by threeness, is given to us in our ordinary experience. Unless we are in moods of debilitating anxiety, we are largely at home in the world.

The Baconian criticism is, on the one hand, quite right. Aristotle "mingles" the human with the non-human. He projects the human experience of meaning and order, the essential ingredients of commonsense, onto the cosmos itself. The Baconian might well agree with Aristotle's analysis of commonsense, but then deny the move that attaches it to things in the world. Aristotle, by contrast, has enormous confidence that commonsense, the phenomena, the *endoxa,* the way people speak is fundamentally informative of the way things are.

Rosen rightly says that "it is a fundamental condition of human existence that we intend to respond correctly to things, experiences, events, and so on, as they actually are" (263). According to Aristotle, this intention regularly meets with success. As he puts it, "human beings are naturally and sufficiently disposed towards the truth and most of the time attain the truth" (*Rhetoric,* 1355a10).[10] We are beings who live in truth, who "truth" (*alêtheuei*: see *Nicomachean Ethics,* 113915), and so can trust commonsense. He expresses this sentiment as follows:

> The study of truth is in one sense difficult, in another easy. This is shown by the fact that whereas no one person can obtain an adequate grasp of it, we cannot all fail in the attempt; each thinker makes some statement about the natural world and as an individual contributes little or nothing to the inquiry; but a combination of all conjectures results in something considerable. Truth is like the proverbial door which no one can miss, in this sense our study will be easy; but the fact that we cannot, although having some grasp of the whole, grasp a particular part, shows its difficulty (*Metaphysics,* 993a30-b10).[11]

10 Translation is my own. The Greek text is W. D. Ross, *Aristotelis "Ars Rhetorica"* (Oxford: Clarendon Press, 1959).

11 Translation is my own. The Greek text is W.D. Ross, *Aristotle's Metaphysics* (Oxford: Clarendon Press,1970).

To summarize: Aristotle has enormous confidence in the human capacity to perceive and then to understand accurately the "natural world." Natural beings show themselves to us as they really are. Appearances and the ordinary language used to articulate them can be trusted. We are, most of the time (or "normally"), at home in the world.

This essay must close with some (necessarily inadequate) remarks about the syllogism, the logical means by which the phenomena are projected onto the heavens. Recall that Bacon derides it: "the syllogism is...no match for the subtlety of nature. It commands assent therefore to the proposition, but does not take hold of the thing."

Three lines of Aristotelian response: First, "things" or nature itself is syllogistically arranged, at least insofar as the syllogism expresses the logic of class inclusion. Consider, for example, Aristotle's conception of the hierarchy of living beings or of "souls." All living beings have the "nutritive soul," i.e., share in metabolic activity and reproduction. Animals have in addition a "perceptive soul," minimally the sense of touch, maximally all five senses. Human beings have "mind" in addition. Each of higher order of life must have all the biological functions of those orders below them. A human being engages in metabolic activity and perception. (See *De Anima* II.1–5.)

Syllogisms can easily be extracted from these biological observations. For example: all human beings are animals; all animals engage in metabolic activity; therefore, all human beings engage in metabolic activity. Or: all animals have sense perception; a rabbit is an animal; therefore, a rabbit has sense perception. These are not merely sterile logical formalisms. Instead, they express the order of nature itself.

Second, Aristotle's conception of the syllogism emerges not from an analysis of the abstract forms of thought, but from the give and take of dialectical exchange. Such, at least, is Ernst Kapp's argument. He begins by noting that the *Topics* is the earliest and thus the seminal logical work, and that its purpose is to establish a method for the kind of argumentation that goes on between questioner and responder in a dialectical "game." He then notes that the definition of the syllogism there asserted–namely, "an argument in which, certain things having been laid down, something other than these things necessarily results through them" (*Topics,* 100a25–26)[12]—is virtually the same as that given in the *Prior Analytics.* Equipped with these observations, he concludes:

> Thus it happened that at the beginning of systematical logical research a syllogism was not sought and was not found among or within the thoughts of the solitary thinker or in his books or formal lectures, but that the original

12 I follow Forster's translation in the Loeb edition (Cambridge: Harvard University Press, 1976).

subject matter of logic was the "dialectical syllogism," the syllogism that develops in conversation.[13]

The syllogism, then, is not a mere formalism, but an organic development of the way people argue with one another when playing the game of dialectic, which itself is the distillation of the practices of ordinary conversation (and which of course was depicted in the Platonic dialogues.) To quote Kapp again: "logic was originally conceived as science of what happens, not when we are thinking for ourselves, but when we are talking and trying to convince one another."[14]

Third: the much maligned syllogism expresses its own kind of wholeness, which like that of good stories, our experience of the intelligibility of the moral life, and of the directionality of place, is triadic in nature. It depends, after all, on a "middle" term.

The remarks above on the nature of the syllogism (which obviously require much elaboration) should clarify the meaning of the verb "project" used throughout this essay. It is not meant to suggest the Freudian sense of transference. Instead, it is intended to bring to mind something like "an overhead projector," one which throws, but retains the form and proportions of, an enlarged image of an original onto a big screen. Aristotle's cosmology uses the syllogism to project an image (an *eikon* not a *phantasm*) of the structure of phenomena familiar to us here on earth onto the heavens. The result is a cosmos, a world infused by commonsense.

To close: in a lecture titled "Philosophy and the Crisis of European Humanity," written in the dreadful year of 1935, Husserl wrote "The European nations are sick. Europe itself, it is said, is in crisis" (270).[15] Husserl was specific in his diagnosis: "The European crisis has its roots in a misguided rationalism" (290).

A materialist, mechanistic conception of nature, studied by a mathematically based science and taking place in an infinite space, not only spawned the powerful technologies we now both take for granted and deeply fear, but has come to dominate western culture itself. Like a giant shadow, modern science and technology have blotted out all other forms of human knowledge and inquiry. Most important, the hegemony of modern science, based always on the paradigm of mathematical physics, has obliterated the possibility of gaining knowledge of the "meaning" of human life itself. For this "meaning" requires natural or ordinary language, and resists mathematical or scientific articulation.

13 Kapp, Ernst. *Greek Foundations of Traditional Logic.* New York, Columbia University Press, 1942), p. 17. Thanks to Bret Doyle who brought this to my attention.

14 Ibid., p. 19.

15 Husserl, E. 1970: *The Crisis of European Sciences an Transcendental Philosophy.* Translated by D. Carr. Evanston: Northwestern University Press.

What Husserl said about Einstein typifies his critique of modern European rationality:

> Einstein's revolutionary innovations concern the formulae through which the idealized and naively objectified physics is dealt with. But how formulae in general, how mathematical objectification in general, receive meaning on the foundation of life and the intuitively given surrounding world-of this we learn nothing; and thus Einstein does not reform the space and time in which our vital life runs its course (295).

To make the same point, Husserl says this: "the scientist does not become a subject of investigation" (295). In other words, modern science, always speaking the language of mathematics, "objectifies" the world. It understands how the material things work, but has nothing whatsoever to say about the unique "meaning" or "the vital life" human beings, including the scientists themselves, actually experience. "No objective science can do justice to the very subjectivity which accomplishes science" (295). Modern science is in this sense dehumanizing. It presents the technician with the opportunity to manipulate the natural world, but says and knows nothing about what it is like for a human being actually to live in it.

Consider the simplest possible example, one already mentioned. Since Copernicus we have known that the earth revolves around the sun and so is not, as Aristotle thought, the center of the universe. On the one hand, this scientific fact allows no dissent. On the other hand, it also conceals a compelling truth: for human beings, the center of our daily lives will always be the earth. It is where we live. To describe the dawn, we invariably say "the sun has risen," even though, from an astronomical perspective, this is false. Ordinary life, as well as ordinary language, speak against the Copernican revolution.

The purpose of Aristotle's cosmology is precisely to speak for ordinary life, i.e., to articulate the phenomena and explain how the natural world appears from a human perspective. What Aristotle achieves is exactly what Husserl called for, namely a *logos,* a rational account, of how the world presents itself to earth-bound human beings. Unlike the modern scientist and, as Rosen has argued, far better than the twentieth century phenomenologist, Aristotle can explain what the world means to us.[16] For him, the scientist, as well as the experience of the ordinary human being, is indeed "a subject of investigation."[17]

16 Rosen's critique of Husserl perhaps could be summarized thus: "the ordinary is . . . replaced within philosophical analysis by a theoretical artifact" (1–2). Aristotle, by contrast, allows the ordinary to speak for itself.

17 I trust Stanley Rosen would not be entirely displeased with the sentiments of this paper. But if there are mistakes, either in its reasoning or its reading of Aristotle, they are surely mine alone.

The Politics of the Afterlife in Plato's Gorgias

Damjan de Krnjevic-Miskovic

Stanley Rosen recited a verse of scripture to me the first time we met. It was in response to a question about the nature of wisdom. "She is a tree of life to those who hold fast to her," he had said, referring to the definition of wisdom or *hochma* in the *Proverbs*. In Judaism, the ascent to the Tree of Life is accomplished through the study of Torah. In Rosen's case, this ascent is accomplished through the erotic pursuit of wisdom or *sophia*. In Judaism, the contemplation and application of Torah to one's life brings about *tikkun*, the correction and repair of the world. God talks to man through Torah and the tradition, and man talks to God through *avodath* or service and *tefilah* or prayer. For Rosen, the quest for wisdom through *eros* is the way to *eudaimonia* or flourishing, the way up from nihilism and poetry.

In his *The Quarrel Between Philosophy and Poetry*. writing on Heidegger and Plato, Rosen remarks on the fundamental peculiarity of the philosophic endeavor: "although in one sense a part of the whole, it is that part which mirrors or reveals the whole *as* a whole. By virtue of the synoptic character of philosophical thought, one may see an image of the whole through a consideration of some of its parts." Soon thereafter, without a trace of false humility, Rosen comments on the ambition of the essay in question—and, I think, by analogy applicable to Rosen's whole enterprise: "The most I dare hope for . . . is such an image; I shall be quite content if the reader regards it as a *muthos* rather than a *logos*. It is an inquiry (*historia*) that 'looks for' (*zetein*) as it 'looks at' (*theorein*)" [QBPP 127].

Rosen could have added that the place from which he 'looks for' as he 'looks at' is high up among the finest branches of the Tree of Life: Rosen has ascended mightily without somehow having reduced himself to leaping from mountaintop to mountaintop. Rosen's antidote to the art of mountain climbing is the art of tree climbing. Philosophic *eros* is the antidote to will to power. Philosophic wonder destroys the will to destroy without curing one of the revolutionary zeal necessary for philosophy to take place. The apparent obscurity of these paragraphs of introduction will become clearer as we enter the universe of Plato's *Gorgias*.

* * *

Every day, Rosen demonstrates what he writes about, namely what it means to be guided by the Heracleitean affirmation that if one does not hope, one will not find that-for-which-he-does-not-hope, believing that that it was not to be found and inaccessible. Rosen interprets this 'hope' "to stand for the *pathos* or *Stimmung* which opens the soul to the otherwise unseen light of Being." As he says, "the mood of hope is frequently called 'wonder' (*thauma*) by the Greeks; both Plato and Aristotle tell us that it is the origin of philosophy. In my own interpretation of Plato's image of the cave," Rosen continues, "Socrates silently alludes to wonder when he asks Glaucon to suppose that one of the cave dwellers, 'having been released [from his chains], is forced instantly (*eksaiphnes*) to stand up, to turn his head, to walk toward and look at the light [of the fire]' [*Republic* 515c6–ff.]. The *periagoge* or 'conversion' is not originally *paideia* or 'education', but the instantaneous illumination of wonder which permits *paideia* to occur. It is," concludes Rosen, "this instant conversion which drags the released man up into the light of sun. Wonder opens man's eyes to the light of the good through the divine spark, the *theia moira*, the *mania*, or gift of the gods, as Plato variously calls the horizon of instantaneous vision" [QBPP 127–28]. Rosenian wonder is awesome to see (Homer would say, *thauma idesthai*), combining as it does the humility and hubris of philosophers unwilling to gaze at the permanent contemporaneity of nihilism with resignation.

Plato's *Gorgias* ends with a Socratic telling of the politics of the afterlife in the form of a *logos* disguised as a *muthos*. Rosen has declared that Plato's political philosophy is the "attempt to purge political life of the dangers of Sophistry without returning entirely to the privacy of Herodotus" [QBPP 55]. I will seek to gain deeper access to a part of the whole of Plato: his politics of the afterlife, uncovering the connection in philosophy between the rhetoric of truthtelling and mythmaking in the context of affirming the ontological priority of the good.

For Rosen, sophistry—of which "Protagoras is the theoretical model" [QBPP 53]—"is the attempt to share in political power without surrendering the status of the theoretician" [QBPP 55]: sophists wish neither to rule directly nor to conceal their wisdom. In a dramatic turn in the *Sophist*, the Eleatic Stranger characterizes the property properly belonging to the sophist as contradiction or disputation [*Sophist* 232b]. The association of the sophist with the art of disputation signals agreement with the thesis of Socrates in the *Gorgias* that sophistry is similar to, if not the same as, oratory [520a]. In the *Republic*, Socrates says that the sophists teach public opinion, gathering together in one place what the people say and "call[ing] it wisdom, having organized it as an art" (*Republic* 493a6–ff). For the sophist, then, opinion is higher than knowledge; the sophist is like the contemporary pollster in America. Socrates' criticism is founded on his being able to claim that there is a difference between wisdom and the ability to persuade the people about the common good on the basis of their own opinions about the what that good is. The necessary implication of this is that the philosopher has knowledge about the common good, and that that not only this knowledge but all non-technical knowledge is not based on the publicly held opinions of the common good but on something more permanent, namely knowledge of human nature, of the human soul. Only thusly can the Socratic claim to rank-order the ways of lives of human beings have any standing, for rank-ordering properly implies knowledge of the common good. This does not solve the problem of demonstrating to the many that popular opinions—their opinions—about the common good are invalid. This can require a particular combination of *muthos* and *logos*, and in due course, this essay will explore this theme, for that is what Socrates' presentation of politics of the afterlife in the *Gorgias* is about.

In contemporary language, sophists are public intellectuals who engage in the "potentially revolutionary publication in a partly-concealed form of the truth about nature," as Rosen says [QBPP 31]. The danger of sophistry is rooted in its view that nature is change, "and so too that *nomos* is lacking a divine foundation. The good is the pleasant, which is to say that the truth is defined by desire. This is the vulgar version of the classical formulation of Nietzsche's doctrine of the will to power" [QBPP 31]. This denial of the unity of *nomos* and the divine is, in Rosen's account, accomplished first by Herodotus.

For Herodotus, "*human affairs are not divine*. Man is independent of the gods (assuming that the gods exist), and Herodotus's subject is the affairs of man as so independent. If all men know the same about the gods, and this knowledge takes the form of *nomos*," Rosen reasons, "then the *nomos* of one city is exchangeable for the *nomos* of another. To say that *nomos* is the king of all men is to say that men do not perceive this equivalence; they do not understand the truth about the gods. [. . .] The extreme consequence of this is that human affairs are not divine because the divine does not exist in a humanly useful or accessible form. How could it if the cosmos is pervasive change?" [QBPP 35–36]. The intellectual roots of sophistry are thus to be found in that which undergirds the Herodotean inquiry.

Further along, Rosen reasons that the "distinction between men and gods leads to the distinction between nature or change and custom or rest. Man is by nature independent of the gods because nature is change. There can be no eternal and hierarchical relationship between man and the gods; it is precisely *nomos*, not the gods, that rules all men." Rosen concludes: "Herodotus thus reverses the Parmenidean distinction between the appearance of motion and the reality of rest. Nature includes gods, men, and the world. All have a common nature because all are changing. There is no distinction between divine and human nature, not because men are divine, but because there are no gods. [. . .] [Herodotus] thus denies the eternal, or rest, or the Being of the Parmenidean, and hence Socratic, philosophers" [QBPP 37]. According to Rosen, what is required as a remedy is not popular piety and religious customs, but a movement toward what late moderns would call a teleological ontology, requiring a surface stillness of the sort the famously pious Egyptians maintain—"because they have not thought through the consequences of their piety"—as well as "intellectual wonder" [QBPP 37]. The political health of Greece, in other words, "depends upon the capacity of Greek wise men to make a judicious adaptation of Egyptian piety" [QBPP 38].

But a direct approach to this problem—i.e. a straightforward pursuit of this teleological account of the whole—is impossible for reasons which are intelligible to those familiar with the philosophical implications of the second sailing image: Plato has no "ontology" in the sense that Hegel claims to have. In more than a few cases, the approach outlined in the *Gorgias* seems to be the best possible one. However, before turning to that dialogue, I ought to complete my consideration of Rosen's definition of Plato's political philosophy.

The first political dialogue in the Western tradition takes place in the context of a conversation in Persia about regime change, as we say now, by the men who had brought about its very destruction. Its hero is Darius, the future king. It teaches: (1) that "men lie or tell the truth for the same reason: gain, either immediate or eventual"; (2) that "justice and freedom may depend upon lies and murder, just as political debate is rooted in conspiracy and violence. Herodotus anticipates Machiavelli by suggesting that good states may depend upon a foundation of violence"; and (3) that "political action is the redistribution of natural changes in an attempt to postpone chaos" [QBPP 41]. Political order's establishment depends on human self-interest, not the gods. As Rosen says, "gain is the link between chaotic origins and surface piety: *Gain replaces the gods*" [QBPP 41].

Later in the same essay, Rosen suggests that Darius is to Herodotus what Socrates is to Plato, and that Darius and the Callicles of the *Gorgias* have much in common. Rosen characterizes Callicles as "provid[ing] us with a mediation between Sophistry and rhetoric [. . .]: he reveals what the weak conceal" [QBPP 49], that is, what Rosen calls "our actual and natural opinions" about politics: that "the conventional teaching of virtue is in fact a *noble lie* at best, and at worst, an ignoble attempt by the many weak individuals to protect themselves against the few strong citizens" [QBPP 49]. This "law of nature," this "natural right" teaching [483e3, 484b1], Rosen calls the "*esoteric teaching of the many*" [QBPP 48].

The ignoble lie upon which political life is based for Callicles and Darius is presented by both of them in relatively private settings. If pushed in public, say at a trial, they could (and would, unhesitatingly) offer denials that could maintain a ring of objective plausibility. Rosen says that for both Darius and Callicles,

> philosophy is an erroneous or childish inference from the nature of things. If nature is change and life is war, then the purpose of intelligence is to copy nature: the warrior is the highest form of philosopher. However, even for the warrior, the purpose of war is in some sense peace, the necessary condition

> for the enjoyment of the fruits of conquest. A secure peace can never be enforced by arms or deeds alone; speech is also necessary. *Nomos* is the force of speech; it is the king of all men, including kings. The warrior-king must conceal his duplicity beneath the veil of *nomos*. Differently stated, *nomos* is a duplicitous appearance of force which pretends to be peace. But the warrior-king *requires* duplicity, which places him at the mercy of the skilled talkers or interpreters of *nomos*. This is the step from the wise men to the Sophists. The wise men are unwilling to engage in rivalry with Darius for political power[. . .] . The pleasure of the wise men consists in looking and talking; their duplicity is exercised in the intricacy of their speech about the visible. They are unwilling to compromise the purity of theoretical pleasure by the exigency of action. Eventually, however, the pleasure derived from the power of speech overcomes the pleasure derived from the capacity of vision. At this point, Sophistry is born [QBPP 47–48].

Sophistry gives birth to itself out of the ambitious desire to have the vain claim of its adherents to being the best teacher of virtue validated in the light of day, that is, publicly and by the many (as well as by the few). "In order to satisfy his vanity," Rosen writes, "the Sophist is required to become a revolutionary" [QBPP 48].

Recalling Rosen's definition of Plato's political philosophy—"the attempt to purge political life of the dangers of Sophistry without returning entirely to the privacy of Herodotus" [QBPP 55]—yields the following insight: Socrates' conversation with Callicles, the spokesman for the esoteric teaching of the many, which culminates in the necessarily mythic presentation of the politics of the afterlife by him who is presented as his opponent, shows the necessity of sustaining intelligibly the conversation between poetry and philosophy, change and stability. This dialogue, more than others, points to the fact that the desirability of philosophy—itself by nature revolutionary—is connected to its ability to engage in what Rosen has called concealed revolution. In a letter to Alexandre Kojève dated 22 April 1957, Leo Strauss takes a different approach. "the meaning of the *Gorgias*," writes Strauss, is that "the relation of the philosopher to the people is mediated by a certain kind of rhetorician who arouses fear of punishment after death; the philosopher can guide these rhetoricians but can not do their work." Indeed, Strauss continues, "I do not believe in the possibility of a conversation of Socrates with the people." This difference in emphasis notwithstanding, both would agree that to philosophize with a hammer, or with the *esprit de géometrie*, may become necessary, but only when that which needs knocking down is otherwise unable, or unworthy of the privilege, to remain standing.

* * *

The final proof or demonstration Socrates offers to Callicles at the end of the *Gorgias* concerning the fact that he would bear death easily if he were to come to his end through lack of flattering rhetoric, through the right practice of politics, is offered in the form of what Socrates says is a very noble or beautiful *logos* but what he says he thinks Callicles will consider a *muthos*. The easy bearing of death is predicated on putting one's hand to the true political art and being or becoming, as Socrates says at various times, a political man, a good man, a good citizen; put differently, Callicles will bear death lightly if he were to continue the right practice of politics, namely to the giving of speeches with a view to articulating what is the best for the Athenians and for himself. In the immediate sequel, Socrates says that he will tell to Callicles the things which compose the *logos* as being true [523a2–3]. This, of course, is different from Socrates saying that he will tell Callicles that these things are simply or fully true. Socrates' careful formulation leaves room for lies—as long as they are presented as being true. Socrates next says to Callicles that the things which compose the *logos* consist in the fact that "no one fears dying itself, who is not, all in all, most irrational and unmanly, but he fears doing injustice; for to arrive in Hades with one's soul full of many unjust deeds is the ultimate of evils" [522e]. The *logos* then is a teaching about true or final judgment on one's life or soul by the gods in Hades.

Callicles, the partisan and invoker of pleasure, does not express pleasure at the possibility of hearing a Socratic myth. The philosopher is not the unmanly one in truth; rather, the unmanly man is he who insists on self-preservation at all costs Later on, Socrates indicates with greater strength that the true manly man is the philosopher. Ironically, by Callicles' own definition, Socrates is more manly than he—not that he would accept that. (In the same letter to Kojève mentioned above, Strauss writes "in the *Republic* everyone is just and moderate, but only the elite is manly (and wise); manliness and wisdom belong together, for philosophy does not wish to be edifying as your hero [i.e. Hegel] says.") To return to the thread of the argument: the criterion of true or final judgment on one's life by the gods in Hades is justice: more specifically, whether one had lived his life by the proper standards of justice or not. I suggest, provisionally, that the theme of the *Gorgias* as a whole, which is not apparent at first blush, is somehow connected to the theme of its final part, the drawing out of which I shall concern myself in this essay.

This theme is connected with the problem of the two "great use[s] of rhetoric" as defined by Socrates in his conversation with Polus: the first is self-accusation [480a1–2, 480c1–3] the second is the conditional or possible ("if") necessity of having to "do evil to someone, either enemy or whomever," that is, the necessity to "provide in every way, by acting and by speaking, that he not pay the just penalty [. . .], and if he has done unjust deeds worthy of death, that he shall not die—above all that he never die but [. . .] be deathless in being wicked, and if not this, that he [. . .] live for as long a time as possible in being such" [480e5–6, 480e7–481b5].

The first "great use of rhetoric," the first type of medicine for the soul, so to speak, is useless for the just man, for he has no cause for self-accusation (this problem is mitigated but not eliminated by the fact that he can still make use of it in case his friends, relatives or city act unjustly; the second use, the punishment of the enemy through what would be understood commonly to be non-punishment, even encouragement to injustice, seems problematical for two reasons. First, as Socrates makes clear, it would not be desirable from your own point of view for this unjust man to do injustice to you [480e7]. Second, the basis for this discussion of the punishment of the enemy, that is, a discussion of the standard of right judgment, occurs only at the end of the dialogue (in the context of what seems to be *logos* but which reads like a *muthos*). In brief, both stated uses of right rhetoric point to the superiority of the good to the just. This is curious considering that the subject matter of just rhetoric is justice, understood to be either self-accusation of injustice—the first use—or punishment—the second use—of the enemy through active prevention of just punishment being served to him. Let me put that alongside with what Socrates says to Callicles right before he begins the *logos*, as noted already above. Socrates says that he will tell to Callicles the things which compose the *logos* as being true [523a2–3], which is different from him saying that he will tell Callicles these things as being simply or fully true. As already noted, Socrates' careful formulation leave room for the telling of lies—as long as they are presented as being true, that is, as long as the appearance of truth is maintained. (We *hold* these truths to be self-evident, you could say.) Telling the truth is different from telling the full truth. And so, telling the full truth, which can mean that to tell the truth it is necessary to tell lies as being true, and a *muthos* disguised or presented like a *logos* seems to conform to my hypothesis that Plato's Socrates in the *Gorgias* points to the superiority of the good to the just.

The actual telling of the *logos* is divided into two sections [523a3–c1; 523c1–524a7]. The *logos* is then followed by Socrates' own hermeneutical restatement and a series of urgings to Callicles. The first section of the telling of the *logos* begins by a Socratic appeal to or reliance on the authority of Homer. Socrates says that Zeus, Poseidon, and Pluto divided the empire among themselves after they inherit it peacefully (*parelabon*) from their father, Kronos. Socrates is referring to *Iliad* 15.187–92 where Zeus warns Poseidon that he must step away from the battle or else face his wrath. Socrates does not mention this threat of violence. Neither does he mention the even more explicit statement in *Iliad* 14.203–4 that Zeus revolted violently against the rule of his father. This seems perfectly consistent with the silence, which runs throughout almost the whole dialogue, concerning violence (cf. 447a1). Justice is to be rightly understood in abstraction from conventional ways of (bodily) punishment. Justice is not subservient to motion, to *kinesis*, but is rather an essential component of rest, of the permanence of things, of things which remain after motion ceases. Just judgment concerns itself with the soul, which is another way of saying that the intimate connection human beings have with the good can only be established via the just (hence the latter's necessarily lower ontological status). This intimate connection seems unable to be established in the context of concern for the body.

Socrates says next that from the time of Kronos to this day there has existed and "always" will continue to exist a *nomos* among the gods concerning human beings. This *nomos* is defined as "he among human beings who went through life justly and piously, when he came to his end, would go away to the islands of the blessed to dwell in total happiness apart from evils, while he who lived unjustly and godlessly would go to the prison of retribution and judgment," This *nomos*, the origin about which Socrates is silent, covers the fates of human beings in the afterlife through the binding together of the human and the divine, or of justice and piety. Note that Socrates does not mention in this context the connection between justice and moderation and courage as he does earlier in the dialogue.

Socrates says next that in the time of Kronos and while Zeus' rule was still new, the methods of judgment were flawed in two ways: both the judges who judged the men and the men who were themselves judged were still alive. Justice and motion seem to be in tension with each other. And so, says Socrates, "the judgments were decided badly"; i.e. unjust and impious human beings were ending up in the islands of the blessed while just and pious men were ending up in Tartaros. The age of Kronos (and the pre-reform age of Zeus) is characterized by the problem of outcome not being always suited to desert. This is the theme of the dialogue as a whole. Socrates' afterlife is one of accountable self-remembering whose purpose it is to illustrate that putting one's faith in something other than virtue leads to deception. Both the judges and the judged are alive and can be deceived because of the perception that the body and the soul are one, in the sense that the actions of the body can mask the real condition of the soul even after the body has become separated from the soul. It may also have something to do with the separation of justice from moderation and courage.

In the age of Kronos, the *nomos* which regulates fate is fallible. While it "exists always and to this day" among the gods, this *nomos* is as fallible as any merely human law is, for the gods, just like human beings, change their minds and want different things at different times. The age of Kronos personifies the problem of justice which the age of Zeus will claim to solve. Before moving on to the second section of the *logos* itself, I ought to make clear my speculation. It is or will be clear that the *nomos* outlined in the first part of the *logos* is subject to change. Does it not then follow that the question of the permanence of all things pious come to the fore? In other words, the attempt by the gods, by Zeus, to correct or solve the problem of justice brings to light the problem of the gods themselves. The attempt to resolve the political problem brings to a new, brighter light the theologico-political dimensions of the problem of the origin of authority (this is made more obvious by Socrates' explicit omission of the necessity of violence or injustice in any regime change—even one which leads to the establishment of justice).

The second section of the telling of the *logos* begins by Socrates taking the place of Homer, the champion of motion over rest. Socrates dispenses with the authority of Homer and puts directly into the mouth of Zeus the remainder of the telling of the *logos*. Socrates' beautiful or noble *logos*, the contents of which he had said he tells as being true, contains the words of Zeus spoken to one of his brothers and to other gods long ago, at the time of the founding. It is literally impossible for Socrates to have knowledge of what was said—unless he is a god or a poet. Socrates nowhere in this dialogue claims such things (although this impossibility may be explainable by the temporal illogic of its dramatic presentation. However, the implication is clear: as Socrates presents Zeus to be the new (and improved) Kronos, so Socrates presents himself as the new and improved Homer. Justice is at home when all is at rest, it rests while motion dominates rest. One could say that Socrates is a Homer who does not require the frenzied song of the Muse. The Socratic philosopher is the new Homer. The philosopher knows nothing about that which he knows everything about; the poet can be made to know everything about that which he knows nothing about—for only the Muse knows. This is paramount to telling stories or myths as if they were true, or telling "lies like the truth"—as the Muses in the proem to Hesiod's *Theogony* put it. Perhaps the understanding of Socrates as the new Homer may explain Socrates' reluctance to explicitly acknowledge the violence, the *de facto* patricide, of the transition from the age of Kronos to the age of Zeus.

Socrates' Zeus begins by saying that he will make the problem of outcome not necessarily corresponding to desert stop from coming to pass *in the afterlife*, when motion loses its pride of place or appearance. Even Zeus cannot return men to before the Fall, so to speak. Zeus cannot fight the power of the body; the most he can do is wait for it to die. Men are judged badly because they are tried clothed, that is, while they are still living, while they are still in motion. Hence, many who have base souls cover them up with beautiful bodies, lineage, and wealth. When the time of their trial arrives, many witnesses, presumably of good repute, go with them to bear witness that they have lived justly. The judges are deceived by such men because they too have bodies, thus confirming the human confusion as to the difference between body and soul, motion and rest. And so their souls are fully covered over, like a screen, with clothing. In other words, they pass judgment on the fully clothed themselves fully clothed.

Sight of the true state of the soul is screened or obscured by the body and its pleasant accouterments. The appearance of pleasure to another concerned with pleasure is enough to (sometimes) mask what lies underneath. The age of Kronos is dominated by the senses (from the human perspective, the age of Kronos is Calliclean in orientation and goal; it also seems to correspond more faithfully to the everyday experience of human beings in motion). According to the Zeus of

Socrates, human beings and their judges do not know how to recognize what is inside (soul) from what is outside (body). This is the main obstacle to proper judgment. Zeus must reform the judges' inability to recognize without prejudice in order to make the attempt to resolve the problem of justice (this is precisely analogous to the way Socrates will present the right practice of politics).

Of course, the above reform pre-supposes the possibility that the distinction between body and soul, between appearance and reality, is a real and relevant one. Included in the pre-supposition of a distinction between surface and depth is an awareness of inequality, for some souls deserve to dwell in complete happiness and away from evil while other souls deserve to go to the prison of retribution and judgment, as Socrates has already said (it is important to note that Callicles must and indeed does accept this awareness of inequality but chooses to accept or prefer the opposite of inequality's corollary). In the age of Kronos, the necessity for such distinctions is not recognized by human beings but only by the gods. Pluto and those in charge of the islands of the blessed, as well as Zeus, are aware of the relevance of the distinction between body and soul in judging human beings rightly or justly. The conduct of judges and the judged in the age of Kronos is similar to the actual and advocated conduct of accuser, accused, and judge(s) in the law courts, the citation concerning which I have given above. This is to be taken in contradistinction to Socrates whose situation he had himself earlier described in the language of the conditional possibility of human judgment as being "tried as a doctor accused by a cook would be tried among children" [521e3–4]. The supremacy of the body in motion articulated by the domination of the senses or appearances in judgment is called into question by the one who has *nous*. The concern with reputation, and the inability to distinguish truth from lies like the truth as well as from lies simply, is perhaps *the* chief characteristic of the age of Kronos from the point of view of human beings, as well as maybe from the point of Kronos, in the sense that the god did not take care to enforce the distinction about which he may have known. Perhaps *the* chief characteristic of the age of Zeus from the point of view of Socrates (and his Zeus) is the separation of truth (mind or soul) from appearance (body). The mind rules in the age of Zeus, not the senses. Socrates strongly implies that he is a human being from the age of Zeus living in the Calliclean age of Kronos. This and other things suggest further that Socrates points to a fundamental similarity between himself and Zeus and to a fundamental difference between himself and the human types represented by Gorgias, Polus, and Callicles. Socrates presents himself as living as a god among men in *their* world, regulated as it is by *their* laws, laws which place undue emphasis on the body, on motion. This is understandable given that we all live in the world of things and not in the world of the mind, of course, but it points, it seems to me, to the proper rank-ordering of the two worlds.

Socrates' Zeus now presents the details of the reforms of his father's *nomos*. These details implicate both those to be judged and the judges. Note that Socrates presents Zeus as acting when confronted with the problem of desert not always conforming to outcome—even in the afterlife. Zeus says that human beings must be stopped from foreknowing their death. This allows one to make timely preparations to conceal the true state of one's soul, to adorn one's soul. Foreknowledge of death allows human beings to confuse the last day of life with the first day of death. As a result, human beings do not consider the body and soul to be separate (in the age of Zeus, they somehow know that their souls will survive their bodies). In the age of Kronos, death, understood as the coming forward of the soul, had no significant meaning because in the age of Kronos, motion reigns over rest.

Zeus then says that Prometheus has already been told to stop human beings from having access to the foreknowledge of death. It is unclear why Prometheus appears not to have done what Zeus had already told him to do—that is, before Hades and the others had arrived. This of course means that Zeus knew of the problem before it was brought to his attention, perhaps because he is in possession of that which characterizes the age of his rule, *nous*. Socrates does not here say why Zeus did not act on his knowledge, although it may have something to do with the consolidation of political power after a regime change. If this is the case, the politics of the afterlife aren't so different from the politics in this life. Prudential statesmanship appears to be a factor in the instauration of divine justice in the afterlife as well. The administration of justice is impossible without a *phronemos*.

Next, human beings must be tried naked, without soul-screens, i.e. without their bodies, without cosmetics, that is to say, they must be tried when they are dead, when their bodies are at rest. Thus, human beings are no longer in control of their own trials, of their own fates. Moreover, the decider of the trial, the judge, must also be naked, dead, and must with *his* soul contemplate the soul of each man immediately upon that man's unwarned death. He must also leave behind on earth all his kinsfolk and adornment. The key ingredient of just judgment is the contemplation of the judged's bare soul by the equally bare soul of the judge. The judges, Zeus tells us, are his sons, themselves gods. It is necessary to infer that they must possess *nous*, for Zeus does not suggest that his sons got the job of judging because of their lineage but rather because of their natural qualifications. So, the resolution of the desert-outcome problem—the apparent impossibility of which (coupled with a lack of understanding of the possibility of anything higher than the just) drove Callicles and those like him to those like Gorgias, is contingent on the imposition of an order which guarantees that the judges, the rulers, possess *nous* and are able *and willing* to act on it.

Socrates' Zeus does everything in his power to ensure the resolution of the problem of justice. This is indicated most directly in the closing words of the *logos*, when the Zeus of Socrates says "that the decision about the journey for human beings may be as just as possible." The formulation "as much as possible" recalls the final formulation of what at the time Socrates was about to present as a *logos*, namely, that he will tell the things to be told "as being true" [524a6, 523a2]. In the latter case, I had suggested that Socrates' careful formulation had left room for lies—as long as those lies were presented as being true. This had further suggested a distinction between telling things as being true and telling true things truthfully. The full truth is truer than what seems to be the truth; the second understood in light of the first shows why the second cannot be and thus is not really a *logos*.

That Socrates tells Callicles he will consider the *logos* a *muthos* is, I believe, a compliment the meaning of which Callicles does and will not understand. Callicles is not persuaded by Socratic *logos*, whether adorned or not, because he equates erotic ascent with love of the people. The *muthos-logos* is meant, in part, to demonstrate what it is about Callicles that prevents him from understanding the consequences of Socrates' reply, namely that this problem is not a cause for infuriation for those who have "*nous*, as the *logos* indicates" [511b7]. Eros points upward only with *nous*. Eros divorced from *nous* leads to what Pascal called distractions or *divertissements* and to what in Greek is called *kinesis*. Zeus then cannot fully solve the problem of justice, which amounts to saying that Zeus cannot overcome the human fact of corporeality, i.e. that which encourages immoderation and cowardice. Plato here yields much to Callicles—whose thinking is an admixture of materialism and hesitant nihilism—but in such a way as to overcome him.

In *Hermeneutics as Politics*, Rosen writes that "esoteric as well as exoteric Platonism is grounded in the thesis that we have a satisfactory understanding of the natural articulation of life that is not the same as the assumption of the eternal order." Nature provides unassisted human reason with the "basis for learning from experience, or engaging in calculation (*logismos*) of a mathematical as well as a political kind. But this type of natural reasonableness is not sufficient to grasp intellectually the eternal order of the whole. At this point, divine madness is required." It may be that what man learn from experience leads him to discover the "natural foundation for willing the eternal order to be" [HAP 126–7], but this is not enough for those who believe that man can jump straight to being and avoid nothingness. However that may be, the attempt to solve the problem of justice through *nous* and *psuche* by going through what appears to be a beautiful *muthos* instead of bland *logos* points to the idea that there is something higher than the just, namely the good, for otherwise there could be no such thing as an uncondemnable lie. That which seems to move Zeus toward a regime of justice is an understanding that the Calliclean appeal to injustice and the corresponding denial of the good is a denigration of human beings in the name of their self-exaltation. Near the end of the dialogue Socrates assures Callicles that he will suffer nothing terrible, as long as he practices virtue as Socrates does, "And after we have practiced in common thus, then at least, if it seems we ought, shall we apply ourselves to political affairs; or we shall take counsel on what sort of thing seems good to us then, when we are better at taking counsel than now" [527]. This liberation, through the *muthos,* from nihilistic freedom, literal truth, and negative justice is necessary for the soul to have any meaning or significance. What remains unclear to me is whether this meaning is anything more than a myth.

Kant's Philosophical Use of Mathematics

Negative Magnitudes

Eva Brann

St. John's College, Annapolis

I hope that this consideration of a peculiar little work of great interest by Kant will do honor and give pleasure to my friend Stanley Rosen. The text is an essay called "An Attempt to Introduce the Concept of Negative Magnitudes into Philosophy (*Weltweisheit*)." Its date is 1763.

Its appeal to me has these three aspects: First there is the tentative mode expressed in the title; here we hear Kant's pre-critical voice—not yet the magisterially conclusive notes of the *Critique of Pure Reason* (1781) but a tone at once spiritedly daring and gropingly uncertain. A second and more specific aspect is the inchoate appearance of major elements of the first *Critique*; we can see its thinking come into being. The third appealing aspect of the essay is its pedagogic suggestiveness; for a teacher seeking to help students reflect on mathematical formalisms, it is a useful source.

The piece on negative magnitudes has been eclipsed by its much longer contemporary, "The Only Possible Basis of Proof for a Demonstration of God's Existence (*Dasein*)," dated 1763. This essay was subjected to an extensive and deep analysis by Heidegger in his lecture course of 1927 (*The Problems of Phenomenology*, translated and edited by Albert Hofstadter, Indiana University Press, 1982, ¶ 8); his elucidation of Kant's use of the term "reality" is particularly relevant to the essay on negative magnitudes.

What evidently drew Heidegger's attention to this essay, however, was its brisk definition of *Dasein*—his central word—as "absolute position." When the verb "is" is used not as a copula to relate a subject to its predicate as in "God is omnipotent" but is asserted abruptly, *absolutely*, as in "God is" or "God exists," it signifies, Kant claims, a mere *positing* of an object. By this, in Heidegger's interpretation, Kant means that the object is affirmed by a *knowing subject* as available to *perception*. (I observe, incidentally, that in order to express the character of existence as non-attributive absolute position more adequately, Kant proposes language that anticipates the existential quantifier of propositional logic: We should say not "A narwhal is an animal" but "There exists an animal, the narwhal, which has unicorn-attributes.") In other words, existence is not a predicate and adds no objective attribute to God's essence. Since it is the crux of what Kant first called the ontological argument (whose best known proponent is Anselm) that existence is a necessary attribute of God's essence, Kant's understanding of existence as a non-predicate seems to be a refutation of that proof.

Kant's own demonstration calls on the concept of a "real-ground" (*Realgrund*) that emerges in the essay on negative magnitudes, to be discussed below. This concept in turn involves the postulate that essence is prior to existence and actuality to possibility. Since Heidegger's thinking is dominated by the reverse claim, he is a severe if respectful critic of Kant's understanding. He regards Kant's exposition of existence as a half-way house, situated between the notion of existence as one predicate among others and his own understanding of *Dasein* as "extantness," i.e. "being-at-hand," with respect to things and "being in the world" with respect to human beings.

There is yet another contemporary essay that has bearing on the essay about negative magnitudes, the "Enquiry Concerning the Evidence of the Principles of Natural Theology and Morality, in Answer to a Question Posed by the Royal Academy of the Sciences at Berlin for 1763." The aim of this essay (which did not win the prize) was to establish what evidence and certainty natural theology is capable of; it is thus a discourse on method. It begins with an investigation of the difference between mathematics and metaphysics (a difference that plays a major role even in Kant's last work, the *Opus Postumum*).

Thus both pieces, the one on God's existence and the other on theological certainty, illuminate the essay on negative magnitudes, the former through its concept of an ultimate reality and the latter through its restrictions on the use of mathematics in first philosophy. I will draw on them in my exploration.

* * *

Anyone who has stepped out for a moment from the routine familiarity of operations with signed numbers will have wondered just how, say, 5, +5, |5| differ from each other, and, furthermore, whether +5 and –5 are operations on or qualifications of the number 5. Although his essay concerns numerable magnitudes, especially those discovered in nature, questions of that sort seem to have been going through Kant's mind, as he considered the illuminations that the actual quantification of experience might offer to philosophy.

In the essay on natural theology Kant sets out four definitive reasons why the mathematical *method* is inapplicable to philosophy and is not the way to certainty in metaphysics (¶ 1–4):

1. Mathematical definitions are "synthetic," in the sense that the mathematician does not analyze a given concept, but first synthesizes or constructs it, i.e., puts it together at will. (In the first *Critique* synthesis will have acquired a deeper meaning; it will no longer mean arbitrary construction but an act of the

understanding expressing in the imagination the formative givens of the intuition.) In philosophy or, as Kant says interchangeably, *Weltweisheit*, "world-wisdom" (as distinguished from the scholastic philosophy of mere, unapplied concepts, see *Logic*, Intro. III), on the other hand, definitions are analytic, in the sense that concepts are given to, not made by, the philosopher, and he then endeavors to analyze them into their implicit elements. (In the *Critique* a way will be found for the philosopher too to form pure synthetic judgments.)

2. Mathematics is always concrete, in that the arithmetician symbolizes his numbers and operations perceptibly, and the geometer visibly draws his figures. (In the *Critique* these inscriptions will be within the field of the imaginative intuition.) Philosophers, on the other hand, use words exclusively, and these signify, in Kant's understanding, abstractly, non-pictorially. (In the *Critique* this rift between word and picture is closed.)

3. The mathematician tries to employ a minimum of unproved propositions (i.e., axioms and postulates), while the philosopher makes indefinitely many assumptions, as needed. (In the *Critique* the principles of experience will be systematically restricted.)

4. The objects of mathematics are easy and simple (!), those of philosophy difficult and involved.

In the *Preface* of "The Attempt to Introduce the Concept of Negative Magnitudes into Philosophy" Kant accordingly eschews the introduction of mathematical *method* into philosophy, but censures the neglect of the application of mathematical *matter* to the objects of philosophy. The really useful mathematical doctrines are, however, only those that are applicable to natural science. (This restriction prefigures the use of mathematics in the *Critique*, where its role is the constitution and understanding of the system of nature, i.e., of matter in quantitative and qualitative change.) As a preliminary example, Kant gives the continuity of space, which is, if inexplicitly, postulated in the Euclidean geometry he assumes. The concept of continuity will give insight, he thinks (but explains no further), into the ultimate ground of the possibility of space. (The claim does prefigure the arguments for the establishment of a spatial intuition in the *Critique*.) The main example in this piece will, of course, be the concept of negative magnitudes, which Kant now proceeds to clarify and apply. I shall follow his arguments through the three sections of the essay.

First Section

There are two types of opposition: *logical*, through contradiction and *real*, without contradiction. If contradictories are logically connected, the result is a "negative nothing, an unthinkable" (*nihil negativum irrepresentabile*; now as later in the *Critique*, *representabile* = *cogitabile*, i.e., to think is to represent in the cognitive faculty). Thus a body in motion is a "something" (which is in the *Critique* the highest objective concept, i.e., that of an object in general); so is a body at rest. But a body at the same time in motion and at rest is an unthinkable nothing. It is not so much a non-object incapable of being as a less-than-nothing incapable of being thought.

Real-opposition (*Realentgegensetzung*), on the other hand, involves no contradiction and thus no unthinkability. For this opposition does not cancel the being of the object thus qualified; it remains a something and thinkable (*cogitabile*). Suppose a body impelled in one direction and also driven by a counterforce in the other. The resulting motion may be none = 0, but the body so affected is not a no-thing. Kant calls this result *nihil privativum representabile*, where *privativum* has a dynamic sense, as of an achieved condition. This nothing is to be termed zero = 0.

Kant also refers to real-opposition as real-repugnance (*Realrepugnanz*) because two precisely antagonistic predicates of an object cancel each other, though they do not annihilate the object they qualify. Moreover, it is somewhat arbitrary (or rather, determined by extraneous human interests) which pole is called negative. For example, "dark" may seem to us intrinsically negative, but it is cancelled by its own negation "not-dark" (which might, of course, actually be light). Thus one may say that in real-repugnance both opposing predicates are affirmative.

Kant gives, among others, the following example. Suppose a person owes 100 dollars and is, at the same time, owed this sum. This debtor-lender is worth 0 dollars, since the two conditions cancel each other, but this fact does not cancel *him*, the bearer of these modifications.

Kant then offers an example (slightly adjusted by me) which expands the concept of real-opposition. Suppose a vessel going from Portugal to Brazil is carried due west by an east wind with an impelling force that would cause it to run 12 miles on a certain day, and is also subject to a countervailing current retarding it by 5 miles; the boat's total progress is seven miles a day. Here the result is not = 0. It is clear that Kant regards real-opposition as taking place along a scaled spectrum of quantifiable qualities at whose center there might be (though there is not always) a neutral fulcrum, 0.

If there *is* an "origin," then on one side there are the positive quantities, on the other those that can be regarded either as the relative negatives of the former, or as opposed positives in their own right. Thus the opening question, what is really meant by +5, –5 and |5|, *might* be answered by Kant like this: The plus or minus sign is neither an implicit operation nor a qualification of the number as itself inherently positive or negative, for the number is, like its "absolute" expression |5|, always positive. The plus and minus signs signify rather the *relation of numbers to each other*: –5 is the negative of +5; it is negative only in relation to a positive five. To be sure, since Kant is not speaking of bare numbers but of magnitudes symbolizing quantified properties such as are representable along one dimension, being in real-opposition, so the application to pure numbers is conjectural.

Objects in real-opposition have, of course, many negations besides those directly opposing a positive: a ship sailing westward is also not sailing southward, but its course is in real-opposition only to the eastern direction. Moreover, there are cases, say of lack of motion, which are not the result of real opposing forces but of a total absence of impelling force. Negation that is the result of real-opposition Kant calls *privatio*, that which has no positive ground is called *defectus* or *absentia*. His example of an absent or null result is what we would call potential energy (not to be confused with "potential-opposition," see below): "Thus the thunder that art discovered for the sake of destruction lies stored up for a future war in the threatening silence of an arsenal of a prince, until, when a treacherous tinder touches it, it blows up like lightning and devastates everything around it." Aside from Kant's pacifistic poetry, this example shows that Kant is considering only the magnitudes of *actualized* forces.

It is pretty clear that what Kant is struggling to do is to present a conceptual underpinning for what we call directed magnitudes as they occur in the world, including signed numbers insofar as they represent natural qualities, whose plus or minus tells us whether we are to move respectively to the right or the left along the line-spectrum (conceived as a straight line, where left is negative by convention). Not that Kant is thinking of our mathematical number line.—He does not even mention an origin (=0), and his opposition-spectra are evidently not necessarily infinite in either direction. While he does insist on the relative directionality of negative numbers, insofar as they countermand their positives, he also reiterates that the negatively directed magnitudes are *not* negative numbers if these are regarded as being less than 0.

For the use of directed magnitudes in philosophy it will in fact be essential that the opposed quantities are indeed inherently positive, as will be shown in Section Three. Hence a debt can be called negative capital, falling negative rising, and so on, where it is our perspective that gives a negative emotional tint to one of the terms. Kant sums it up in a basic law and its converse: 1. Real-repugnance takes place between two positives, power against power, which cannot be contradictories but must be of the same kind (while the complement class in a contradiction, e.g., "non-dark objects," is not necessarily of the "same kind" as "dark objects"; they might be invisible objects). 2. Where a positive opposes its proper positive, a real cancellation will occur.

Furthermore certain rules of operation follow. For example, if the opposites are quantitatively equal, their sum will = 0, or A – A = 0, which shows, Kant explains, that both A's are positive (since A = A). Also A + 0 = A and A – 0 = A, since no oppositions are involved. But 0 – A is philosophically impossible since positives cannot be subtracted from nothing: There are no inherently negative qualities and so, as was said, no directed *magnitudes* inherently less than 0 (!). This odd-sounding but unavoidable consequence will have important metaphysical implications.

Real-repugnance, strange though its label be, has an Aristotelian antecedent. It is, I want to argue, a dynamic version of the logical opposition Aristotle calls *contrariety* (*Metaphysics* X, 4). Kant himself says as much in his *Anthropology* of 1798; he there contrasts contradiction or logical opposition (*Gegenteil*) with *contrariety* or real-opposition (*Widerspiel,* ¶ 60).

As a formal logical opposition contrariety occurs in the Square of Opposition, which is a tabulation of the Aristotelian doctrine on the subject: If the basic proposition is "Every S is P," its contradictory is "Some S is not P" and its contrary is "No S is P." Contradictories cannot both be true nor can they both be false, but contraries, though they cannot both be true, *can* both be false; for if not every S be P, yet might it be false that no S is P. Contrary propositions bear a certain formal relation to contrary *terms*, for these cannot both at once belong to an object but they might both fail to belong to it. Thus an object could not be at once pitch black and pure white, but it needn't be either, which is untrue of contradictories, such as black and not-black.

The above paragraph is really a digression to show that it is not contrary propositions but contrary terms denoting qualities that are related to Kant's real-opposition. Contraries are qualities which are not simply in abrupt polar opposition (though their extremes delimit a maximum difference) but are connected through a spectrum of gradations. Aristotle makes privation a particular case of contrariety, and for Kant negation, interpreted as *privatio* (in German *Beraubung*), "deprivation," introduces into some of the ranges of opposition a kind of null point or zero through which the quality goes by degrees into a negative or oppositional mode. (As was noted, not all the spectra have such a center; for example when bodies are brought to rest = 0 by countervailing forces this 0 is not an origin in the spectrum of forces but is a net effect in the bodies' position, measured in spatial extension rather than as qualitative intensity.) Some of Kant's examples will be given below.

What turns contrariety into real-repugnance is the dynamic view Kant takes of this opposition: It means not just being supinely, matter-of-factly opposed; it means being antagonistically, aggressively opposed. Moreover, this striving in many different dimensions of quality is quantifiable in degrees of intensity, as Kant's examples will show.

Second Section

Kant now calls for examples from 1. physics, 2. psychology, 3. morality.

1. In physics his prime example is impenetrability, which is a positive force, a true repulsion that might thus also be called "negative attraction." For attraction is a cause, contrarily directed, by which a body compels others to push into its own space.

2. From psychology (*Seelenlehre*) come Kant's most pungent examples of real-opposition. He raises the question whether aversion could be called "negative pleasure." The fact that in German aversion, *Unlust*, looks like a direct contradictory of pleasure, *Lust*, gives him pause, but he observes that in "real-understanding"

(*Realverstand*), meaning in actual psychic perception, aversion is not just a negation of desire or even its diminution, but a real-repugnance, a positive perception. Then, to illustrate, comes an almost comical quantification: A Spartan mother hears of her son's heroism; a high degree of pleasure ensues, say of 4 degrees. Then comes the news of his death. If the resulting *Unlust* were a mere negation it would equal 0, but 4 + 0 = 4, as if the death made no difference to her delight. Kant concedes however (some notion of a mother's feeling!) that the positive *Unlust* of his death, the real-repugnance, will diminish the mother's *Lust* at her son's bravery by one degree, which will therefore = 3.

In the same vein, disgust is negative desire, hate negative love, ugliness negative beauty, error negative truth, and so on. Kant warns against regarding this terminology as mere word mongering: It is a philosophical pitfall to regard the evils of positive privation as mere defects. Thus Kant is denying, surely quite incidentally, the theological doctrine (found in Plotinus, Augustine, Thomas) of evil as privation of good (*privatio boni*), for in Kant's view in this essay evil, though a relative negation, is yet a positive force.

3. Kant naturally regards his concept of real-opposition as having important uses in "practical prudence" (*Weltweisheit*), that is, applied morality. Non-virtue (*Untugend*) is, in human beings, not a mere denial of virtue (*Tugend*), but a positively negative virtue, vice. This is the case because humans, unlike animals which are morally unendowed, have an "inner moral feeling" that drives them to good actions. For instance they harbor a law of neighborly love. To do bad deeds, human beings have to overcome this natural inclination to good. (A quarter century later, in the second *Critique*, the *Critique of Practical Reason*, 1788, Kant will, on the contrary, see the test of true morality in the overcoming of natural inclinations.)

Thus certain people must make a noticeable effort to engage even in sins of omission (such as neglecting to offer neighborly help), which differ from sins of commission (hurting one's neighbor) only in degree; hence the slide from the one to the other is all too smooth, though the beginning is effortful.

Kant apologizes for what may seem to enlightened readers the prolixity of his exposition. He is writing for a "indocile breed of judges, which, because they spend their lives with a single book, understand nothing but what is contained therein." The book is, I imagine, the Bible.

In an appended Remark, Kant forestalls the notion that the world conceived in such a dynamic balance is capable neither of augmentation nor perfection. He points out 1. that in potential oppositions (to be explained below) though the total quantity of effect may = 0, yet there may be an increase in apparent change, as when bodies widen the distance between them; 2. that it is the very antagonism of natural forces that keeps the world in its perfectly regular courses; and 3. that though desire and aversion do balance each other considered as positive quantities oppositely signed, who would claim that aversion is to be called a perfection? Moreover, though the net quantity of moral action in two people may be the same, yet the quality of the one who acted from the better intention is to be more greatly valued. Kant adds that these calculi don't apply to the godhead which is blessed not through an external good but through itself.

Third Section

Kant introduces this section, which contains his startling application of the concept of real-opposition to metaphysics, by insisting once more that it is a mere attempt, very imperfect though promising: It is better to put before the public uncertain essays than dogmatically decked-out pretenses of profundity. This section is accordingly called "Containing Some Reflections Which Can Be Preparatory for the Application of the Concept Here Thought Out to the Objects of Philosophy." I dwell on this language because it is not a tone familiar to those of us who have spent time with the three *Critiques*.

Everyone easily understands how it is that something *is not*—the positive ground for its being is absent; there is no reason for it to be. But how does something *cease* to be? The question arises because we must understand every passing-away as a negative becoming. As such it requires a real or positive ground.

In the first two sections Kant had spoken of real-opposition or real-repugnance, by which were meant normally apprehensible contrarieties. Now, in the third section, he introduces real-grounds (*Realgründe*). As far as I can make out from the examples, real-grounds are natural, including psychic, causes: forces, powers, and acts exercised by material or psychic agents. "Real" here is used not as in real-opposition, which is opposed to logical contradiction, but it seems to mean "affecting perceptible existence." Real-grounds seem to be a first-level, underlying causal reality, apprehended through its effects. Thus Kant uses "reality"—and, as we shall see, "existence," "being" (*Wesen*), as well as "actuality" (*Wirklichkeit*)—quite loosely in these exploratory essays; Heidegger shows that Kant's later systematic meaning of reality is the "whatness" of a thing, all its possible predicates, its essence, while existence is perceptibility.

Kant's examples are mainly from the soul. It costs real effort to refrain from laughing, to dissipate grief, even to abstract from a manifold representation for the sake of clarity; thus abstraction is negative attention. Even the apparently random succession of thoughts has real grounds which are "hidden in the depths of the mind (*Geist*)," i.e., in what we call the subconscious. Whether the change is in the condition of matter and thus through external causes, or of the mind and thus through inner causes, the necessity for a causal real-opposition remains the same.

Kant is focusing here, it seems to me, on a partial converse to, and a kind of complement of, a question, evidently not asked by the ancients, which is to become a modern preoccupation: "Why does something exist rather than nothing?" It was first raised as a metaphysical problem with a theological answer by Leibniz ("The Principles of Nature and Grace, Founded on Reason," 1714), and was repeatedly taken up by Heidegger (especially in "What is Metaphysics," 1949), who treated it as "the basic question of metaphysics," though to be resolved without recourse to theology.

Leibniz asks for a reason, sufficient and ultimate, to account for the *existence* of a universe of things in progress and finds it in God. Kant, on the other hand, asks for an adequate reason why a present condition in the world should *go out of existence* and finds real-opposition as the cause, though an *unexplained* cause which, Kant says at the end of the essay, he has been and will be thinking about and will in the future write about.—This appears to be a harbinger of Critical works not to appear for almost two decades. Meanwhile the metaphysical consequences are exceedingly strange: *The sum total of all real grounds equals zero*, and "the whole of the world is in itself Nothing." More of this below.

2. Kant says that the theses to be here proposed seem to him "of the most extreme importance." First, however, he distinguishes real-opposition, or as he now calls it, "actual" opposition, from "possible" or "potential" opposition. The latter type of opposites are also each other's negatives, real to be sure, but not, as it happens, in conflict. Thus two forces, each other's opposites, may be driving two bodies in opposite directions: They have the potential to cancel each other's motion but do not actually do so in the given situation. So also one person's desire may be the other's aversion, yet their ability to stymie each other is only a possibility.

Kant then offers the following first general thesis:

> *In all natural changes of the world their positive sum, insofar as it is estimated by the addition of agreeing (not opposed) positions and the subtraction from one another of those in real-opposition, is neither increased nor diminished.*

Recall Newton's Third Law of Motion (*Philophiae Naturalis Principia Mathematica*, 1687):

> *To every action there is opposed an equal reaction: or, the mutual actions of two bodies upon each other are always equal, and directed to contrary parts.*

It is pretty evident that Kant is struggling to ground in metaphysics and apply to the human world the most dynamic of Newton's Laws of Motion or perhaps the Law of the Conservation of Momentum, which is implied in (or, some argue, implies) the law of equal action and reaction; it states that when the forces acting on bodies in the same and in contrary directions are summed (over time) the quantity of motion (i.e., the mass compounded with velocity = mv) is not changed. Kant says without proof that although this rule of mechanics is not usually deduced from the metaphysical ground from which his first thesis is derived, yet it could be. (The first *Critique* will be partly devoted to giving the transcendental grounds of the laws of motion and conservation.)

Not only bodies in motion but souls in emotion obey the law of conservation, and so do humans in action. Astoundingly, Kant really means this: For every "world-change," i.e., every "natural" change (which includes the psychic realm) there is an equal and opposed change, so that the sum of measured final positions, i.e., states of existence taken globally, is equal to what it was before the change, or the total effect = 0.

Every becoming, then, induces an actual or potential counter—becoming or cessation. It can now be seen why Kant introduced potential real-opposition: Kant's forces not only act in opposed pairs but they may act on *different* objects, i.e., the real-opposition may not be actualized in one body or one soul or even in the same mode in one soul. Nevertheless these potential oppositions enter into the summed effects of the world-total.

Kant then goes on to give more concrete non-mechanical examples—though these are not non-natural, because (as will still be true in the *Critiques*) the soul, excepting in its practical-moral employment of reason, is subject to natural dynamic forces. The examples of this third section differ from the ones in the previous section exactly as the course of the exposition requires: They are cases not of actual but of potential real-opposition. Thus if one person's pleasure and displeasure arise not from the same object, but the same ground that caused pleasure in one object is also the true ground for feeling displeasure in *another*, then in analogy to two bodies moving in contrary directions by repulsion, there is one potential real-ground and cause for the positive and the negative feeling. These feelings oppose but also bypass each other; they may cancel each other but need not do so. This is why the Stoic sage had to eradicate all pleasurable drives—because they always engender an associated but diverse displeasure that affects the final value of the pleasure, though perhaps not the actual pleasure itself. Even in the use of the understanding, we find that to the degree that one idea is clarified, the others may be obscured, though surely not by the clarification. Kant adds that in the most perfect Being the zero sum result does not hold, as will be shown.

Now comes the second thesis, which is simply the translation of the first thesis into its causative grounds:

> *All real-grounds of the universe, if one sums those similarly directed and subtracts those opposed to one another, yield a result which is equal to zero.*

Kant immediately states: "The whole of the world is in itself nothing, except insofar as it is something through the will of someone other." Regarded by itself, the sum of all existing reality = 0; the world is an almost Heraclitean system of balanced oppositions, of mutually negating positivities. In relation to the divine will the sum of all possible reality, of the world's existence, is, however, positive. But it itself is not therefore in real-opposition to the divine will; it is not the godhead's relative negation. Consequently existence, i.e., whatever is perceptibly there in the world, is through its *internal* relations nothing, but in relation to the grounding will of the divinity it is something; it is positive. For there can be no real-opposition of the world to the divine will. (This thought is still to be found in the *Opus Postumum.*)

The nullity of the physical and psychical world in its summed effects, the nothingness of the underlying universe of summed causes, and the positivity of creation only in relation to God—Kant presents these results without any discernible pathos, without acknowledgment that this cancellation of the world-whole of effect and cause might bear a religious or moral interpretation beyond the intellectual proof of God's existence. Nor can I discover that he ever reverted to this nullifying construal of the laws of conservation. Perhaps it is to be regarded as a passing notion that served as a spur to further inquiry into the world's relation to its ground. (Kant does hold on to the "law of the antagonism in all community of matter by means of motion"; any divergence from its reciprocity would, he now argues, move the very center of gravity of the universe, *Metaphysical Foundations of Natural Science* of 1786, ¶ 563. In this essay too the notion of real-opposition is put to work in the specific antagonism of repulsion and attraction, forces which between them are responsible for the way matter, i.e., "the movable," fills space. However, the explanation of these forces in their specificity remains an unsolved problem for Kant into the *Opus Postumum.*)

So Kant concludes by making *explicit* the heretofore assumed conversion: Because the internal sum of existence is zero, it follows that the "real-grounds," i.e., the forces and powers producing effects in the world, must be in a corresponding opposition: The realm of existing and possible reality is in itself shot through with grounding polarities that cancel existence, though in respect to the divine will (Kant doesn't speak of "God" in this context) it has positive being (*Wesen*). This overt conclusion of the last section is surprising since it follows close on the assertion that the zero sum of all existence flows necessarily from the grounding being (*Wesen*) of the world; it is hard to tell whether the zero sum of effects is responsible for or is derived from the underlying real-opposition of causes. I hesitate to detect Kant in unwittingly circular reasoning here. (He is, to be sure, the master of intentional circularity in the *Critique*, where the grounds of the possibility of experience are inferred from experience while experience is certified by the grounds. Perhaps the apparent circle in the above paragraph is a precursor of critical thinking.)

The metaphysical intention is however quite clear: 1. The world exists as a complex of quantifiably opposed effects; negative magnitudes express such relative opposition; when summed with their positives they yield zero. 2. Underlying these existences, there is a realm of grounds; these are forces, powers and actions; they are also in mutually cancelling opposition, and, like their effects, they are so only relative to each other. 3. In respect to an ultimate ground they are positive, yet no real-opposition to it is possible. Kant himself knows that he has not yet sufficiently clarified the character of *real-grounds*, nor their relation to the divine will.

His first definition of a real-ground actually occurs in a *General Remark* appended to the third, final section of the essay. A logical ground is one whose consequence can be clearly seen through the law of identity; for example composition is a ground of divisibility, i.e., it is identical with part of the meaning of the concept and can be educed from it analytically. A real-ground, by contrast, has a relation to its effect which, although quite truly expressed as a concept, yet allows no judgment, no true understanding, of the real-ground's mode of action. In other words, the relation of a real cause to its effect is not apprehensible by mere logical analysis. (Here, of course, is formulated the problem that Kant will solve in the *Critique* by means of the "synthetic judgment *a priori*"—the cognition in which real connections are made—not, of course, by the logical law of identity but through our cognitive constitution.)

In this essay, this understanding of a real-ground raises—for the first time for Kant—the fundamental question of causation: "How should I understand it THAT, BECAUSE THERE IS SOMETHING, THERE IS SOMETHING ELSE?" The will of God is something. The existing world is something else altogether. Yet the will of God is the ultimate real-ground of the world's existence. Kant says that no talk of cause, effect, power and act will help: God and world are totally each other's other and yet through one of them the other is posited. And the same holds on a lower level for the natural causes in the world, be they of an event or its cancellation. Kant promises an explication in the future, but for now he remarks only that the relation of real-ground to what is posited or cancelled through it cannot be expressed in a judgment, i.e., a mental "representation of the unity of a consciousness of different representations," but is in fact only a mere, non-analyzable concept, that is, a general representation or a thought (*Logic* ¶ 1, 17). Kant is saying that the relation of an effect to its cause cannot be articulated as an affirmed attribution of a predicate to a subject. It is his way of expressing Hume's rejection of empirically grounded causation. (In the *Critique* the attempt to make God's causal relation to the world comprehensible to reason will be shown to be hopeless, but causality within the world will be grounded in the very constitution of the spatial intuition.)

So ends the essay in which the reflection on negative magnitudes has led, through the concept of real-opposition, directly to the problem of causal connection and indirectly to God as ultimate cause. I have not done justice to the exploratory tone of the essay, to Kant's witty derision of those who get stuck in premature dogmatism, and to his sense of having made a mere, even insufficiently explicated, beginning, but a beginning of something very important: the inquiry into causation.

* * *

An elucidation of some of the matters left unclear in the essay on negative magnitudes occurs in the essay on "The Only Possible Grounds of Proof for a

Demonstration of God's Existence" of the same year (1763), and it seems to me so daring that I cannot resist carrying this exposition a little further. The reflections I shall refer to are not those that most interested Heidegger, the ones concerning existence as position, but those dwelling on the relation of possibility to actuality (or as Kant says, to existence) and on an absolutely necessary "existent" (*Dasein*; First Part, Second and Third Reflections).

Possibility, Kant says, depends entirely on the law of contradiction: That is a possible something the thought of which accords with what is thought in it. This "comparison" of a subject with its predicates through the law of contradiction is to be called *logical* or formal possibility; a triangle cannot have other than three angles, for that would contradict its definition. But it also has something additional, a given character as a triangle in general or in particular, say a right-angled triangle; these are the *data* of its *material* or *real* possibility.

Therewith possibility without prior existence is abolished. For a thing is not only impossible—a "no-thing"—when contradictory predications are made of it, when it is formally impossible, but also when it offers no real material, no *data*, to thinking. For then all thinking ceases, for everything possible must be something thinkable, must offer stuff for thought. It follows that for Kant possibility is conditioned on actuality.

There is, to be sure, no formal inner contradiction in the brute negation of all existence, since nothing has been posited to begin with. But that there be a possibility and that nonetheless nothing actual exist—that *is* contradictory. For if nothing exists, nothing material is given to be thought about. Therefore to say that nothing exists is, according to the previous analysis of existence (*Dasein*) as a positing act of thought, to think and say that there is absolutely nothing. And then to add that something is possible is clearly self—contradictory, for no material for thinking at all is given. Thinking involves material givens; without them it contradicts its own character. Thus the cancellation of the material data of possibility also cancels possibility. *It is absolutely impossible that nothing should exist.* I understand Kant to mean that one can—logically—deny all existence, but having denied it one cannot then retrieve its possibility.

The only really elucidating example of a necessary existence is, Kant says, that of the unique Subject (i.e., God), to be touched on below. Meanwhile, if we ask, for example, how existence precedes possibility in respect to "body," we may grant that the concept body contains no logical impossibility, yet to call on its predicates of extension, impenetrability, force, to be the *data* of possibility (either assumed or experienced) in the absence of actually existing, given bodies, is quite unwarranted. Without such data the concept "body" is empty. (We see here the forerunner of the dictum in the first *Critique* that the mere functions of the understanding are empty without the givens of intuition.)

Then Kant explains the concept of an absolutely necessary existence. To say that it is that whose contradictory is in itself impossible is a merely nominal explanation. Since existence is no predicate, its denial can never conflict with other predicates. However to deny the positing of the thing itself is not a denial of predicates but of something else, and hence is not contradictory. Kant is looking not for logical but "real-necessity" (*Realnotwendigkeit*), for what cannot be denied in any "real-explanation" (*Realerklärung*). This is it: "What I am to regard as absolutely nothing and impossible must be that which eradicates all thinking." Now total nonexistence in fact cancels all the material and data of thought, and hence it is impossible.

It follows that there is an absolutely necessary being. For all possibility assumes something actual, whose cancellation would itself cancel all inner possibility, i.e., the real coherence of predicates. That part of existence, on the other hand, which *does not* provide the material for all that is thinkable, but without which there would still be matter for thought—and thus possibility—that part is, although in a real sense possible, yet in the same sense conditionally possible, i.e., contingent; not *all* existence is necessary. (In his *Inaugural Dissertation* of 1770 Kant will say that all worldly substances are in fact contingent since they maintain reciprocal relations, while necessary beings are independent, ¶ 19.)

Kant now goes on to show that the *one* necessary, non-contingent existence is God, a being that is one, simple, unchangeable, eternal, and a spirit. But its philosophically most important attribute is that it is (in scholastic terms) the *ens realissimum,* the most real being, that which contains the highest reality. For it contains all the givens, the *data*, of possibility either as directly determining other existences or as being the real-ground of which they are the consequences. (In the *Critique*, the *ens realissimum* will be relegated to the status of an ideal of reason, a regulative idea that marshals our thoughts of the world.)

Does the attribution to God of the most and the highest reality mean that *all* realities, i.e., all real attributes, must be assigned to God? Here the concepts of the essay on negative magnitudes come into their own: It is common doctrine that one reality can never contradict another reality, since both are truly affirmed. But this assertion leaves out of account the notion of real-repugnance, i.e., of real-opposition. Realities may, indeed must, oppose each other without one of them being in itself negative.—That was the essay's main finding. In God, however, even real-opposition cannot take place, because that would result in privation or defect and would contradict God's maximal reality. Thus God contains no realities in opposition to his positive predicates; for example, the real-oppositions attributable to bodies, such as being subject to contrary forces, cannot without contradiction belong to a being that has intellect and will; hence the *ens realissimus* has clear positive determinations.

It is, it seems to me, implicit in these pre-Critical essays that neither existence (*Dasein*) nor actuality (*Wirklichkeit*) is as yet convertible with subjective perceptibility, though both will indeed be so later, as Heidegger observes. Instead these terms mean objective givenness, thereness, be it sensorily received or essentially apprehended. The road to the first *Critique* will be the development of this conversion from the object of experience as given *to* the subject to its being constituted *in* the subject. The roots, however, of the primacy of the subject are already present in one respect, now to be shown.

* * *

There is, then, necessarily a God, a being comprehending not all, but all the highest positive reality. He is a real-ground of the world; the world, in turn, amounts quantitatively to a self-cancelled nothing, though it may well be qualitatively positive. One way to get hold of this—by Kant's own frequent confession—still inchoate complex is to ask just how daring a departure from tradition it is.

Kant, who without naming Anselm is attempting to rebut his argument for the existence of God, calls his own proof "ontological" (later in the *Critique* that is what he will call Anselm-type proofs). Anselm argues (*Proslogium* 2, 4) that God is a maximal being whose essence is to be thought as largely and inclusively as possible; thus it must include the predicate existence. This is what Kant denies, but he accepts something that seems to me even deeper in, or rather behind, Anselm's argument: that when *I must think* that God exists, he exists. But this is thinking of the type Kant himself engages in on an even deeper level when he makes God's existence follow from the existential necessities of thinking: What is required for thinking to be possible must necessarily exist. Here Anselm and Kant are brothers under the skin. I can think of counterarguments to their assumption (though without being quite persuaded by them): Is it utterly impossible that a being which *must* exist in thought fails to exist in fact—is it so totally unthinkable? Is it not possible to think that thinking can do utterly without the material, the data grounded either in a highest reality, as in the essay on God's existence, or in some sensory influx from a transcendent outside, as in the first *Critique?* Is it unthinkable that possibilities do not disappear when actualities fail, but that there is spontaneous, autonomous, self-generated, worldless thinking? Kant has, it seems, levered the Cartesian-type certification for personal existence; *Cogito, ergo sum*, "I think, therefore I am," into a proof of God's existence: *Cogito ergo Deus est,* "I think therefore there is a God." But what if "I think" entails instead: "*I* make the world," if I myself give myself the *data*?

Such misgivings and intimations aside (they will become Kant's own in the *Opus Postumum*), he has found an approach to a question that seems never to have occupied the ancients and was, as was mentioned, first formulated by Leibniz (*Principles of Nature and Grace*, 7): "Why does something exist rather than nothing? For 'nothing' is simpler and easier than 'something.'" Leibniz finds the answer in the ultimate sufficient reason called God. Kant argues the other way around: Nothing is *harder* than something, indeed impossible for thought, and

God becomes necessary not as a sufficient reason inferred from the world's existence but as a necessary being implied by human thinking.

In 1763, having proved in one essay the necessary existence of the highest and most real ground and so (for the time being) answered Leibniz's question, Kant is left with the unanswered next question of the essay on negative magnitudes quoted above, which he prints in block letters: "How can I understand THAT BECAUSE SOMETHING IS, SOMETHING ELSE MIGHT BE?" In other words, having proved God's existence, how can I understand him, or his agents in the world, as causal *grounds*? (This very same question will be presented, as was said, in the *Critique* as unanswerable by logical thinking alone, but solved with the aid of the a priori relations given in the intuition.)

By 1781, the year of the first edition of the first *Critique*, Kant will have given up not only his own so circumstantially prepared ontological proof, the only possible one, as he had thought, but also in principle any expectation of a theoretical demonstration of God's existence—and so, it seems, any rational explanation of the first question, why there is existence at all.

The second question, on the other hand, is just what the *Critique* addresses. Kant distinguishes cosmological freedom, the power to make an absolute beginning, from causality according to natural law, which is rule-governed consequence acting within what already exists. An insight into the first, into absolute causation, i.e., creation, Kant shows, is in principle impossible for us, for it is beyond the limits of human reason. The second causality, that of lawful succession, of cause and effect in natural events, is grounded in the synthesizing character of our cognitive constitution. The essays here considered show Kant—and for my part I find this intellectually moving—casting about for disparate clues to the concepts and claims which would one day come to cohere in his master edifice.

Origins of Enchantment

Conceptual Continuities in the Ontology of Political Wholeness

Waller R. Newell
Carleton University

> "The Greek *form* is replaced by the modern *concept*; this in turn reflects the initially ambiguous shift from nature to subjectivity as the locus of objectivity."
>
> Stanley Rosen, *G.W.F. Hegel*, p. 143.

I

In this essay, I will explore a specific motif in the meaning of political community common to the works of some major European thinkers including Rousseau, Schiller, Hegel, Marx, Nietzsche and Heidegger. My specific aim is to set forth some continuities in the ontology of political wholeness that characterizes German Idealism as a mode of discourse—continuities that converge in what I term (for reasons I will elaborate momentarily) the transposition of eros. Common to the political philosophies I will explore is the exploration of a holistic conception of civic community that provides the existential and theoretical contexts for the practice of citizenship, the elucidation of rights and duties, the debate about justice, the emergence of civic virtue, and the pursuit of satisfaction and meaning on both an individual and a communitarian level. In this respect, the tradition of German Idealism, originating in the influence of Rousseau, attempts to restore the classical conception of political ontology as against the general (although not unexceptionable) assumption of Enlightenment political theory that human beings are individualistic by nature and that, consequently, the social contract has no more than an instrumental value to its members.[1]

1 Shlomo Avineri, *Hegel's Theory of the Modern State* (Cambridge, 1982), pp. 134–35; Isaiah Berlin, *The Roots of Romanticism* (Princeton, 1999), pp. 124–27; Karl Lowith, *From Hegel to Nietzsche,* Green trans. (Doubleday Anchor, 1967), p. 306; Bernard Yack, *The Longing for Total Revolution* (Princeton, 1986), pp. 145–62; Steven B. Smith, *Hegel's Critique of Liberalism: Rights in Context* (Chicago, 1989), pp. 7–9.

Aristotle had consolidated the communitarian tradition in pre-liberal political theory with his conception of the political community as a life-long education, in which the moral and intellectual virtues solicited by the responsibilities of collective self-government also cultivate the soul's potential for happiness, so that informed and vigorous citizenship is at once altruistic with respect to one's fellow citizens and eudaimonistic with respect to each citizen's fulfillment. Rousseau and his German devotees consciously retrieve this expansive and pedagogical understanding of the political community to mitigate what they believed to be modern liberalism's tendencies toward crass materialism, philistinism, plutocracy and political apathy. But at the same time, they believed it was possible to combine the holism of the classical conception of civic community with the positive achievements of modernity: the Enlightenment's insistence on the irreducible autonomy and dignity of every individual *qua* individual, as against the sometimes despotic incursions of feudal and religious collectivism. The grandeur of German Idealism springs from this noble longing for what Schiller called "the third realm" or, as Schelling evoked it with an allusion to Homer, mankind's journey home from the lonely odyssey of modern individualism to the Ithaca of the coming age, a homeland in which human beings are free as individuals, but within the comforting contexts of history, tradition and the indeterminate richness of the life-world.[2]

But if the thinkers I am exploring in this essay share in common the vision of a coming restoration of Aristotelian community and civic friendship without sacrificing modern autonomy, their works are haunted by a problem unique to modernity: the troubling status of reason in relation to life and the pursuit of happiness. For the ancient thinkers, no such conflict between reason and happiness was conceivable, either in principle or in wisely guided practice. Aristotle and the other classical thinkers present civic life as an ascent from lower to higher kinds of perfection, from bodily moderation to informed citizenship and, on the basis of the moral qualities perfected through serving the common good, a final ascent towards the transcendental good that endows the cosmos with harmony, order and proportionality. As Aristotle puts it, the wholeness pursued by the city is ultimately an instantiation of the wholeness and repose that govern the cosmos (*Politics* 1325b23). The polis points to the cosmopolis of reason and happiness by way of the civic virtues. Thus, the mind's ascent toward philosophical contemplation is at the same time the soul's progressive achievement of emotional and aesthetic satisfaction. Transcendence is both theoretically enlightening and psychologically therapeutic.

Modern philosophy, by contrast, begins by demolishing the classical teleology linking the human pursuit of wholeness through the civic association with the

2 Friedrich Schiller, *Letters on the Aesthetic Education of Man,* Snell trans. (Ungar, 1965), pp. 112–13; Schelling, *Samtliche Werke*, Pt.1, vol.3, pp. 628, 341; *The Ages of the World,* Frederick de Wolfe Bolman, Jr., trans. (New York, 1942), pp. 84, 90–91.

wholeness that characterizes the cosmos, whereby, in pursuing civic satisfaction, we are cultivating the divine spark in our souls that connects us to the beautiful harmonies of the world. By reducing the cosmos to the Baconian and Newtonian physics of matter in motion, modern philosophy treats nature as the sub-phenomenal substratum of chance out of which visible phenomena unfathomably issue. The reasoning power by which we classify those random motions and assign their causality is accordingly severed from the objective being of the cosmos and re-conceptualized as an anthropocentric faculty. By this means human beings, finding themselves in a world of dangerously random and morally purposeless forces, impose their wills on nature and re-shape it to provide an artificial state that will protect them from its ravages. This will also protect them from their own propensities to exploitation and mastery—the upsurge of what Machiavelli calls "the malignity of Fortuna" into human nature through the passions.

Whereas the classics conceived of nature in terms of *telos*, form and final cause, modernity identifies nature with origin and genesis. Thus, whereas for the classics nature entails reason, order and virtue, for the moderns—illustrated early on by Machiavelli—nature is a sub-phenomenal void of origination which is indifferent to the superstructures of reason, order and virtue, if not outright hostile to them ("the malignity of Fortuna" again). Consequently, whereas for the classics, reason and man's place in the cosmos are entailed by nature, for the moderns, reason is an anthropocentric quality which enables man to fight back and perhaps control or master Fortuna. Whereas for the classics, the passions properly understood lead to their own self-transcendence, so that in properly fulfilling our erotic longings (as sketched by Diotima in Plato's *Symposium*) our soul is ultimately led to an approximation of the intelligible harmony and repose that characterize the cosmos, for early moderns such as Machiavelli and Hobbes, nature repulses our efforts to find happiness. Fortuna is not beneficent, but she does teach us the valuable lesson that our longings for happiness have no ontological or metaphysical grounding in the non-human world. When we realize that nature is alienating, we will be goaded into summoning from ourselves the willpower to fight back and change our natural circumstances. By attributing to the examples of the most "outstanding virtue" the capacity to "introduce into matter whatever form they pleased," Machiavelli transfers to the "virtue of their (that is, the greatest princes') mind" a capacity to fashion or re-fashion nature *ex nihilo* traditionally reserved for God.[3]

The great counter-movement to these identifications: of nature with genesis and of virtue with the anthropocentric will to assert mastery over nature, is crystallized by Rousseau. Like the early modern thinkers, Rousseau also identifies nature with genesis. Like them, therefore, he also rejects the classical view that

3 Niccolo Machiavelli, *The Prince,* Mansfield trans. (Chicago, 1985), p. 25.

reason, order and virtue are entailed by nature—understood as a teleological conception of the cosmos. Unlike the early modern thinkers, however, Rousseau regards nature as beneficent and as the source of human happiness and repose. He thus restores the classical concern with happiness on the basis of the modern account of nature as genesis. For the classics, happiness was an ascent from the moral virtues to the intellectual virtues, so that the aspirations of the mind for its fullest satisfaction entailed along the way our duties as citizens. A few progressed far enough in the development of the contemplative virtues that their minds were drawn close to, and in some manner harmonized with, the ordered cycles of the cosmos. For Rousseau, by contrast, happiness is the immediate and immanent gift of nature to all human beings. Not only is it not necessary for us to ascend through the moral and intellectual virtues, but these products of civilization alienate us from the sweet sentiment of existence which is given to every human. In his *Reveries*, Rousseau often describes natural happiness as a complete loss of self, of the awareness that one is a self, not through the transcendence of the self in the direction of the eternal, but through a descent behind, or recession from, the self into the pre-self, into the primordial origins "without taking the trouble to think."[4] Rousseau transposes to the origins that erotic wholeness which for the classics could only be aimed at through a teleological ascent solicited and guided by the final end. For the early moderns, nature is bad and reason is the anthropocentric tool for its repression and reform. For Rousseau, nature is good, and therefore modern rationality lacks even the utilitarian or instrumental beneficence that it possesses for Machiavelli or Hobbes. The question inherited from Rousseau by German Idealism is vexing: How can reason be reconciled with nature understood as a beneficent, life-affirming, world-generating void of origination, given that the beneficence of the origins invalidates the modern identification of reason with utilitarian mastery but at the same time prevents any return to the classical account of nature as an orderly cosmos that entails reason?

One answer to this question is broached by Rousseau himself, and given full expression by Kant. Human beings are necessarily divided into (a) a natural happiness to which they cannot return under the conditions of civilization and (b) a self-conscious, rational and willing half that alienates them from the unself-conscious sweetness and repose of the origins. Ordinarily, reason and will are used to stimulate the desires beyond their simple natural equilibrium and devise the means to gratify these sophisticated, inflamed passions. By formalizing the will, by willing only what can be willed for mankind in general, our alienated, unnatural half can turn back against the natural desires corrupted by civilization and paradoxically restore a simulacrum of the equality, austerity and repose that nature originally gave us as an unself-conscious gift for which no such spiritual

4 Jean-Jacques Rousseau, *Les Reveries du Promeneur Solitaire*. Jacques Voisine ed. (Garnier-Flammarion, 1964), pp. 95–105.

striving is necessary. The generalized will has willing itself as its object to the degree humanly possible, and therefore does not have as its object the satisfaction of any natural inclination with its empirical correlates in the world governed by necessity and scientific reasoning. The generalized will, or will to will, cannot heal the division in the self and return it to nature. But it can achieve a certain dignity, employing the purified will as a bulwark against the corruption of whatever remains in us of nature's beneficent residue.

The other answer, developed by Schiller, Schelling and Hegel among others, is to argue that this divided Kantian self is both unbearable and unnecessary. According to Schiller (and, on some readings, the Kant of *The Critique of Judgement*), the divided self can achieve unity through aesthetic fulfillment. Nature as a void of origination expresses itself, achieves a certain kind of flowering, as the work of art—as Schiller puts it, aesthetic education is a path to freedom "through" beauty.[5] We do not so much will art as the product of an isolated individual ego as let it come forth through us, an upsurge from the origins that finds clarity, form and sublimity through its interaction with human creative faculties. In Schelling's and Hegel's idealism, nature as the world-artist develops and expresses itself, rising out of the primordial depths and flowering throughout the millennia, like an enormous symphony made up of many cultural and artistic achievements. History unifies world and self. For the classics, the soul achieves unity by rising toward and approximating, through the cultivation of the moral and intellectual virtues, the eternal harmonies of the cosmos. For German Idealism, nature as genesis unifies the human self by enveloping the self in its mutable, time-bound processes, and expresses itself by rising to culture through the human self. As Schelling describes the ages of mankind, the history of the world mirrors Homer's *Iliad* and *Odyssey*, a modern period of struggle, mastery and the emergence of human subjectivity, individuality and autonomy, followed by the current era in which this liberated individual, longing for a reconciliation with nature, history, culture and an organic feeling of unity with other people, embarks on the journey home to Ithaca.

II

Let me sum up my argument to this point: When Rousseau and his German heirs attempt their noble return to the holistic politics of the ancients, they are faced with a dire difficulty. Whereas, for the classics, reason was the sole reliable path to natural satisfaction, the early moderns saw it very differently. For them, reason

5 M. H. Abrams, p. 185, *Natural Supernaturalism* (Norton, 1973), p. 185; Arthur Lovejoy, *The Great Chain of Being* (Harvard, 1936), pp. 293–98; Hans-Georg Gadamer, *Reason in the Age of Science*, F.G. Lawrence trans. (The MIT Press, 1983), p. 35.

is an instrument for the conquest of nature, including our own natures, which, lacking any intrinsic potential for virtue, are necessarily prone to war unless they are curbed by the artificial restraints of the social contract. Whereas, for the ancients, human reason is but a reflection of the noetic harmony that structures the cosmos, making nature both intelligible and beneficent, for the early moderns, reason has no necessary mooring in the patterns of nature; these regularities are evidently indifferent and perhaps even hostile to human longings for happiness. I now want to argue that the tensions within German Idealism, the profound and sometimes even hostile debates among its major expositors, flow from their differing attempts to reconcile this modern conflict between nature and reason, or, as it is variously expressed, the is and the ought, the real and the ideal, or happiness and virtue.

The key to their resolution of this conflict is a fundamental re-thinking of being, in which the modern understanding of nature as non-teleological sub-phenomenal motion is endowed with the capacity of the classical conception of nature to offer human beings a trans-human grounding and communal context for their longings for moral and intellectual self-cultivation. I term this fundamental re-thinking the transposition of eros. I use the term eros in the Platonic sense of an ordered longing for wholeness. That longing for wholeness is now transposed from an orientation toward the motionless super-sensible stability identified by classical metaphysics with the transcendental Good to the mysterious richness of genesis and indeterminacy, the enchantment of the origins. Ontologically, this re-thinking of nature as beneficent (as in the classical view of the cosmos) but also time-bound and generative (as in the modern view of nature as motion) provides a common conceptual substructure for Schelling's understanding of Absolute Identity ("the infinitely finite"), Hegel's concept of Spirit as a "self-originating wealth of shapes," Marx's concept of species-being, Nietzsche's concept of the whole as the "world artist" expressing itself as will to power, and what Heidegger evokes as the call of Being.[6] What generates the turbulent debate within German Idealism from Schelling to Heidegger is how this organic, holistic conception of nature as a dynamic equilibrium of life forces expresses itself through its human agents in the mediating forms of civic and aesthetic wholeness. In other words, does Being develop itself out of its matrix of origination into a transparent metaphysics and a final teaching about politics, culture and justice? Does Being progress?

Thus, I am suggesting that German Idealism can be usefully understood as an internal dialogue about the meaning of the transposition of eros, the fundamental Rousseauan inversion of classical teleology whereby nature is identified

6 Stanley Rosen, *G.W.F. Hegel*, (Yale, 1974), pp. 56–62; F.W.J. Schelling, *Bruno or On the Natural and Divine Principle of Things*, Vater trans. (SUNY 1984), pp. 146–53.

with a limitless and teeming *Ursprung*, a self-revealing, life-affirming and spiritually energizing matrix of origination. The internal dialogue centers around how that matrix of origination issues through human action so as to come to presence, to be immanentized, within the phenomenology of observable human civilization. All of the thinkers within this continental tradition of political philosophy are radical de-subjectivists. Not one of them shares the prevailing assumption of the Enlightenment that human beings are first and foremost individuals with no intrinsic connection to one another or to the currents of time, history and heritage. Every one of them believes that human beings find themselves always already enmeshed with a tacit underlying communality, more or less accessible under the more or less alienating conditions of the present epoch of modernity. Each argues that, in order for human beings to be free and happy within a co-operative association, they must somehow break the shackles of their current alienation and re-orient themselves toward this immanent communality.

Of course this question sharpens the debate concerning the precise relationship between the immanent communality granted us by the matrix of origination, and the phenomenology in which it manifests itself. To what extent is the phenomenology the dialectical ladder to the sought-for communality? To what extent is it, on the contrary, an iron cage of determinacy and reified social and political hierarchies that cut us off from the life-world? On the basis of this debate over the relationship of the phenomenology of everyday experience (including authority, civic life and aesthetic culture) to the underlying ontology of the origins (and Rousseau's transposition of eros) emerge the more familiar debates between Hegel and Marx or Heidegger and Nietzsche concerning the philosophy of history, religion, art and the question of the best social order.

Hegel locates in the mediating circumstances of the historical process those limitations on human will and spontaneity that the classics had located in the eternal structures of the cosmos. Progress for Hegel is thus cumulative rather than revolutionary. Marx and Nietzsche, despite profoundly differing views on other issues, both object to so much of the agenda for active historical creativity being reserved for the objective dimension of the historical process and claim it instead for the dynamic transformative powers of the human bearers of emancipation. Heidegger in turn rebels against what he sees as this increasing subjectivization of the immanent self-presencing of history as "destining" (*Geschictlichkeit*).[7] He identifies the will to creative liberation through historical action as the cause, rather than the remedy, of modern man's alienation and calls instead for a pensive submission to the currents of temporality that ground our tacit experience of being-in-the-world and being-with-others prior to all assertions of will to reconstruct the environment.

7 Martin Heidegger, *Sein und Zeit* (Max Niemeyer, 1979), p. 385.

Hegel had famously argued that the grand historical symphony evoked by Schelling must include the unedifying world of modern Lockean liberalism, utilitarianism and analytical and empirical rationality. Schelling had understood nature in terms of an unfathomable primordial genesis which expresses itself by distinguishing itself from itself as a delineable aesthetic experience, a work of art, music or literature. For Hegel, too, Being is a genesis that distinguishes itself from itself in order to "be" in the concrete phenomenal sense. But, Hegel argues, Being negates its own distinctions cumulatively, and therefore actually progresses teleologically, in contrast with Schelling's view that Being is a plenum within which discrete aesthetic phenomena emerge alongside each other without a dialectical resolution in one direction over time. Hegel's understanding of Spirit transposes the classical account of teleology as a recurrently repeatable ascent from origins to ends *sub specie aeternitatis* to a single ascent by the entire human species in time from the earliest epochs to the present, so that in the *Phenomenology of Spirit* he uses the imagery of Plato's Divided Line to describe the progress of history from the parti-colored mists of the dawn of self-consciousness to the "spiritual daylight of the present."[8] By presenting *Geist* as a process that unfolds and flowers by progressively negating itself "by crucifying its own distinctions and preserving them through their crucifixion" Hegel claims to have synthesized the modern conquest of nature (Machiavelli and Hobbes) with the anti-modern or what we would now term post-modernist longing for immediate wholeness and immanence (Rousseau and the Romantics). Both poles of modernity, Hegel argues, are abstractions from Spirit, independent from one another only in the act of analytical understanding, always unified in experience and therefore always mediated and tempered by one another. Truth, in Hegel's formulation, is the unity of Subject and Substance.[9] That is to say, truth is the synthesis of the modern subjectivistic conquest of nature with its anthropocentric and utilitarian conception of rationality and the Schellingian longing for the self's reabsorption into the primordial void of origination. This synthesis is meant to prevent both a Romantic flight from the muck of politics into merely personal aesthetic enjoyments and the Jacobin impulse to shatter and re-construct all human institutions so as to return us to the Arcadian bliss of the origins.

With Heidegger, we reach the dismantling of this grand Hegelian edifice, the science of Spirit, and hence one of the explicit founders of post-modernism. Heidegger's philosophy may be characterized briefly but not misleadingly as historicity without teleological progress or development. Much like Schelling in some ways, for Heidegger, Being is a genesis that unfolds, that presences itself as an art work or a historical community, but does not develop. Unlike Hegelian

8 G.W.F. Hegel, *Phanomenologie des Geistes*, Hoffmeister ed. (F. Meiner, 1952), # 177.

9 Hegel, *Phanomenologie*, #17–19; Michael Rosen, *Hegel's Dialectic and its Criticism* (Cambridge, 1982), pp. 78–84; Abrams, pp. 217–37.

Geist, for Heidegger, Being does not seek a focal point within itself, does not seek to become self-conscious, does not try to become an object "for itself," thereby using its human agents to develop itself through struggle, negation, victory and progress. Being reveals. Being gives. Because Being is to be understood in terms of the primordial origins rather than in terms of the ontic, thingly or metaphysical end, Being is fundamentally characterized by finitude, impermanence and perishability. Historicity without progress might also be termed existentialism. But Heidegger also claims in *Being and Time* to ground phenomenology (including the historical existence of peoples) in his primordialist account of Being. Heidegger's phenomenology, however, is not like Hegel's, for whom phenomenology reveals the "shapes" of self-consciousness as they cumulatively and progressively unfold Spirit's odyssey. Heidegger's phenomenology, by contrast, limns the cycles of existence, of time-bound being in the world, that form the deep ontological structures of any possible world.

Like many of his generation, Heidegger did not think it possible to believe in the teleological progress of history after the events of World War One and the crisis of modernity they both expressed and radicalized, leading to the prolonged political, economic and cultural upheavals of the twenties and thirties. The modern, subjectivistic side of *Geist* that Hegel thought would be tamed and mediated by the longing for wholeness (while simultaneously shaking the latter out of its tendency to Romantic flight, sentimentality and despair) had burst forth from the constraints of Hegelian mediation to reveal itself as the imperative for global technological domination. Heidegger's response to the failure of the Hegelian science of Spirit to contain the modernist pole of the dialectic was to dismantle this dialectic altogether so as to liberate Being from its entanglement with reason understood as culminating in modern technological rationality. Heidegger's phenomenology deconstructs the historical evolution of reason and returns to the sheer indeterminacy out of which, in Hegel's account, it had dialectically developed. Heidegger's remedy for the assimilation of reason to technology is to re-inaugurate the transposition of eros at is most original and primordial level, prior to all causal and analytical mediation, and all positive accounts of the teleological progress of history. No Hegelian synthesis of Subject and Substance is possible, according to Heidegger, because history itself has revealed that Western reason as such (not just modern rationality, but down to its very origins in Plato and even the pre-Socratics) is metaphysical and hence, even since Anaximander and certainly after Plato, incipient global technology.

For Heidegger, the collapse of modern rationality is the collapse of Western philosophy as such, the discrediting of its search for eternal clarity and permanence. Now, instead of this ocular assault upon Being, we can only listen and wait for Being to touch us again from within the depths of its finitude through our finitude as mortals. This involves returning to the origins of the Western tradition of philosophy and re-thinking works such as Plato's in light of the contemporary withdrawal of Being. This is not a question of exposing Plato as wrong, because Being needs to "presence" as form. But we do need to re-think Plato in order to see how what is properly only one moment in the unfolding of Being the moment of visible "presencing" or "lighting" was at the very outset of the West's destiny elevated as the only intelligible perspective on Being, so that Being was reified as another and higher kind of thing.[10] When Being is reified as an exclusively thingly mode of being, the primordial origins of Being are then stigmatized and banished to a lower realm of mere appearance, becoming, change and decay. Being as *eidos, telos* and final cause then turn back on Being as genesis and attempt to reconstruct the latter in light of these stable archetypes of perfection, the ontological origin of technology, which for Heidegger is the distinct destining of Being for the West. Thus, whereas Leo Strauss, for example, would argue that only with modern thinkers like Machiavelli and Hobbes does reason become an instrument for the conquest of nature and technological domination, for Heidegger, the West's destiny as "the working out of metaphysics as technology" is already launched in Plato.

III

I should make it clear at this point my own preferences in this debate over the transposition of eros. For, although Hegel's philosophy is only one variant of what I have termed the transposition of eros, my approach to the whole paradigm of continental political thought is in a sense Hegelian. As we have observed, Hegel's answer to the question of how freedom and nature might be reconciled through educational culture is the teleological progress of history. For us moderns, in other words, the place occupied by the soul in the classical understanding of political community is replaced by history—or, in Hegelian terms, the historical process—in a deliberate assimilation of theological terminology, by *Geist* or Spirit. History is a phenomenology of the (Holy) Spirit.[11]

The key to understanding Hegel's conception of Spirit is his argument, already touched upon, that "truth is the unity of subject and substance," or, as he otherwise expresses it, the unity of Understanding (*Verstand*) and Love. By the former, he means (as had Schiller) the cold analytical thought premised on modern man's alienation from nature and his growing power to master it through scientific knowledge and technique. The political parallel of this analytical dissection of nature's parts came with liberalism's vision of human beings as

10 Heidegger, *Sein und Zeit*, pp. 3–7.

11 Hegel, *ibid.; Early Theological Writings*, Knox trans.(University of Pennsylvania, 1971), pp. 303–13; Werner Marx, *Hegel's Philosophy of Spirit* (Harper and Row, 1975), pp. 54–57; Charles Taylor, *Hegel* (Cambridge, 1975), pp. 48, 67–68; Smith, pp. 184–86; Fred R. Dallmayr, *G.W.F. Hegel: Modernity and Politics* (Sage, 1993), p. 33.

isolated individuals impersonally represented by the contractual state. Indeed, for Hegel, the category of *Verstand* comprehends the whole complex of phenomena that we identify with modernity—the interlocking modalities of rights discourse, behavioristic reasoning, and the derivation of empirical observations in a logically necessary manner from Newtonian general laws.

Love, by contrast, embodies our feeling of unity with our fellow human beings and with nature. Spirit reconciles these two dimensions of existence. For Hegel, history is a double-sided quest for solidarity and fulfillment. The progressive pursuit of Understanding (including individual rights and the scientific power to master nature which those rights both maximize and pre-suppose) itself unexpectedly brings about the reign of Love. The human race pursues its freedom through the outward and ostensible conquest of nature. But the Spirit of history has all along been simultaneously embarked on an odyssey of fulfillment that it pursues through its locus: mankind's pursuit of freedom. The result is the embodiment of reason and freedom in the present age, specifically in the form of the nation-state with its representative institutions, personal liberties, tolerance, cultural and religious communities and its recognition of human dignity whether it is expressed through our autonomy as individuals or through our overlapping memberships in the various communal contexts that are open to us.[12]

Viewed subjectively or from a strictly secular and human perspective, this historical process is the human pursuit of freedom beyond the contradictions placed on it by the present. However, viewed more comprehensively and therefore more adequately from the perspective of Objective Spirit, the progress of history is Spirit's own development as it supersedes itself through the agency of man. Because of this double-sided "negation of the negation," history can be viewed as the cumulative progression through an ever-richer series of mediations. In this way, the Hegelian dialectic tries to provide a way of understanding social and political existence that gives fair weight to both the communitarian longing for repose and reconciliation and to the more aggressive and transformative aspects of modern autonomy, the "labor of the negative" in history, embracing mankind's pursuit of political, economic and technological mastery over the natural environment. For Hegel, both dimensions—both Love and Understanding—are essential for a stance toward civic existence that is both humane and realistic. Guided by this synthesis, we can steer between the extremes of Jacobin fanaticism—the attempt to impose from above, by revolutionary fiat, a single global pattern for rational political and economic organization—and the Romantic retreat into a purely apolitical realm of aesthetic bliss. Hegel's successors tend to exaggerate one side or the other of this synthesis of community and autonomy and choosing either communitarian spontaneity bereft of purposive rationality or the limitless reconstruction of the world.

12 Avineri, pp. 180–84.

In the lectures published as the *Philosophy of History*, Hegel remarks that "nothing vanishes in Spirit."[13] Contrary to a persistent misconception, Hegel does not embrace a "stage theory" of history in which one era is seen as manifestly and decisively outmoding its predecessor in a relentless march forward. Indeed, his phenomenology is among other things an attempt to moderate this hubristic modern assumption that the past has nothing to teach us about freedom or culture, an arrogance wonderfully summed up by Flaubert in the masterpiece of his fictitious artist Pellerin taking the shape of a giant canvas depicting Christ piloting a locomotive through a virgin forest, entitled "Progress." Although Hegel does present an historical chronology tracing the history of self-consciousness through such "shapes" (*Gestalten*) as mastery and slavery, Stoicism and Skepticism, Christianity and the Enlightenment, this phenomenology should not be viewed so much as a straight arrow pointing forward as a series of circles rippling out from and back toward their origin, evolving into more complex patterns as they intermingle. Although, for Hegel, we cannot literally return to any past civilization, or restore it in the present, the positive contributions of past epochs to the deepening of Spirit (and therefore of the human spirit) remain with us as an organic heritage that can be raised to consciousness through a dialectic of recollection. Phenomenology is not only the philosophical recollection of these multiple historical moments, but their actual therapeutic crystallization in the life of the present. We cannot literally be Stoics or Epicureans, we cannot experience tragedy precisely as the Greeks did, but we carry in us as a collective heritage residual experiences of Stoic nobility, Epicurean skepticism, and tragic resignation that form the well-spring of experiences and culture from which we derive our moral energies as citizens and human beings in the present. In this respect, Hegel was arguably the last great philosophical friend of liberal modernity, precisely because he believed its narrow account of human experience needed supplementation from a friendly outside source, the organic communitarianism that would ground liberal rights within a shared culture that might approximate, for the citizens of modern representative states, the pedagogical community extolled by Aristotle.[14]

My hermeneutical approach to German Idealism is Hegelian in the sense just described. I bring to it a three-fold purpose. On one level, these political theories can be read independently of one another, since each thinker presents a powerful and persuasive argument about the meaning of political community that to a very large degree stands on its own merits, and does not need to be treated as a pre-cursor or consequence of another philosophy. On another level, however, the thinkers under consideration in this essay do consciously address and criticize each other,

13 G.W.F. Hegel, *The Philosophy of History*, Sibree trans. (Dover, 1956), p. 79.

14 Avineri, p. 69; Hegel, *Early Theological Writings*, pp. 325–28; Dallmayr, pp. 249–51; George Armstrong Kelly, *Hegel's Retreat from Eleusis* (Princeton, 1978), pp. 113–15.

deliberately joining an inherited ontological pedigree in order to transform or subvert it from within. The works of Schelling, Hegel, Marx, Nietzsche and Heidegger are saturated with similar pre-occupations, and often with the same technical vocabulary. In this respect, they do form a genealogy for the exploration of the transposition of eros and the grounds it might offer for a just and fulfilling account of political community, a genealogy with a leitmotif of problematics stretching continuously from Schiller to Heidegger. Finally, however, the respective political philosophies remain independent *Gestalten* in our on-going reflections on political ontology, sturdier in their independence (in proper Hegelian fashion) precisely through their comparison and contrast with one another. They thereby remind us that the adequacy of our reflections will stand or fall by their capacity to embrace without reductionism, distortion or caricature the autonomous alternative that each philosophy offers in illuminating the relationship between happiness and life. Nothing vanishes in Spirit.

To situate my hermeneutical approach within the broader and more familiar terrain of political theory, it bears re-emphasizing that for Hegel, Spirit is concretely embodied in the nation-state. This, and this alone, in contrast with a recent misunderstanding, is what he means by the now super-charged term " the end of history." In the coming synthesis, Hegel tells us, the nation-state will emerge as an organic mingling of political, aesthetic, religious and cultural bonds. The nation-state will educate and acculturate. It will embody the history and traditions of a people, or of an association of peoples, so as to mediate the abstract, universalistic and sometimes distant relationship between the state's representative institutions and its citizens. The healing force of religion in history, reconciling the sometimes seemingly hopeless antagonism between Understanding and Love—between rights and community, or the ought and the is—this is the ultimate basis for Hegel's hopes for a renewed sense of civic community within the prevailing world-view of modernity.

Hegel attempts to synthesize liberalism with communitarianism by arguing that the nation-state embodies universalistic principles of rights and legitimacy in the distinct historical evolution of particular peoples or associations of peoples. In this way, the nation-state is the best hope for avoiding the characteristic extremes of modernity: the Jacobin utopianism which tries to destroy all vestiges of historical community, and the tribalism which tries to liberate the existentially authentic "people" by dismantling the overlay of modernity.[15] Accordingly, just as Hegel's successors attempt to dismantle the Hegelian synthesis ontologically by de-constructing its polarities and exaggerating either our direct, tacit and unmediated immersion in the immanent wholeness of the life-world (the realm of Love) or our untrammeled subjective power to assert our wills over this life-world and reconstruct it (the realm of Understanding), so do they, as the political and

15 Avineri, pp. 44–48, 228–29.

civic corollary of this ontological critique, tend to attack the legitimacy of the nation-state as the concrete embodiment of Spirit, pulling it apart either in the direction of globalizing technological rationalism or of tribal belonging.

In this way, the internal debate within German Idealism over the ramifications of the transposition of eros, and the successive critiques launched against Hegelian Spirit by the philosophies of Marx, Nietzsche and Heidegger, bring us directly to our own era, and remind us again that political philosophy always emerges from the crucial dilemmas that we ourselves face as citizens grappling with the problematic relationship between liberalism and community. It is no longer possible for us to embrace Hegel's progressive teleology of history in all aspects of its positive, outward structure (for instance, its Eurocentricity, occasional insensitivity toward or ignorance about non-Western cultures, and its assertion that Christianity has a privileged place among modern faiths as "the religion of the Absolute"). Nevertheless, the internal structure of Spirit as the unity of subject and substance mediated by historical context remains promising as a quasi-transcendental but non-monistic account of civic community that is, in its respective moments, both integrative and differentiated. Freed from the determinacy of a particular account of progress the immanent structure of Spirit as the preservation of dynamic unity through its ensemble of tensions can help to illuminate democratic citizenship as an equilibrium of overlapping and mutually reinforcing spheres of public, private, familial, erotic, cultural and religious avocations whose tension with one another enliven, invigorate and enrich the elusive unity they pursue in common.

For these reasons, I am broadly sympathetic to Habermas' argument that, while we are obliged to jettison Hegel's claims to have established the "absolute science of Spirit," along with other ill-fated claims to the unity of theory and practice including Leninism, a return to Hegelian "forms of consciousness" and the "shapes" that contextualize the polarities of individualism and communitarianism within a distinct historical life-world is most desirable. Such a move can help us to avoid the extremes either of Leninist "monism" or of "irrational decisionism" without conceding politics entirely to the realm of the technical interest.[16] Hegel's "shapes of consciousness" ground liberal autonomy within the hermeneutical self-interpretation of communities mediated by a commonly held discursive heritage. This returns us to our earlier discussion of the assault on Hegelianism launched by his successors, and especially to Heidegger's critique of the Hegelian science of Spirit for its irredeemable propensity to assimilate itself to global technology. That critique can be answered from within Hegel's philosophy by de-constructing the positive outward form of the science of Spirit and returning it to its own underlying and more fundamental ontological flexibility without sacrificing the mediating structures of civic and moral experience.

16 Juergen Habermas, *Theory and Practice,* J. Viertel trans. (Beacon Press, 1974), pp. 41–44, 254–55.

On Giving Oneself the Law

Robert B. Pippin
University of Chicago

1. Kant's claim that morality is a matter of rationality clearly counts as a legacy to contemporary philosophy. Thanks largely to the influence of John Rawls and his legions of Kant scholar students, this Kantian position has again become a contemporary option in debates about moral theory. It was also a great living legacy to his German Idealist successors, although the nature of that linkage is still not well understood. So before addressing what I want to claim is the central issue in the contemporary appropriation of idealist moral theory (the idea of "self-legislation")[1] I would like to begin with a brief comment about Hegel, the relevance of which will, I hope, become clear by the end of this paper about Kant.

A common and understandable view of Hegel's ethical theory has it that Hegel has a "social role" theory of right human conduct. What it is "right" to do is supposed to be accounted for by appeal to the social role one occupies. Since Hegel also regularly describes modern ethical life as rational, this last point must mean that appealing to such ethical roles is for him a normative or justificatory appeal, that such an appeal can function as a practical reason, a justification.[2] "Because I am a father," "because that is what a good business man should do,"

1 The appeal to autonomy or self-legislation is also why Stanley Rosen regards Kant as having started modern philosophy on a slippery slope, eventually culminating in the Nietzschean creativity theory and in "hermeneutics as politics." See the new second edition of his book by that title (New Haven: Yale University Press, 2003). I am concerned here with a preliminary issue: how the difficult idea of "giving oneself the law" could even be understood. One could thus see the following as preliminary to an engagement with Rosen's charge against modern German philosophy.

2 Since Hegel denies philosophy any prescriptive role, many assume that any such account is a purely descriptive or an explanatory, not a normative account. But that would be the wrong inference to draw, since Hegel also clearly insists that occupying such modern roles *is* rational, that the roles in some way manifest the work of reason, even while denying that this means "what a purely rational agent would will." See "Hegel's Ethical Rationalism," in my *Idealism as Modernism: Hegelian Variations* (Cambridge: Cambridge University Press, 1997), and my "The Realization of Freedom: Hegel's Practical Philosophy," in *The Cambridge Companion to German Idealism*, edited by Karl Ameriks (Cambridge: Cambridge University Press, 2000).

or "because I am a citizen" would be the obvious sorts of candidates for what Hegel must regard as practical reasons.

On the face of it, this is unsatisfying. Any practical argument which concludes with this sort of justification appears clearly incomplete, to require another, final step in which the justifiability and goodness of there being these roles at all is defended universally and objectively. Only such a final step, it would seem, could complete the invoking of this consideration to someone who demands a justification. We might up the stakes by adding that such roles have become "essential" to a person's identity, that I couldn't even begin to reflect on what to do were I not to begin reflecting qua something or other, family member, producer/worker/professional, or qua citizen. But that move only adds to the suspicion that such considerations are not really playing a normative role, that they instead describe some psychological or social necessity that delimits the possibility of practical reasoning. There might be something interesting to say about someone's social identity, but without the further step we are looking for there is no clear reason to think that "what my social identity requires" could be the sort of practical reason whose binding force others ought also to acknowledge. Likewise, trying to make this next move and complete the argument by claiming that such social functions are indispensable elements of any good or flourishing life, or that they should be seen as the outcome of a rational historical process, has come to look hopeless to most modern philosophers, almost all of whom have come to accept a "plurality" of equally legitimate and incommensurable claims about ultimate human ends or goods, and who, after the twentieth century, would view any notion of historical progress as Panglossean.

This is a natural and plausible way to think about the limitations of what is taken to be the Hegelian position. Assertions about the normative dimensions of social roles, especially if they are understood to involve rights or entitlement claims, must be able to survive, we think, a full "*reflective* endorsement," a reasoned defense that does not presuppose our social roles, but concludes in affirming them (if it does), and only thereby can such claims be said to count as binding practical reasons for any reflective individual.

This line of thinking seems natural and unavoidable. It is however, already quite theoretically "thick," and leads fairly directly to a Kantian position on obligation, or on the binding "source of normativity."[3] If every sort of consideration can count as a justifiable practical reason only if it survives some sort of reflective endorsement test, and there are such tests, and some considerations do survive them, and we can accept or reject such proposals *because* they pass or fail, then we

3 Indeed one other initial way to stress the differences between Kant's and Hegel's approach is to note that Hegel must be striking out in some very different direction because he appears to have no interest at all is any refutation of moral or normative skepticism, appears to think it is wholly unnecessary.

have claimed that reason can be practical in some way, that passing this reflective endorsement test is, at some basic, fundamental level, what most matters, is the crucial component in the rational source of normativity, and that it at least can motivate agents. And we have at least opened a clear path to the claim that the question of what we ought to do (especially the question of what we may never do) is finally a matter of *pure* reason being practical, that there is a form of reflective reason not already tied to any pursuit of contingent, material ends, and it too "can be practical," that all our actions can be judged permissible or not by appeal to such an a priori endorsement test. On such an account, *being* in a certain social role could never of itself count as a reason to do anything. I must reflectively *adopt* the requirements of such a role as a principle of action, actively require of myself a course of action, determine that what I find myself engaged in ought to be engaged in or not.

3. And therewith the other, now very familiar side of the Kant-Hegel dialectic on this issue begins to come into view as well. The list of counter-questions is well known: in what sense can we be said to be normatively bound to, committed to, what a purely practically rational agent would legislate as required? In what sense am I, just qua agent, "committed" to the requirements of reflective endorsement? Is there any such test? That is, does anything action-guiding really follow from such a commitment, and is there any coherent theory of human motivation that could account for the motivational efficacy of such an always over-riding commitment? On the Hegelian picture, our claims on each other, our normative rules, arise out of and are grounded in already on-going ways of life, attachments, institutions and dependencies. Some such attachments and dependencies are said to be constitutive of being an individual human agent (at some historical period), and any reflective abstraction from such involvements creates an artificial construct, whose putative endorsements (if any determinate ones can be made out) amount to a philosophical fantasy world, bear no relation to the requirements of a concretely human life.[4]

And so the familiar back-and-forth. According to Hegel's theory, such social commitments and dependencies do not merely reflect *beliefs* about value held by individuals for various reasons. They are much "deeper" than that, are in some sense forms of life or, in Hegel's terms, "shapes (Gestalten) of spirit." On the Kantian picture, this all ignores how radically we certainly *can*, in concreto, detach ourselves from, reflect on, and possibly reject such inheritances, and can thereby determine in some purely rational (or impersonal or not at all self-regarding) way, what ought to be done. (In Korsgaard's words: "A good soldier obeys orders, but a good human being doesn't massacre the innocent." (CK102))

However, we should also immediately note that, for *both* Kant and Hegel, to understand each other as merely passively shaped by, and in our practical lives

4 Most obviously for the Hegelian side, the long period of childhood dependency in a particular community counts as one of the un-abstractable features at issue.

merely expressing, the influences of socialization and habituation, communal mores and roles, is to fail to accord each other the appropriate respect, dignity and worth as the kinds of creatures we are. We are entitled to such respect because the lives we lead *are* up to us, are actively *led* by us.[5] Whatever social roles we inhabit or conventions we act out, we have somehow made them our own; they function as norms and ideals for us that we must actively and with some justification to ourselves and others sustain, and which, like any ideal, we can hold and yet fail to live up to. They are certainly not, according to Hegel, just regularities and dispositions. The worth of our lives is tied to their being free lives, and their being free lives is tied to a capacity for some sort of reflection, and such reflection is reflection if genuinely reasoned, not merely expressive. The disagreement at issue turns on the nature of this act of "making them our own" or "acknowledging their authority" and so on Hegel's disagreement with equating such a dimension (which Hegel calls simply "subjectivity") with individual "reflective endorsement," especially when that is understood as the practicality of pure reason. And this finally brings me back to my main topic: Kant on the self-imposed norms of reason.

4. The clearest way to state the radicality of the Kantian claim about the only possible origin of normative commitments is to repeat his claim that we are always only obligated to what we can, from our own first-person perspective, rationally obligate *ourselves* to.[6] That is Kant's solution to the problem of obligation descended from the dead ends created by the divine command and natural law traditions.[7] If human beings can be duty-bound, can be subject to a universal law, then we must be able to explain how this is consistent with another indispensable premise in Kant's Protestant enterprise: that human beings are full *subjects of* their own lives, not *subject to* any normative authority they cannot, from their first-person perspective, reflectively endorse. And the only way this is possible is if they are *both* legislators of and subject to the laws they obey. Nothing about the state of things, history, my social role, nature or even God can function as a practical reason unless I count such a consideration as a reason to act, and in

5 On the importance of reflective, subjective allegiance in Hegel's theory of objective spirit, see my "Hegel, Freedom, The Will: *The Philosophy of Right*, #1–33," in *Hegel: Grundlinien der Philosophie des Rechts*, ed. Ludwig Siep, (Berlin: Akademie Verlag, 1997); "Hegel on the Rationality and Priority of Ethical Life" in *Idealism as Modernism op. cit.*; and "Hegel on Institutional Rationality," in *The Southern Journal of Philosophy*, Vol. XXXIX, Supplement, "The Contemporary Relevance of Hegel's Philosophy of Right" (2001).

6 On what it means to occupy, necessarily, such a first-person perspective, see Christine Korsgaard, "Morality as Freedom," in *Creating the Kingdom of Ends* (CKE) (Cambridge: Cambridge University Press, 1996), pp. 162–87.

7 A solution many now understand as descended from Pufendorf. See especially Chapter Seven of J.B. Schneewind, *The Invention of Autonomy. A History of Modern Moral Philosophy* (Cambridge: Cambridge University Press, 1998), pp. 118–40.

doing so, in Kant's language, I am giving myself the law. And I can only be said to be genuinely conferring such value (as opposed to, say, just expressing an inherited, socialized attitude) if I do so with reason.[8] It is a big and controversial step to go on to say, as an extension of this claim, that since reflective reasoning is the "source of value" in this way, we are, therefore, as a consequence of some sort of "regress" argument, unconditionally bound to reason itself and its pure, universal requirements, all with a kind of moral necessity, and in a way that can guide a life, but it is an understandable step, and we shall examine it in due course. As Korsgaard rightly put it, engaging in such reflective endorsement "is not for Kant a way of justifying morality; it [subjecting myself only to what I can reflectively endorse] is morality itself." (89)[9] (From here on, I will be making use of Korsgaard's version of Kant as representative of contemporary Kantian approaches. There are of course other approaches, but several aspects of her project seem to me to capture best the appeal of this reflective endorsement ideal.)

So, in sum, both the attractiveness of the Kantian position against the supposedly Hegelian, and its potential paradoxes, are evident in this famous, densely dialectical claim from the *Groundwork.*

> The will is thus not merely subject to the law [*dem Gesetze unterworfen*] but is subject to the law in such a way that it must be regarded also as legislating for itself [*selbtsgesetzgebend*] and only on this account as being subject to the law (of which it can regard itself as the author [Urheber].) GL, Ak. 431.[10]

Surely the first point to make about Kant's claim is that it is *metaphorical* The image of some sort of putatively law—less person making or originating or legislating a principle and "only" thereby being bound to it—otherwise not bound at all—makes it very hard to imagine on what sort of "basis" such a law-less subject could decide what to legislate. Unless you are *already* bound to the constraint of reason, on what basis could you "subject yourself" to such constraints? If rational reflection and ultimately reflective rationality itself are the source of all human value, then the whole idea of authoring or legislating *that* principle looks groundless, and the picture coming into focus looks more like

8 Cf. Korsgaard's account in "Kant's Formula of Humanity," CKE, ". . . in our actions we view ourselves as having a value-conferring status in virtue of our rational nature. We act as if our own choice were the sufficient condition of the goodness of its object: this attitude is built into [a subjective principle of] rational action." P. 123.

9 Clearly, this claim will then also, in a different way, raise again the question of the justification of morality *so construed.*

10 This from Paul, Romans 2:14. See Christine Korsgaard, *The Sources of Normativity* (SN) (Cambridge: Cambridge University Press), p. 100.

a melancholy Dane ready to "leap" or an anguished, near-sighted Frenchman "condemned to be free," than the dutiful sage of Königsberg.[11]

Of course, some aspects of the metaphorical dimension of "authoring the law" are not that obscure. "Reason legislates" when we simply determine what to do on the basis of reasons, and when we do so, *we* are determining what will count as decisive; it cannot be anyone else or any other authority unless *we* also so determine. And in so determining, we are always relying on a principle of some generality. "Because I felt like it" cannot ever be our legislated norm, even if we think it is. But "Always to do what I feel inclined to at the moment" can be. But this still leaves the basis of such determination—"ourselves as authors"—obscure and so does not help explain Kant's paradoxically reflexive formulations—that reason has itself for its object, that the will wills itself, and so forth.

Of course, again, at a sufficient level of generality, even very unKantian predecessors like Christian Wolff could adopt such rhetoric. "Because we know through reason what the law of nature prescribes [haben will], a rational person needs no further law; he is rather by reason a law unto himself."[12] And

> Since a rational person is a law unto himself and besides natural obligation needs no other, so neither rewards nor punishment are for him motives for good action and for the avoidance of bad ones. . . . And hence someone rational performs the good because it is good and omits the bad because it is bad, in which case he becomes like a god, as one who has no superior who can obligate him to do the good and omit the bad . . . but rather by the perfection of his nature, does this and omits that.[13]

Wolff's autonomy language is of course quite restricted by his rationalist perfectionism (reason has an intelligible object in such legislation, not, as in Kant, itself) and by his helping himself to the notion of "intrinsically motivating by nature," a dodge that Kant cannot afford, but the emphasis on a kind of autonomy

11 Perhaps the clearest contemporary expression of the principle Kant is assuming can be found, not surprisingly, in Rawls, *A Theory of Justice* (Cambridge: Harvard University Press, 1971). "(T)he self is prior to the ends which are affirmed by it." (p. 560) The spirit of my response to that claim is similar to Nagel's concluding objections to Korsgaard in SN. He is objecting to Korsgaard's account of *why* someone might sacrifice his life for others. Korsgaard she says it is because his very "identity" is at stake and he could not live with himself if he betrayed the others. Nagel says, quite rightly I think, "The real explanation is whatever would *make* it impossible for him to live with himself and that is the non-first-personal reason against the betrayal." p. 206. This can be the right response without, I think, any necessary commitment to what Nagel calls "realism."

12 Christian Wolff, *Gesammelte Schriften* (New York: Olms, 1976) Abteilung 3. *Deutsche Ethik*, (DE) §24.

13 DE, §38.

and the flexible interpretability of being a law unto oneself, are still quite striking. But the contrast with Kant's version is also striking. Kant is not just claiming that we exclude empirical considerations and rely on what pure reason and no other consideration can determine we ought to do. He is claiming something like "*pure practical reason determines that its law should be the constraint of pure practical reason, and it thereby submits to the authority of this law.*" This separation of pure practical reason from itself and then this re-union is what is so metaphorically puzzling. (For one thing, without some non-metaphorical gloss, the situation looks like one Nietzsche might describe, where self-rule or self-mastery is simultaneously and perhaps indistinguishably, self-enslavement.)

Using some of the passages from Kant's *Religion* book, we might also make more plausible the idea of someone's responsibility for "legislating" a life-plan in which she determines that the moral law and not self-love is to be the always super-ordinate principle in all her decisions. That would be a way of "electing" to subject oneself to the law.[14] But that would not be an explanation of her *being* duty-bound in the first place (which is the problem), only of the *extent* to which she acknowledges and obeys the already binding law over the course of a whole life. We surely do not want to be in the position of saying that the moral law is obligatory only for those *who have actually made it binding*, and not binding otherwise. The passage surely cannot be opening that door, but it obviously forces on us the question of the compatibility between Kant's emphasis on autonomy and the human source of value with his emphasis on unconditional, or, let us say, unavoidable obligation.

5. Later in the Growundowrk it is at least clearer what Kant means to *exclude* by his author or "Urheber" principle, and that points in a clearer direction. He says that accepting the authority of any "external" command, or accepting a course of action necessary to satisfy a sensible impulse, is an evasion of our very status as actors at all, of what is involved in inhabiting the unavoidable first-person viewpoint from which we must direct the course of our lives. (It is a little unclear how to state this, since it is quite obviously important to Kant that the appearance of just *being* commanded or *being* determined is itself a delusion, in many cases a willful self-delusion. By "letting ourselves" be commanded or determined we are actually not passive at all, but are determining ourselves to act on such a principle, and this claim gets us closer to the "inescapability" that Kant's *Urheber* principle must involve. A representative passage:

> Now it is impossible to think of a reason that in full consciousness [mit ihrem eigenen Bewußsein] receives direction [eine Lenkung empfinge] as regards its judgments from elsewhere; for then the subject would ascribe the

14 Cf. Korsgaard's "Morality as Freedom," CKE, pp. 164–67, and what she calls the "Argument from Spontaneity."

> determination of his faculty of judgment not to his reason, but to an impulse. Reason must regard itself as the author [die Urherberin] of its principles independent of foreign influences. Therefore as practical reason or as the will of a rational being reason must regard itself as free. GL, Ak 448

6. Various possible ways of rendering Kant's "authorship of the moral law" claim less metaphorical can now suggest themselves. As we have already begun to intimate, most such ways are, paradoxically, ways of denying what the metaphor itself suggests is possible: some state of not-being-obligated, which then becomes, by an act of authorship and subjection, a state of being obligated. The arguments amount to such a denial, and the strategy is already evident in the passage just quoted, with its denial that it is "possible to think" that reason *could* receive direction from elsewhere than reason, and with its claim about the practical necessity of acting always "under the idea of freedom," and so on reflectively considered reasons. Such a strategy must accomplish this goal while also showing that is nevertheless in *some* sense (if not the obvious one) "up to us" whether we are guided by reason or not. That is, for Kant what is wrong in immoral or unjust actions consists in a violation of the minimal, formal constraints of rationality, and it is only by being subject to such constraints that we can be said to be actors at all. It must also be said that it is in some way up to us whether we subject ourselves to such constraints or not, even though attempting to avoid such requirements must also manifest that we are nonetheless already so subject. A simpler way to put the point would be to say that for Kant, despite the surface grammar, "person" is in no sense a substantive or metaphysical category, but in some way or other, a practical achievement, and the attribution of the notion to an other is an ascription not a description. As Fichte would say, the I posits itself; as Hegel would say, Geist is a "result of itself." But we digress.

One way to show this (that there really can be no such literal "act" or that the act of self-subjection must always already have gone on) is to show that we have somehow always already undertaken the basic obligation in whatever we do, and to be able to show that somehow that "already," and the claim of unavoidability and necessity, do not cancel out the self-legislation demanded by the active language of "authorship." (One wants to say that we are not bound to reason because we bind ourselves to it, but that reason is "constitutive" of the "binding" legislation without which there are no norms, and so without which there is no way to lead a life.)[15] This has been called a "regress" argument and has received a well known formulation by Korsgaard, although a somewhat different version has also been proposed recently by Allen Wood.[16]

15 Korsgaard uses this phrase at SN, p. 234.

16 Cf. Korsgaard's "Kant's Formula of Humanity," CKE, and her analysis of Kant's Groundwork, pp. 428–89 on the practical version of reason's "regress to the unconditioned." P. 119–31. Wood's account in his *Kant's Ethical Theory* (Cambridge:

7. I'll return to the moral dimensions of this sort of case later in this paper. But first, before we reach the issues of practical unavoidability and implicit, undeniable commitments, we need to make less metaphorical the whole idea of *our* legislating rules or norms to ourselves, and our being bound to them by "binding ourselves." And Korsgaard and others have argued that ordinary cases of hypothetical imperatives can show this rather easily, and so demystify the self-legislation language. This is important because the instrumental form is usually taken as an unproblematic application of practical reasoning, and so it allows a clear view, one would assume, of what practical reason can be said to require of us (what the so-called "normativity of instrumental reason" amounts to)[17], and thereby whether this language of self-legislation and authorship makes any sense in that context.

The basic idea in such an approach is not complicated. When I set an end, or do not merely "wish" (in Kant's sense) to pursue an end, but "will," actually resolve to pursue it, I can also be said thereby "to have committed myself" to achieving the means necessary to attain it. By "authoring" one rule for myself (to pursue an end) I have authored another and bound myself to it (to obtain the means), *whether I explicitly realize this or not. I* set the rules for the game I decide to play, and so can be said to have bound myself to play by them. If I am "rationally bound" to obtaining such means then "I *have* bound myself" just by setting the end, and reason will have been shown *already* to be practical, to have satisfied the "internalism" requirement, or to have been shown really to motivate an action. Not everyone, for example, must take organic chemistry to succeed in college, but if I resolve to go to medical school, when I learn how important for admittance a good grade in "o-chem" is, I must either give up the end, or follow through on my commitment by attaining the relevant means. And the important point here, from a Kantian perspective, is not at all the predictive point that someone who resolves to go to medical school will very probably, almost certainly, sign up for that chemistry class. That would be a kind of third-person viewpoint which treats beliefs about means as a kind of gate or shunt for desire, such that beliefs about means merely direct the flow of motivational desire, which desire for the end is still doing all the real motivational work. In this case, it seems quite artificial to say, with the Humeans, that my desire to be a doctor remains the motivating force in this way, and that it has been "guided through o-chem," so that

Cambridge University Press, 1999) depends on a strong claim about the "objective" goodness which his Kant maintains must be claimed by anyone willing rationally in setting that end (any end). His regress then turns on the value of the "source" of this *goodness*. I have presented some objections to this approach in "Kant's Theory of Value: On Allen Wood's *Kant's Ethical Thought*," *Inquiry*, Vol. 43, (summer, 2000).

17 Christine Korsgaard, "The Normativity of Instrumental Reason," in *Ethics and Practical Reason*, ed. By Garrett Cullity and Berys Gaut (Oxford: Clarendon Press, 1997), pp. 215–54.

I somehow also "pick up a desire for it" on the way. Something more than that is clearly going on here, since, speaking from the first-person perspective, I can genuinely have that belief about the usefulness of o-chem and *not* "automatically" head for the registrar's office. I can fail to live up to what I know *it is rational for me to do*, even while I really do commit myself to the end in question and the relevant means. And if this is so then we must admit something that Hume, in effect, never did: that there is such a thing as *practical reason*, that there is a "normativity of instrumental reason" as Korsgaard has put it, or there is a question, as Kant put it, about the rational "necessitation" (or constraint, *Nötigung*) of the will in instrumental cases (GL, Ak, 417). The ultimate point of seeing things this way is quite important (and one Hegel would agree with): that "to be rational just *is* to be autonomous,"(my emphasis) or "to be governed by reason and to govern yourself, are one and the same thing." (CK, NIR, 219) There are no laws out there which we need to see and adopt our behavior to. There are only laws we give ourselves, to which we are bound because we have committed ourselves to them, such that, if we don't follow through, we won't have decided anything at all; we won't be rational, *that is*: subjects, persons, agents.[18] (The somewhat confusing but very important point here is that being a subject *means being able to fail to be one*, something that already tells us a lot about the uniquely practical, not metaphysical status of subjectivity in the post-Kantian tradition.)

There is an awful lot packed into this last claim. The difficulties come when we try to state in this case as well as the more ambitious case about moral commitment or self-legislation, what all of this amounts to in detail, how to gloss what it means to "govern ourselves" in cases like these. And, I want to show, the model of individual agents "detaching" or disengaging themselves from their concerns and lives, and then reflectively committing to or endorsing very general principles of action by reliance on some "pre-commitment" form of practical reasoning, will lead into one paradoxical situation after another. As we have seen, the question is a very large one; it goes to the purport of this quintessentially modern insistence that some consideration can count as a genuine reason for action only if we "make it our own," adopt it in a way that we can defend (even just to ourselves), and when we can be said to have adopted it because of such a recognition of these justificatory considerations. On Korsgaard's account, this means that a person is not being *instrumentally rational* and so not "governing herself," her life is not her own, if she merely wants an end, has a certain belief about the right means, and *is* pursuing those means. For Korsgaard, she must also be pursuing the means *because* she believes she ought, that that is the rational thing to do, that that rational identification of the means is a norm she can live up

18 Cf. the indispensable article by Dieter Henrich, "The Concept of Moral Insight and Kant's Doctrine of the Fact of Reason," in *The Unity of Reason: Essays on Kant's Philosophy*; ed. Richard Velkley; transl. Jeffrey Edwards (Cambridge: Harvard University Press, 1994).

to or not, all in order for her to count as self-governing and not "accidentally rational."

This is quite a controversial way to put the matter because there is already an ambiguity in such an account between being "guided" by reason and being "motivated" by it (terms that Korsgaard tends to treat as synonymous). Again, a Humean could certainly accept the former. As just noted, this is precisely what practical reason does in Hume: guide us to the means that in fact themselves lead to an end. In so far as we are being rational at all, we follow that guidance, where here being rational at all just means that nothing has gone causally haywire. But in *that* sense of guidance (as Korsgaard points out), *not* going where such guiding reason leads is nothing like a failure of rationality. It has to be a mistake, a breakdown, or ignorance or failure of memory, etc., or a change of heart about the end. To show *rational failure* we have to show that we are motivated by what reason requires when we act rationally, and that we can fail to heed this claim, even though we acknowledge and accept it. That is a much different and more controversial matter, and I don't think that anything Korsgaard says supports that claim. At least at this point, the whole notion of "committing oneself" to an instrumental norm and "following through" or "failing" even while still committed, is still vague and metaphorical and needs to be clarified.

8. A major problem with all of this stems from Kant's complicated claim that,

> (W)hoever wills the end, so far as reason has decisive influence on his action, wills also the indispensably necessary steps to it that he can take. This proposition, in what concerns the will, is analytic; for, in the willing of an object as an effect, my causality, as an acting cause of this effect shown in my use of the means to it, is already thought, and the imperative derives the concept of actions necessary to this purpose from the concept of willing this purpose. (GL, Ak, 417)

But if it is *analytic* that "whoever wills the end, *wills* the means," then we have not *imposed* a normative law on ourselves *with respect to these means*, and the direction we were just following is irrelevant; we should u-turn back to Hume. According to Kant's strong analyticity claim, someone who does not pursue the means necessary to the end that he has committed to is not being irrational, is not failing to conform to a norm that he has imposed on himself. He simply reveals that he had not "really" willed such an end after all; he merely wished it. The criterion, the test, for having "really" willed it *is* willing the means.[19] You may tell yourself and everyone else that you are working to dismantle capitalist class inequalities, and you may give away a certain amount of money, but your Lexus

19 Cf. the "already thought" above, and the "derives the concept of actions necessary to this purpose".

and your Brioni suits and your Tuscany villa tell us much more about your genuine ends.

But there is an escape clause in this passage; the clause "so far as reason has decisive influence on his action." And it is a good thing too, because besides making this claim about analyticity, Kant also claims that hypothetical imperatives are *imperatives*, and that must mean "norms that we adopt and can fail to observe." Perhaps we can admit, in other words, that there may be self-deceived cases like our limousine socialist. But there are also cases where the right analysis of what happens when the means to an end are not sought is more directly a failure of rationality; we are being irrational, and that just means: not abiding by the norms we have legislated for ourselves, bound ourselves to. Surely this can happen too. We want to go to medical school with every fiber of our being, but math anxiety takes over when we face o-chem, and we sign up for art history classes instead. That is, we can genuinely will an end, but fail to will the means simply because the normative claim of reason fails. In such cases we should state the analyticity principle more carefully: anyone *who has reasons* to pursue an end *has reasons* to pursue the means relevant to it. Or whoever *ought* to pursue an end (setting a goal is a normative matter too, after all), *ought* to pursue the means. We have to state it this way because what is crucial about instrumental reason being reason, normative, is that it must be able to fail; to be adopted and held, but avoided and ignored at the relevant moment. Otherwise the language of norms and hypothetical imperatives is inappropriate, and we should be talking about what people are very likely going to do, given what else they are doing.

And Korsgaard gives a few plausible examples. A man who believes that an injection will spare him from a deadly disease, and who wants to be spared, nevertheless refuses the injection because he is terrified of needles. He does not give up the end of survival and adopt as a priority the end of avoiding being stuck by needles. And there is the classic Western or civil war movie scenario. Tex has been shot in the leg and will die if the leg is not amputated. As his comrades prepare to amputate, Tex begs them, in agony and fear, not to amputate. But we, and his comrades, do not take such protestations as what he genuinely wills. We (presumably) know that what he must really will is to stay alive, and we know that his protestations are the irrational irruption of anxiety and fear, that he doesn't *really* prefer avoiding amputation at all costs, prefer even death, to undergoing an operation like that without anaesthetic.

9. This last case seems right, but we should be careful about concluding too much from it. There are three problems.

In the first place, it simply is not easy to tell when a person has "really" willed an end and is just irrationally "failing" to pursue the means he has normatively committed himself to. Unless we want to beg all questions from the outset and just require as a condition of agency always being prudentially concerned with long-term benefit over short-term gains (as Nagel ultimately does), we don't have any clear right, certainly not a priori, to tell what a person's "true end" really is in cases like the above. In the case of our limousine socialist, it seems much more appropriate to say that he hasn't really set any end of abolishing the class structure, even when he sincerely reports that belief, and the best evidence for such a denial is that his actions show no serious intention of attaining the means to do so. What distinguishes this from other cases, where we might want to say: he *has* set the end but is "weak," and cannot muster the resolve to seek the means? Why not say: his not seeking the means is very good evidence indeed that he has not really set, willed, the end? In the case of Tex and our needle-avoider, we rely on the assumption that the end of staying alive is an obvious one to impute, and so we go the "weakness" route. But is it so outrageous to suppose that someone might reckon a distant probability not as important as avoidance of an immanent pain, that there is nothing that requires us to say that he is "weak"; or to reject a priori that someone might rather die than undergo a procedure that, to him, might be worse than death itself; or that someone has no idea what is most important to him and can argue himself into either position? (Korsgaard wants to claim that "obligation in general is a reality of human life." (113). But what is going on here hardly seems like Tex is "avoiding an obligation." It would certainly be odd if one of his buddies pointed out to him, "But Tex, just by being alive and wanting to live you have rationally obligated yourself to have your leg amputated.") I would venture the bet that in most cases like this, where people profess (even to themselves) to have set an end, and do not seek the necessary means, that it is much more likely that they have either not really set such an end, have changed their mind about the end when confronted by difficult means, or, what is most likely, have usually set the end in some qualified manner; as in—so long as it doesn't cost me something else I value very highly. (This seems exactly how most people adopt the end of staying married "'till death do them part.")[20]

Secondly, it is not at all clear just how, from a Kantian point of view, we are supposed to state the elements in our irrational failure to live up to a norm we have supposedly committed ourselves to. When Korsgaard mentions factors that might explain how people can be said to become "irrational and weak-willed," she mentions such things as "terror, idleness, shyness or depression," and she goes so far as to call these "forces" that "block" "susceptibility to reason." (NIP, 229). With respect to Tex, we hear: "The right thing to say is that fear is making Tex irrational." (238) And in a similar passage, we read that "timidity, idleness and depression . . . will attempt to control or overrule my will." (246) For me to be leading my life, she insists I must actively seize control of my own destiny,

20 There is a passage in SN where Korsgaard seems to make just this point. She points to case where "rules and principles are *constitutive of*, and *therefore internal* to, the activities themselves. If I am to walk I must put one foot in front of the other: this is not a rule that externally constrains my walking, or boxes me in like the walls of a labyrinth, or that I can with much coherence rebel against." My emphasis, p. 234.

"consciously pick up the reins, and make myself the cause of the end." When I don't do this "I, considered as an agent, do not exist" and therefore "Conformity to the instrumental principle is thus constitutive of having a will, in a sense it is even what gives you a will."

Surely the first thing to say here is that Korsgaard has let her Kantian admiration for autonomy get out of control. If, in not conforming to an instrumental principle, I have *ceased to be an agent*, then surely what we have here is not *my* failure of rationality. It sounds like: *I* haven't failed to realize a commitment; something has happened *to me*, in all these examples, that prevents this realization. Something "*blocks*" the motivating power of reason; fear "*makes* me irrational," and so forth, all exactly as our Humean wanted to say earlier. This may be a breakdown in the power of reason to motivate, but it all here sounds like a disease or exogenous interference, not *my* failure or weakness. What has happened to the Kantian "incorporation" principle (which Korsgaard accepts)[21], according to which fears and desires and inclinations, while they may incline me to do something, can never be counted, just by their occurrence, as motives to act, that they must be incorporated in a maxim, taken as good reasons by an agent, for them to count as my motives? If we take this incorporation principle to heart, it becomes even less plausible to appeal to Korsgaard's "failure" or "weakness" account since I must be counting some present anxiety, aversion or anticipation as worth acting on, and if I am doing so, then I am diverting *myself* my from the original end, not failing to follow through on a commitment.[22] It makes a great deal of difference, in other words, whether these emotional factors are said to "control" *or* "overrule" my will, to use the two terms Korsgaard uses

21 Cf. especially her "Kant's Formula of Humanity," in CKE, pp. 110–14, and her citation of passages from the *Metaphysics of Morals* (e.g., pp. 387 and 392—these passages have been quite influential in recent discussions of Kant, as the work of Tom Hill evinces), and especially also the *Conjectural Beginnings essay*, and the *Religion book*.

22 What is going wrong here, I think, originates in the Christian language of "weakness," and so the corresponding appeal to "strength" of resolve. The common-sense description of this as a case of irrationality is a good place to start. It would say that Tex's refusal is "irrational" because the urgency of the situation, the sheer lack of time and crisis conditions, require Tex to make a decision in such unusual circumstances that he does not decide what he very likely *would*, were he to be able to reflect calmly and in full awareness of the facts and consequences. We might (and usually do) add that he would like to identify as the "Real Tex" that calmly reflective agent. But this is a bit of a fantasy as well. In resisting the amputation, Tex is not "too weak" to be the "Real Tex." He expresses and discovers something about this real Tex in such resistance, something about the nature of his commitment to life, the weight of his fear of pain, his ability (or lack of it) to invoke and rely on an ideal picture of himself, and so on. He is not, in resisting, "weakly" the Real Tex. *He is just Tex*.

synonymously.[23] They are not synonymous. If the former, "control," which Korsgaard's examples suggest, we don't have an irrational action, but no action at all, a breakdown in agency not its failure; if the latter, "overruling," we have a case of counting something as worth more than something else, and so perhaps a case of ignorance or foolishness, not weakness or wantonness.

Moreover, if we try to take a few steps back and argue that I am originally responsible for the kind of character that would produce these emotional storms, (that I have "chosen" it and so must live with the current consequences as my fault, even if I can't do anything about it now) we will not only introduce all sorts of "moral luck" problems involving the social conditions and opportunities (or lack of them) under which such a character was formed (and so will have undermined any strong "responsibility for my character" view), we will thereby introduce again the implausible picture of some character-less agent choosing a character as if a suit of clothes.[24] Indeed that implausible picture is already suggested by Korsgaard's unusual language: that by committing yourself to some instrumental norm, you "give yourself" *a will* in the first place. While we couldn't ask for a better contemporary evocation of the route from Kant to Fichte (and his *Ich* that posits itself), I'm not sure we want to open up that Pandora's box.[25]

23 Cf. also, in her "Morality as Freedom," CKE, "The person who acts from self-love is not actively willing at all, but simply allowing herself to be controlled by the passive part of her nature, which is in turn controlled by all of nature. From the perspective of the noumenal world, ends we adopt under the influence of inclination rather than morality do not even seem to be our own." P. 168. Something is clearly going wrong here because *most* of our sensible ends are adopted "under the influence of inclination," and strictly speaking, the idea that someone can "allow" themselves to be controlled, but is *not* thereby "actively willing" is incoherent. Not much is gained, I would argue, when one simply bites the bullet on this one and claims that, therefore, on the basis of these considerations, "evil is unintelligible." p. 171.

24 For Korsgaard's attempt to make the notion plausible, see "Morality as Freedom," CKE, p. 181.

25 What Korsgaard wants to say (very clearly in the second of her recent Locke lectures) is that it cannot just be *tautologous* that someone who wills the end wills the means (and so: someone who doesn't will the means must not have willed the end), because then the clear normative force of claims like "You really should see the dentist about that tooth" would be hard to explain. But the Humean has no problem denying there is such a thing as practical reason at all, so it is no objection to point that out to him. (That is, he accepts that it cannot be said to be more irrational to prefer the continuing toothache to a speedy resolution at the feared dentist's.) More broadly, I think Korsgaard is right to criticize the Humean for explaining how the motivational efficacy of some end pursued works causally, but do not agree that this means hypothetical practical principles are norms in her sense. An "expressivist" account of action, and an account of a revisable-over-time, provisional theory of motivations (we very rarely *know* whether we have really opted for an end or not,

Finally, third, while it is important to stress that we cannot be living norm-governed lives unless we can both acknowledge the authority of, and yet fail to live up to, such norms, there are other ways of expressing and accounting for such failure than by the problematic (and in Kant paradoxical) appeal to weakness, or any other such Christian notion of a frailty usually tied to sensibility (or any such notion of sin). When we find that we do not seize an opportunity to acquire means to an end we had believed was an end of ours, something we had willed to pursue, we simply could be said to fail to live up to an ideal we had of ourselves. Someone simply finds out that she wasn't who she thought she was; all these years firmly convinced that she was seeking A; it turns out she wasn't. We could of course put this by saying that finds she did not have the "will power" or strength of resolve, even though she had committed to A, but we have already seen the paradoxes of that view. It seems more appropriate to invoke the language of self-knowledge and self-assessment, and to concentrate on what her actions reveal about the ends she really does care about.[26]

10. However, at this point, it may be that our search for some de-metaphor-ized account of the strong "authorship" interpretation of autonomy needs to take into fuller account an aspect of the issue mentioned briefly earlier. We seem to be getting into some trouble taking too literally some pre-law situation, whereas we might want to try harder to undermine the possibility of such a putative option, even while still trying to retain the authorship and self-subjection issues. Entertaining such an option in order to show its normative impossibility, would be the required argument. This gets us more directly to the "what we must be taken to have obligated ourselves to" position.

Indeed, even in the instrumental case, we have not addressed all of what it means to have "failed to live up to" a norm of instrumental rationality. As we saw, in Korsgaard's account that involves somehow failing to be an agent; not to have set the course of my life, but to have allowed it *to be set* exogenously. (We have also seen that it is unclear on a Kantian account how we should describe our doing that, since, despite the hedge words, "letting" or "allowing," it *is* a doing.) But the point at the moment is that we should describe the stake we have in our commitment to observing the claims of reason a bit more fully. We don't just "come that way," susceptible and responsive to such demands automatically. The point is that we must commit and hold to the commitment or else we will not be subjects of our lives; or the point is: what the commitment *means* to us. Since, according to Korsgaard's Kant, when I don't hold to such commitments, "I, considered as an

until we see what we actually are willing *to do*) could fill out such a picture of a non-causal account. See my "Hegel's Practical Philosophy: Rational Agency as Ethical Life," forthcoming.

26 That is, the idea would be: those who pursue an end that a full or fuller use of reason would not endorse are being "irrational," even if that pursuit cannot be traced to a weak act of "will."

agent, do not exist," then this stake in reason "issue(s) in a deep way from our sense of who we are." (SN, 18). Our very "practical identity" is at stake.

Practical identity in general ". . . is better understood as a description under which you value yourself, under which you find your life worth living and your actions to be worth undertaking." (SN, 101) There will be many contingent versions of these—professor, husband, friend, American—so, even though in all of them, I can be said to have a practical identity only by maintaining a commitment to the norms which constitute each, I could be said to "adopt" one, "abandon" another, and nothing about mine need have any claim on you.[27] But it is the next step in the development of this line of thought that returns us to Kantian moral theory. Are there "particular ways in which we *must* think of our identities"? If there are, these will be the sought-after "moral identities," such that losing that would be "worse than death"?[28]

We might first say that being a human being at all, or some universal feature of being human, can function like this inescapable identity, such that "losing" it would mean losing a recognizable human life, any course of existence that could have value to a human being. Or at least we might say it as long as we keep faith with Kant's "authorship" principle here too. We cannot *lead* a life at all without authoring, and without commitments to, such practical identities, but therefore the "value" of having any practical identity itself, and also the necessary conditions for any such identity, *does not have the same status as such particular roles or identities*. The value of reflective reasoning itself-the condition for anything mattering to us in a distinctly human way—doesn't arise out of contingent attachments and dependencies; it is what we must keep faith with if we are to sustain *any* identity at all. We have value as human beings because we value ourselves as human beings, and the introduction of this notion of practical identity is supposed to make more transparent, by means of this sort of regress, *why we could not but*

27 Cf also SN, pp. 239–41. Korsgaard often appeals to a claim like: ". . . at the moment of action, I must identify with my principle of choice if I am to regard myself as the *agent* of the action at all." (p. 241)

28 Clearly these claims about practical identity have put us somewhere in the neighborhood of the "social role" considerations that we noted at the outset. The differences are also becoming clearer too. On this view of Kant, such roles, if they are to function as normative constraints, must be seen as products of reflective endorsement by each individual. An individual must be able to see himself as the author, *Urheber*, of the role and its relationships. For Hegel on the other hand, the practical roles are the prior conditions for any reflective content, and this not as a matter of fact limitation, but as expressing the objective normative structure of modern ethical life itself. But more famously, on Kant's account there is an ultimate moral identity and attendant obligation that trumps any other contingent obligation, and his case for that will return us to the most important manifestation of the self-legislative metaphor.

"value" our humanity.[29] The direction suggested by the authorship principle is supposed to lead to this argument form. To value anything and hold oneself to the commitments necessary to attain it, is already to have valued this capacity itself, to have acknowledged that we cannot be human just *by being*; we must posit ends and hold ourselves to norms, and so valuing that capacity above all is inescapable.[30]

In this way all value depends on the value of humanity; other forms of practical identity matter in part because humanity requires them. This "human" identity and the obligations it carries with it are therefore *inescapable and pervasive*, even though, given the kind of feature of human life it is, it is not an identity one can be said simply to have, like a substance's identity through time. This claim—that our human identity is a kind of result, a posit that we make and sustain over time—would be taken up eagerly and would provoke much speculative gymnastics by later idealists, especially since, now that the very identity of a subject is at issue, the dialectical dimension of a subject as an unusual "result of itself" is clearly on view. And it is the source of some of Kant's own most speculative moments. (The second *Critique's* invocation of a "fact" of reason in what appears to be an unusual "exposition/demonstration" of the reality of human freedom already appeals to this notion of making in the root, *facere*, or "making," of *Faktum*. In this sense "acknowledging" the normative claims of reason is exactly not what the ordinary meaning of fact, or knowing a fact, would imply; it is much more like the "authoring" or self-legislation and self-subjection to such a norm. Or, a commitment to practical reason is a deed, a "Faktum," something we do, not something we passively notice or accept; it is effected.)[31]

11. But all of this only gets us so far, and not yet to any *necessary moral identity*. In the first, and most well known place, this argument only shows that in order to preserve any basic coherence in acting, you must be presumed to value humanity in *your own person*, must value *your* reflective capacity. To argue for some inescapable moral identity would be to argue that you cannot so legislate such a value without valuing humanity, respecting such a reflective life-leading

29 SN, 121. Wood's version of this move is similar, but, because it involves quite a substantive commitment, is considerably more controversial: I reveal "an esteem for myself which . . . is what holds me to my rational plan." *Kant's Ethical Theory*, op. cit., p. 119. I should think that I hold to my plan simply because I still want the end, even when my desire has turned into a calm passion, barely noticed as such.

30 "If we do not treat our humanity as normative, none of our other identities can be normative, and then we can have no reason to act at all." SN, 129.

31 Or at least, that would be one, rather adventurous way of reading the Faktum claim, in the spirit of Korsgaard's rather Fichtean Kantianism. For a general discussion of the Faktum passage, see Karl Ameriks, "Pure Reason of Itself Alone Suffices to Determine the Will" in *Kants Kritik der praktischen Vernunft*, ed. Otfried Hoeffe (Berlin: Akademie-Verlag, 2002).

capacity, in everyone. To show this, some try to demonstrate that we can start with our own private, unavoidable, normative commitment to our own humanity, and then reason in some "transcendental-argument" way that we are thereby committed to acknowledging the value of humanity in another, in anyone at all. But even if successful, this appears to show at most that I must acknowledge the value of each person's humanity *to* him or her, and not that *I* must value *your* humanity. More ambitious attempts, like Korsgaard's and Nagel's, start by attempting to deny that my valuing my own humanity can really be understood as just *my* valuing *my own* humanity. They argue in different ways that whatever reasons I have, originally, from the outset, must be reasons to value humanity itself, and that means to be committed to the value of humanity anywhere there are human beings. I *can't* value it in just my case alone, goes the argument; there couldn't be any "*reasons*" to value it *like that*. And since I must value humanity itself in order to value my instantiation of it, I am committed to respecting humanity as an end it itself, and we would thus have shown a moral identity.

The question of whether this argument establishes such a moral commitment to a universal value is one that would obviously require at least another paper. But it is also unclear exactly what is being established by the claim, what "the value of our own humanity," and so the inherent value of humanity itself, involves. Korsgaard makes extraordinarily generous use of the argument form, so generous as to render it immediately suspicious. She claims, for example, that our valuing, taking care of and pleasure in, our animal nature presumes a commitment to the value of animal sentience wherever we find it, and so gives us a way of thinking about our duties to non-human animals. This seems to me like a quite a stretch, and the source of the discomfort resides in how much is being deduced by noting that we must value our animal nature in some sense. I don't think I have any views about whether *animality* is a valuable thing, even if I take some pleasure in *mine*, and I can't see that I am expressing such a view when I avoid cold and pain and so forth. And this question points to the larger, similar issue at stake in the universal value of humanity. Any such moral identity, that view of ourselves as merely one among many is, in the Rawlsean terms that Korsgaard adopts, merely a "concept," a statement of the problem, not yet a "conception," a specification of the substantive answer. That is, let us assume that taking the source of value to be this capacity for reflective endorsement commits me to that value itself, and that I can't be holding such a commitment, and so cannot be an agent, have an identity, if I do not respect that capacity in others. But this too is still a concept, not a conception, a statement of the problem and not the solution. We don't for one thing, know *how* important that value should be. If it is automatically a trump against all other values, it would be hard to understand the kinds of real conflicts (not just resistance to duty) that emerge in the conflicts between our contingent practical identities and such a putative moral identity. And if it is so important as to be of inestimable value, then, when I take risks for my own amusement, and so value the pleasure of driving fast over safely maintaining my reflective endorsing capacities, am I being immoral?

12. But more importantly, we cannot derive from a deductive analysis of a rational agent alone any content for such a commitment, any sense of what makes up this value of humanity, or the essence of freedom as reflective endorsement. Given a "general" concept of ourselves as one-among-many, and as not relying on any consideration in my evaluating that I am not also willing to grant you entitlement to (which is all the regress argument allows us to say), the various "conceptions" that could manifest such a commitment are far broader than the specific "post-Enlightenment" ones that Korsgaard cites. As she often points out, which conception satisfies such a concept does so "by way of practical identity." We need to understand the distinctly human way in which persons acknowledge and hold themselves to values before we can understand what in particular they may not rationally ignore in others. As she points out,

> . . . human identity has been differently constituted in different social worlds. Sin, dishonour, and moral wrongness all represent conceptions of what one cannot do without being diminished or disfigured, without loss of identity, and therefore conceptions of what one must not do.[32]

And,

> The concept of moral wrongness as we now understand it belongs to the world we live in, the one brought about by the Enlightenment, where one's identity is one's relation to humanity itself.[33]

Exactly right, say we card-carrying Hegelians, but such a sweeping admission concedes the whole match between Kant and Hegel, and brings us round full circle to the alternatives with which we began. If the distinctly moral realization of the requirement of reciprocity inherent in any reflective end-setting is a matter of "history" in this way, and there is *nothing more* we can say about the normative authority of this historical epoch, then the formal requirements everywhere in force are nowhere near as important as the fact that the realization of these requirements is socio-historically specific. This makes it unlikely that there could be any deductive account of someone's core practical or moral identity and that whatever legitimating account there might be will probably be developmental, not deductive.

13. In this respect, Hegel may prove to be the more Kantian than this Kant. As we have seen several times, the obvious Kantian thing to say here is that there is no particular reason to grant our historical location in "late modernity" any normative authority unless that form of life can be itself reflectively endorsed.

32 SN, p. 117.
33 *Ibid.*

But given the road we have traveled, just trying to do so, fulfill such a criterion in the way "we" would understand such an attempt, would be merely, and in a question-begging way, *manifesting* again the form of life we wanted to authorize. In Hegel's language, the rational status of Enlightenment modernity can be established, but not by means of a deductive methodology nor by an analysis of the concept of agency. We still need some alternative way of accounting for how we can be said to make these historically specific attachments, dependencies, social roles and social ideals "our own," some alternate way of accounting for their legislated character and our submission to such legislated results. Hegel's intuition is here quite a useful one. He focuses our attention on the experience of normative insufficiency, on a breakdown in a form of life (a situation wherein we cannot make them any longer "our own"), and thereby, through such a *via negativa*, tries to provide a general theory of positive normative authority.

But that is of course another topic, and it would take a good deal of work to show that everything changes when we regard norms as collectively legislated over time, rather than elected by individual rational endorsement. I have only tried to suggest here that it is unlikely that an account of the subjectivity of moral life could rely on an appeal to something like such an individual endorsement test.

Christianity Is Platonism for the "People"

A Reinterpretation

Robert Rethy
Xavier University

1

In a notebook entry from around the time that many of the aphorisms that form *Beyond Good and Evil* were being composed, Nietzsche wrote the following: "To make an *evil* book someday, worse than Machiavelli . . ."[1] This is an important hint for reading *Beyond Good and Evil*, which could be viewed, at least in part, as a Nineteenth-Century version of *The Prince* and *The Discourses*, the advice to the new philosopher-prince echoing the former as the vision of a return to the *virtu* of the ancients corrupted by Christianity mirrors the central impulse of the latter. In the twelfth chapter of Part II of the *Discorsi* we even have an anticipation of the locution "will to power," when Machiavelli speaks of the "natural hatred" that republics and princes have for one another, a hatred which arises, especially among republics, due to the greater *virtu* of their members, from their

1 Nietzsche, *Kritische Gesamtausgabe: Werke* (*KGW*) (ed. G. Colli and M. Montinari, New York-Berlin: de Gruyter, 1967 ff), VII, 2, 26[349]. (All quotations of Nietzsche's works will be from this edition, and all translations my own.) The whole note is as follows: "To make an *evil* book someday, worse than Machiavelli and that very German and sweetly-nasty, most subordinate devil of a Mephistopheles! /Its qualities: cruel (pleasure in viewing how a beautiful type is destroyed)/seductive (inviting to the doctrine that one must be *both* the one *and* the other)/mocking toward the virtues of the monk, the philosopher, the self-important artist, etc., also the good upright herd man/noble toward the curious, importunate, proletarians of knowledge, also toward the pedantic, dissembler: no laughter, no rage." Nietzsche's interest in Machiavelli at this time is indicated by another note in a notebook from Spring 1884. Another projected book, entitled : "The New Enlightenment" has chapters "Against the churches and priests/against the statesmen/against the good natured, pitying/against the cultivated and luxury/in summa against Tartuffery/like Machiavelli" (25[296]) Henning Ottmann has a valuable discussion of Nietzsche's interest in Machiavelli in *Philosophie und Politik bei Nietzsche* (Berlin-New York: de Gruyter, 1987), pp. 281–92.

"ambition to dominate" [*ambizione di dominare*].[2] It is thus certainly not fortuitous that the Preface to *Beyond Good and Evil* begins with a reminiscence of the famous conclusion of the penultimate chapter of *Il principe*, entitled "Quantum fortuna in rebus humanis possit, et quomodo illi sit occcurrendum." Fortune has great power in human affairs, especially when human *virtu* does not intervene, although even then, when fortune changes, men rarely do and they thus suffer the consequences of their obstinacy. Machiavelli finishes advising his "new prince" by saying that, nevertheless, with regard to fortune, "it is better to be impetuous than respectful. Because fortune is a woman and it is necessary, wanting to hold her underneath, to beat her and to jolt her. And it is seen that she lets herself be conquered more by these than by those who proceed coldly. And she is always, as a woman, a friend of the young, because they are less respectful, more ferocious and command her with more audacity."[3] The changeableness of fortune can be overcome, if only for a little while, by force of arms, though the mutability and volatility of Dame Fortune can never fully be conquered.[4] The comparison with the beginning of *Beyond Good and Evil* is instructive: "Assuming that truth is a woman—well then, isn't the suspicion well-grounded that all philosophers, insofar as they were dogmatists, understood women badly?" Their seriousness, importunity, awkward flat-footedness were hardly the way to entice a woman. The complexity, contradictoriness, and hiddenness of truth is such that a less straightforward approach is called for. As we discover in the body of the text: not an earnest face but a series of masks; not a logical argument, but a rhetorical flourish; not exoteric clarity, but esoteric hints, not the plodding argument of the pedant, but the wild leaps of the enthusiast are appropriate to such a task. If truth is a woman, then conceptual dogma is less likely to ensnare her than a dancing god, who is revealed at the work's end, and who is shown to be one who understands how to enchant his woman, Ariadne.[5]

2 Niccolò Macxhiavelli, *Discorso sopra la prima deca de Tito Livio*, ed. Sasso/Inglese (Milan: Rizzoli, 1984) , p. 513.

3 *Il principe* (Milan:Arnoldo Montadori, 1986), p. 113. Note the kinship between this advice and the old woman's infamous advice to Zarathustra in "Of the old and young female" (VI, 1, 82) Perhaps Zarathustra is being advised how to "love fate." The supposition of a connection is strengthened by *JGB* 147, which echoes Zarathustra's female informant (in Italian) and attributes the thought to "old Florentine novellas."

4 For fortune in the *Discorsi* see III, 9: "How it is proper to change with the times if one wants always to have good fortune." Machiavelli is dubious that human nature can change as quickly and seamlessly as necessary, though presumably his advice is meant to help encourage it. (III, 9, 4: p. 496)

5 See *Beyond Good and Evil* (*JGB)* 295. One of the early titles of *Beyond Good and Evil* was *Dionysus or the Holy Orgies*. (VII, 3, 29[65] (Fall 1884–Beginning 1885) There are many similar titles in the notebooks of this time, particularly those of April–June 1885. See, e.g. 34[182]: "*Dionysus./Attempt at a divine manner of/philosophizing.*/By Friedrich Nietzsche."

Nietzsche permits himself the hope, as the Preface moves away from the trope of "woman," that "all dogmatizing" has been a bit of childishness and a mere beginning, a "promise spanning millennia." As the false hopes of astrology helped develop astronomy, and the false hopes of an afterlife gave rise to the "grand style of architecture in Asia and Egypt," so may it be hoped that dogmatic philosophy, the Vedanta-philosophy in Asia, Platonism in Europe, may also be a "grand thing" that must first have appeared as a "monstrous and fear-inducing grimace." The worst and most dangerous error has been a dogmatic error, "Plato's invention of pure mind [*Geist*] and the good in itself," which denies "the perspectival, the basic condition of all life." The final section of the Preface begins with a discussion of the meaning of the "battle against Plato, or, to make it more intelligible and to speak for the 'people', the battle against the Christian-ecclesiastical pressure of millennia—because Christianity is Platonism for the 'people'—has created a glorious mental tension [*Spannung des Geistes*] that has never yet existed on earth, and with a bow so tensed one can now shoot for the furthest goals." Though "European man" experiences such tension as a state of distress, and democracy and the Church—Jesuitism[6]—have tried to relieve this tension by reducing the contradictions within the soul and among men, Nietzsche confirms that "we" as "good European and free, *very* free spirits," ourselves have them still: "the full distress of the spirit and the full tension of its bow. And perhaps, the arrow, the task, who knows? The goal . . ."

It is not *our* task fully to analyze this complex document of Nietzsche's high maturity, but only to put the phrase we are studying—"Christianity is Platonism for the 'people'"—into the proper context. The preface, appropriately for a work concerned with the "*philosophy* of the future," focuses on Plato and "Platonism" almost to the exclusion of Christianity. It is somewhat unsettling to find Plato's name among the "dogmatists," aware as we are, and as Nietzsche surely was, of the derivation of dogma from *doxa* and of the low standing of this latter in the Platonic schema: the starting point, not the end of philosophy.[7] Nor could Plato's method be characterized as a "dogmatic" method, but rather as dramatic, a philosophical *agon*.[8] Indeed, *Beyond Good and Evil* is notable precisely for its nuanced view of Plato,[9] one that does not match the rather "dogmatic" view of Plato in the Preface. Between the assertion that "Christianity is Platonism for the 'people'" i.e. that Platonism is the source of the "dogmatic errors" of millennia, and

6 For the role of Jesuitism, see VIII, 1, 1[179] (Fall 1885–Spring 1886).

7 See, for example, *Rep.* V, 477b.

8 "Socrates the common man: sly: becoming master of himself through clear understanding and strong will. . . . Dialectic is *plebeian* according to its origin. Plato's fanaticism that of a *poetic* nature for its *opposite*. At the same time he notes, as *agonal* nature, that here the means for victory is given against all other fighters, and that the capacity is rare." (VII, 2, 25[297]; Spring 1884)

9 See aphorisms 14, 28, 190, 204. This will be discussed below.

a suspicion, even in the Preface, that dogmatism is an inadequate characterization of the form and matter of Plato's thought, we are left with a puzzle.

2

Two of Nietzsche's letters to Franz Overbeck will help unravel this puzzle as they will shed light both on Nietzsche's relation to Plato and some much larger issues as well. The first letter was written on March 31, 1885, approximately two months before the Preface itself. Surrounded by seven paragraphs of mostly personal information—about his state of health , travel and publication plans, the problems of mutual acquaintances—Nietzsche writes : "I read, yesterday, for relaxation, the Confessions of St. Augustine, with great regret that you were not here with me. Oh this old rhetorician! How false and how theatrical! How I laughed. . . . What psychological falsity. . . . Philosophical value equal to zero. *Plebeian Platonism* [*Verpöbelter Platonismus*], that is to say, a way of thinking that was invented for the highest aristocracy of the soul arranged for slave natures. By the way, in this book you see into the belly of Christianity. I stand by with the curiosity of a radical physician and physiologist."[10]

We can be fairly certain that the reading and interpretation of St. Augustine's *Confessions* forms the basis of the epigram we have been examining. "Plebeian Platonism" as the "belly of Christianity" becomes "Platonism is Christianity for the 'people'." This is St. Augustine's "null" contribution to philosophy, the union of Platonism, neo-Platonism and Christian doctrine, presumably as found in *Confessions* 7, 9, 13 ff. For Nietzsche, the attempt to unite Platonism and Christianity does violence to Platonism's essentially noble character, which is to say that it mistakes Plato and Platonism by viewing it "from below" and thus is blind to its heights: in terms used in *Beyond Good and Evil*, by an exoteric, not esoteric reading of this most subtle of philosophers.[11] "Platonism for the 'people'" is then a contradiction. As aristocratic, Platonism is a teaching about the order of rank, animated by a pathos of distance, precisely the opposite of the pathos of

10 *Sämtliche Briefe: Kritische Studienausgabe*, (*KSB*) ed. G. Colli and M. Montinari, (Munich: dtv/New York-Berlin: de Gruyter, 1975–1984), *KSB* 7:34. The emphasis is in the original text.

11 On Plato's complexity, see VII, 3, 34[66] (April–June 1885), an earlier version of *JGB* 190. For "exoteric-esoteric", see *JGB* 30. See also the important notebook entry, contemporary with the publication of *Beyond Good and* Evil, and headed "Exoteric-Esoteric" (VIII, 1, 5[9]: Summer 1886–Fall 1887.) I offered an interpretation of this fragment in an unpublished paper, "'Exoteric-Esoteric': Nietzsche's Metaphysics," delivered March 8, 1991 at the Metaphysical Society of America meeting in State College, Pennsylvania. Contrast Rosen, *The Question of Being* (pp. 226 ff.)

equality of souls, the humility that animates Christianity.[12] Far from equating Christianity and Platonism, Nietzsche's epigram, when viewed from this perspective is a critique of the Christian conception of Platonism. Indeed, one might say that this view of Platonism is part of the Jewish-Christian inversion of values, as it transforms an aristocratic into a plebeian way of thinking. As we will discuss below, the references to Plato and Platonism in *Beyond Good and Evil* are *correctives* to the Christian democratization of Plato, as they emphasize the aristocratic, ironical, hidden nature of Plato. "Christianity is Platonism for the 'people'," then, is not a characterization of Plato or even Platonism, but rather a critical comment on Christianity, and a remark about one of its early interpretive victims.[13] Yet Plato had been mentioned before in the Preface: we read of "Plato's invention of pure mind and of the good in itself," the opening events in the nightmare of dogmatic philosophy from which Europe is just beginning to awake.

To complete our view of the Plato being addressed in the Preface to *Beyond Good and Evil*, we may turn to another, earlier letter to Overbeck, who had supplied Nietzsche with a copy of Gustav Teichmüller's *Die wirkliche und die scheinbare Welt*, published in 1882. In a postcard dated 22 October 1883 he wrote: "Dear old friend, on reading Teichmüller I am more and more struck with amazement about how little I know Plato and *how much* Zarathustra *platonizei*."[14] The precise meaning of this phrase with regard to Zarathustra is probably connected to Teichmüller's interpretation of Plato, which views Hegel as a "Platonist" and Heraclitean whose discussion of non-being in the *Logic*, for example, adds nothing to Plato's in the *Parmenides*.[15] Using the *Parmenides and Sophist* as his point of departure, Teichmüller takes Plato to be the first and chief "pantheist," a perspective that philosophy has never been able to overcome and that reached its culmination in Hegel.[16] The explicit textual reference in the letter may involve his discussion of *parousia*, where there is a striking anticipation of Zarathustra's language: "The idea can do nothing with its wealth [*Reichthum*] and needs the needy [*Bedürftigen*] that allows itself to receive gifts. [*der sich schenken und geben läßt.*] Thus Plato allows it to descend from the intelligible heaven down into the darkness of the world and there in the appearances be

12 Augustine must supplement neo-Platonism with St. Paul in order to attain to the proper humility of a true Christian. See *Confessiones* 7, 21, 27.

13 Criticism of Christian "hermeneutics" is a consistent element through Nietzsche's career. See, e.g. *Dawn* 84 (V, I, 72) and *Antichrist* 42.

14 *KSB* 6:449. Stanley Rosen refers to this letter on pp. 22, 185 of his *The Mask of Enlightenment*.

15 Gustav Teichmüller, *Die wirklich und die scheinbare Welt: Neue Grundlegukng der Metaphysik* (Breslau: Wilhelm Koebner Verlag, 1882), pp. 94, 143 ff.

16 pp. xix, 108.

'present.' This *Katabasis* of the idea is its *Parousia*."[17] For Teichmüller, the teaching of such dialogues is of the necessary dialectical interplay—an interplay that is indistinguishable from contradiction—between the ideal and the actual, and pantheism amounts to the denial of any real being outside of this exchange.

Equally important in this context is Teichmüller's view of Plato's esotericism, explicitly with respect to the idea of "pure mind" as later taken over by Christianity. In fact, the keystone of Teichmüller's "new foundation of metaphysics" is the indispensability of Christianity, and particularly the Christian conception of the individual soul or I, grasped in intellectual intuition, for an exit from the circle of idealism which can never get past a "transcendental ego" and hence is without an ontological ground, trapped in the cycle of insubstantial "eidetic" giving and "phenomenal" receiving.[18] Thus, Teichmüller vigorously denies that Plato, "even in a dream, could think of the immortality of the soul, or of individual beings generally who were not somehow mere appearances."[19] This view is supported by a lengthy note in the work's Preface distinguishing "exoteric, orthodox Platonism" and "esoteric Platonic dialectic," the former used by the Church fathers, the other with its pantheistic element misunderstood or rejected by them.[20] There is no determinate concept of the individual and of personhood in Plato. In a pointed statement about Christianity and Platonism, he explicitly asserts that "we have no reason to hold that the conceptions of Plato which we find among the Church fathers and many moderns are authoritative in establishing the true teaching of Plato."[21]

Nietzsche's debt to Teichmüller is evident in *Beyond Good and Evil*. The discussion in its tenth aphorism of the "zeal and refinement" with which the "problem 'of the actual and apparent world'" is confronted "everywhere in Europe today" memorializes the title of his book.[22] The use of "perspectival" in

17 p. 342. For Zarathustra, see, e.g. the first section of the *Vorreden* (published even earlier as *Gay Science* 342, *Incipit tragoedia*); Night Song (*Zarathustra* II, VI, 1, 132 f.); and most explicitly in the later "Of the Poverty of the Richest," the final *Dionysus Dithyramb*, which were originally associated with Zarathustra. (VI, 3, 441ff, esp. 444 f.) Nohl noted Teichmüller's influence on Nietzsche in this and other respects in an early article, "Eine historische Quelle zu Nietzsches Perspektivismus—G. Teichmüller, die wirkliche und die scheinbare Welt, in *Zeitschrift für Philosophie und philosophische Kritik* 149 (1913), pp. 106–15.

18 p. 170.

19 p. xix.

20 p. xix n.

21 p. xx n.

22 In German, *JGB* 10 begins: "Der Eifer und die Feinheit, ich möchte sogar sagen: Schlauheit, mit denen man heute überall in Europa dem Problem 'von der wirklichen und der scheinbaren Welt' auf den Leib rückt . . ." (VI, 2, 16) The well-known section in *Twilight of the Idols* entitled "How the 'True World' Finally Became a

the aphorism and elsewhere in Nietzsche shows his indebtedness to Teichmüller's favored term for the world of semblance.[23] When Nietzsche speaks a bit later of Plato's opposition to sensualism, reminding his readers that the Platonic way of thinking was a noble way of thinking, and refers to the "sense-mob" [*Sinnen-Pöbel*], a reader of Teichmüller might be reminded of his `characterization of "sensualists and positivists, who according to Cicero's assumption are the plebeians among the philosophers."[24] The emphatic recognition of the importance of the esoteric and exoteric in *JGB* 30 along with the use of the terms might also be due to Teichmüller's use of the terms in his discussion of Plato.[25] The enduring influence of this view of Plato is testified to in the note of Spring 1888, i.e. the last year of Nietzsche's philosophically productive life. After contrasting Platonic "decadence" and sophistic honesty reading Greek culture, the note characterizes Plato as a "grand Cagliostro," and Nietzsche proceeds to raise questions about his honesty : "We know, at the least, that he wanted to have *taught* as absolute truth what was not even conditionally held by him as truth: 'the individual existence and individual immortality of 'souls.'"[26]

From the perspective of Teichmüller's work, then, the two doctrines named by Nietzsche in his Preface are no longer identifiably Platonic: the "good in itself" is a victim of a *katabasis* that necessarily involves it in the world of appearances if it is not to be a mere will of the wisp, and the "pure mind" is a myth for the "people" who could not manage the implications of the full pantheistic doctrine of Platonism, which, for Teichmüller, involves an acceptance of the contradictory nature of things.[27]

Fable," is a final *hommage* to Teichmüller's "new metaphysics" (VI, 3, 75). Note also its cyclical interrelation of Plato, the beginning of the true world (not necessarily the "error," and Zarathustra, at error's end. See the conclusion of Rosen's interpretation of this passage, *The Question of Being*, p. 175.

23 See pp. xvi, xvii, 183 ff.

24 *op. cit.*, p. 15.

25 For indications of an early awareness of this in Nietzsche's understanding of Plato, see the *Einleitung in das Studium der platonischen Dialoge* (1871–1872), II:4:2: 55. Rosen notes the importance of esotericism in *Beyond Good and Evil* in many publications, most recently in *Metaphysics in Ordinary Language* (New Haven: Yale University Press, 1999), pp. 1f.

26 VIII, 3, 14 [116].

27 See the passage on the educability of the people in Plato: "it didn't occur to him to teach children and the mob pure mathematics or pure philosophy. As a statesman he knew that the people [*Volk*] must believe something in order to live correctly and obey they laws since they are incapable of philosophical freedom and can neither control themselves nor others." (xii) The passage about Plato and contradiction is on p. 234. The whole passage, pp. 233–37 repays study about the relation of Plato and Hegel.

Thus, the "indictment" of Plato in the Preface, and the identification of Christianity and Platonism, are both evidence of the prevalence of historical misappropriation. For Nietzsche, such a conflation of Christianity and Platonism is evidence of the interpretive violence of Christianity, as exemplified by St. Augustine, and its slavish impossibility of affirming a true order of rank; reading with Teichmüller, it grants "dogmas" to a fundamentally dialectical teaching. Platonism as Christianity for the people cannot survive a sociological or metaphysical analysis. It remains to be seen what Platonism, or Christianity might actually be.

3

We would only be repeating Nietzsche himself if we said that the Plato presented in the Preface to *Beyond Good and Evil*, and particularly in the parenthetical phrase on which we have been concentrating, is a caricature.[28] As already noted, the references to Plato in the work itself give us a very different view, and focus on Plato the aristocrat, the man of refinement and complexity, while the ideal of the philosopher of the future, particularly as articulated in *JGB* 211, is not far from the Platonic philosopher king. Nonetheless, as often, this caricature has had a more vigorous life than the more detailed picture. It is one of the most visible masks under which the philosopher, indeed Nietzsche's "neo-Platonic" philosopher, lives in his writings.

Most notable is the role that the identification of Platonism and Christianity in the Preface to *Beyond Good and Evil* plays in the most influential interpretation of Nietzsche of the past century. Indeed, Heidegger's use of this apparent identity is not only central to his interpretation of Nietzsche, but also of metaphysics and nihilism, and hence of great consequence for the whole of "post-modern" philosophy. It is a tribute to the power, as well as the admitted violence of his interpretation that he has been able to build such an imposing edifice on such negligible foundations.

If we survey the classic Nietzschean texts on nihilism, texts that, in a selective manner, Heidegger himself examines in his different interpretations, we see that there is an element common to all of them that is absent, or virtually so, from Heidegger's interpretation: Nietzsche's focus on the "Christian" or "Christian-moral" dimension.[29] A few quotations of familiar texts will make this plain: "Nihilism stands before the door: whence does this most uncanny of guests come to us: 1. Point of departure: it is an error to point to 'distressful social

28 See VIII, 2, 10 [112] (Fall 1887).

29 Löwith objects to this in his early (1962) review of Heidegger's *Nietzsche*, the subject of Strauss' letter discussed below (p. 15). See *Aufsätze und Vorträge, 1930–1970* (Stuttgart: Kohlhammer, 1971), p. 83 See also p. 98 for the independent importance of Christianity to Western philosophy, unmentioned by Heidegger.

circumstances' . . . as *cause* of nihilism. . . . Nihilism is set in a totally specific interpretation, in the Christian-moral interpretation. . . . 2. The downfall of Christianity—due to its morality . . . which turns against the Christian God (the sense of truthfulness highly developed by Christianity . . ."[30] Another note, from the same period, has, as the "plan of the first book": 1. The oncoming nihilism, theoretical and practical. Fallacious derivation of it. . . . 2. Christianity perishing from its morality. 'God is the truth' 'God is love' 'the just God'—the greatest event—'God is dead—dully sensed.'. . . The signs. The European nihilism. Its cause: the devaluation of the previous values."[31] The well-known text entitled "The European Nihilism," itself the title of the lengthiest chapter in volume II of Heidegger's and the name of the first book of the plan used for the posthumously published *Will to* Power, begins "1. What advantages did the Christian moral hypothesis offer?"[32]

Yet Heidegger manages to mention Christianity, and Christian morality, only in passing in his lengthy treatment of "the European nihilism." He is contemptuous of any contribution of Christianity to philosophy in its thirteenth chapter, "Metaphysics and Anthropomorphy." According to this chapter, "a 'Christian philosophy' remains even more senseless than the thought of a square circle."[33] To preserve Nietzsche for philosophy, and to remove religious questions from his examination of nihilism, Heidegger regularly uses the passage from the Preface to *Beyond Good and Evil* that has been the subject of this paper. Thus, in the seventh chapter, "Nihilism and the Man of Western History," he notes that the "two-world doctrine" is what Nietzsche understands as the metaphysics of Plato, with its opposition of a world of "being" and "appearance." "Insofar as Christianity teaches that this world, as a vale of tears, is only a temporal transition to an eternal bliss that lies in the beyond, Nietzsche can understand Christianity as a whole as Platonism (two-world doctrine) for the people."[34] The crucial importance of this phrase for Heidegger's interpretation of Nietzsche is visible in his treatment of it in the first volume of this work, toward the end of the first lecture series in the chapter entitled "Truth in Platonism and in Positivism. Nietzsche's Attempt at an Inversion of Platonism out of the Basic Experience of Nihilism." Discussing Nietzsche's view of the ideal as a negation of life, he writes: "Here is a new interpretation of Platonism. It arises from the fundamental experience of the fact of nihilism and sees in this the original and determining ground for the possibility of the advent of nihilism, of nay-saying to life. Christianity for Nietzsche is nothing other than 'Platonism for the people', as

30 VIII, 1, 2[127] (Fall 1885–Fall 1886) Also published as *Will to Power* 1.

31 *ibid.*, 2[131].

32 *ibid.*, 5[71] Summer 1886–Fall 1887 . Portions of this lengthy, sixteen part notebook entry were published in different sections of *The Will to Power.* This was published as its fourth aphorism.

33 Heidegger, *Nietzsche* (Neske: Pfulllingen, 1961), p. 132.

34 *ibid.*, II:83.

Platonism however nihilism."[35] The Heideggerian strategy is clear: the interpreter can move seamlessly from references to Christianity to references to Plato, hence avoiding any embarrassing "theological" or "ethical" discussions, and then move straight to a discussion of nihilism as a metaphysical event. The degree to which Heidegger shares this view of Christianity—one which we now know that Nietzsche himself did not but which was formulated by a Father of the Church with whose writings the Jesuit-educated Heidegger must have been well-acquainted—is evident from the following important passage in his *Beiträge zur Philosophie (Vom Ereignis)*, written around the time the Nietzsche lectures were delivered. In §110, the second longest in the book, entitled "The *idea*, Platonism and Idealism," after having (in no. 21) accused Nietzsche of being a final consequence of Platonism in the very attempt at inverting it, he concedes, in number 22, that "[o]n the other hand Nietzsche is the one who first recognized the key position of Plato and the significance of Platonism for the history of the west (advent of nihilism). More exactly: he had intimations of Plato's key position." He remained Platonic in his use of Platonic categories in his interpretation of pre-Platonic philosophy. "However, and what weighs more, Nietzsche had detected Platonism in its most hidden forms: Christianity and its secularizations are all 'Platonism for the people.'"[36]

We can see the weight of this insight in Heidegger's essay, "Nietzsches Wort, Gott ist tot." which gives a sort of summary of the Nietzsche lectures. Particularly in this essay, which poses as a commentary on aphorism 125 of *The Gay Science*, entitled "The madman," it is crucial for Heidegger to move swiftly from religion to metaphysics, the "death of God" to the "absence of a supersensible world."[37] Heidegger makes it very plain that if we take "God is dead" as "formula for unbelief" we remain stuck in a "theological-apologetic" view and cannot grasp what is important for Nietzsche, namely "what has happened with the truth of the supersensible world and with its relation to the essence of man."[38] The elision of God, theology and belief from the discourse of this essay is made possible by an allusion to the passage under discussion. In the first paragraph of his interpretation, after a reproduction of the aphorism itself and a quotation from aphorism 343 of *The Gay Science* that makes explicit the reference to the "Christian God," Heidegger explains that though the saying about the death of God is clearly about the Christian God, "the names 'God' and 'Christian God' are used in Nietzsche's thought for the designation of the supersensible world. God is the name for the region of ideas and ideals. This region of the supersensible has been held, since Plato, more exactly, since the late-Hellenic and Christian interpretation of

35 *Ibid.*, I:182 f.

36 Martin Heidegger, *Beiträge zur Philosophie (Vom Ereignis)*, ed. F-W von Hermann, (Frankfurt a. M: Vittorio Klostermann, 1989), p. 219.

37 Martin Heidegger, *Holzwege*, (Frankfurt a. M.: Vittorio Klostermann, 1950), p. 200.

38 *ibid.*, p. 202.

Platonic philosophy, as the true and genuinely actual world. . . . The temporal world is the vale of tears in distinction from the stronghold of eternal bliss in the beyond. . . . The saying 'God is dead' means: the supersensible world is without effective force. It dispenses no life. Metaphysics, i.e. for Nietzsche Western philosophy understood as Platonism, is at an end."[39] Once this identification is made, Heidegger is free to ignore the apparently essential role that "God" or the "Christian God" plays in this aphorism, as he leaves unmentioned the role played by Christianity in the unpublished, programmatic pieces on nihilism.

The power, if not the accuracy, of Heidegger's interpretation is evident simply by looking at the history of the interpretation of Nietzsche and post-modernism, for which this essay and perspective on Platonism is canonical. Even Leo Strauss, in a recently published letter to Karl Löwith (March 15, 1962), written soon after the publication of Heidegger's Nietzsche lectures and Löwith's review of them, wrote: "I agree with Heidegger against you concerning the subordinate status of the issue of Christianity as distinguished from Platonism. I believe that the preface to *Beyond Good and Evil* is decisive in this respect."[40] Yet there is little doubt that the identification of Christianity and Platonism robs Christianity of what, for Nietzsche, were two of its defining characteristics, i.e. its denial of an order of rank among souls and its affirmation of the Jewish "morality of pity," while it neglects the aristocratic aspect of Platonic philosophy that was important for Nietzsche from the very beginning of his philosophical career, and that only grew in importance as he learned, perhaps influenced by Teichmüller, to read Plato more carefully.

4

In *The Birth of Tragedy*, Nietzsche viewed Socrates as the "mystagogue of science" responsible for the death of tragedy and the subsequent "net of thought" that has spread over the globe, as "the one turning point and vortex of so-called world history."[41] As Plato's teacher he brings an end to the great tragic age and is the "type of a form of existence unheard of before him, the type of the *theoretical man*."[42] Emblematic of this age and of his effect is the act of erstwhile tragedian,

39 *ibid.*, pp. 199 f. Note the similarity of language—"vale of tears"—in this passage and the one on *Nietzsche* II, 83, Christianity is finally dismissed as an object of Nietzsche's attention, and hence Heidegger's, on pp. 202 f.

40 Leo Strauss, *Gesammelte Schriften: Band 3* (ed. Heinrich and Weibke Meier, Stuttgart-Weimar, 2001) p. 686. In this letter Strauss, perhaps surprisingly given his other hermeneutical positions, indicates his preference for Heidegger's interpretation of Nietzsche, at odds with the author's own views, to Löwith whose views, Strauss concedes, are more congruent with Nietzsche's own.

41 *KGW* III, 1, 96 (*GT* §15).

42 *ibid.*, p. 94 (*GT* §15).

Plato, who is said to have burned his poems in order to become Socrates' pupil.[43] The three stages of history as enunciated in *The Birth of Tragedy* are the tragic age, the theoretical age and, as we reach the nineteenth century, the post-Kantian, Schopenhauerian-Wagnerian *rebirth* of Greek antiquity, the rebirth of tragedy.[44] Neither Christianity nor Judaism plays a role in this historical schema: history is a story told in Classical Greek and modern German.

However, despite the repetitions of Heidegger, his acolytes and his critics, by the time of *Beyond Good and Evil* the task is no longer the reversal of Platonism, but the transvaluation of values, and the transvaluation involves the overcoming of "slave morality,"—the overcoming of Judaism and its successor religion Christianity.[45] According to the central section of the central chapter of this work, it is due to the Jews and their "miraculous feat" of the inversion of values "that life on earth in the past 2,000 years has taken on a new and dangerous attraction." What is new is the institution of the "slave rebellion" as a normal state, the devaluation of the highest values. The danger it brings with it is that "most uncanny of all guests," nihilism. The work's very title testifies to the centrality of the "slave rebellion" in the resentful generation of values that are hostile to the "master" values which alone permit the expansion of life. To go "beyond good and evil" is not to "reverse Plato" or go "beyond Plato," but to declare war on the representative of the slave rebellion in modernity, i.e. Christianity.[46] Nietzsche's late works could not be clearer about this: *The Antichrist* was conceived as the first book of the *Transvaluation of all Values*, then as the *Transvaluation of Values tout court* before it received its final subtitle: *A Curse Upon Christianity.* [47] The penultimate section of *Ecce Homo* ends with the Voltairean "*Ecrasez l'infâme*," referring to Christianity, and the book ends with an even stronger plea for comprehension: "Have I been understood?—*Dionysus vs. the Crucified* . . ."[48]

The central historical roles have thus been exchanged. Socrates and Plato have been replaced by Moses and Jesus, or Moses and Paul. Nietzsche's view that

43 *ibid.*, p. 88 (*GT* §14).

44 *ibid.*, pp. 127 f (*GT* §20).

45 Nietzsche notes the absence of any discussion of Christianity in his later "Attempt at a Self-Critique," §5, published in 1886, and interprets this as a "wary and hostile silence." (*ibid.* p. 12).

46 Contrast Heidegger's remarks (*Nietzsche* I, 180) about Nietzsche's early note which, along with the phrase we have been examining, is a pillar of his interpretation: "My philosophy reversed Platonism." (III, 3, 7[156]). This note is crucial to Rosen's interpretation of Nietzsche as well: note the subtitle of *The Question of Being*—"A Reversal of Heidegger," and the title of the work's second half, on Nietzsche: "Reversed Platonism." See the introductory remarks to the section, pp. 137–39.

47 See VI, 3, 162–64; also Nietzsche, *Kritische Studienngesamtausgabe*, ed. G. Colli and M. Montinari, (Berlin: de Gruyter., 1980), 14:434 f.

48 VI, 3, 372.

Christianity, particularly Christian morality is at the basis of the nihilism and decadence of the nineteenth century, though fully developed in *Beyond Good and Evil*, makes its first serious appearance in *Dawn*, published in 1880.[49] Barely visible in this work, however, and only making its public appearance in later works, are considerations of the indebtedness of Christianity to Judaism. Nevertheless, the complex interaction of Jews, Romans and Germans is a particular theme of the notebooks of this time. In one of the earliest Nietzsche wrote: "Christianity *arose out of* Judaism and from nothing else . . ."[50] Christianity's victory as the hidden triumph of Judaism is also an explicit theme of Nietzsche's "Transvaluation of All Values," i.e. *The Antichrist*. Although Jesus is presented, á la Tolstoy, as a kind of Buddha explicitly opposed to the Jewish tendency toward revenge through his major teaching, non-resistance to evil,[51] or alternatively as a Dostoevskian "idiot,"[52] St. Paul, still "one of the most Jewish Jews who ever existed," in his "rabbinical impudence"[53] falsifies the history of Israel and the meaning of the life and death of Jesus and finally turns Christianity into a new Jewish sect, a new "elect" opposed to the "chosen people" of an "Old Testament, so that, finally, "The Christian is only a Jew of a 'freer' confession."[54] Far from being Platonism for the people (*das Volk*) Christianity is Judaism for the peoples (the *gentes*).

To quote "Christianity is Platonism for the 'people'" as if it were Nietzsche's considered characterization of Christianity and Platonism is completely to miss the force and depth of Nietzsche's later hostility to Christianity, present precisely in *Beyond Good and Evil* and *Toward the Genealogy of Morality* as well as in later works such as *The Antichrist*. Christianity remains a successor, but now a successor *religion*. The two-world thesis presented by Heidegger as "Platonic," arising out of an application of this phrase, is more appropriate to the criticism of

49 See the later Preface of 1886, V, I, 8 (§4). For the text itself, see the whole second half of Book I (§§57–92).

50 V, I, 3[137] (Early1880). The consequence of this for Europe and the Germans is drawn in other notes: "Europe has allowed an excess of Oriental morality to run rampant in it, as the *Jews* have thought and worked it out. One will not be the happiest and most sensible of people when one is so excessive when it comes to the moral and transposes it into the divine, humanly impossible." (3[128]) Regarding the Germans more specifically: "If one wishes to say that the Germans [*Germane*] are pre-formed and predestined for Christianity, then one is certainly no lacking in shamelessness, for the opposite is not only true, but even palpable. How should precisely the Germans make a better home than other peoples for the invention of two distinguished Jews, of Jesus and Saul, the two most Jewish Jews that have perhaps ever existed." (3[115])

51 See *The Antichrist* §§29, 31, 35, 42: VI, 3, 198, 200, 205 f., 213.

52 *Ibid.*, §§ 26, 29, 31: pp. 194, 198, 200.

53 *Ibid.*, §41: p. 213. In on the final sections of the work, Paul is called "the Jew, the wandering Jew, the eternal Jew *par excellence* . . . (§58; VI, 3: p. 244).

54 *ibid.*, §44 : p. 218 f.

Christianity we find in Bauer, Feuerbach or Marx. Perhaps it is the resonance of this phrase with the Marxian apothegm: "religion is the opiate of the 'people'"[55] that has allowed so many interpreters to forget the different valence of *Volk* in the two thinkers.

5

As the common interpretation neglects the growing significance of Nietzsche's moral critique and of the moral dimension of his conception of nihilism, so does it overlook the ever-greater, or ever more explicit complexity of his evaluation of Plato.[56] Even at the time of *The Birth of Tragedy* Nietzsche found Plato's political conceptions of the greatest interest and importance. In his final "Overview" to the introductory portion of the lecture notes for his *Introduction to the Study of Platonic Dialogues* from Winter 1871–72 he wrote : "His *legislative mission* must be understood as being at the center of the Platonic impulse. He counts himself among the Solons, Lycurgus', etc. Everything he does he does with a view toward this."[57] It is not surprising, then, that a good number of the notebook entries from this time concern the Platonic *Idealstaat* as the "model of a true *Denkerstaat*."[58] The only printed evidence of such reflections, and of the importance of the Platonic "ideal state" to Nietzsche at this time, is in his short essay *The Greek State*, one of the "five forewords to five unwritten books" privately printed and presented to Cosima Wagner as a Christmas gift in 1872. Its theme is the positive connection between the "highest" culture and the "lowest" things, especially the inseparability of slavery from culture. Its final paragraph is a peroration of the "perfect state of Plato," "something greater than even the most warm-blooded among his admirers believe." Plato had an intuition into the "genuine goal of the state, Olympian existence and ever-renewed generation and preparation of genius, in contrast to which all else is only a tool, resource, enablement." Nietzsche excuses Plato's rejection of the artistic in favor of the "genius of wisdom and knowledge" as a "rigid consequence of the . . . Socratic judgment of art, which Plato had made his own in battle against himself." The essay ends with a rhetorically charged characterization of the Platonic state as a "hieroglyphic of a profound and eternally to be interpreted *mystery doctrine of the interconnection*

55 Karl Marx, "Zur Kritik der Hegelschen Rechtsphilosophie" in S. Landshut, ed., *Die Frühschriften*, (Stuttgart: Kröner, 1971), p. 208.

56 An excellent summary of Nietzsche's views of Plato, and a recognition of their fundamental ambivalence may be found in Dieter Bremer, "Platonisches, Antiplatonisches." (*Nietzsche-Studien* 8: 1974, pp. 39–103.)

57 II, 4, 54.

58 III, 3, 7[17] End 1870–April 1871, p. 148. For other similar notes, see 7[25. 113], 29[170] Summer–Fall 1873 and 30[17] Fall 1873–Winter 1873–1874.

between state and genius."[59] In a notebook entry from this time, Nietzsche writes at the end of a list of topics regarding Plato: "Parmenides: Prelude, skepticism about the theory. Plato fundamentally legislator and reformer, never skeptic about that."[60]

The turn to the Platonic ideal, as the "noble Hellenic ideal," in *Beyond Good and* Evil, and its view that "genuine philosophers are commanders and law-givers,"[61] is thus a return, now purified of any suspicion that Plato himself was responsible for the downfall of the pagan ideal and nourished by a theory of will to power rather than artistic genius.[62] The role of Plato in *upholding* this ideal of "order of rank" with its return to the pre-eminence of the philosopher and the "master task and masterfulness of philosophy"[63] is visible in the book we have been calling Nietzsche's last version of *Transvaluation of All Values*, namely *The Antichrist*. At the work's end he contrasts the Christian teaching of equality with the Aryan Book of Manu. Part of the "naturalness" and "higher reason" of the latter is its "order of castes," which sanctions a "natural order" of "three types with a physiologically different gravitational field." The first of the three types are the few, the spiritual, the artistically gifted, "who rule not, because they want to, but because they *are*, and they are not free to be second." The second are the "guardians of right," the "noble warriors" who are the "executives of the most spiritual." Third are the "mediocre," the most numerous, the "broad base of the pyramid" that constitutes a "high culture." The kinship between this structure and that of the *Republic* is manifest. We need not belabor either this or the fundamental difference between a "natural" polity in a Platonic cosmos and one in which "the world is will to power—and nothing else." Nevertheless, far from overturning Platonism, the deepest protest against the Christian is made on the basis of a newly formulated Platonic state. The Aryan-Platonic "order of castes, the *order*

59 III, 2, 270 f. Ottmann (*op. cit.*) discusses Nietzsche's early "aestheticizing Platonism," pp. 44–48, along with other issues surrounding Nietzsche's political Platonism, pp. 146 ff., 276 ff., 312 ff. It is tempting to view Nietzsche's affirmation of the connection of slavery and art in these pieces sent to Cosima Wagner as a silent critique of Richard Wagner's position in *Art and Revolution*, where the presence of slavery was seen as the reason for the downfall of Greece's great artistic age, while the contemporary hope was for a rebirth of an artistic age on the basis of universal liberty and equality.

60 III, 3, 29 [174] Summer–Fall 1873, p. 196.

61 §211 (VI, 2, 149).

62 See *Antichrist*, §51: "It is not, as it is believed the corruption of antiquity itself, of *noble* antiquity, that made Christianity possible. . . . The great number became master; the democratism of the Christian instinct was *victorious.*" (VI, 3, 229 f.) On Plato as representative of noble antiquity, see also Bremer, pp. 76–80.

63 §204 (*ibid.*, p. 135) Nietzsche here speaks of the absence from our modern world of the "whole type of Heraclitus, Plato, Empedocles, and whatever other names these royal and splendid spiritual solitaries might have had."

of rank, merely formulates the supreme law of life itself . . . the inequality of rights is the first condition for their being any rights at all," while the claim for "equal rights'" is injustice. The Christian's denial of the order of rank manifested in Plato and the Book of Manu shows why "Christ" and "Anarchist" are of the same origin: they both deny the natural *archē*.[64] In affirming a "long ladder of the order of rank and value difference" [65] among human beings, Plato shows that he, unlike modern "free thinkers," knows the answer to the question asked by the last chapter of *Beyond Good and Evil*, "What is Noble?"

6

In the beginning was the word, the famous saying by a great smithy of phrases. What do we have now, in the end? We may first ask what Nietzsche hoped to achieve by saying that "Christianity is Platonism for the 'people'"? If we think of *Beyond Good and Evil* as a self-proclaimed renewal of the esoteric art of philosophy—a renewal of a Platonic art of whose Platonic roots we have seen that Nietzsche was well aware—we might raise the question this way: what is the exoteric meaning—the meaning "from below"—and how does it relate to the esoteric meaning—the meaning "from above"? From below, that would be from the crowd, here the crowd of free thinkers and atheists discussed in sections 44 and 58, filled with their "modern ideas" and animated by the nineteenth century's own "divine form of naiveté," its sense of superiority to religion as well as to philosophy, its sense of the hegemony of science and the scientist which includes the reflexive materialism and sensualism of sections 10 and 14. For the crowd of "modern thinkers," two outmoded systems of thought are conjoined, and the "two-world" interpretation of both, favored by post-Kantian critics and particularly the Hegelian left, is joined. If Christianity is but a popularization of Platonism, and Platonism, in an age of criticism and science, is itself a dogmatic relic of a pre-scientific, pre-critical age, then both may be dismissed as philosophies of the past, and philosophers of the future, already mobilized by Feuerbach in the 1840's, may be ready to fight once again. Such warriors remain a large segment of the Nietzschean cohort even today, readers for whom Nietzsche is an apostle of freedom and of social diversity, an enemy of repressive Christianity and rigid categorical structures.

From the esoteric view—from Nietzsche's point of view—such an interpretation is not unexpected. It is ill-considered in its own terms, since it does not conceive of the consequences of such an affirmation: the overcoming of

64 *The Antichrist*, § 57 (VI, 3, 239–42).

65 *JGB* 257. This phrase is in the first sentence of the first section of this last chapter. (VI, 2, 215) Compare the conclusion of Rosen's "Remarks on Nietzsche's 'Platonism'" in *The Quarrel Between Philosophy and Poetry* (New York-London: Routledge, 1988), p. 203.

Christianity and Platonism in this sense, of the two (or one) major world-interpretation(s) of the past 2,000 years, leaves nothing standing. Science itself is undermined by the rejection of Platonism, and the ethical certainties of nineteenth century democratic humanism are dissolved by the rejection of Christianity's "slave morality." The advent of that "uncanniest of all guests" is near at hand as the "self destruction of morality" and the "self-destruction of truth" work themselves out. But this is only to work out the hidden consequences of the surface interpretation. The interpretation itself is inadequate, and symptomatic of the interpreters, since it neglects the crucial role of the *Volk*, and is thus protected from the deepest and most dangerous impulse, the dynamite[66] that, a contemporary reviewer correctly saw, animates this work: a call to the destruction of a civilization based on universal human rights and human dignity, characterized by Nietzsche as herd or slave morality, and its replacement by one based on the "pathos of distance," the "order of rank," and "slavery of every sort."[67] From such a perspective, to think of "Platonism for the people" is to make a joke, either unintended—as in the *Confessions*—or intended, as in the Preface itself. Whoever takes it seriously has already condemned himself as plebeian, has already shown that he is not sensitive to the vast difference between a noble way of thinking—Platonism—and that way of thinking by means of which the slave has rebelled and the mob has poisoned the source of all nobility.

Interpreted from above, the very title and subtitle of the work bespeak the difference between the two teachings identified in this phrase. "Beyond Good and Evil": that is, beyond Judeo-Christianity and its inversion of value. "Prelude to a

66 Nietzsche himself uses the term, presumably picked up later by Widmann in his well-known review: J.V. Widmann, "Nietzsches gefährliches Buch," *Der Bund* 16/17, September 1886, reprinted in C.P Janz, *Nietzsche: Biographie* III (Munich: Carl Hanser Verlag, 1979), p. 257ff Nietzsche gleefully acepted this characterization. The third sentence of the final chapter of *Ecce Homo*, "Why I am a Destiny," asserts: "I am not a man, I am dynamite." (VI, 3, 362). Nietzsche refers to this review as evidence that he has been understood by at least one reader, in many subsequent letters: to Köselitz, 20 Sept. 1886, to Deussen (same date), to Fritzsch, his publisher, 24 Sept. 1886, to von Meysenbug, 24 Sept. 1886, to Köselitz again, 10 October 1886, to his mother, (same date), and to his sister, 3 November 1886.

67 Compare Burckhardt's letter after reading *Beyond Good and Evil*. Burckhardt, one of Nietzsche's three "intended readers" (cf. *KSB* 7:270: Taine and Bauer were the other two) summarized its central themes as follows: "on the will in the peoples and its current paralysis; on the antithesis of great assurance of well-being vs. a desired education through danger; on industriousness as destructive of the religious instincts; on the present herd man and his claims; on democracy as heir of Christianity; most particularly, however, on the future strong on earth! Here you ascertain and exhibit the probable conditions of their genesis and life in a way that must arouse the highest sympathy." (Burckhardt to Nietzsche, 26 Sept. 1886, Nietzsche, *Briefwechsel: Kritische Gesamtausgabe* (Berlin-New York: de Gruyter, 1975 ff), III:4, 221 f.)

Philosophy of the Future": that is, toward a reinstitution of the order of rank and of the task of the philosopher-lawgiver, of the Platonic view of the just polity and the philosopher's task, based in the new interpretation of the commanding authority of the philosopher.

Another group of readers remains: we are neither the crowd of nineteenth century free-thinkers nor Nietzsche himself. What have we gained by this exhaustive examination of a six-word phrase? Once we recognize the gulf of "rank" between Christianity, with its roots in the "Jewish slave rebellion," and Platonism, which arises from the culture that defines nobility for Nietzsche, we are led to review his conception of nihilism, as fundamentally a moral or, more exactly, moral-political phenomenon. The Heideggerian interpretation of nihilism as a metaphysical or ontological event has little or no basis in Nietzsche's texts once "Christianity is Platonism for the 'people'" has been eliminated as a straightforward identity. For Nietzsche, to be sure, nihilism demands a philosophical response, which is not the same as a lucubration about being. The philosopher of the future, about whom Nietzsche speaks, is a lawgiver and ruler. Only in this sense can we confirm Heidegger's Nietzscheanism: his actions of 1933 are the practical truth as the later lectures and writings are the theoretical retreat from the "explosive" message of "Nietzsche's dangerous book." Knowing what we know now, we can approach Nietzsche, Christianity, and Plato differently. We can learn much from Heidegger's mistakes, both practical and interpretative, and substitute theoretical boldness for his intellectual retreat, practical caution for his political decisiveness. We need to try to grasp the true nature of Platonic nobility, as we consider the deeper sources and consequences of Christianity and its denial, if we are to understand the lesson of Nietzsche, self-styled antichrist and Platonic philosopher of the future.

Where My Spade Turns
On Philosophy, Nihilism, and the Ordinary

Sharon Rider
Uppsala University (Sweden)

> If I have exhausted the justifications, I have reached bedrock, and my spade is turned. Then I am inclined to say: "This is simply what I do."[1]

Introduction

The title of this essay may be startling to those readers who recognize the reference as a quote from Ludwig Wittgenstein. And, I will in fact be discussing certain recurring themes in Wittgenstein's philosophy which I take to be in harmony with a number of central insights in Rosen's thought, although the focus throughout will be on ideas, and not authors.

I have three reasons for undertaking this task. The first reason is purely autobiographical. I have been deeply influenced by Wittgenstein's work for the last decade, but in the most fundamental respects, I see this influence as a continuation of the philosophical training I received under the tutelage of Stanley Rosen. Second, and more importantly, precisely because their work is so very different in form, the reflections offered here have to do with what I take to be serious intellectual and ethical concerns motivating the work of both men, rather than with the technical arguments to which those concerns give rise, or with schools of thought, traditions of interpretation, and so forth. They are questions such as: What is the relationship between reason and the good, i.e. in what way, if any, is intelligibility bound up with values? Or: What is the relationship between "everyday life," "ordinary experience" or "the life world" on the one hand, and philosophical insight and conceptualization, on the other? Third, I believe that making clear where there is more agreement than may be assumed between these two so radically different ways of viewing and engaging in the philosophical enterprise can provide instructive cues to answering those general questions. Because the point of the essay is conceptual rather than expository, I will take the liberty of

1 Ludwig Wittgenstein, *Philosophical Investigations,* (1953) transl. G.E.M. Anscombe (Basil Blackwell: 1958), §217.

focussing primarily on issues discussed in Rosen's most recent treatment of Wittgenstein (in *Philosophy and Ordinary Experience* and *The Elusiveness of the Ordinary*),[2] although familiarity with his other writings will be assumed. What I offer below is a way of understanding Wittgenstein that I take to be both deeper and more philosophically interesting than the received view(s). While this way of reading Wittgenstein is something that I in fact have learned from others, the claims I make are to be taken as my own reflections, inspired by my understanding of Wittgenstein.[3]

Let me begin by saying something about what I do *not* take Wittgenstein to be saying. A common picture of the later Wittgenstein's project is that it is intended to help us delineate *rules* for meaningful speech on the basis of *de facto* speech. Commenting on Wittgenstein's emphasis on ordinary language, Rosen writes:

> He begins from the conventional or historical fact of the linguistic community whose members speak in more or less the same way. It is as a member of this community that the philosopher or speech therapist has access to standard idioms and rules of linguistic use, by which to eliminate mistakes arising from misuse of those idioms and rules.[4]

I would say that one of the driving motivations behind the *Investigations* (in contrast to the *Tractatus*) is the attempt to find a legitimate function for serious philosophical thinking, given that philosophy has lost its mandate to legislate norms. In itself, however, this insight need not entail the view that classical philosophy was wrong or confused insofar as it attempted to assimilate the logical and the ethical, but rather reflects the sober recognition that philosophy, as a

2 Stanley Rosen, *Metaphysics in Ordinary Experience* (Yale University Press: 1999; St. Augustine's Press, 2006), and Stanley Rosen, *The Elusiveness of the Ordinary: Studies in the Possibility of Philosophy* (Yale University Press: 2002).

3 A few interpretations and applications of Wittgenstein's philosophy that have inspired some of the ideas sketched below are: Sören Stenlund, *Language and Philosophical Problems* (Routledge: 1990); Martin Gustafsson, *Entangled Sense* (Uppsala University Press: 2000); Pär Segerdahl, *Language Use* (Macmillan: 1996); Lars Hertzberg, "Wittgenstein and the Sharing of Language," in *The Limits of Experience* (Acta Philosophica Fennica: 1994) and "On the Need for a Listener and Community Standards," in *The Practice of Language,* Martin Gustafsson and Lars Hertzberg (eds.), (Kluwer: 2002), and James Conant, "Wittgenstein on Meaning and Use," in *Philosophical Investigations* 21 (1998).

4 Rosen 2002, p. 141. Perhaps the most prominent Wittgenstein interpreters who hold something like this view are Gordon Baker and Peter Hacker (*Wittgenstein: Rules, Grammar and Necessity,* Blackwell 1985). The issue of rule-following is crucial to, and therefor, pervasive in Wittgenstein scholarship and interpretation, but clearly beyond the scope of this essay. The reader is referred to an excellent review and analysis of the problems in Martin Gustafsson (2000).

matter of fact, no longer has a morally legislative function. In this respect, there is clearly a Nietzschean element to Wittgenstein's thought.[5] But, as I will try to show, this recognition does not make Wittgenstein a nihilist, but rather, like Nietzsche, a philosopher who is grappling with the problem of nihilism (among other things).

For Nietzsche, as opposed to many of his disciples, "the problem of nihilism" was not a theoretical issue, nor a rhetorical or literary trope, nor an intellectual mannerism. His pronouncements on the revaluation of all values, the death of God and so forth have overshadowed a more matter-of-fact expression of the same concern: there seems to be nothing more worth taking seriously.

When Nietzsche denies that there are "moral facts," or when he derides Kant's notion of the will as a "faculty," in other words, when he criticizes metaphysics and theology, he does so, one might say, on *ethical* grounds: the kinds of "facts" presented in theological and philosophical discourse, rather than expressing incontrovertible truths as they claimed to, in effect, expressed moral demands. Nietzsche rarely criticized ethical practices or personal beliefs *per se*; what he criticized was the tendency of normative systems to parade around as logically binding facts (this is especially clear in *Twilight of the Idols* and *The Antichrist*). On this reading of Nietzsche, he is not making a negative metaphysical claim when he says, for example, "there are no moral facts whatsoever". He is saying that it *makes no sense* to talk about "moral facts" at all. Thus it makes no sense, really, to make the claim that nothing is morally true, if by that one means that the truth of all ethical questions lay somewhere else, in, let us say, some materialist conception of human life, for instance. The problem with philosophers, as Nietzsche describes it in *Beyond Good and Evil*, *Twilight of the Idols* and *the Gay Science*, is that they have been concerned with justifying a certain moral order.

Nietzsche's assertion that "God is dead" is commonly treated as if it were Nietzsche himself who committed deicide, as if Nietzsche *demanded* of his readers that they cease believing in God, as if Nietzsche wanted to replace God with "the absence of God" as a metaphysical starting-point, i.e. atheism as a philosophical position. But one can also understand, for instance, book III of *The Gay Science*, as simply *pointing out* that the language of guilt, punishment and reward, right and wrong, good and evil, which were part of the religious way of life, had lost their meaning, and that what remained were abstract codes and empty forms. In this light, we can see Nietzsche's often trying praise of hardness, strength, will, and nobility of character as words of encouragement to those who had the same

5 Despite deficiencies in his discussion of Wittgenstein's ostensible "faith" in ordinary language, Erich Heller's comparison of Nietzsche and Wittgenstein is worth reading in this context. See Erich Heller, *The Importance of Nietzsche* (University of Chicago: 1988), chap. 8.

suspicions. Nietzsche was encouraging what Heidegger would later characterize as *Beschlossenheit*, resoluteness, in the face of the new *facts of life*. In this respect, Nietzsche's ethical teaching is indistinguishable from his conceptual analysis.

But we can appreciate his attempt to save humanity from nihilism, from the sense that "there's nothing more worth taking seriously," without accepting his proposed solutions. While it might have seemed plausible to Nietzsche that a great work of philosophy, or art or literature could revivify culture by introducing new values, or even re-introducing ancient ones, that is not a viable option for us today, since even nineteenth-century ideas of literary or artistic greatness have become obsolete.

Yet the problem of nihilism might not be the same problem for us today as it was for Nietzsche. One might say that everything that Nietzsche feared has come to pass, but then, looking at our lives and our culture not as a future possibility or an historical event waiting to be interpreted a hundred years from now, but from *within*, so to speak, it is not so certain that the situation is as bad as all that. While we are constantly being bombarded with claims that we *must,* as enlightened denizens of this the most enlightened epoch, see ourselves as atoms whirring meaninglessly in the void, we have now, as always, the option of meeting such claims with circumspection and even suspicion. We can follow Nietzsche's advice in *Beyond Good and Evil:* "So let us, for once, be more cautious, let us be 'unphilosophical'."[6] I take the later Wittgenstein's philosophy to be "unphilosophical" in precisely this regard.

Certainty and the Unsayable

It is true that the later Wittgenstein most certainly would say that the hypostatization of the transcendental I as the source and guarantor of certainty is impossible for us to take seriously anymore. This does not, however, entail the impossibility of certainty, even in moral issues, that is often assumed to follow from that impossibility. It is not that certainty is impossible; it just turns out to be something other than what philosophers have thought. Certainty is something attained on the basis, infamously, of the "unsayable". In what follows, I will attempt to show the respect in which the *unsayable* is not the same as the *silent*. The unsayable is actually quite articulate (if not garrulous). That is, it is constantly *showing itself* in any number of things that we are inclined to say and do. But the things that we are inclined to say and do are so complex and variegated that they cannot be stated

6 Friedrich Nietzsche, *Beyond Good and Evil*, (1886) transl. R.J. Hollingdale (Penguin: 1973), "On the Prejudices of the Philosophers" §19.

in this or that doctrine. Nonetheless, something can be said about our various and sundry practices: this is what is meant by the notion of a *rule*. The notion of rule-following is misleading, however, because we tend to think that first there is a rule, and then we either follow this existent rule correctly, or incorrectly, or not at all. For Wittgenstein, the rule derives its determinate meaning from practice, and not the reverse. Thus, Rosen is naturally right when he describes Wittgenstein's project as finding meaning in *de facto* praxis. Nonetheless, I think that one should take great care to understand the import of this *conceptual* point regarding the relationship between rules and practice, namely, that anything we can *say* about what it means to do something presupposes the practice the statement is intended to describe. This is the respect in which a full description is "unsayable," that is, it never hits bottom. But Wittgenstein is not suggesting that there are two kinds of knowledge/language, "propositional" or "discursive" on the one hand, and some sort of "tacit knowledge" or "non-discursive insight," on the other. What makes Wittgenstein's later philosophy so difficult is that his studies of "depth grammar" are comparable to Kant's transcendental reflections insofar as they are not propositions about states of affairs at all. They are rather meditations on the conditions for making such propositions (given the fact that we can and do engage in such discourse) and, as such, "say nothing" about anything:

> We feel as if we had to penetrate phenomena: our investigation, however, is directed not towards phenomena, but, as one might say, towards the "possibilities" of phenomena. We remind ourselves, that is to say, of the kind of statement that we make about phenomena[. . .] . Our investigation is therefore a grammatical one. Such an investigation sheds light on our problem by clearing misunderstandings away. Misunderstandings concerning the use of words, caused, among other things, by certain analogies between the forms of expressions in different regions of language.[7]

Grammatical investigations naturally use language, presuppose language and take place in language, since the whole point is to describe our form of life from the point of view of lived experience (that is, from the point of view of the user of language). The "given" for Wittgenstein is not "the contingent practices and conventional ways of speaking of our historically particular culture"; such a description presupposes our language and form of life as an *external object* for consideration, a point of view which is parasitic upon the first-person, or internal, perspective we all have in our everyday dealings with language.

7 Ludwig Wittgenstein, *Philosophical Investigations*, (1953) transl. G.E.M. Anscombe (Basil Blackwell: 1958), §89.

One may describe Wittgenstein's project as the attempt to do philosophy *given* that we cannot lift ourselves up by our hair or step out of our skin: he describes our linguistic practices as *ours*. And, for *us*, as language users and livers of our form of life, that is, from the first-person perspective, there is nothing accidental, historically contingent *or* conventional about most of the things that are important to us, least of all, moral and religious practice. There is plenty of room for ethical *truth*: what you (we) *really* want. There is equal room for logical or philosophical *truth*: what you (we) *really* mean. But these truths are not statements of fact in the scientific sense, and the tendency to waffle between these sorts of insights and statements of fact leads inexorably to philosophical confusion. Yet certainty in these questions can be shown (most often in and through language, or discursive practice, or whatever term one prefers), although not "stated" as such. Once more, Rosen is certainly right to point out that if ordinary language is understood as "the changing idiom of history," then it is indeed a theoretical construction. But from the first-person perspective, language cannot be seen thus; and for Wittgenstein, for whom genuine communication about the world is not only a possibility but an actuality (and thus the starting point for all philosophical investigation), the goal of philosophizing is to understand what we actually (really) *mean*.

If philosophy is about what we really can meaningfully say, this is neither because meaning is prior to use, nor because there are conventional rules determining what is an allowable move in a language game. It is rather because in learning our native language, we "take in" the world. We cannot simply choose "alternative" pictures or uses at will and still be able to mean at all. To mean is not the same thing as to apply a theory of meaning (the choice of which makes not the slightest difference for how we live our lives). For Wittgenstein, the failure of philosophy to describe adequately and accurately how it is that we can "mean," rather than suggesting that meaning is arbitrary or uncertain, indicates that there is something fundamentally wrong with the question. Another way of putting it is to ask, with Wittgenstein: "You ask how meaning is possible? In what respect?" Posing the question this way, Wittgenstein hopes to show how meaning is possible, in a way that is not a general statement of fact (because the question of how meaning is possible is not a question about a state of affairs).

Compare now what I have said above with the following remark, in which Rosen criticizes what he takes to be Wittgenstein's implicit historicism:

> Since grammars define families of language games or constitute a "life-form," and life-forms are multiple as well as diverse, or in other words, since there is no universal life form, any more than there is a universal form of the proposition, it seems that human nature, and so what counts as ordinary or healthy use, is a function of history, that is to say, of chance.[8]

8 Rosen 2002, p. 140.

To begin with, Rosen states that "grammars define families of language games" or constitute a life-form. But what is meant by *grammars* here? Wittgenstein writes:

> In the use of words one might distinguish "surface" grammar from "depth" grammar. What immediately impresses itself upon us about the use of a word is the way it is used in the construction of sentences, the part of the use—one might say—that can be taken in by the ear.— And now compare the depth grammar, say of the word "to mean," with what its surface grammar would lead us to suspect. No wonder we find it difficult to know our way about.[9]

Wittgenstein would not accept the idea that surface grammars (such as the rules formulated by grammarians, or the logical combination of meaningful sentences in the manner of Carnap's logical syntax) define forms of life. It's not as if Wittgenstein thinks that the most important things we can know about a form of life is the prevalence of gendered articles or the prevalence of strong verbs within a language group, or linguistic theory. Those sorts of rules are obviously arbitrary insofar as they were developed precisely for scholastic instruction (primarily, in fact, for foreign language instruction, that is, "official Greek"),[10] in the one case, and developed within the particular history of the philosophy of language stemming out of Frege and Russell, on the other, and are thus the result of historical contingency. Historically speaking, the world of lakes and the practice of swimming existed long before the grammarians parsed up language into verbs and nouns, or the logicians formulated the rules for well-formed sentences. Furthermore, in cultures in which speakers have no notion of verbs or nouns, people talk about lakes and teach their children to swim, *using* language. The suggestion that there is some grammar dictating these practices that these people are implicitly following is, to say the very least, highly speculative, and, I do not think a view that Wittgenstein would hold. So what is being suggested here? It must be that *depth grammar* is what is definitive of a language and form of life. And, insofar as we are philosophizing, that would be Wittgenstein's view. Depth grammar describes, as it were, a horizon of our understanding, a point at which

9 Wittgenstein 1958, §664. Richard Sørli points out that, while the standard reading of the distinction is to identify surface grammar with the "obvious syntactic features of sentences and the words of which it is composed," and depth grammar with "the combinatorial possibilities and impossibilities, of the circumstances of its use, and of its consequences" (Hacker, cited in Sørli), this reading neglects the importance Wittgenstein ascribes to *use*. Thus what Wittgenstein intends by "surface grammar" is close to the standard reading of "depth grammar." I follow Sørli in my use above. See Richard Sørli, "Wittgenstein, Grammar and the Orthodoxy of the Ordinary," unpublished manuscript, 2002.

10 R.H. Robbins, *A Short History of Linguistics* (London: 1967), p. 13.

nothing more can be said *about* meaning, although meaningful speech that is revelatory of that horizon is both possible and actual (but not as an intellectual discourse about *some thing*).

In the rest of the quote, a number of consequences are drawn from Wittgenstein's refusal to engage in generalized discourse about "human nature," "a universal form of the proposition," etc., in particular that it results in historicism. But Wittgenstein is not advocating an historicist view, simply by criticizing an ahistoricist view. Once more, he is trying to avoid "saying too much," and thus risk saying nothing ("nonsense"). Wittgenstein would presumably grant a number of historicist assertions about particular cases, without embracing historicism as such, that is, he would grant its point as critique in any number of contexts, but refuse to grant it as a philosophical thesis or doctrine.[11] As a general thesis, historicism assumes in advance of the formulation of any specific problem that the problem *ought* to be formulated in such a way as to be amenable to historical explanation. But Wittgenstein would first demand that we are clear about what it is that we want to know before assuming an historicist stance.

As critique, historicist works mostly describe the *de facto* conditions in which past thinkers worked, the intellectual debate of the period, the connotations of certain terms in a given epoch and so forth. The motivation behind such studies is presumably the prevalence of treating philosophers in the past as if there were no such conditions, as if philosophers did not in fact write in a certain context and not another.

As a general thesis or starting-point, however, historicism seems inevitably leads to a number of perplexities. First, the prioritizing of questions concerning cultural bias, for example, is often assumed to be unproblematic given the historicist starting-point. The historicist position provides a kind of metaphysical justification for posing certain questions, and simply disregarding others, as those become nonsensical within the historicist framework. Second, it presumes that one can say something sensible about a culture as a whole, and thus moves from being a modus operandi to an ontology. If we follow this line of thought to its natural conclusion, we seems to be forced to embrace one of the following, to my mind absurd, conclusions:

Past thinkers (or actors) were culturally limited. We, however, can see the conditions of their thinking better than they could because of our historical distance.

We are culturally limited, we cannot understand anything at all except for our own cultural projections.

11 Here Koselleck's historicizing of historical thinking in *Critique and Crisis: Enlightenment and the Pathogenesis of Modern Society* (MIT: 1988) is relevant. The historical coincidence of the development of "historical thinking" in the modern sense and the advent of "critique" is a useful reminder to us that we are not nearly as self-critical in our perpetual gesturing to "historical contingency" as some kind of neutral fact as we ought to be.

Interestingly enough, few draw these drastic conclusions, but at the same time, neither do they draw a lesson from the fact that they are unprepared to do so. I would say that the lesson to be drawn is that our own experience inoculates us from such theoretical extremism in practice (although not in philosophy).

I take the Wittgensteinian position toward historicist claims to be that it is something that must be decided from case to case, issue to issue. We cannot, in advance of inquiry, decide, for instance, that either (i) there is no such thing as sex and death *per se*, but only different cultural practices of, say, courtship and religious mysticism, or (ii) there is only copulation and expiration, and these are the basis for various arbitrary cultural expressions such as marriage and religious institutions. The question of the constancy of human nature can only be decided in the context of a much more specified question, and with respect a predetermined and presumably narrow use of the notion of constancy. As a hermeneutic principle, this means that the extent to which ancient texts, for example, are intelligible or unintelligible to modern discourse is simply the extent to which they are intelligible or unintelligible. The question is, what problems are you trying to solve? If an ancient text does, effectively, shed light on a problem, then it is apparently intelligible in the relevant sense (even if only to a few). As Rosen writes, "[i]t is our perception of human nature that makes Plato and Aristotle intelligible to us."[12] But to ask if such perception *in general* is an historical artifact or a part of the natural order is to pose a question that cannot be decided once and for all. In Wittgensteinian terms, it is not a question we can "get clear about".

More importantly, such a stance can only be taken towards an object of inquiry, that is, towards language or culture as an object. Wittgenstein's remarks are not about linguistic practice as an object of study, but are "internal" to actual language use. In this respect, there are "logical" or "grammatical" remarks that are not in the least arbitrary, that is, which show *necessary* relations, *given* the language we have. There are certain facts about our language that cannot be otherwise, whereas the philosophical explanations we develop to explain these *may well be* historically contingent.

The concept of a line, one might want to say, is relative to the cultural and linguistic horizon it inhabits. What would it mean, however, to say that there are lines that lack length? However fuzzy and confused our idea of the dark side of the moon as a possible object of perception, we can at least get started thinking about it. And we certainly have no trouble grasping the claim that dogs perceive odors that human beings cannot. Thus we may be tempted to say that there is or could be a society or language in which lines were not always perceived as having some length; say, a tribe in which all members suffer from some kind of hereditary congenital blindness. In the imagined case, the tribe has survived without the

12 Rosen 1999, p. 221.

capacity to perceive lines at all, and this might seem to provide evidence for the notion that attributing length to lines is a convention, or as counter-evidence to the notion that the association between length and lines is some sort *of biological* fact about human psychology. But from the point of view of depth grammar, the relationship between length and the notion of a line is internal; length belongs to the meaning of a line. A notion of line without length would be a *different use* of the word, a different concept, than the ordinary geometrical one. As a grammatical remark, the foregoing is neither normative (it is not a prohibition against using words as one wishes) nor informative (it provides no explanation); it is a description of a defining feature of the ordinary use of the word line.

Neither psychologistic nor conventionalist explanations of how we have the notion of line that we have can get off the ground without assuming the meaning of line, lest they not know what it is they are explaining or disagreeing about in the first place. In fact, they would have nothing to explain (they would have no problem to pose). *All* empirical explanations (that is, explanations about things) rely upon "grammatical facts" of this kind. To say that a line necessarily has length is to reach the point at which "my spade turns". It's the sort of remark that few would dream of questioning, but not because it's an implicit or tacit theory. Rather, it's the sort of remark one arrives at when trying to define what it is that one is talking about, what it is one is trying to explain, what it is that one "really means". But it is, in a sense, a "transcendental" remark insofar as it tells us nothing that wasn't already there with us from the moment we learned how to use the word "line," and which simply has no use outside of the context of such reflection. I take this to be Wittgenstein's point when he remarks: "The work of the philosopher consists in assembling reminders for a particular purpose. If one tried to advance *theses* in philosophy, it would never be possible to debate them, because everyone would agree to them".[13] The various ways we were trained to use "line," the nearly infinite number of circumstances at home, in the playground and even the first-grade classroom cannot be cursorily stated in a philosophical theory without falsification or unwarranted speculation (which is not to say that such speculation and even simplification is always unwarranted. One can imagine uses for it in, for example, early childhood development studies, where one is interested in testing various methods of early instruction to improve geometric understanding among schoolchildren).

In response to the objection that *either* there is a natural order *or* there is only construction, I would say that Wittgenstein simply refuses to accept that dichotomy as helpful in a number of important philosophical issues, because the terms are formulated at the outset before the posing of the particular question. That lines have length is not a "construction," if by that we mean a convention that could be

13 Wittgenstein 1958, §127, §128.

otherwise. Objections with reference to non-Euclidean geometries or Poincaré's conventionalism are irrelevant here, since we are not talking about a working definition, say, a line as the shortest distance between two points. Poincaré's conventionalist view of mathematics is largely in harmony with Wittgenstein's, but the internal relation between the notion of line and the having of length is not a part of mathematics. But is it a "natural fact"? Hardly. In an important sense, it's not a "fact" at all. Rosen reads Wittgenstein as seeing nature as a theoretical construction, but I do not think that Wittgenstein sees ordinary use as theoretical in this way. There is, however, a use of nature that *is* a theoretical construction, namely, the "nature" of the natural sciences (which is often assumed in an unspecified and fluid manner in philosophical discussion). Borrowing a phrase from Rosen, one could say that it is not Wittgenstein's analysis of the "ordinary" that is endless, with "no bottom and no top," but rather generalized philosophical notions of "nature," "custom" and so forth that are endless (because fluid). Words such as "nature" and "culture," like words such as "object" or "I" tend to play the field in philosophical discussion. When we "bring back words from their metaphysical to their everyday use," we are, Wittgenstein says, bringing them back to the language-game which is their original home,[14] or rather, calling them back to work when they've gone, as Wittgenstein says, "on holiday".[15] This is the sense of the "extraordinary use" of words in philosophy that we have to learn to resist if we are to attain the clarity that is for Wittgenstein the goal of philosophy. But is clarity certainty? Can we say that we are "certain" that lines have length?

The goal of certainty in modern philosophy seems to involve starting with what cannot be doubted even in principle, and building up arguments on that basis. For Wittgenstein, this philosophical notion of certainty that is both the starting-point and ultimate goal is problematic. I will not rehearse Wittgenstein's discussion of certainty here, but will rather limit myself to a few points relative to the discussion above. I wish to say that clarity is not certainty, but that we should perhaps not be concerned with certainty in philosophy, precisely because certainty is something we aim at with regard to facts. Philosophy, however, can provide us with clarity such that the issue of certainty never arises (because the kinds of insight philosophy provides cannot be doubted). In "A Central Ambiguity in Descartes," Rosen notices that the rejection of everything that can be doubted in principle presupposes the capacity to identify with certainty what constitutes dubious knowledge. But is our distinct recognition that we are uncertain about something, something about which we can be certain? Carl Page writes:

> Certainty in all its forms entails a meta-reflection, an assessment that a given judgment has been made properly and correctly. It is a retrospective certification that the evidence is in order and that the train of thought leading up to

14 Wittgenstein 1958, §116.
15 Wittgenstein 1958, §38.

> the judgment has followed adequate procedures. Declarations of certainty in actual cases are thus relative to the standards of evidence and ratiocination presupposed for different types of judgement.[16]

I take this to be an accurate and succinct description of the use of the notion of certainty. And it invites the question, are all insights that cannot even in principle be doubted, amenable to demands of justification, standards of evidence and procedures of ratiocination? How could I, even in principle, satisfactorily demonstrate that all lines have length? Or more to the point, how can I even begin to doubt that lines have some length? What would such doubt mean? If I am looking at two lines written on a blackboard two meters away, and describing what I see for someone on the telephone, he might question whether or not my *observation* about the relative lengths of the two lines is correct. And, in such a case, I may well squint my eyes for a few seconds (checking the equipment, as it were), and then I might be inclined to say, "Yes, I'm quite certain now. Line A is longer than line B." In this case, I have reason to distrust the testimony of my senses, and indeed, there is a procedure for checking the accuracy of my original statement. The extent to which we speak of evidence is exactly the extent to which the statement refers to a state of affairs, that state of affairs being the relative length of the two drawn lines. Similarly, my certainty is tied to my assessment that the evidence is in order.

What are we to make of the internal relation between lines and length then? I would certainly want to say that it is indubitable, but this precisely because it is not a fact or state of affairs, and therefore not susceptible of proofs either. Evidence and justification belong to cases in which doubt has been introduced. To state the matter perversely, we can only be certain about what can be doubted. But this does not open the floodgates of nihilism, since accepting that certain things simply cannot be doubted, that we have hit rock bottom, is merely to admit the *limits of philosophy*. Wittgenstein's proposal is that philosophy is still possible if it takes as its task to remind us of what we as *human beings* cannot doubt, and leave the work of justification and meeting evidentiary demands to the special sciences. To return to Rosen's critique of Descartes, one might say that Descartes' "mistake," if one wishes to call it that, is to take the impossibility of his doubting that he is thinking *substantively*, that is, as a fact (as if he has identified some thing, namely, the act of doubting). As Rosen argues in "Philosophy and Ordinary Experience," the way out of the doubt raised by the rhetoric of science is a "reconsideration of ordinary experience, and so too the rediscovery of the starting points of philosophical investigation."[17]

16 Carl Page, "Symbolic Mathematics and the Intellect Militant: On Modern Philosophy's Revolutionary Spirit," in *Journal of the History of Ideas*, vol. 57, no. 2, p. 237.

17 Rosen 1999, p. 238.

"The Highest Things"

One important theme in Rosen's work is the ranking of forms of life: distinguishing between good and bad, better and worse, coherent and incoherent, etc., or analyses and evaluations as two sides of the coin of judgment and discernment. Both in the *Preface* to *Metaphysics and Ordinary Language* and in the essay "Philosophy and Ordinary Experience," for example, Rosen suggests that rank-ordering of forms of life are an essential element of philosophy, without addressing explicitly certain objections that I take to be Wittgensteinian. In particular, one could say something like the following: A rank-ordering is a kind of systematization; but as Rosen has repeatedly pointed out, everyday life is not systematic. A rank order that does not bear the mark of a systematic structure, if it were an honest and intelligent appraisal based on the facts of lived experience would be an expression of wisdom, to be sure, but why philosophy? (It is, among other things, the assimilation of the logical and the ethical in the *Tractatus* that the later Wittgenstein takes issue with in *Philosophische Bemerkungen*).

Isn't the point of an immanentist view of philosophy in the manner of Wittgenstein to leave wisdom to the wise, and the analysis and dissolution of philosophical problems to philosophers? Of course, there are wise philosophers, as the example of Rosen strikingly illustrates, but there are wise men who are not philosophers insofar as their wisdom is simply not relevant to problems of metaphysics or epistemology. Similarly, there are "working philosophers" who have made important contributions to our collective thinking, but who few of us would be inclined to describe as "wise" in broader and deeper respects (Frege would, I imagine, be an example of the latter). A philosopher may well combine deep insight into human existence with trenchant conceptual analysis and breadth of erudition (I suppose this is what we mean by calling Plato or Kant "great philosophers"), but it is not clear that the relation is *internal*. Indeed, the sheer prevalence of the one unaccompanied by the other would seem to indicate an external relation. The philosophical rank-ordering, from whatever depths it may emerge, is bound to be taken as doctrine and dogma among disciples, and, at the same time, hardly needs to be stated for those who are capable of such discrimination. But once again, this does not mean that the insights are false, uncertain, subjective or contingent.

Rosen is concerned that "by forbidding us to speak of that which cannot be completely clarified, Wittgenstein condemns us to silence about what is of the highest importance."[18] On the reading proposed here, Wittgenstein does not forbid discussion of the highest and deepest things. He does, however, call into question the idea that philosophy, by attaining conceptual clarity, provides moral insight (what we referred to above as the assimilation of the moral into the

18 Rosen 2002, p. 144.

logical). Another way of putting the point is to say that intellectual or philosophical or scientific problems are inseparable, even unintelligible, in isolation from the intellectual discourse(s) which give rise to them. Existential or moral problems arise in the sphere of human action and intention, they are not problems that can be solved by achieving clarity into the context in which they arise, that is, they do not disappear just because we have understood them. In this respect, they are "real problems," problems that may well be irresoluble, not because we're not clever enough, but because they belong to human life: they may require of an individual that he make a substantial decision, or take a stand that cannot be justified on morally neutral grounds.

There is, of course, a clear connection between "wanting to know what I really mean," and "wanting to know what I really want," namely, they are both cases of "wanting," or, in Rosen's terms, desire. But isn't it interesting for our understanding of philosophy as being about "the highest things" of concern to us as human beings, that "there are neither idealists nor materialists in everyday life"?[19]

On the face of it, it would seem that philosophy is about very important matters, since it calls into question our most basic assumptions, precisely in order to secure certainty, to deliver us a sense of confidence and trust in our capacity to understand the world around us. It would be a terrible thing indeed if we were to be mistaken about what is most *essential*.

Let me, for a moment, caricature the problems of philosophers. A philosopher asks himself to what extent we can trust science or our everyday experience: are there really cars, women, antelopes, neutrons, the square root of two and black holes, and if there are, are they real in the same sense and in the same way? After much blood, sweat and tears, he may come to the point at which he feels that has come to grips with his problem. Perhaps he becomes an idealist, and maintains that physical objects can only be described as objects *for us*, that is, that phenomena are real only insofar as they are objects for a consciousness. He feels compelled to draw this conclusion from the insight that all knowledge presupposes a knower, every object that is observed or perceived presupposes the existence of an observer, and so forth. Even the psychologist who, in his role of psychologist treats the I as an object is himself a subject. If he attempts to observe himself when observing something else, what he observes then is actually not what he intended to observe, but rather the act of observing itself. And when I observe myself, there is always something missing in the description, namely, the observation that describes the I. If we take that observation into account in the description, we have yet another observer, etc. This relationship between the object and the subject of knowledge is unavoidable, according to our idealist. It is quite simply a condition for consciousness. Thus the naive belief in a reality independent of our thinking is eschewed.

19 Rosen 1999, p. 238.

Another philosopher may take the realist position, and take for granted either an immediate correspondence between objects and our ideas about them, or attempt to show how thought and perception organize the "raw material," that is, sense impressions. In both cases, the emphasis is on the knowledge we have of *objects*, and the task becomes to explain the constitution of the world and our knowledge of it (in our day, it is common to think in terms of brain function). One may describe this view as a sort of epistemological optimism.

Regardless of whether our philosopher is an idealist or a realist, it is important for him to feel that he has arrived at a deeper understanding in his meditations on these questions, and not satisfied himself with how things ordinarily seem, when he's not thinking philosophically. The point is, after all, to see through and beyond our everyday ways of seeing and acting.

The question of to what extent and in what respect the world can be said to be as it seems, and how much of what we perceive and experience is effected, or even produced, by our consciousness, or neurobiological processes, or habituation and training in Indoeuropean linguistic and cultural practice, is a hotly debated topic in philosophical journals, conferences and seminar rooms. Naturally, since it concerns nothing less than the existence or non-existence of the outer world.

Wittgenstein expresses a certain discomfort with the form of the question. In order to see more clearly the weight of the question for us, for how we live our lives (since, after all, these are very important questions), he tries to imagine a use or application of this set of questions outside the journals, conferences and seminar rooms. He writes in *Zettel*:

> §413. One man is a convinced realist, another a convinced idealist and teaches his children accordingly. In such an important matter as the existence or non-existence of the external world, they don't want to teach their children anything wrong.
>
> What will the children be taught? To include in what they say: "There are physical objects" or the opposite?
>
> If someone does not believe in fairies, he does not need to teach his children "There are no fairies: he can omit to teach them the word "fairy". On what occasion are they to say: "There are . . ." or "There are no . . ."? Only when they meet people of the contrary belief.
>
> §414. But the idealist will teach his children the word "chair" after all, for of course he wants to teach them to do this and that, e.g. to fetch a chair. Then where will the difference between what the idealist-educated children say and the realist ones? Won't the difference only be one of a battle cry?
>
> §415. For doesn't the game "That is probably a . . ." begin with disillusion? And can the first attitude of all be directed towards a possible disillusion?
>
> §416. "So does he have to begin by being taught a false certainty?

> There isn't any question of certainty or uncertainty yet in their language game. Remember: they are learning to *do* something?[20]

Wittgenstein wants to bring philosophical questions, and answers, *back to life*: back to the life, the world, which gave rise to them. And notice that the realist and the idealist do to a great extent inhabit the same world. If my three-year old has never seen a film or book in which fairies are represented or mentioned, nor heard songs about fairies or heard them mentioned at all, how am I to make him understand that they do not exist? Well, by showing him certain books and singing certain songs, until he understood what a fairy is. Only then can I help him understand that they do not exist in the same respect as an armchair or his big sister. In the same way, I can eventually, if I am so inclined, train him to understand that the world isn't always what it seems to be. But in order for him to understand such comments, he must first be familiar with a world in which one pours milk in a glass, turns on the light-switch when entering a room, waits for the green light before crossing the street; in this familiar, homey world, the world in which he learns how one says things and how one does them, there is still no room for the sort of doubt out of which idealism and realism are born.

Is Wittgenstein's solution to the "big questions" with which philosophy has struggled for two thousand years to return to the innocence of a three-year old? Doesn't this way of reasoning amount to an exaltation or romanticizing of the simple, the primitive, the everyday? I don't think so. Rather, the case is this: Tinkerbell *is* a fairy, as much for the philosopher as for his young son. The difference consists mainly in that the father has already gone through the disappointment that accompanied the insight that he would never meet Tinkerbell "in real life". But recall Wittgenstein's question: "Can the first attitude be directed towards a possible disillusion?" Shall a mother say to her son: "Jimmy, fetch the chair, which furthermore exists!" Or express to him her meaning intention of his brushing his (by her intended) teeth?

One obvious objection to the intentional absurdity of such a scenario is that children are quite simply not capable of such abstractions. They have not learned the intellectual discourses in which such abstractions are used. The question is if *we* adult philosophers, who must in our daily dealings with the world, open doors, turn on lights and pass the salt to each other at the dinner table are capable of it either as *a way of life*. In other words, the question is whether it is possible to be *mistaken* about the existence of the outer world. How often can such a question be posed in such a way that it means something concrete, that *it makes a difference for what we do*, to be right or wrong?

Towards the end of "Sad Reason," Rosen takes up what he considers an intimate connection between analytic thinking and evaluation. And there may indeed

20 Ludwig Wittgenstein, *Zettel*, transl. G.E.M. Anscombe (Basil Blackwell: 1967).

be some sort of "family resemblance" between the hardness of the logical must and the hardness of the moral must, but they are clearly distinguishable, and, in fact, distinct. In a certain respect, the latter is both logically and temporally prior. I must already implicitly accept the obligations imposed on me by a sense of logical responsibility if the logical must is to have any force. But it is precisely the nature of that sense of responsibility that is so problematic. Isn't traditional metaphysics exactly the attempt to state that nature and its necessary consequences? And isn't the failure of such statements in the past the cause of the disillusionment with reason in our day? Rosen and Wittgenstein agree that the philosopher has access, through his very humanity, to the standards, purposes and values that underlie theoretical reflections and technical productions. But Rosen thinks that we are forced to assume, explicitly or implicitly, "the constancy of human nature as underlying historical change," if we are not to end up in "historically relative dialects". I take it that Wittgenstein would reject the general nature of the formulation of the question that leads to this either/or. It seems to me that the difference between Rosen and Wittgenstein on this point consists in this: for Rosen, philosophy is the activity *par excellence* that tells us who we are. For Wittgenstein, the answer to that question can only be found in our living our lives.[21]

21 I thank Sören Stenlund, Mats Persson, Anders Odenstedt, Michael Gustavsson and Niklas Forsberg for helpful comments, insights and suggestions.

Freedom from the Good

Heidegger's Idealist Grounding of Politics

Richard L. Velkley
The Catholic University of America

I. Introduction

Commentators on Heidegger often note three phases in his thinking as it relates to politics: (1) the analysis of human existence or *Dasein* culminating in *Being and Time* of 1927 and ending in 1933, which is apolitical or at least has only implicit and rather vague political implications; (2) the explicit political engagement with the National Socialist revolution from 1933 to around 1936, in which Heidegger sees the chance to link his philosophical efforts for spiritual renewal of the West to the dominant political forces in Germany; (3) the withdrawal in the middle to late 1930s from an active political approach to the overcoming of Western nihilistic technology, with the adopting of a stance of awaiting the next dispensation of Being in the arrival of new gods, as heralded by Hoelderlin, the poet of the German nation who speaks for Germany's spiritual leadership of the West.

But it has also been claimed that the authentic comportment toward existence described in *Being and Time* entails, in its account of the resolute affirmation of fate, a radical decisionism which is continuous with Heidegger's political engagement of 1933, even if specific features of National Socialism, such as its biological racism, are not indicated by, or not even compatible with, Heidegger's existential analysis.[1] Indeed one might discern an underlying continuity to all three phases. Herman Philipse in his recently published *Heidegger's Philosophy of Being*, has put forth the interesting hypothesis that the project running through Heidegger's work is theological: *Being and Time* pursues a "Pascalian strategy" of characterizing human existence as miserably fallen so as to provoke rejection of the spiritually devastated rationalism of Western civilization and therewith a search for redemption, whose features are essentially Christian;[2] Heidegger then in the years just following *Being and Time* (1929–1932) attempts to find what Philipse calls the "metaphysical grace" for which the analysis of *Dasein* was

1 See Herman Philipse, *Heidegger's Philosophy of Being: A Critical Interpretation* (Princeton: Princeton University Press, 2000), 256–66.

2 Philipse, 223–29, 239–44.

preparation, an effort that ends in failure; Heidegger takes refuge in Nazism, a desperate action which Philipse describes as religious conversion; that too ends in disaster, and Heidegger's later thought consists in developing what Philipse terms "postmonotheist theology" to save the West.[3] Philipse argues that in Heidegger's later theological or eschatological scheme, Nazism still plays a positive role insofar as it furthers the completion of the technological age through its absolute assertion of the will to power. Since moral criticism of any agent in the fulfillment of the West's historical destiny is beside the point, Heidegger's disavowal of Nazism could never be more than equivocal at best.[4]

Philipse's formulation has helpful features, but it overlooks some explicit statements of the later Heidegger that strikingly show that the political reality of the National Socialist movement held for him, even from the standpoint of utter defeat and personal disgrace in 1945, a promise that he believed that he and others in positions of authority in the early 1930s failed to fulfill. These assertions shed important light on Heidegger's political thinking; they indicate that Heidegger perhaps never learned the "lesson" that *all* political engagement on behalf of his philosophic vision is inherently mistaken.[5] They point to a conception of politics that, paradoxical as it may seem, might be called "idealist." I want to show that this conception of politics, which surely in the years of Heidegger's service to the revolutionary regime contains no hint of a basis in traditional revelation, is well grounded in Heidegger's thought of the period 1929–1932. It is philosophically a kind of idealism that drastically rejects theological or "metaphysical" grace, or any turn to an infinite (superhuman) reality.[6] And it is an idealism in crucial ways descended from the great tradition of German Idealism, by Heidegger's own avowals. It also contains, I argue, an internal paradox which illuminates the

3 Philipse, 246–76.

4 Philipse, 276: Heidegger's view of National Socialism is "never unambiguously negative." Philipse goes further. He characterizes the later theological thought as "spiritual Nazism" (270–72): grounded on the experience of the death of God as proclaimed by Nietzsche, and thus on the total withering of Christianity and its Platonic roots, this pious thinking awaits new gods who support the particular folk, the German folk, in its struggle with Western decadence. Heidegger's account of the history of the West gives no place to Judaism, even though its eschatological structure has unmistakably Biblical sources. This is a special sort of Nazism to be sure: the greatness of the folk is based not on biology but on the spirit of language and poetry.

5 See Leo Strauss, *Studies in Platonic Political Philosophy* (Chicago: University of Chicago Press, 1983) 34: "One is inclined to say that Heidegger has learned the lesson of 1933 more thoroughly than any other man."

6 See the account below of the Davos disputation with Cassirer, and the essay contemporary with it (1929) "Vom Wesen des Grundes," part II, conclusion, in *Wegmarken*, vol. 9 of Heidegger, *Gesamtausgabe* (Frankfurt: Vittorio Klostermann, 1976), 161–62. Henceforth volumes from this edition will be cited as *GA* followed by the volume number.

so-called "turn" (*die Kehre*) in Heidegger's thinking, and which can be viewed as the hidden link between the Kantian idealism of the Davos disputation of 1929 and the post-Kantian idealism of later writings. Philipse's continuity-hypothesis must undergo revision through more attention to this philosophical stratum in Heidegger.

II. History as Metaphysics

Heidegger penned a remarkable document in 1945, "The Rectorate 1933/34: Facts and Thoughts," which he gave to his son Hermann with the instruction to publish it at "a specified time," and which appeared with the rectoral address of 1933, "The Self-Assertion of the German University," in 1983, seven years after Heidegger's death.[7] It is a self-serving and in verifiable ways mendacious document, to be sure.[8] Yet it is not simply dismissive of the National Socialist movement; indeed Heidegger offers what is perhaps his most articulate justification for participating in the revolution of 1933. "I saw at the time in the movement that had come to power, the possibility of an innner gathering and renewal of the people (*das Volk*) and a way for it to find its historical Western destiny. I believed that the self-renewing university could be called on to work as the standard for the inner gathering of the people."[9] In hindsight he does not say that this perception of the movement was a mere delusion, although he does grant that "mediocre and incompetent" persons in the movement stood in the way of achieving higher goals. Instead Heidegger poses a remarkable "what if" question—a sort of question he acknowledges to be risky. "But the question may be put: what would have happened and would could have been prevented if in 1933 all the competent forces (*vermoegende Kraefte*) had aroused themselves and slowly, in secret persistence, purified and moderated the movement that came into power?"[10]

7 *Die Selbstbehauptung der deutschen Universitaet. Das Rektorat 1933/34: Tatsachen und Gedanken*, with foreword by Hermann Heidegger (Frankfurt: V. Klostermann, 1983), 6. These writings are reprinted in *GA* 16, *Reden und andere Zeugnisse eines Lebensweges, 1910–1976*, which appeared this year (2000). I will cite the more accessible earlier edition, referring to it as *SdU*. But the volume of *Reden* contains many important things—speeches, lectures, official documents, exhortations to students and faculty—that make evident the full range and intensity of Heidegger's support of the new regime, even after his resignation from the rectorate in spring 1934.

8 See Philipse, 248–49, whose chief source for biographical data is Hugo Ott, *Martin Heidegger: Unterwegs zu seiner Biographie* (Frankfurt and New York: Campus Verlag, 1988).

9 *SdU*, 23.

10 *SdU*, 25.

Heidegger never anywhere suggests that another regime or movement, actual or possible, had the possibility for such direction from the "competent forces." Certainly no Western democratic regime could be directed in this way. Thus the Heidegger of 1945 had not broken with the Heidegger of 1933 as to the philosophical rightness of his placing his prestige and talent behind the National Socialist revolution, as rector of the University of Freiburg. His error was only in underestimating the difficulties he would face in his efforts to shape the regime toward higher ends.[11] Behind Heidegger's affirmation of the philosophical rightness of his move is a conception of the relation of philosophy to practical life that persists in his thought from early to late.

Scholarship on Heidegger has lacked the proper terms for describing this relation. It is seldom noted that the hope of shaping the direction of political life through the university, and the project of subordinating political life to higher philosophical or cultural aims, are both well-established in the tradition of German Idealist thought.[12] Even when this is noted, the deeper philosophical premises behind this account of the relations of university, politics and philosophy are not uncovered. This failure is not unrelated to the fact that contemporary scholarship takes for granted the truth of many or most of these premises, in some form. Most basically, this account assumes that philosophy is, or can be, the dominant force in human affairs, and that human history is most fundamentally the history of philosophy. Accordingly the principles of ordinary actors in political and social life express, more or less directly, principles arrived at philosophically. This must mean that politics, morality and religion ultimately are derived from philosophical thought; the ordinary moral actor is thus in possession of a metaphysical principle of morals, as Kant says. The spheres of politics, morality, and religion do not maintain any degree of autonomy from philosophy; but conversely, philosophy does not maintain any degree of autonomy from practical life. Philosophy's meaning becomes that of wholly transforming practical life; or rather, it becomes that transformation itself, the historical spirit effecting such transformation. This is not to deny that certain individuals—philosophers, poets, and statesmen—can have central historical roles as the leading spokesmen of that spirit.

Heidegger's version of this idealism is supported by another assumption bearing an unmistakable Kantian stamp: the core of existence for all human beings is a kind of freedom, a capacity for transcending concerns variously described as empirical, heteronomous, anthropological or ontic. As Heidegger puts it, the core of human existence is the understanding of Being; the transcendence that makes all human thought and action possible is philosophical

11 To accusations that he harmed individuals, groups, the university or Germany itself by his actions, Heidegger's response is one of full denial.

12 A start is made by Miguel de Beistegui, *Heidegger and the Political: Dystopias* (London: Routledge, 1988), 32–39.

transcendence. As thus capable of transcending mere beings (*Seienden*) toward the whole of Being (*Sein*) the human essence has the ability to look past the vulgar concerns with comfort, security, and happiness, to face resolutely the totality of existence, which is limited only by death. As becomes evident in the Davos disputation, Heidegger is fully aware of the idealist and more specifically Kantian origins of this acccount of freedom. It is not possible to argue here how this idealist notion emerged in the eighteenth century in response to the perception that modern scientific naturalism failed to provide an adequate account of the unity and the ends of human knowledge.[13]

It would also be very helpful in this context to show that Heidegger, in his effort to provide the foundation of metaphysics in the analysis of *Dasein*, saw himself as addressing in the early twentieth century a situation much like that Kant faced: the dominance of mathematico-empiricist philosophies that overthrew the authority of metaphysics as the ground of the unity of the sciences and as the reflection on the highest human *telos*.[14] Heidegger is much aware of his debt to the German Idealist tradition, and this debt has also been widely discussed in the scholarship. What has not been seen is the full scope of what that debt means. When Heidegger asserts that Kant is the first philosopher since Plato and Aristotle to take a further step in metaphysics,[15] the place of freedom in Kant's metaphysical thought is present to Heidegger as central to that advance. But with the Kantian account of freedom comes a particular conception of the relation of metaphysics to practical life. I will argue that a version of this conception always underlies Heidegger's thinking—at times quite plainly, at others more covertly. Heidegger's version certainly no longer supports Kant's Enlightenment-universalist idea of human dignity, but after 1932 it undergirds a Romantic exaltation of particular people or folk (Greeks, Germans) with a universal mission of a philosophical nature.[16] My concern is with showing how Heidegger grounds his *voelkisch* thinking in idealist premises. I begin with the Kantianism of the Davos disputation and tutn to later utterances in where the *voelkisch* element is pronounced.

13 See the author's *Freedom and the End of Reason: On the Moral Foundation of Kant's Critical Philosophy* (Chicago and London: University of Chicago Press, 1989).

14 See *Schelling: Vom Wesen der menschlichen Freiheit (1809), GA* 42, 61–72, and Barash cited in note 16 below.

15 *GA* 9, "Vom Wesen des Grundes," 133, note.

16 In one notable self-accounting, Heidegger claims his thought renews and deepens a concept of the essence of freedom emerging at the end of the 18th century: "Freedom now (in that period) has for the Germans a new sound and meaning. Freedom means: adherence to the law of the folk-spirit, that manifests itself preeminently in the works of poets, thinkers and statesmen . . . Freedom: responsibility for the destiny of the folk," "Die deutsche Universitaet," in *GA* 16, 291. This is two addresses, previously unpublished, that Heidegger gave in a "course for foreigners"—clearly a performance

III. The Revision of Kant

The theme of freedom is a crucial link between the writings before and after 1933; a central factor in Heidegger's thinking on freedom is his study of Kant, which is especially intense in the late 1920s and early 1930s.[17] For the significance of Kant to Heidegger one of the most important documents is the spring 1929 disputation with Ernst Cassirer in Davos, Switzerland.[18] Heidegger was at the time writing *Kant and the Problem of Metaphysics*; this interprets the *Critique of Pure Reason* as providing the foundations of ontology in the productive imagination, which provides temporal intuitions as "schemata" for the categories of the understanding·[19] Heidegger saw in Kant's argument an anticipation of his own account of the temporal openness of human existence as the condition for understanding Being.[20] In the dispute with Cassirer, Heidegger defends his interpretation against the Neo-Kantian view of Kant as providing a theory of the natural sciences. Cassirer for his part asserts that he is not a Neo-Kantian as

of public service—at the University of Freiburg in November 1934, after his resignation from the rectorate. Heidegger traces this new concept to all of the leading thinkers and poets of Germany of the age, and claims that it was the principle behind the founding of the University of Berlin. This is one of Heidegger's most detailed statements linking his thought to earlier German political thought and it concretely ascribes a common root to his philosophy and National Socialism. Special praise is given to Savigny, who "showed in relation to the essence of the state, that political freedom and unfreedom does not depend on the form of state (*Staatsform*) but above all on whether the power of the state is rooted in the nature and history of a folk, or is entirely used up in the will of individual power-holders and governments" (294). For the relation of Heidegger to the "historical school" of Savigny and Niebuhr, and to the Romantic approach to history in general, see Jeffrey A. Barash, *Martin Heidegger and the Problem of Historical Meaning* (Dordrecht: Martinus Nijhoff, 1988).

17 Noteworthy in this regard are the seminar of winter 1927–28 on Kant's *Kritik der reinen Vernunft* (*GA* 25) and that of summer 1930 on Kant's account of freedom in the Dialectic of the same work (*GA* 31), bearing the title *Vom Wesen der menschlichen Freiheit. Einleitung in die Philosophie.*

18 This appears as the fourth appendix in the fourth edition (1973) of *Kant und das Problem der Metaphysik*, which edition was reprinted as *GA* 3 (1991). The Davos disputation occupies pages 274–96 of *GA* 3. I will not give page references for each passage cited and discussed in what follows, but refer the reader to the entire text.

19 In a lecture given at Davos during the same *Hochschulkurse* (third appendix in *GA* 3), Heidegger put forth the famous thesis, argued in the book, that "Kant through his own radicality brought himself before a position from which he had to draw back in fear (*zurueckschrecken*). That is to say: destruction of the foundations theretofore of Western metaphysics (Spirit, Logos, Reason)" (*GA* 3, 273).

20 In the fourth edition of this book Heidegger says that Kant was for him just a "refuge" (*Zuflucht*) whom he could treat as the spokesman for his own account of Being; he says that he misunderstood both his own question and Kant at that time.

Heidegger defines Neo-Kantian, and that for two reasons: (1) he inquires into the productive imagination for understanding the symbolic as the basis for a general theory of culture; (2) he sees that the central problem for Kant is ethical: How is freedom possible? In this latter inquiry Kant takes a remarkable step into the supersensible, the *mundus intelligibilis*, wherein he discloses a universal moral law that establishes the reality of freedom. At this point Cassirer challenges Heidegger to make sense of this aspect of Kant on his interpretation. If Heidegger treats Kant as a philosopher of finitude, for whom all knowledge is relative to human *Dasein*, then what place can Kant have for the move into the infinity of the supersensible and the eternal truths of the ethical?

Heidegger's reply is impressive and in part convincing. He notes that in the *Critique* Kant is not concerned with "regional ontologies" of the physical (nature), or the psychic (freedom or culture) but with *metaphysica generalis*, the basis for any ontological inquiry. Heidegger then denies that the move into ethics is for Kant a move into the infinite; ethical imperatives can hold only for finite beings; the moral is identical with autonomous or self-supporting reason and is not derivable from a higher eternal ground; it is the transcending of the creatural that can be carried out only by a finite creature. But now Heidegger calls ethics itself into question, by claiming it is an error to stress the normative function of the moral law. Through self-legislation *Dasein* constitutes itself, thus disclosing the ontological significance of the law. Human existence does partake of a certain infinity, the free "self-giving" or *exhibitio originaria* whereby the transcendental imagination projects Being as a whole. Only a finite creature can have an ontology; God as eternal being has no temporal projection of Being. Thus Heidegger links the moral law to a finite being's understanding of Being as "thrown project": *Dasein*'s projective effort to illuminate Being which remains fundamentally opaque and mysterious, as simply given to *Dasein* and not created by it.

Then more radically Heidegger asserts: the truth of Being exists only if a finite human being, such as *Dasein*, exists. Eternity has meaning only within such a being's "inner transcendence of time"; there is no eternal "beyond" finite being. He then pronounces the task of his *Destruktion* of the philosophical tradition: his whole critique of that tradition is that only on the basis of time as the gathering together of past, present and future, is anything like substance, *ousia*, idea, and the eternal law intelligible; since antiquity the problem of Being has been interpreted in terms of time, which was always addressed to the subject-matter in an unintelligible way. Kant made the first step toward uncovering this presupposition, and to this end he raised the question "What is man?," therewith initiating

GA 3, XIV. For learned and penetrating discussions of Heidegger's relation to Kant see Stanley Rosen, *The Question of Being: A Reversal of Heidegger* (New Haven and London: Yale University Press, 1993), 192–211, and *The Elusiveness of the Ordinary: Studies in the Possibility of Philosophy* (New Haven and London: Yale University Press, 2002), 94–134. See also the references in note 43 below.

the metaphysics of *Dasein*. Heidegger says that as with Kant, his raising of the question "What is man?" is not anthropological but metaphysical: it discloses *Dasein*'s temporality as the condition for metaphysics. And as with Kant, his analysis emphasizes the finitude of *Dasein*. Accordingly such anthropological themes as anxiety and living toward death are adduced only for illuminating the structure of human temporality.

Heidegger poses at this point the delicate question of the relation of his philosophy to "world-view," a question that clearly relates to that of the moral significance of freedom. Is Heidegger's analysis of *Dasein* pre-ethical, perhaps ethically neutral? He handles this question with ambiguous, not to say obfuscating formulations. Philosophy does not have the task of providing a world-view, although world-view is the presupposition of philosophizing. This presupposition is not, however, a doctrine, but solely the philosopher's effort to disclose in the act of philosophizing the highest freedom of human existence. He shows freedom not as an object of theory but as the act of setting-free. This at the same time discloses metaphysics as a human happening, as historical. The philosopher pushes human freedom to its limit, and forces man to confront at the limit of existence the Nothingness that is inseparable from Being. This exposure of *Dasein* as free is for Heidegger the *terminus a quo* of philosophy, and the entire problematic of his thought. He has not formulated the *terminus ad quem*, which is the first concern of Cassirer, namely, a philosophy of culture. But can Heidegger deny that his renewal of the question of Being is motivated by a view of the worth and end of human existence?

He proceeds to say that the philosophic exposing of the nothingness of human *Dasein* is "not an occasion for pessimism or melancholy." Rather one must grasp that an authentic existence needs opposition, and that philosophy must "throw man back into the hardness of his fate, away from the lazy aspect of a man who exploits the work of the spirit." Thus genuine philosophy must be destructive, a radical "bursting-open" (*Sprengung*) of tradition, as in the case of Kant, who in attempting to lay the foundation of metaphysics was pressed toward finding that foundation in the abyss (*Abgrund*). The foundation of philosophizing never ceases to be questionable; the *terminus a quo* and the *terminus ad quem* to this extent coincide. The form of life that affirms the inescapable questionability of the starting-point is the highest form of existence. Yet man finds himself thrown into Being in an historical, even accidental way. Echoing Aristotle's remark on the nature of the theoretical life, Heidegger says that man is allowed only a few rare glimpses, at the pinnacle of his possibility, of the totality of existence. Otherwise his life is overwhelmed by the beings (*Seienden*) in terms of which he tends to view himself: as something "ontic," an empirically given object, not as the "eccentric" being open to beings as a whole and himself at the same time. Human life ordinarily is either dispersed among beings or withdrawn into itself: the hardest thing is to see that the self is inseparable from Being, openness to which makes possible openness to self.

As an aside, Heidegger remarks that interpreting Kant's problematic in this way precludes viewing it in an "isolated ethical" sense. The radicality of questioning precludes assuming an ethical end or justification for that questioning. Moreover, it seems for Heidegger to preclude an orientation of radical questioning toward the ethical or political questions, as the subject-matter for a thinking that tries to answer the question "What is man?" Here Heidegger strikingly separates himself not only from Kant, but from the entire tradition of philosophy since Socrates. Still one discerns an indebtedness to Kant, the first philosopher to propose that the inquiry into the moral, or the good, can be divorced from man's nature, and specifically, the human natural concern with happiness. Heidegger advances further in this direction by divorcing freedom from the good entirely.

IV. The Idealism of the Volk

In the memoir of 1945 Heidegger offers a sketch of the philosophic prehistory to his assumption of the rectorate. He mentions first his 1929 Freiburg inaugural address, "What is Metaphysics?" whose concern, he notes, was to uncover the essential ground of the scattered multiplicity of academic disciplines in a concept of truth.[21] It thus took the first step toward a philosophic reform of the university on the basis of the questioning of *Being and Time*, which sought the ground of the possibility of metaphysics in the analysis of human existence as temporal. Heidegger then mentions a seminar and lecture on Plato, and a lecture on the essence of truth, from the period of 1930–1932.[22] The Plato seminar and lecture are centrally on the cave-image of the *Republic*. One can surmise that Heidegger mentions them because they are the basis for an anti-Platonic *paideia*, in which liberation from the cave advances not toward the truth as *idea*, but as the unconcealment (*Unverborgenheit*) of beings that was uncovered by the Presocratic philosophers. Plato's doctrine ambiguously presupposes and conceals that original ground of thinking, with fateful consequences for the West. Heidegger claims that these lectures were censored by the Nazi authorities.[23]

The crucial moment in this prehistory of the rectorate is Heidegger's account of "how he saw the historical situation at that time."[24] In 1930 and 1932 Ernst Juenger published the essay on "Total Mobilization" and the book *The Worker*; Heidegger notes that he discussed these in a small circle with his assistant Brock, and in these discussions Heidegger "tried to show that in these writings an essential understanding of Nietzsche's metaphysics was expressed, insofar as in the

21 *SdU*, 21. "Was ist Metaphysik?" *GA* 9, 103–22.

22 *Vom Wesen der Wahrheit: Zu Platons Hoehlengleichnis und Theaetet, GA* 34 (seminar winter 1931/32); "Vom Wesen der Wahrheit," *GA* 9, 177–202; "Platons Lehre der Wahrheit," GA 9, 203–38.

23 *SdU*, 22.

24 *SdU*, 24.

horizon of this metaphysics the history and the present of the West were seen and foreseen." The circle reflected on what was coming (*das Kommende*) and later events, Heidegger adds, confirmed what Juenger foretold, namely, the universal domination of the will to power as the planetary destiny. Nietzsche declared the advent of this reality with his pronouncement that "God is dead," which expresses not just ordinary atheism but that within the history of humanity the supersensible world, especially Christianity, has lost its moving power (*wirkende Kraft*). Heidegger quoted this line of Nietzsche in the rectoral address of 1933.[25] The event of God's death, Heidegger now states, alone makes intelligible the two world wars. In sum, Heidegger claims that in the period 1930–1933 he became aware of nihilism as planetary destiny, which awareness forced on him a radicalizing of the problem of the search for the ground of the sciences and the renewal of the university.

It made clear to him the need to reflect on the overcoming of the metaphysics of the will to power through a conversation with the Western tradition that returns to its origin.[26] This remark refers to Heidegger's efforts in the same period to go behind Plato, in whom he saw the roots of the metaphysics of the will to power, to the origin of the West in Presocratic thinking about Being. And he now asks rhetorically, if the urgency of the problem did not warrant, for the sake of this reflection on the part of the Germans (*bei uns Deutschen*), the awakening and the leading into the field (*ins Feld zu fuehren*) of those places that are considered the seat of the pursuit of knowledge and learning—the German university? "With the assumption of the rectorate I dared to make the experiment to save, purify and secure the positive (in the National Socialist movement)."[27]

What did Heidegger see as positive in this movement? He asserts that in the rectoral address his attempt was to see beyond the "deficiencies and crudities" of the movement, toward its potential "to bring, one day, a gathering of the Western-historical essence of the German."[28] His failures as administrator, he observes, should not distract from the essential: that we stand in the midst of the comsummation of nihilism and the death of God, and every "time-space is closed off from the divine." At the same time "the overcoming of nihilism is announced in German thinking and singing," although the Germans do not perceive this and instead measure themselves by the standards of the prevailing nihilism. Thus they "misunderstand the essence of an historical self-assertion." Heidegger's thought can be reconstructed as follows: only the Germans are capable of leading the West out of nihilism because only they have the capacity to recover the forgotten

25 *SdU*, 13.

26 *SdU*, 25. Heidegger perhaps reads some thoughts of the later 1930s back into the period 1930–1932. All the same, the memoir makes evident the persistence in Heidegger's thought of the "idealist" orientation.

27 *SdU*, 26.

28 *SdU*, 39.

beginning of the West; if the Germans are to fulfill this mission, they must be led by the spiritual leaders in the universities; the latter must have the support of political authority; only a movement that is both anti-democratic and intent on asserting German superiority among the nations has the requisite authority; such a movement came to power in 1933. Heidegger states that less possibility exists in the present moment of 1945 than existed in 1933, "of opening blinded eyes to a vision of the essential."[29]

Whereas Heidegger carefully grounds his 1933 assertion of the world-historical destiny of the Germans in earlier reflections, it is striking that the writings before 1933 lack stress on Germanness. Section 74 of *Being and Time* briefly connects the resolute affirming of destiny to the history of a people (*Volk*) as the destiny to be affirmed.[30] Yet that work's analysis of human existence as preparation for raising the question of Being does not give a special role to the Germans in fulfilling that analysis. It seems to characterize the human situation in universal and even timeless fashion. According to Heidegger's own account of how his eyes were opened, it was Juenger who portrayed the darkness of the present in such terms as to make evident the need for a radical overcoming of the nihilistic age, through an historical recovery of the origins of the West. Such overcoming, since it was to be realized in the world as a whole and not only in exceptional philosophic individuals, would have to be carried out by a people or folk, the modern successors to the Greeks. In no other way, it appeared to Heidegger in 1933, could the original question of Being be raised again.

This national or *voelkisch* grounding of philosophy is found in statements such as this one in the rectoral address: "For the Greeks science (*Wissenschaft*) is not a 'cultural value' (*'Kulturgut'*) but the innermost determining center of the whole popular-national existence (*volklich-staatlichen Dasein*)."[31] For related thoughts one can turn to the lectures of 1935, *Introduction to Metaphysics*, which Heidegger published as a book in 1953.[32] Heidegger writes that philosophy cannot be immediately effective in practical life, or expect resonance quickly, even though it may be in accord with "the inner history of a people."[33] He speaks of the depth of the connection between *Volk* and philosophy in the following: "Philosophy opens up the paths and perspectives for the knowing that establishes measure and rank, in which and out of which a people (*Volk*) grasps its existence (*Dasein*) in the historical-spiritual world, and brings to completion the knowing that inspires, threatens and necessitates all questioning and judging."[34]

29 *SdU*, 39.

30 For discussion of this passage, see Philipse, 260–62.

31 *SdU*, 12.

32 *Einfuehrung in die Metaphysik* (Tuebingen: Niemeyer Verlag, 1953 and later editions), reprinted as *GA* 40. I will cite the Niemeyer edition as EM.

33 *EM*, 7.

34 *EM*, 8.

Philosophy fulfills the destiny of a people, not by lightening human burdens, as in securing the foundations of a culture, but through inducing struggle and hardship, since these are the condition for greatness.[35] In Heidegger's account the Germans have already been granted the gift of struggle testing them for greatness, by an historical fate that places them in a pincers between Russia and America.[36] These powers embody the technological nihilism of modernity: "The same dreary technological frenzy, the same unrestricted organization of the average man."[37] In this situation the Germans, who are the "metaphysical folk," must decide to move themselves and the history of the West into the primal realm of the powers of Being, or suffer the spiritual annihilation of Europe. The Germans alone can overcome the modern misinterpretation of spirit (*Geist*) as cleverness, technical skill, and cultural value, by raising anew the question of Being.[38]

But how can a folk accomplish this; what does it mean to say that a folk thinks metaphysically? Heidegger in another set of lectures quotes approvingly the line of Hegel that "a cultivated people without a metaphysics is like a richly decorated temple without a Holy of Holies."[39] Yet Heidegger asserts that only a few actually philosophize. "Which few? The creative transformers, the converters." They arouse the folk to gather its forces, teaching it that its destiny is to further philosophical questioning and thereby to assert spiritual leadership in the world. But as in other contexts, Heidegger indicates here a paradoxical character to this effect of the few with respect to the many: the teaching of the thinkers works slowly through imperceptible pathways and detours, until at last their thought is no longer original philosophizing, but "sinks down into the self-evidence of daily existence." It therefore must always be the task of the thinkers to unsettle the comfortable state of metaphysical certainty that eventually arises out of their own thought, and to expose once again the people to the hard truths of their spiritual destiny.

I conclude this discussion with a general observation: the writings of Heidegger that discuss political matters directly show that these are of interest to him only insofar as they can be brought to bear on the renewal of the question of Being. Heidegger's political engagements show that the furthering of that renewal takes precedence over any considerations of the good, the moral, and the just, as these have been understood in in the philosophic tradition as having some universal articulation, reflecting ends (happiness, perfection, virtue) inherent in human nature or reason.[40] Indeed for Heidegger the meaning of the renewed question

35 *EM*, 9.

36 *EM*, 29, 34.

37 *EM*, 28; cf. 35.

38 *EM*, 35–37.

39 Hegel, preface to first edition of *Logik* (1812), cited by Heidegger in *Parmenides* (seminar winter 1942/43), *GA* 54, 148–49.

40 *GA* 16, 294: "Savigny showed that right (*das Recht*) arises not solely and not primarily from the formal legal thinking of legislation (*Gesetzgebung*), but rather, as in the

entails a reinterpretation of such concerns as modes of fallenness, to the extent that they tend to be placed ahead of the primary human historical concern of "gathering forces" for the renewing of the question. Such a fall occurs when discussions of National Socialism stress its moral evil rather than inquire about its role in the history of Being's disclosure. It is wrong to think of Heidegger's failure to comment on the moral evil of Nazism as merely a personal failure, unrelated to his thought. Nor can one say that Heidegger simply did not get around to discussing moral good and evil, because his concentration was on the preliminary task of uncovering the ground in Being for such discussion. The turn to Being is understood by Heidegger as entailing a complete reevaluation of the meaning and place of "morality" in human affairs, such as very few people are prepared to undertake or accept, as Heidegger himself discovered.

V. Idealism Without Freedom

Heidegger in 1929 and after is forced to confront a certain paradox, not unrelated to one in Kant. On the assumption that human beings possess universally a radical kind of freedom, in an openness to Being that transcends all given beings, how is it that human beings are universally "fallen" into the forgetting of Being? And how has the present age emerged as an especially deep forgetfulness? How can freedom be gained and lost, if it has no empirical or ontic basis? Heidegger saw that his move from analysis of *Dasein*'s temporality to Being (*Sein*) itself, by passing through the "destructive" history of the ontology of time which he planned as the second half of *Being and Time*, could not provide him with the answer to that question. The freedom for openness to Being has been occluded by technological domination of the world; this has its roots not in an ordinary "fall-enness" of *Dasein* into beings, but in the planetary-historical fate in which Being withdraws into oblivion. Accordingly Heidegger introduced a new formulation about freedom: man is possessed by freedom, not freedom by man.[41] In the last analysis freedom for openness to Being is a gift of Being, granted to certain peoples in certain epochs.[42] It was such a gift that, in Heidegger's view, Germany and therewith the West were granted in 1933, with the ascent to power of Hitler

case of language, from the folk-spirit of the peoples (*Voelker*), with their belief and their customs."

41 "Vom Wesen der Wahrheit," *GA* 9, 190; see also *Schelling* (1936), GA 40, 15; "Der Spruch Anaximanders" in Holzwege (Frankfurt: Klostermann, 1950), 340–41.

42 For a formulation which has explicit reference to the contemporary political situation (Germany's withdrawal from the League of Nations) see GA 16, 333: "True historical freedom as the independence of the recognition of one folk by another has no need of the organized illusory community (*Scheingemeinschaft*) of a 'League of Nations' . . . The true historical freedom of the peoples (Voelker) of Europe is the presupposition for the West's returning once again spiritually-historically to itself

and his revolution—a gift that was misunderstood and improperly used by the Germans. At the same time, Heidegger's noting the universal fallenness or *Seinsvergessenheit* of the epoch implies a greater gulf between the philosopher and his milieu, than was implied in the analysis of *Being and Time*. Even as the philosopher would ground his insight more deeply in the folk's potential for openness to Being, he necessarily separates himself more sharply from its historical actuality. This peculiar combination of identification and distance is possible only on the basis of a transmutation of the folk into the "ideal" such as occurs in Heidegger's thought.

In sum, the radicality of freedom that has no ground in human nature can appear, or disappear, only at the whim of history, or fate, which demands the proper attunement of mankind for its reception. Indeed the promise of such freedom will appear most forcefully in those moments when ordinary reality, with its ontic or merely "natural" concerns, is most threatened with destruction. In this way nihilism, as the complete immersion in beings, can destroy itself when its negative force is turned against the beings, thus compelling human life to be free for openness to Being. The scourge of the earth is its savior: "Where danger is, there grows salvation." Since, however, the promise of the 1933 revolution was not fulfilled, and in 1945 the darkness of the American-Soviet imperium descended over the world, mankind must await, indefinitely and indeterminately, in the long convalescence (*Verwindung*) of the technological world-night, for the saving of mankind by other, more efficacious deities than those that appeared in 1933.

Heidegger has a profound grasp of the radicality of philosophical questioning comparable with that of the greatest figures in the tradition.[43] But his divorce of questioning from any natural-teleological basis, for which the German Idealist concepts of freedom helped set the stage, has a paradoxical consequence. Such questioning is unable to see clearly the political-moral phenomena which must nourish it; a questioning that cannot see these phenomena cannot gain true distance on them, and so risks becoming their slave. The paradox is not mitigated if the servitude is not unwitting but voluntary, as in the case of Heidegger.

and for its securing its destiny in the great decision of the earth against the Asiatic." That this last term refers to the Judaic and Christian heritage of the West cannot be missed.

43 This perhaps emerges most forcefully from Heidegger's dialogues with philosophers from the past. For accounts of his "dialogue" with Kant see the following: F. Schalow, *The Renewal of the Heidegger-Kant Dialogue: Action, Thought, and Responsibility* (Albany: SUNY Press, 1992) and C. Sherover, *Heidegger, Kant and Time* (Bloomington and London: Indiana University Press, 1971).

The True and the Bad Infinity

Donald Phillip Verene

Emory University

Philosophy as a branch of literature requires images. It is a kind of prose, interspersed with poetry. The poetic moments of philosophical prose occur through metaphors. These moments, as Horace says, are pictures. Although reflective philosophy has its prose adorned by such pictures and is never without them, speculative philosophy especially depends upon them. Speculative philosophy is akin to poetry. Like poetry it attempts to express the True, which is beyond language. Like Plato's philosophy, speculative philosophy can never be written down. Although speculative philosophy is akin to poetry, it is not the same as poetry. Poetry, as Hegel says, is immediate. It attempts to recover the immediacy that is present in the myth, the immediacy of perception.

In reflective philosophy all that is thought is mediated. Immediacy itself is left behind. In speculative philosophy immediacy is brought along in its mediacy, in the way that poetry is brought along in its prose. It is not a perfect union because philosophy has within it a propensity toward the concept. The thought of the concept is by its nature prosaic. Speculative philosophy thus struggles to be poetic. This struggle is true of Hegel, who announces in one of his earliest fragments the need for a "mythology of reason." The mythology of reason is a conception of what speculative philosophy is. Hegel opposes it to the thought of "our literal-minded philosophers." Literal-minded philosophy is limited to the thought of reflection. The idea of reflection as an act of mind turning back upon itself is brought into English philosophy by Locke and into French philosophy by Descartes and thus into modern philosophy generally.[6]

1 R. G. Collingwood, *An Essay on Philosophical Method* (Oxford: Clarendon, 1933), ch. 10.

2 Horace, *Ars poet.*, 361.

3 Plato, *Letters*, VII, 341 c–e.

4 G. W. F. Hegel, *Vorlesungen über die Ästhetik, Werke*, 20 vols. (Frankfurt: Suhrkamp, 1971), 13: 140–42.

5 G. W. F. Hegel, "Das älteste Systemprogramm des deutschen Idealismus," *Werke*, I: 234–36.

6 For the history of "reflection" in philosophy, see my *Philosophy and the Return to Self-Knowledge* (New Haven: Yale University Press, 1997), ch. 1.

Modern theory of language is founded on the discovery of the "understanding," which produces a knowledge of the object by means of reflection—what Kant summarized in his doctrine of "transcendental reflection." As Hegel says, in modern philosophy "*reflective* understanding took possession of philosophy," reflection became a slogan.[7] Reason is lost. It becomes, as Kant sees it, the fog banks of illusion that surround the blessed isle of the understanding, Kant's "land of truth."[8] In the security of the understanding Kant has found the kingdom of Prester John, an epistemological inner Africa.

With the loss of reason is the loss of mythology. For mythical thought the true is the whole grasped in its immediacy. Reason, the agency of speculative philosophy, is the attempt to recover the wholeness of the mythical world in a new, prosaic form. What happens in mythology in terms of a narrative of gods, men, and nature happens in the mirror of reason in terms of a narrative of categories of the real. The narrative of the myth holds together contradictions, reversals, coincidences, and juxtapositions. The narrative of speculative philosophy holds the phenomena of the world and their categories together through dialectic. The narrative of speculative philosophy, unlike that of history, tells the one true story under the idea of necessity. History is guided by Clio and orders events in terms of what was, is, and is to come. Speculative philosophy is guided directly by Mnemosyne, whom Hegel calls "the Absolute Muse."[9] To narrate the world *per causas* is to add necessity to what was, is, and is to come by relating events as what had, has, and will have to be. Necessity is internal to dialectic.

As Hegel describes dialectic in the *Phenomenology of Spirit,* consciousness can be said to have experience only when it passes from an awareness of being-in-itself to being–as-it-is-for-consciousness. These two moments, the double-*Ansich*, are in an absolute bond such that each requires the existence of the other for its own existence.[10] One does not have being without the other. The passage from one to the other is necessity itself. Neither movement is in any way derived or derivable from the other because there is no specifiable principle by which this movement can occur. The dialectic these two moments exhibit is primordial and allows for speculative philosophy to narrate the True as the whole.[11] All that there is stands as an array of opposites.

7 G. W. F. Hegel, *Wissenschaft der Logik*, ed. Georg Lasson, 2 vols. (Hamburg: Meiner, 1971), I: 26.

8 Immanuel Kant, *Kritik der reinen Vernunft* (Hamburg: Meiner, 1956), A 235–36; B 294–95.

9 G. W. F. Hegel, "Über Mythologie, Volkgeist und Kunst." Manuscript in the Staatsbibliothek Preussischer Kulturbesitz, Berlin. For a translation of this passage and comment, see my *Hegel's Recollection: A Study of Images in the Phenomenology of Spirit* (Albany: State University of New York Press, 1985), 36–37.

10 For discussion of the double *Ansich*, see *Hegel's Recollection*, ch. 2.

11 "Das Wahre ist das Ganze," *Phänomenologie des Geistes*, ed. Johannes Hoffmeister, 6th ed. (Hamburg: Meiner, 1952), 21.

The *Phenomenology of Spirit* records the fact that the constant feature of experience is conjunction. All experience has the form of in-*and*-for-itself. In its attempt to overcome the "andness" of its life consciousness undergoes illusion after illusion, passing through the whole "gallery of pictures" of experience.[12] Andness is the key to the mythic apprehension of the world. For myth andness remains unproblematic. Myth simply joins one immediacy to another. In mythical thought anything can be conjoined with anything else. But at the level of consciousness that has begun to become philosophy, one thing is joined to another through recollection. The andness of myth is collective; the andness of dialectic is recollective.

Recollection requires, as Aristotle claims, a causal ordering of what is recalled.[13] Consciousness is unable to attain the natural equilibrium of mythical thought because it can never attain a complete unity of the two sides of its apprehension of the object. Each time consciousness believes itself to have found such a union the unifying moment dissolves into an illusion. All of these illusions are the stages of the *Phenomenology of Spirit* and are the objects of the "science of the experience of consciousness." At the final moment of "absolute knowing" the shape of wisdom appears. It appears in the act of acceptance of the andness of things, the realization that consciousness is a coincidence of opposites. The last illusion that the life of consciousness is one thing is gone. The activity of absolute knowing is the ontology of the *Science of Logic*. The andness written into the inner life of consciousness cannot be *aufgehoben* at the level of consciousness. But once this andness is accepted for what it is, it can be thought.

Thought is distinguished by principles or categories. Categories are the ultimates through which the real is formed. The category becomes a deliberate way to confront the andness of experience and the inherent disjunction within experience that conjunction implies. Logic is speculative philosophy and it is a melancholic activity, for it is predicated on the truth that the doubleness internal to consciousness can never be eliminated. It can be confronted as a moment of thought—thought now without illusion. All of the categories through which thought manages andness can be articulated as a system. The whole can never simply be an object of one form of experience or another but an object of one form of thought or another. It is melancholic, but it is not without humor, not without the irony that is originally present in the idea of a dialectic in which one

12 *Ph.G.*, 563.

13 Aristotle, *On Memory*, 453a6–10.

14 Bertold Brecht, *Flüchtlingsgespräche* (Berlin and Frankfurt: Suhrkamp, 1961), 108–11. My translation.

15 Brecht likely has in mind the Berlin irony found in the remark made on visiting the gravesite of a friend and finding a large flower growing from it: "My, how you've changed, my friend!" I have found this in a poem in Berlin dialect, titled "Die Seelenwanderung" ("The transmigration of souls"):

thing is *aufgehoben* in another. The surprise of the *Phenomenology of Spirit* is not that some stages do not seem to follow from those before them but that any of them seems to necessitate the next.

The melancholy side of both the *Phenomenology of Spirit* and the *Science of Logic* is that they are like dreams. They are like what Hegel says of the art work that it is not alive in our time and so the artist must "place his imagination in a past world; he must dream a world, but the character of dreaming, of not being alive, of the past, is plainly stamped on his work."[16] The *Science of Logic* is recollection because it takes the categories of the real from what is already collected in language. The speculative philosopher is not present when language is actively forming the world. The philosopher, like the owl of Minerva, comes to language only after it has been formed, and discovers what is there. The philosopher's melancholy comes from the fact that the immediacy of language, that activity that is distinctly human, can never be fully recaptured, any more than can the artist recapture the original life of the art work. The philosopher is, and must remain, a memory expert.

The Hegelian John Findlay once expressed the view that the *Phenomenology of Spirit* is an *auto-da-fé*, a labor of the negative that makes way for the great truth of the *Science of Logic*.[17] I have never been comfortable with this view. It would suggest a comparison of the *Phenomenology of Spirit* with the justified *supplizio* of Savonarola in the Piazza della Signoria of Florence, as well as with the mysterious and unnecessary burning of Giordano Bruno in the Campo dei Fiori of Rome. The *Phenomenology of Spirit* cannot be merely abandoned—the Hegelian ladder of experience simply kicked away. Yet in some sense the *Phenomenology of Spirit* cannot simply be dwelt upon as if it were the sum and substance of Hegel.

A turning point in my own thinking on this question occurred when I first saw Stanley Rosen's book on *G. W. F. Hegel: An Introduction to the Science of Wisdom,* when we were colleagues at Penn State. My eye immediately fell on the chapter title, "From Logic to Phenomenology."[18] I knew that Rosen's attraction, in Hegel, was primarily to the *Logic*. It was the work on which he was presenting graduate seminars at that time. The Kojèveian title of Rosen's book moves the reader immediately from "the science of the experience of consciousness" of the *Phenomenology of Spirit* to the science of the logic, reminding me of what I have always found most interesting in Alexandre Kojève's lectures on the phenomenology—his striking identification of absolute knowledge with the wise man.[19]

16 See *Hegel's Recollection*, 36.

17 This is the approach in John Findlay, *Hegel: A ReExamination* (London: Allen and Unwin, 1958).

18 Stanley Rosen, *G. W. F. Hegel: An Introduction to the Science of Wisdom* (New Haven, Conn.: Yale University Press, 1974), ch. 6.

19 Alexandre Kojève, *Introduction à la lecture de Hegel,* ed. Raymond Queneau (Paris: Gallimard, 1947), 306–35.

Rosen's chapter title is intellectually deft. Simply by reversing the order of the *Phenomenology of Spirit* and the *Science of the Logic*, he suggests a new way to look at Hegel's project. Findlay's *auto-da-fé* is a formulation of the British Hegelian view, that the *Phenomenology of Spirit* is an earlier work of Hegel and not part of the system, similar to what in Kant would be seen as a "pre-critical" period. The approach of British Hegelianism led to a serious overlooking of the true genius present in the *Phenomenology of Spirit* that had to be discovered by the French, notably Jean Hippolyte, and especially Kojève. Rosen takes a step beyond the French fixation on the *Phenomenology* by moving to the greater *Logic*, but in so doing he finds a way to look back at the *Phenomenology.* I wish to suggest my own version of this art of *Wiederfinden*, through attention to two images that dominate the Hegelian system—the master-servant and the true and bad infinity.

Of all the pictures or images in Hegel's *Galerie von Bildern* none has been greater in its effect than the *Herrschaft und Knechtschaft* section of the *Phenomenology*. There is no section of the *Science of Logic* more crucial to Hegelian ontology and to the Hegelian system generally than that which Hegel calls the true infinity (*die wahrhafte Unendlichkeit*) and the bad infinity *(die schlechte Unendlichkeit)*. Both of these images are great, I wish to claim, because each contains below its surface a portrait of the true or speculative philosopher-of who the philosopher in fact is. It is this sub-surface portrait of the philosopher that attracts the philosophical reader to these images, even if this attraction is not apparent to the reader. Only if we look between the two works, suspending them in air and looking from the *Phenomenology of Spirit* to the *Science of Logic* and back, can we see what these master images hold in common in Hegel's circle.

All of the Hegelian philosophy is directed to the question of what it means to be a philosopher. Hegel's passion is to know what philosophy is. His system is not directed primarily to reform of the nation, to the unification of knowledge, or to the meaning of history. What Hegel says on such issues is extremely valuable but it is not the essence of his thought. He, like any philosopher, is occupied with penetrating the question of what philosophy is, of the nature of its *philia* and the nature of *sophia*.

The *Phenomenology of Spirit* is not the story of consciousness as such, rising from its earliest forms. If this were so, the *Phenomenology* would begin with a stage of mythical consciousness, a stage in which the world is simply felt and expressed in terms of benign and malignant forces.[20] The *Phenomenology of Spirit* is a work for philosophers. It begins when consciousness first experiences skepticism toward the object, the response to which is sense-certainty. Thus the *Phenomenology of Spirit* is the story of the rise of philosophical consciousness

20 Ernst Cassirer, *Philosophie der symbolischen Formen*, vol. 2, *Das mythische Denken* (Darmstadt: Wissenschaftliche Buchgesellschaft, 1969), ix–xi.

within consciousness in general. The pursuit of certainty in the earliest stages of the *Phenomenology* is a response to the uneasiness of a natural skepticism, the beginning of wisdom.

Wisdom begins in the quest for certainty as the answer to skepticism, but wisdom can begin to take shape only when consciousness has outgrown its attachment to sense experience as connected to the understanding. The turning point is the inverted world (*die verkehrte Welt*), the result of which is a twofold commitment by consciousness, one to the reality of itself as the basis of the object, and at the same time, a commitment to dialectic as the means to form oppositions. The experience of freedom that releases consciousness from its being simply as consciousness rests on the realization that the object is made. That the object is made is the basis of self-knowledge. Realization that the object is made by consciousness is the first step toward overcoming certainty on behalf of the true, for the true requires a knowledge through causes, something the understanding, with its attachment to reflection, cannot comprehend. The sense of the object as made is the beginning of speculation. All that is made occurs through opposition, the subject matter of speculation.

Dialectic is the internal logic of opposites. It shows how one thing is produced through the agency of the other. The flaw or illusion that consciousness has as it passes from consciousness to self-consciousness is that it takes its newly found self-reality as a certainty. It grasps that its object is made from its own reality, but it fails to grasp that its own self-reality is also something made. It has yet to penetrate the sense in which the dialectic is something self-caused. In this way it has failed to master opposites.

The failure to master opposites, that is, to accept the genuine being of "twoness," issues in the life-and-death struggle of masterhood and servitude. The master or *Herr* is certain of his own being because of his dominance of the *Knecht*. The illusion of Masterhood is the belief that the other can be dominated. The work of the master is the management of the other as a means to the mastery of the object. The master has a problem with his own reality, for his reality becomes inconceivable apart from the means of the servant. The servant, not the world, is the master's object. Without the servant, the master is not. The servant is a vacuous actuality as long as the servant-self looks to the master as real. When the servant remembers that there is a world of objects, the servant is free.

The servant is not just the opposite of the master, he is the opposite of the objects of the world, the products of consciousness. The medium of the servant's relation to these objects is his work. The work of the servant on the world is a dialectic independent of the dialectic between master and servant. The master is powerful but thoughtless. He does not know that his central problem is his own reality. He must keep up the picture of his own reality or lose his position. Once the servant ceases to believe in the reality of the master, the master is lost to himself, but he can do nothing but struggle to claim his position.

The master sees all as politics. The servant has come to disbelieve in politics. The servant is freed from politics because of his grasp of the reality of the nature of things. For the master, politics is an absolute activity. But the servant, through his work, has grasped the possibility of the absolute in the sense of acting in terms of the nature of things. This sense of what is beyond politics is writ large by Hegel's "absolute spirit" that emerges at the end of the *Encyclopaedia*, in which absolute spirit emerges through art, religion, and philosophy.[21] Even in political theory, for Hegel world history is a larger reality than the nation.[22] The philosopher has no belief in politics, that is to say, in what the master believes.

In the *Phenomenology of Spirit*, the struggle of master and servant results in the philosophical life-forms of the stoic, the skeptic, and the melancholic, or what Hegel in one of his powerful images calls the unhappy consciousness (*unglückliches Bewusstsein*). The unhappy consciousness is the bad infinity, not as a thought-form but as a phenomenon experienced by consciousness. The stoic, skeptic, and melancholic are the three sides of the philosophical life. They are the results of the realization by emerging philosophical consciousness that philosophy, although existing within the dominance of the *Herrschaft* of the state, is not of it. The philosopher is a threat to the state but assumes the guises of the stoic, skeptic, or melancholic so as to appear harmless to its *Herrschaft*. The philosopher cannot be dispensed with by the state because the philosopher as its servant holds the key to the politician, the man of the state's reality. The philosopher appears variously as a master of self-sufficiency and endurance, as a standard of criticism, or as simply unhappy and harmless.

In the *Phenomenology of Spirit* what comes after these forms of self-certainty is the stoicism of reason, the attempt to live within the natural order of the world. This is followed by the social forms of spirit, in which the faith consciousness has in each of them breaks down into skepticism. Society is certainly the highway of despair, for consciousness, because it above all else is a world of its own making. Absolute knowing is melancholic because it is the acceptance of the ultimate twoness of consciousness, that there is no possibility of unification with itself, of undifferentiated self-identity. The truth of the whole is that it is two. There is no transcendent moment of unity. Acceptance of consciousness as it is, is the key to wisdom.

There is no melancholic politics because the politician always believes in politics and insists on apprehending the world on his own terms. The philosopher never believes in politics, but believes in thought. When politics enters the room, thought always leaves. The philosopher, faced with life in the state, practices the

21 G. W. F. Hegel, *Enzyklopädie der philosophischen Wissenschaften im Grundrisse* (1830), ed. Friedhelm Nicolin and Otto Pöggeler (Hamburg: Meiner, 1959), 440–63.

22 G. W. F. Hegel, *Grundlinien der Philosophie des Rechts*, 4th ed., ed. Johannes Hoffmeister (Hamburg: Meiner, 1955), 288–97.

logic of the mask, the logic that Hegel says is never understood by the physiognomist or the phrenologist.[23] The philosopher thus moves among the disguises of stoic, skeptic, and melancholic.

Because in the very construction of consciousness, in the actual dialectic of its birth, the master has fallen prey to the cunning of the servant, the politician is uneasy with the philosopher. The politician is as uneasy with the philosopher as was Leon the Tyrant of Philus, when he asked Pythagoras whether he was wise. Pythagoras' s answer was stoic, skeptical, and melancholic; he said that only the gods were wise, that he was a lover of wisdom. The answer is stoic because it is a stance of acceptance, skeptical because human wisdom is open to question, and melancholic because wisdom is beyond us. Leon is then satisfied, because the philosopher is as harmless and admiring as the pure spectator at the great games, to whom Pythagoras likens the being of the philosopher.[24]

The speech to Leon is the mask that covers Pythagoras; what Pythagoras leaves unsaid is whether the philosopher may possess human wisdom, a claim Socrates openly makes in his final appearance before the State.[25] It is the claim Hegel makes in the preface to the *Phenomenology of Spirit*, when he says he will produce not the love of wisdom but wisdom itself, by means of his dialectic.[26] What he will produce is self-knowledge. The *Phenomenology* is the greatest treatise on self-knowledge since the ancients. The *Phenomenology of Spirit* is the necessary introduction to wisdom understood as a knowledge of things human and divine and their causes. Divine wisdom is itself a kind of human wisdom. It rests on the power of the philosopher to make the distinction. Politics can do nothing in such an affair. Politics becomes a stage-play for the philosopher to observe. The philosopher can watch each of the moments of common life illustrate the logic of the illusions of Hegel's stages in the *Phenomenology*—his ship of fools, his spiritual zoo writ large.

The spectation of the philosopher requires the speculative sentence. The language of reason is the speculative sentence (*spekulativer Satz*). Speculative philosophy requires a prose in which the sentence is a circle accomplished by a dialectic internal to the subject and predicate. The meaning of the speculative sentence moves from the subject to the predicate and back to the subject. The returned meaning of the subject contains within it the meaning of the predicate, now *aufgehoben* in this dialectical movement. Hegel says his system is a circle, in fact a circle of circles.[27] The system returns to itself in this most perfect of geometric forms. What is true of the system is true of its smallest unity of expression. The speculative sentence is an ouroboros.

23 *Ph.G.*, 233.
24 Cicero, *Tusc.* 5.3.7ff.
25 Plato, A*pology*, 20 d–e.
26 *Ph.G.*, 5.
27 *Logik,* 2: 504.

The reflective sentence that is the medium of the understanding is not circular but classificatory. The predicate is simply the container of the subject, as explicated in the principles of class logic. The language of the understanding is tied to the separation of truth and falsity. What it can say is either true or false. The language of reason is always a doubling-up, a speech in which the subject and predicate are the partial truths and the partial falsities of each other. The reflective sentence is declarative, an assertion either describing or prescribing (in the case of ethics) a state of affairs. The speculative sentence corresponds in ordinary speech to the suggestion.

The logic of the suggestion follows neither the logic of imperatives nor the logic of descriptions. A suggestion is a possible truth but not a mere possibility because the suggestion, to be genuinely suggestive, must reflect an actual state of affairs that is subject to true or false description. At the same time it must be prescriptive in that it projects a meaningful course of thought or action in response to a particular, problematic state of affairs. The suggestion has a doubleness of mind. The suggestion is implicitly a likely story, in the way that any metaphor is a fable in brief.[28]

The likely stories of the Platonic dialogues are the foundation of the speculative sentence. They suggest the nature of what is. As likely, these stories are both partially true and partially false. The speech of the true and the false, of partial truths, is the speech of civilized interchange. Our speech to others, when it is mannerly and civilized, is never flatly a truth stated or a lie fabricated. It is a way of responding to others that is adjusted to the particular situation governed by the coincidence of opposites, including that of truth and falsity. A model of this is the Italian ideal of speaking *con buon garbo*, the ability to convey something negative and unfortunate in a manner that can soften its blow, make it acceptable. It is an ideal of the proper speech of human events.[29]

Speculative speech is rooted in human speech. It is not extraordinary. Reflective speech, the logic of the understanding, is what is extraordinary and in a sense anti-human, appropriate to the production of a knowledge of natural objects but not appropriate to self-knowledge. It is not the speculative philosopher who thinks abstractly, it is the reflective and common-sense thinker. The speculative philosopher, when confronted with such literal-mindedness, can only open his metaphysical overcoat and let loose the flashing star of wisdom.[30] In

28 Giambattista Vico, *Princìpi di scienza nuova d'intorno alla comune natura delle nazioni*, in *Opere*, vol. 1, ed. Andrea Battistini (Milan: Mondadori, 1990), par. 404. On metaphor see Eva T. H. Brann, *The World of the Imagination: Sum and Substance* (Lanham, Maryland: Rowman and Littlefield, 1991), pt. 4, ch. 3.

29 This ideal has its zenith in the Renaissance, in Baldassare Castiglione, *Il libro del cortegiano* (*The Book of the Courtier*) (1528) and Giovanni Della Casa, *Galateo ovvero de'costumi* (*Galateo, or On Manners*) (1552–55).

30 G. W. F. Hegel, "Wer denkt abstrakt?" *Werke* 2: 575–81.

speculative speech the self confronts its own nature and the world as a part of its own reality, as a familiar other, a *Du*. In this relationship, speculative reason assumes the relation to the other present in mythical thought, in which the world is an alter-ego.

The subject of the speculative sentence is being, the category with which Hegel begins the *Science of Logic*. The philosopher can produce no discourse on being as such because as such being is as indeterminate as nothing.[31] Hegel's discourse on being, as it moves from the "nothingness" of being toward its determinate sense, has a crucial moment when it reaches "infinity."[32] Distinctive to the philosopher is his ability to speak about infinity, for what is infinite is beyond thought. The philosopher, unlike the physicist or the religionist, speaks of infinity as such. The philosopher speaks of infinity as both within and beyond experience.

In the *Logic,* the phenomenon that has made consciousness unhappy in the *Phenomenology*, that has produced the original basis of philosophical melancholy, becomes an object of thought. The result is the idea of "bad infinity." Bad infinity is undialectical "andness." that is, andness that cannot double-up, that cannot become ambiguity. Bad infinity is the thought of an endless series in which the last member of any given series can have a next member simply conjoined to it. There are the members of the series and then there is another and another and another, and so on. The infinite is not unlimited because its limit is the finite. The infinite in its bad form is the negative of the finite, its opposite. It evolves its endless series simply by conjunctions, not by any principle of determination. Andness is not a principle. It is repetitive addition in the sense that Hegel describes it in the *Phenomenology of Spirit* in relation to the adding of properties to a thing.[33] Adding property after property to a thing does not achieve a principle of the internal determination of its nature. The process of conjunction does not supply consciousness with the grasp of how the thing has these properties. The bad infinity can never produce a whole.

The principle proper to speculative philosophy is that the True is the Whole. Without the ability to think the whole speculative philosophy is illusion, its thoughts are the fogbanks beyond Kant's blessed isle of reflection. The true infinity is the key idea to the nature of the whole, the idea that the speculative philosopher cannot do without. It is his only relief from melancholy. The true infinity shows the structure of thought upon which the dialectic itself depends. It is speculative philosophy's secret and it is completely simple. The problem is to find a way to visualize it. Josiah Royce has offered two ways to approach the true infinity: through Georg Cantor's system of transfinite numbers, which shows how orders

31 *Logik*, 1: 69.
32 Ibid., 1: 125–46.
33 *Ph.G.*, 90–93.

of numbers can infinitely and determinately generate further orders of numbers; and through the imaginary example of making a map that maps itself.[34] Royce has shown that the key to true infinity is the process of systematic self-representation.

Cassirer has given us the best way to grasp the true infinity as a principle of abstract thought, for he realized that the internal structure of Hegel's concept (*Begriff*) is analogous to the indissolvable bond between the principle of a series and its members, that can be symbolized as (x).[35] The (*Begriff*) is a "concrete universal." The ϕ is the universal principle by which the series represented by x is constructed. The universal has no meaning in and of itself without its realization in the series. Without their bond with the universal rule that makes them a series, the members of the series are simply random particulars. Cassirer regards $\phi(x)$ as the basis of function-concepts (*Funktionsbegriffe*), as opposed to substance-concepts (*Substanzbegriffe*). The substance-concept, the basis of Aristotelian class logic, is expressed in the reflective sentence. It has no inherent bond between the class and its classified members leading to all the metaphysical debates over *quidditas*.

Quiddity or haecceity is not an issue for the functional concept or the dialectical concept. Any series of the form $\phi(x)$ can be extended indefinitely, yet every new member of the series is joined to it by the definite principle of the series. It is not merely conjoined as in the bad infinite. Further, the ϕ of the original bond can be a member of another series of another logical order, and any member of a series x can be a universal principle of a series of another logical order—similar to the map that maps itself. The $\phi(x)$ bond can expand in every direction. The logic of the functional concept is an analog to the logic of the whole. There are no limits to what can be included in a total pattern of expansion, but the expansion is determinate at each of its moments. This logic is the thought of the absolute in abstract terms. It is the double bond of the in-itself and the in-itself-for-us. The $\phi(x)$ is being in-and-for-itself.

How can this process of the functional concept be transposed into an account of the actual, to produce the True as the Whole? It requires an act of genius. It is what is required for the schematism, which Kant says depends upon "an art lost in the human soul."[36] The schematism is the speculative moment that makes the understanding possible. Kant understood the necessity of the schematism, but his commitment to the terrestrial bonds of critical philosophy rendered impossible any development of its possibilities. Every stage of Hegel's dialectic is a schematism, a schematism not separated from the thing-in-itself.

34 Josiah Royce, *The World and the Individual*, vol. 1 (New York: Macmillan, 1899); see the "Supplementary Essay," secs. 3 and 4.

35 Ernst Cassirer, *Philosophie der symbolischen Formen*, vol. 3, *Phänomenologie der Erkenntnis* (Darmstadt: Wissenschaftliche Buchgesellschaft, 1958), 351–55.

36 *Kritik der reinen Vernunft*, A 141; B 180–81.

The philosopher is freed from his servitude to the master by becoming the master of the true infinity. The true infinity is the abstract portrait of freedom because, like freedom, for Hegel it is the structure of self-determination.[37] Self-determination is the philosopher's natural stoicism. It is classical stoicism *aufgehoben*. Classical stoicism is withdrawal from society. Its freedom is the moral correlate to the logic of the bad infinity because in his solitary ethics the classical stoic has no principle of self-development. His life is limited by society in a way analogous to the limitation attached to the bad infinity by its opposition to the finite. The philosophical self is in society but not of it. Speculative philosophical stoicism is the stoicism of Socrates, whose activity is in the *agora* but never of it. Having seen through the illusion of politics, the speculative philosopher is in possession of the vision of the absolute. This possession is the reason for the mask. The classical stoic is an open book; thus he can have only a partial answer to the power of the master, the power of the state.

The philosophical ideal is the life of self-determination, the dialectic realized. The master has not, nor he can have, a vision of the whole. He tells no likely story but is a problem solver, a director of work for his own desire. The master has the cunning of Ulysses, the cunning of the fox to solve the problems before him through the dominance of the servant. The philosopher as servant acquires the cunning of reason. He can comprehend the whole through spectation. The story of the whole takes him beyond the state. If this became known, what would be the reaction of the master and his believers?

The answer to this question is already known since the myth of the cave. It is a lesson learned. Knowledge of the whole is the basis of prudence. In the modern world the cunning of reason begets the logic of the mask. It is as simple as that.

37 See Stanley Rosen, "Theory and Practice in Hegel: Union or Disunion," in *Hegel's Social and Political Thought*, ed. Donald Phillip Verene (New Jersey and Sussex: Humanities Press and Harvester Press, 1980), 34–46.